ONE WEEK LOAN

14 DEC 2011

06 FEB 2012

D1381656

CLARENDON LAW SERIES

AN INTRODUCTION TO THE LAW OF TRUSTS

THIRD EDITION

SIMON GARDNER

BCL (Oxford) MA (Oxford)
Fellow of Lincoln College Oxford
Faculty of Law, University of Oxford

OXFORD
UNIVERSITY PRESS

OXFORD
UNIVERSITY PRESS

Great Clarendon Street, Oxford OX2 6DP

Oxford University Press is a department of the University of Oxford.
It furthers the University's objective of excellence in research, scholarship,
and education by publishing worldwide in

Oxford New York

Auckland Cape Town Dar es Salaam Hong Kong Karachi
Kuala Lumpur Madrid Melbourne Mexico City Nairobi
New Delhi Shanghai Taipei Toronto

With offices in

Argentina Austria Brazil Chile Czech Republic France Greece
Guatemala Hungary Italy Japan Poland Portugal Singapore
South Korea Switzerland Thailand Turkey Ukraine Vietnam

Oxford is a registered trade mark of Oxford University Press
in the UK and in certain other countries

Published in the United States
by Oxford University Press Inc., New York

First published 1990
Third edition published 2011

British Library Cataloguing in Publication Data
Data available

Library of Congress Cataloging in Publication Data
Library of Congress Control Number: 2011924933

Typeset by Newgen Imaging Systems (P) Ltd., Chennai, India
Printed in Great Britain
on acid-free paper by
Clays Ltd, St Ives plc

ISBN 978–0–19–954574–2
ISBN 978–0–19–954575–9 (Pbk.)

1 3 5 7 9 10 8 6 4 2

Preface

The previous edition of this book appeared in 2003. Since then, the law has moved on somewhat, maybe the most significant change being the advent of the Charities Act 2006, together with judicial revision of the rules regarding family homes. Academic endeavour too has continued, perhaps the most striking new work being that concerning the duty to account and its significance. And my own thoughts, and ideas about expressing everything, have evolved as well. This new edition aims to convey such developments.

Just as the previous edition was more detailed and subtler than its predecessor, moreover, this one in turn offers rather greater substance, and a more overtly scholarly style. Much of this change consists in the provision of more extensive footnotes. But even where the text too has become fuller (as it has especially in the treatment of remedies and of remedial constructive trusts), I hope that it will continue to offer an accessible and stimulating treatment of the subject. It is aimed above all at undergraduates studying Trusts as part of their law degree. Although it can valuably be read before embarking on an in-depth study of Trusts, it is probably best used alongside or after such study. I hope it will help undergraduates understand the subject better, both by the reflections it makes on the material they are studying and, perhaps more importantly, by encouraging them to develop such reflections for themselves. Other readers too may find that it serves their needs, especially those looking for a brief account of this area of the law, explained in terms that may strike chords with other fields of interest.

To help in the exposition of the material, I have divided some otherwise over-long chapters: those previously covering both remedies against trustees and the position of third parties; resulting trusts and the principles behind constructive trusts; and various instances of constructive trusts. I have also moved all the material on resulting and constructive trusts to the end of the book, where it can take advantage of a now earlier discussion of account liability, this being an arguably influential factor in shaping a number of kinds of constructive trust.

The text was finalized at the end of November 2010. At this point, certain further developments were nonetheless anticipated. Readers should be on the alert for these. In particular, we expect, in the winter of 2010–11, a decision of the Court of Appeal about the rule in *Re Hastings-Bass* (*Pitt v Holt*, *Futter v Futter*—cases reaching the court as a result of the Revenue having belatedly interested itself in this issue); and in the spring or early summer of 2011, decisions of the Supreme Court regarding family home constructive trusts (*Jones v Kernott*), and the nature of a beneficiary's interest (*Colour Quest Ltd v Total Downstream UK Plc*—this being litigation over the fire at the Buncefield oil depot, a rather improbable vehicle for raising the topic). There is also the question whether s 199 of the Equality Act 2010, abolishing the presumption of advancement, will be brought into force, something about which I could obtain no information from the Ministry of Justice at the time of writing.

Once again I must, and gratefully do, acknowledge the help that others have been generous enough to give me. Much of this has been in the background, but it is not the less appreciated for that. In a specifically academic vein, I have received it above all from Michael Ashdown, Mindy Chen-Wishart, Elizabeth Cooke, Kate Davidson, Anne Davies, Joshua Getzler, Jonathan Herring, Mike Macnair, Christopher McCrudden, Charles Mitchell, Jenny Payne, Lionel Smith, Margaret Stevens, and Bill Swadling. The publishers have once again been most supportive.

This book is dedicated to the county of Devon.

Simon Gardner
December 2010

Contents

Table of Cases

Table of Statutes, Statutory Instruments, and International Conventions

I

The Nature of Trusts

Our first task is to form a general idea of what trusts are.[1]

I.I   A DEFINITION

The most basic legal concepts are often not easy to define with complete precision, and trusts are no exception. The difficulty arises partly because, in English law, many of the concepts (including trusts) are developed by the judges rather than being established by Act of Parliament, so there is no single, completely authoritative statement of their nature. But it arises also for a more fundamental reason. There can be a variety of different ideas as to the proper mission of the law in the area in question—whether it should reflect this consideration, or that—and therefore as to the proper work that the concept should do. These ideas are often in conflict with each other. If one idea were altogether to vanquish its rivals, this would not prevent the emergence of a clear-cut definition. But that does not normally happen. For one thing, human affairs are too complicated and compromised to allow only for clean answers. For another, the definition has (as a result of the doctrine of precedent) to be assembled from judicial utterances over many years: some from periods when one policy slant dominated, others from periods when another view had come to the fore.[2]

So no definition of a trust can be given which is beyond contention, either in terms of its technical fit with the substance of the law or in terms of its freedom from political controversy. It would therefore be entirely reasonable not to offer a definition, but to move directly into a discussion of the various points which might feature in any definition, and of the different possible accounts of them. Such a discussion certainly cannot

---

[1]   The nature of trusts today differs in some respects from that of their ancestors, known originally as 'uses'. On the early period, see A Simpson *A History of the Land Law* (1986) ch VIII.

[2]   For an account of the effort to define trusts, and the predictably problematic experience with the venture, see J Anderson in W Cornish et al *The Oxford History of the Laws of England, Volume XII: 1820–1914 Private Law* (2010) Part One VI, 238–46.

be dispensed with. But it is probably easier to follow, and more rewarding, if at the outset we do posit something having the look of a definition, to provide a starting point.

The 'definition' thus offered here is as follows:

> A trust is a situation in which property is vested in someone (a trustee), who is under legally recognized obligations, at least some of which are of a proprietary kind, to handle it in a certain way, and to the exclusion of any personal interest. These obligations may arise either by conscious creation by the previous owner of the property (the settlor), or because some other legally significant circumstances are present.

The task now—for the remainder of this chapter, and indeed of the book—is to explain the significance of the various aspects of this 'definition', and to record and explore the ways in which it is contentious.

1.2 AN EXAMPLE

Many of the terms of the 'definition' just offered are abstract or not matters of ordinary usage. So, in order to be able to focus our discussion more solidly, it will be helpful at this stage to give a concrete example of a trust. To do so is itself a contentious undertaking, however.

It will be noted that the 'definition' offers two alternative ways in which a trust can arise: 'either as a result of the conscious creation of these obligations, or because some other legally significant circumstances are present'. The reference to 'some other legally significant circumstances' is unspecific, hinting that these circumstances are various in nature. And there is no stipulation as to the content of the obligations which lie at the heart of the 'definition'. Taking all this together, it can be inferred, correctly, that trusts can arise in many situations and be made to do a wide range of work. If we take an example, however, we immediately focus upon the particular kind of situation, and upon the particular kind of work, that the example illustrates. And we thereby tacitly privilege this situation and work over all other situations and work that can in principle equally well be associated with trusts. To explain the danger is, however, hopefully to go some way towards allaying it. At all events, the usefulness of giving an example seems worth the risk.

Imagine that an elderly grandmother wants to give £100,000 to her baby grandson Adam. As he is so young, however, she does not want him simply to have all the money straight away. Under other circumstances, she might have kept it herself and paid it over to him in amounts, and at times, of her own choosing. But, given her age, this is not a satisfactory option for her. So she makes a trust for him. She does so by transferring the £100,000 to a trustee (a close friend, maybe, or her bank) with instructions how to deal with it: say, to invest it and accumulate the income, to pay Adam the capital and accumulated income on his eighteenth birthday, but meanwhile to pay out anything that might be needed to give him a good education, plus an annual allowance of £1,000 once he reaches his teens.

This illustration certainly falls within our 'definition' of a trust. We see that, as a result of the conscious creation of the arrangement by the grandmother, property is vested in a trustee, who comes under obligations not to treat it as his own but to handle it in a defined way, ie to provide the stated benefits to Adam. But we can also see that there are many respects in which the 'definition' allows for trusts which do not follow the pattern of the example. That is what now needs to be explored.

No other example would have avoided the danger of privileging its content any better than the example just given. But it may nevertheless be asked why the particular kind of situation inherent in that example should have been singled out for attention. This situation features an effort at structuring of the use of wealth between generations of a family. This situation and effort are characteristic of the principal use made of trusts as a matter of history (though the example of Adam and his grandmother is much simpler than most real parallels). The trust concept was thus predominantly developed against the policy considerations relevant to this situation and effort. Beginning from material such as the example should help us, therefore, to understand and appraise many of the concept's features.

I.3 THE WAYS IN WHICH TRUSTS CAN COME ABOUT

The grandmother in the example may have established her trust by paying the money over to the trustee during her own lifetime. If she did, the resulting arrangement—even though designed to endure after her death—is known as an '*inter vivos*' trust. Alternatively, she might have chosen to establish the trust by providing for the payment to the trustee in her will. This would have created a 'testamentary' trust.

In the example, the trust came about as a result of someone (the grandmother) wanting to make it. Such a person is called a 'settlor'. The establishment of a trust by a settlor is a very common situation, but it is not essential to the idea of a trust. Trusts are also found in cases where they are not consciously made in this way, but for one reason or another the circumstances demand that the holder of some property should nevertheless be regarded as a trustee and subjected to duties concerning its handling accordingly. Trusts that arise because they are consciously made, like that in the example, are called 'express trusts'. Those arising for other reasons are called 'constructive trusts'. The underlying point, however, is that these various circumstances in which constructive trusts arise, and the conscious actions of a settlor in the case of express trusts, are all different reasons for coming to the conclusion that someone who holds some property should be under a duty as to its handling. (There also exist 'resulting trusts'. These are trusts in which the trustee, receiving the property from another person, holds it on trust for that very person. They are customarily regarded as a category additional to express and constructive trusts. From the present point of view, however, they add nothing, for although the basis on which they arise is contentious, as discussed in Chapter 16, it is either the wish of their settlor, like express trusts, or some other legally significant circumstance, like constructive trusts.)

Sometimes, the idea of 'the circumstances demanding a constructive trust' is left without explication, and thus read as an invitation to the judges to impose such a trust whenever their own individual notions tell them to. That position, or one approaching it, is prominent in the jurisprudence of Canada. The constructive trusts to which it gives rise are called 'remedial'. It has attracted less support in England. Here, constructive trusts are more commonly viewed as arising, without such active judicial mediation, in circumstances laid down by the law (though of course that does not preclude innovation and development in the latter). The contrast between the two positions, and the bases on which, and the main circumstances in which, constructive trusts arise in English law, will all be discussed further in Chapters 15, 17, and 18. But a few examples of English law's constructive trusts, drawn from that discussion, may be given now. Where property is transferred to someone on the understanding that he[3] will hold it on an express trust, but a rule requiring such an express trust to be made using writing is not complied with, a constructive trust arises to oblige the transferee nevertheless to hold the property on the agreed terms. Where property belongs to one person, but he and another member of his family have operated on the understanding that it should be shared with the latter, a constructive trust arises to give effect to the understanding. And where an agent makes a profit for himself by using his employer's property, that profit will be subject to a constructive trust.

---

[3] Here, and (unless the context indicates otherwise) throughout this book, masculine pronouns are intended to refer to both sexes.

It is sometimes said that whilst express trusts (especially within families) were historically the more important species of trust, constructive trusts nowadays occupy that position. How does one measure 'importance', however? Many such statements implicitly look to the relative frequency of litigation. It appears likely that there is nowadays more litigation over constructive trusts than over express trusts, and that this reverses the historic position. But although comparison on this ground does possess significance (for example, for priorities in the education of advocates, and for the organization of court business), it is not the only possible approach. If one looks instead to the relative frequency with which clients consult lawyers over the two types of trusts in a non-litigious context, express trusts will probably emerge as the more 'important'. This measure too has its significance (eg for the organization of solicitors' firms). But the real conclusions are that no measure of 'importance' has value outside its own terms, and that neither type of trust can therefore be represented as more 'important' than the other in a global sense. They both matter, but differently.

1.4 THE SETTLOR

An express trust therefore arises as a result of a decision on the part of the settlor to make a trust of it. It follows that an express trust must have a settlor.

In the example given above, the settlor (the grandmother) transferred the property to the trustee in order for the latter to hold it on trust. This step, however, is not essential. It is possible for the settlor and the trustee to be the same person. Instead of transferring his property to a trustee who will then have the duty of dealing with it as specified, a settlor may keep it but undertake the same duty himself. If the grandmother in the example had not perceived her remaining period of life to be short, but had still wished to establish a trust (perhaps valuing its structured nature in preference to a series of ad hoc gifts), she might have chosen to do so in this way, rather than by transferring the property to a trustee. Establishing a trust in this way is known as 'declaring a trust': the settlor declares that he holds the property in question as trustee, and stipulates that in that capacity he will deal with it in a certain manner for the beneficiary. What is essential, therefore, is not a transfer of property from a settlor to a trustee, but rather for the property to be with the trustee, and for the trustee to be under a duty in regard to its handling.

In a case where a constructive trust arises, indeed, the position will always be that the owner of some property will come under some duty to deal with the property in a certain way, ie will become trustee of it. There will not be a settlor, ie a person whose intention to place his own property on trust is effectuated by the law.

The grandmother in the example was a human being. Where a trust does have a settlor, that settlor may alternatively be any other entity recognized by the law as having the same capacities, in regard to the enjoyment of property, as a human being. In other words, it might be a 'legal (or juristic) person', notably an incorporated company.

1.5   THE BENEFICIARY

The trust in the example was constructed so as to provide, ultimately, for payments to Adam. A person who has a claim to receive payments from a trust is known as a 'beneficiary'.[4] Many trusts have at least one beneficiary and, of those that do, most have more than one. The beneficiaries' entitlements may be arranged concurrently (eg 'for Adam and Briony in equal shares') or in succession to one another (eg 'to pay the income to Adam for his lifetime, then to pay the capital to Briony'), or in some mixture of the two.

A beneficiary may be either a human being, like Adam, or some other legal person.[5] But many trusts do not have a beneficiary, human or otherwise, at all. A trust might instead provide for payments towards the achievement of some purpose: for example, to investigate whether the plays attributed to Shakespeare were really the work of Bacon, or to establish and maintain a dogs' home, or to provide a public recreation ground, or to further the aims of some organization. Such trusts without beneficiaries are called 'purpose trusts'. Collectively, beneficiaries and such purposes are called 'objects' of trusts. Many purpose trusts have certain characteristics—most centrally, the offer of benefit to the public generally—making them 'charitable', and as such they receive special treatment from the law. We shall examine these in Chapter 6.[6] The law has also allowed certain non-

---

[4] Or 'cestui que trust', pronounced 'settee key trust'; plural correctly 'cestuis que trust' ('cestuis que trustent' is also found), pronounced (in either case) 'settees key trust'.

[5] For the extent to which there must be clarity over a beneficiary's identity, see further sections 8.4–8.5, 9.4, and 9.8.

[6] There also exist 'public trusts' in another sense (see generally J Barratt (2006) 69 MLR 514): situations in which a body holds public money. Historically, those responsible for the use of the money were seen as fiduciaries, ie as owing duties analogous to those owed by (other) trustees, and exposed to the same sorts of correction if they breached these duties: see *A-G v Dublin Corporation* (1827) 1 Bligh NS 312. This vision has resurfaced from time to time, including, relatively recently, in *Bromley London Borough Council v Greater London Council* [1983] 1 AC 768; *Porter v Magill* [2002] 2 AC 357; *Westminster City Council v Porter* [2003]

charitable purpose trusts, as described in section 12.3, but according to one point of view, no such trusts should be valid. The argument against non-charitable purpose trusts springs from the thesis, described in section 12.2 and usually referred to as 'the beneficiary principle', that trusts must necessarily feature not merely duties upon the trustees, but rights on the part of beneficiaries amounting to something like an interest in the trust property. Indeed, this thesis not only underlies the argument against purpose trusts, but also manifests itself in certain features of the law regarding trusts that do have beneficiaries. Its merits, and the considerations and rules antagonistic to it, are explored in section 12.4. But it is not reflected in our 'definition' as it does not fully capture the existing state of the law. Instead, the 'definition' stipulates for duties on the part of the trustees, it being possible for these to exist whether or not they mirror, or are mirrored by, rights on the part of any beneficiaries.

A beneficiary of a trust may also be a trustee of it. Such an arrangement makes some sense: since the point of the trust is to provide for the beneficiaries, it is reasonable for them to be involved in running it. So if Adam's grandmother had created a trust for his parents as well as himself, she might have made the parents not only beneficiaries but also trustees. But this effect can occur only in trusts with more than one trustee and/or beneficiary. Otherwise, if a person were both sole trustee and sole beneficiary, the trust would consist in him owing an obligation purely to himself, which dissolves into nothing: he would remain the absolute owner of the property in question.[7]

Sometimes, too, a trust's beneficiary may be the same person as its settlor. The settlor of an express trust may stipulate that he will be its beneficiary: ie he may make a trust for himself. The idea of doing so may at first sound strange. In medieval times, however, it was a common

---

Ch 436. The contemporary idea of an 'NHS Trust' trades upon it, but more rhetorically than substantively; see D Hughes (1991) 54 MLR 88, 92–5, 103. The vision further connects with the treatment of, in particular, feudal lords and indeed the monarch as on some level obliged to exercise the powers vested in them for the good of their tenants and subjects; and with one of the origins of company law in the control of the directors of the old semi-public companies such as the Bank of England (see eg *Charitable Corporation v Sutton* (1742) 2 Atk 400); on some of which see J Getzler in A Burrows and A Rodger (eds) *Mapping the Law: Essays in Honour of Peter Birks* (2006) ch 31, 592–3, 595–7.

[7] While it is thus technically feasible, understandable, and indeed quite common for a person to be both trustee and beneficiary, the possibility obviously puts pressure on another feature of the trust concept, namely that a trustee must not have a personal interest in the trust (see section 1.10). The relationship between the two rules has not been sufficiently explored in general terms, though some work has been done regarding particular contexts: see eg M Milner [1997] Conv 89.

practice, used above all so as to avoid certain forms of taxation. It is also quite common today: for example, when people put money into pension schemes or invest it in unit trusts, they can (simplifying somewhat) be seen as placing it with trustees on trust for themselves. Sometimes, too, such a trust will arise without a settlor—the transferor of the property—so stipulating. Trusts that arise in this way are mostly called 'resulting trusts'. A resulting trust occurs, certainly, when I give you property to hold on trust, but do not fully specify the objects for whom or for which you are to hold it, or where I give you property gratuitously, but you cannot prove that I did so as a gift; and arguably in certain other circumstances too. The law regarding resulting trusts is discussed further in Chapter 16.

1.6 THE TRUSTEE

The trust created by the grandmother in our example had one trustee. A trustee, again, may be either a human being or some other legal person such as an incorporated company. Some companies, known as 'trust corporations' (often subsidiaries of banks), specifically offer their services as trustees of express trusts, but any corporation may find itself trustee of a constructive trust or a resulting trust. If the settlor of an express trust confines himself to human trustees, he is unlikely to use just one: groups of between two and four are commoner.

We have seen that a trust need not have a settlor; nor a beneficiary, as opposed to a purpose. But in all the variations on the trust theme that we have noticed—express and constructive (and resulting) trusts, trusts for beneficiaries and for purposes, and so on—there has always been a trustee. And amongst all the learning on the subject of trusts, it has never been doubted that a trustee is required. This is not an accident. A trust involves an obligation to handle certain property in a particular way. An obligation is a proposition about what a person ought to do. So there cannot be an obligation to handle property in a particular way unless there is also a person, the trustee, who is subject to that obligation.

It is likely that the trustee in our original example agreed to take on the trust. It is usual for the settlor of an express trust to consult the intended trustee, and obtain his agreement to act in that role. If the settlor does not take this step and the intended trustee is not willing to act, the latter may disclaim the trusteeship, in which event the role will fall upon the settlor (or, if the settlor was acting by will, his executors), until someone else can be appointed trustee. Moreover, if a trustee wishes subsequently not to continue to act, it will generally be possible to relinquish the role.[8] So in practical terms, the agreement of the trustee comes close to being a requirement in express trusts. But the trustee's agreement is certainly not required in the case of other kinds of trusts. A constructive trust will arise where the trustee has the relevant property and the circumstances are such that the law imposes such a trust. It is irrelevant whether the trustee agrees to the trust's imposition.[9] On the other hand, such trustees too can—and indeed should—commonly rid themselves of the role, by handing the property over to the beneficiary.

To see the trustee as important only so as to provide a repository of the trust obligations would, however, be to capture only part of the picture. Trustees are important to trusts also for their own qualities, whether as people, in the case of human trustees, or organizations, in the case of trust corporations. The operation of an express trust in particular may, and normally does, require choices to be made. (In the trust in our original example, for instance, the trustee had to choose in what investments to place the trust's assets, and whether and how much to pay out for Adam's education.) The choices made will reflect the individual values and capabilities of the particular trustees. Exceptionable values and low capabilities will lead to trusts being performed unsatisfactorily. The law contains certain measures designed to counteract this possibility.[10] Above the floor created by these measures, however, the operation of trustees' individual values and capabilities is not simply tolerated; it is essential if trusts are to function as usefully as we have come to expect. When a settlor selects a trustee, therefore, he will reflect not only on whether the person in question is honest, but also on whether that person will in a more positive sense conduct the trust—make the choices—in a way that the settlor finds congenial. (Adam's grandmother, for example, will have chosen as trustee someone whom she regards as likely to keep Adam's best interests at heart, and whose conception of 'Adam's best interests' is one which, she feels, resonates with her own.) And the law too relies heavily on the contribution that trustees' qualities make to the operation of trusts,[11] above all as implying that trusts can for most of the time be safely allowed to run by themselves, without supervision by the courts. If it were otherwise, the courts would soon be overwhelmed.

---

[8] See section 11.1.

[9] The same should be true of resulting trusts. Lord Browne-Wilkinson in *Westdeutsche Landesbank Girozentrale v Islington LBC* [1996] AC 669, 708 asserts that a resulting trust arises only if the trustee so intends, but this is implausible: see section 16.3.

[10] See Chapter 11.   [11] See section 11.8.

1.7   THE TRUSTEE'S DUTIES

Although to mention duties and overlook the importance of the trustee's own characteristics is therefore to miss part of the picture, it remains the case that the trustee, holding the trust property, is under duties to handle it in a certain way. There is much to be said on this topic; Chapters 7–9, and also section 18.5, are devoted to it.

All trusts require their trustees to respect the fact that the trust property is not beneficially their own. At the lowest, this means they must keep the property for transfer to the objects, and so transfer it, or else give it up to fresh trustees.

Many constructive and resulting trusts will involve no duties beyond these. Express trusts will often demand more, however. The trust in the example earlier was an express trust. Its trustee had further, or fuller, duties of two kinds. He had to pay money out to the designated person, Adam, in the designated amounts, at the designated times, under the designated conditions; and not to pay it out, or withhold it, otherwise. And in the meantime, he had also to manage the trust property, and invest it appropriately so as to produce the income envisaged. Trustees of express trusts generally have duties of both these kinds, but such duties will vary in their details from the duties upon Adam's trustee. There will always be a duty to devote the trust's property to its object in some fashion; to do so in the right measure, at the right times, under the right conditions; and to do nothing else with it. But in another trust, the manner in which the property is to be devoted to the object might be different (it could aim at providing a house for the beneficiary to occupy, for example, or at carrying out some charitable purpose); and the designation of the object, amounts, times, and conditions will certainly be different (eg 'to pay half the capital to each of my sons on his marriage, save that if any reaches the age of 40 without having married his share shall be divided equally between his married brothers'; 'to relieve famine in the third world'). Likewise, there will normally be a duty of stewardship, requiring the trustee to manage the trust property so as effectively to allow for the enjoyment of it by the objects; but the exact manner of doing so may differ (eg the trust property may include agricultural land, the trusteeship of which evidently requires different practical steps from the trusteeship of stocks and shares). Chapters 7–9 deal with different aspects of the duties that trustees of express trusts can incur.

The 'definition' essayed at the outset referred to 'legally recognized duties'. One function of the words 'legally recognized' (we shall come to the other in the next section) is to establish a contrast with duties that the holder of some property may owe, but that are morally, not legally, operative. The grandmother's settlement for Adam could take exactly the same form, but be composed of moral, not legal, duties. A person subject to a duty might not wish to make anything of the distinction, and might be as ready to comply with a moral as with a legal duty. But the distinction matters if the law needs to establish whether there is present something that it regards as a duty: for that purpose, moral duties do not count. In the case of constructive trusts, there will be no confusion over this matter, as the circumstances recognized by the law as giving rise to such trusts will always, by definition, generate legal duties. The same is true for resulting trusts, in so far as these are not based on the settlor's intention. With express trusts, however, the question could in principle always be asked whether the settlor intended the duties to be legal (so creating a trust) or not. In practice, however, most trust-like arrangements are created in a relatively formal way, which leaves little doubt that legal duties are intended. The matter is discussed in more detail in Chapter 3. But even while we acknowledge that a trust must have such legally operative duties, it does not necessarily follow that these duties must be enforceable. That question is discussed in section 12.6.

1.8 THE OBJECTIVES OF THE TRUST

The device of an express trust lends itself to any purpose that can be translated into the terms of the two principal types of duty discussed above, namely bestowal of rights of enjoyment (often, in the form of payment out) and stewardship. So it can be used, as in our original example, to make payments to a person in a pattern more complex than a simple gift; equally, to a number of people, often according to an intricate scheme; or, as noted in the reference to purpose trusts, to provide for spending towards the achievement of a purpose. And the use of trusts in these ways may itself occur for a range of reasons. Trusts in favour of people might be used to distribute wealth amongst a family, for instance. They also provide the legal vehicle for the holding of contributions in a pension scheme, and the payment out of pensions; or for the pooling of investments, and the payment out of the return upon them.[12] Trusts for purposes might be used, as already noted, for objects such as investigating whether the plays attributed to Shakespeare were really the work of Bacon, or establishing

---

[12] See further G Moffat *Trusts Law Cases and Materials* 5th edn (2009) ch 13.

and maintaining a dogs' home, or providing a public recreation ground, or furthering the aims of some organization.

The element of stewardship is sometimes, as in the case of pooled investments, no less prominent among the reasons for which a trust is employed than that of bestowing enjoyment. Sometimes there will be a desire to procure the talents of the trustee in the active management of the trust's affairs, especially in the matter of investing the money.[13] Sometimes the idea will be more passive, eg to lodge the money with a custodian in such a way that it will remain safe even in the event of the custodian's bankruptcy (such safety being, as explained below, a characteristic of the trust concept).

Sometimes, even when the purposes of the trust are fundamentally ones of bestowal of enjoyment and stewardship, the precise arrangement of its provisions is shaped by a collateral aim: the reduction of tax liability. That is, the precise arrangement is chosen, in preference to other possible schemes for producing roughly the same desired package of stewardship and enjoyment, because it should attract a lower level of tax liability than they.[14] At one time, for example, trust arrangements were used to bring it about that payments, which would otherwise have been classed and taxed as income, appeared instead as a capital gain, and so attracted a lower tax rate.

There are, however, some objectives for which settlors might wish to use the trust device but that are not permitted by the law. This is the other significance of the stipulation, in the 'definition' essayed at the outset, that the trustee's duties be 'legally recognized'. In brief, it is not permissible to make a trust for a purpose that is itself illegal, such as for the furtherance of a criminal or otherwise illegal activity.[15] Arrangements that, while not otherwise illegal, tend to do social damage are also sometimes declared invalid, but the picture is ill defined. Provisions undermining the institution of the family are sometimes struck down, for example, as are those interfering excessively with the freedom of the beneficiaries (say, by attaching intrusive conditions to their entitlements). Trusts calculated to avoid tax are not always permitted to do so. And there seems to be evidence of judicial unhappiness at the economic damage that trusts can do. Ultimately, indeed, the law appears to allow only trusts that conduce to

---

[13]   See further R Cotterrell (1993) 46(2) CLP 75.

[14]   See further G Moffat *Trusts Law Cases and Materials* 5th edn (2009) ch 8.

[15]   For a case involving a trust whose object was a fraud on the social security system, see *Tinsley v Milligan* [1994] 1 AC 340; and for one involving a trust whose object was to defraud creditors, see *Tribe v Tribe* [1996] Ch 107.

human fulfilment. Matters of this kind are considered in more depth in Chapter 2, and also section 12.4.

Within these limitations, it is probably true in the abstract to say that the range of uses to which trusts may be put is infinitely variable. It would therefore be reasonable to suppose that the trust concept itself remains unaltered, no matter to what use it is put. But in practice, particular clusters of use emerge, albeit with detailed differences from one trust to another within each cluster: family settlements, charitable purpose trusts, pension scheme trusts, unit trusts, and so on. To greater or lesser extents, these clusters have attracted rules special to themselves, calculated to deal with concerns special to the area in question. As regards pension scheme trusts, for example, legislation such as the Pensions Act 1995[16] (introduced in the wake of a scandal, the Maxwell affair) secures that the trust property is better protected, and that scheme members are better informed and more closely involved in the running of the fund, than would be the case under the general law about trusts. The existence of such special rules has led some commentators to suggest that instead of thinking about the trust concept, or the law of trusts, as a single entity, we should think about a number of different entities.[17] They undeniably have a point. But it must not be assumed that because some new rule has emerged in a particular context, it cannot apply in other contexts too. If the new rule is compatible with the trust concept (which it must be, to have been accepted even in a limited context), it is worth considering whether it should be extended to some or indeed all other instances of that concept, which is a matter of whether it would advance policy aims favoured in the latter. The move to enhance the rights of pension scheme members, for example, may perhaps be seen as an especially intense version of a similar, if less clear-cut, development in the position of trust beneficiaries generally.

1.9 THE PROPERTY

Our original example involved a grandmother placing property on trust for her grandson. And we have continued to discuss trusts in terms of an obligation upon a trustee to handle some property in a particular way. It is implicit in this that there must be some property.[18]

---

[16] See further now Pensions Act 2004.
[17] See eg G Moffat (1993) 56 MLR 471 and D Hayton [2005] Conv 229 (pension trusts); J Warburton [1999] Conv 20 (charitable trusts).
[18] As regards the extent to which the property must be defined, see further section 8.3; P Parkinson [2002] CLJ 657, 663–76.

Some legal arrangements create obligations having no reference to property. For example, a singer, hired to perform at a concert, has a duty to do so. The use of his voice is not regarded as property.[19] Such a situation cannot be a trust.[20]

But the fact that an obligation *relates to* property does not on its own qualify it to be a trust obligation. The distinctive characteristic of a trust is that at any rate the trustee's most basic obligation regarding the property (that of not treating it as his own) is *attached to* the property, rather than resting on him personally. Obligations attached to property are known as 'proprietary' (or '*in rem*'); those resting on someone personally are termed 'personal' (or '*in personam*'). If I contract to sell you my car, I have an obligation to you (to perform this contract) that relates to a piece of property (the car); but I do not hold the latter on trust for you. Although it refers to a piece of property, my obligation to sell you the car is as personal as the singer's obligation to let the concert impresario have the benefit of his voice.

What does it mean to say that an obligation relating to some property is proprietary rather than personal? The answer is visible in two situations in particular: first, if the owner of the property transfers it illicitly to another person; and secondly, if the owner of the property becomes insolvent, and his property is seized and sold to pay his debts. If I had contracted to sell you my car, the upshot in these circumstances is that the car is validly transferred to the other person, or validly seized in my bankruptcy. Because my obligation to you is only personal, rather than attached to the car, you cannot go after the car itself: you can only have me pay you compensation for the fact that I can no longer perform my duty to let you have the car. So, in my bankruptcy, you become just another of my creditors. On the other hand, if I hold the car on trust for you, the car will commonly[21] not be validly transferred to the other person, and cannot be seized in my bankruptcy—as it is commonly said, you enjoy priority over my ordinary creditors. Because my obligation is proprietary, ie attached to the car itself, you can demand that it be vindicated against the very car, and not just against me.

---

[19] Though the scope of 'property' is neither self-evident nor hard-and-fast: K Gray [1991] CLJ 252.

[20] One sometimes finds the term 'constructive trust' used to describe a situation in which it is asserted not that the 'trustee' holds certain property on trust, but that he owes a purely personal obligation: see sections 15.1, 18.1. This usage is nowadays generally regarded as incorrect.

[21] A valid transfer will occur, however, if the transferee is a bona fide purchaser of the car without notice of your claim to it: see sections 12.1, 17.2.

The characterization of trust obligations as proprietary or personal, and their relationship with the beneficiaries' rights, are matters dealt with more fully in Chapter 12.

1.10 THE ABSENCE OF A PERSONAL INTEREST IN THE TRUSTEE: TRUSTEES AS FIDUCIARIES

The 'definition' given earlier stipulated that the trustee's obligations must extend 'to the exclusion of any personal interest'. The trust in the original example complied with this: the trustee there had no role other than to provide stewardship of the property and to transfer it as stipulated to Adam.

There are some arrangements that, like trusts, involve the owner of some property being subject to a legal duty, attached to the property, to handle it in a certain way; but where the owner does retain a personal interest in the property. Consider an easement. An easement arises where, for example, the owner of some land undertakes to permit his neighbour to walk across the land (the kind of arrangement known as a 'right of way'). The owner thus incurs an obligation to handle the land he owns in a particular way, for his neighbour's enjoyment, and this obligation is attached to the land. But he himself remains very substantially interested in the land: in all respects other than the inability to prevent the neighbour walking across it, it remains his. In particular, if he sells the land, he takes the proceeds for himself.

In the case of a trust, on the other hand, this will generally not be the case. If a trustee sells trust property, the proceeds will not be his to keep, but will in turn become subject to the trust. The exception is where the trustee is also one of the beneficiaries, as discussed earlier. In that case, he will obviously have a personal interest, in the latter capacity.[22]

The rule that trustees should have no personal interest is an important one for the trust concept. Taken with the other things we know about trusts, it means that trustees are fiduciaries. A fiduciary is someone whose role it is to act on behalf of—serve the interests of—another, his principal. A trustee is a fiduciary *vis-à-vis* the objects of his trust. Other

---

[22] A few cases (*Binions v Evans* [1972] Ch 359; *Swiss Bank Corporation v Lloyds Bank Ltd* [1979] Ch 548; *Lyus v Prowsa Developments Ltd* [1982] 1 WLR 1044; *Ashburn Anstalt v Arnold* [1989] Ch 1) hold a 'trust' to arise where the trustee clearly retains a personal interest, just like the owner of land which is subject to an easement. These cases are discussed in sections 15.1 and 18.1, where it is argued that they do not truly involve trusts, on the ground in the text.

fiduciaries include solicitors, who must serve the interests of their clients. Likewise stockbrokers and their clients, employees and their employers, company directors and their companies, and business partners as between themselves.[23]

The ability to entrust our property or affairs to another is valuable. It allows us to have the benefit of expertise or other desirable qualities that we ourselves lack; to deal more distantly, and more frequently; and to effectively multi-task in our affairs, directing our own personal attention to other aspects of them. These boons can be seen, in differing mixes, in the various fiduciary relationships. But there is a downside, 'the principal–agent problem'; for these purposes, the word 'agent' encompassing all kinds of fiduciaries. Entrusting his property or affairs to another leaves a principal more vulnerable than acting in person on his own behalf. Fiduciaries are commonly difficult to supervise. And, perhaps above all, the selfless nature of a fiduciary's role means that his principal's interests are at best neutrally, and sometimes negatively, correlated with his own. Say I hold property on trust for you. I therefore have a number of obligations to you, but their performance is of no benefit to me. Indeed, put most crudely, it would be in my personal interest to disregard the trust and treat the property in question as my own.

To facilitate the use of valuable fiduciary arrangements in the face of this misalignment between a fiduciary's interests and his duty, the law has rules calculated to counteract it.[24] These rules aim, directly or indirectly, to minimize the impact of the fiduciary's own interests, and to maximize his incentive to serve his principal. So, for example, a fiduciary must avoid any situation in which he risks distraction from his principal's interests; and he must 'account' to his principal—an expression covering a number of rules that fix a fiduciary's exact duties and liabilities in a characteristic way that has traditionally borne uncompromisingly, even harshly, on the fiduciary.[25] These features of the law will be discussed in detail in a number

---

[23] Although it is thus easy to identify the main kinds of fiduciary, an abstract definition has proved elusive. See further J Shepherd *The Law of Fiduciaries* (1981) chs 5 and 6; M Conaglen *Fiduciary Loyalty* (2010) ch 9; J Edelman (2010) 126 LQR 302.

[24] The 'principal–agent problem' has also received attention from economists, aimed at designing contracts calculated to meet the difficulties. (See eg D Sappington (1991) 5 *Journal of Economic Perspectives* 45.) Many fiduciary relationships involve contracts and so are in principle amenable to this approach, but trusteeship commonly does not, leaving the rules referred to in the text to do most of the corrective work. These rules also constitute the default position in the contractual context, which the contract can vary.

[25] For the connection between the nature of fiduciary responsibility and the duty to account, see further J Getzler in A Burrows and A Rodger (eds) *Mapping the Law: Essays in Honour of Peter Birks* (2006) ch 31, 590–7.

of later chapters. As we shall see in those discussions, the stringency of the relevant rules is explicable as calculated to address the specific difficulties embedded in the principal–agent problem. But we shall also see that it may simultaneously be unhelpful or even counter-productive, and that signs can be found of a tendency to dilute it.[26]

1.11 THE ESSENTIALS OF TRUSTS

We began, albeit with caveats, by offering the following 'definition' of the trust concept:

> A trust is a situation in which property is vested in someone (a trustee), who is under legally recognized obligations, at least some of which are of a proprietary kind, to handle it in a certain way, and to the exclusion of any personal interest. These obligations may arise either by conscious creation by the previous owner of the property (the settlor), or because some other legally significant circumstances are present.[27]

The various components of this 'definition' have now been reviewed and explained. Although again with caveats, we took an example, that of the grandmother's trust for Adam: more abstractly, a settlor transferring property to a trustee with instructions to handle it for the benefit of a beneficiary. We then saw how the various features of this may be essential or inessential to trusts. This trust arose because its settlor so intended; but trusts are recognized as arising for other reasons as well. It had a settlor, a trustee, and a beneficiary, who were different people; we have seen that whilst there must be a trustee, there need not be a settlor, and, in place of a beneficiary, the object of the trust might be a purpose. The trust must, however, always (like that in the example) involve some property, which the trustee will technically own but as regards the handling of which he will be under certain obligations of legal rather than just moral significance, at least some of which will be attached to the trust property. The example was typical of express trusts in involving duties to disburse the trust property correctly and meanwhile to manage it, but the details of the duties, and the reasons why people wish to create them, may vary

---

[26] Moreover, it is unclear to what extent they apply to constructive and resulting, as opposed to express, trusts. See further section 18.5.

[27] This description of a trust is in most respects similar to that used in Art 2 of the Hague Convention on the Law Applicable to Trusts and on their Recognition. This Convention aims to secure international agreement that countries whose own law does not feature trusts will nevertheless respect trusts emanating from countries whose law does feature them. The principal difference between the description given in the Convention and that given in the text is that the former in effect confines itself to express trusts.

considerably. Trusts must, however, remain within the realm of what is legally permitted, and they must in principle exclude any interest on the part of the trustee.

Taking all this into account, the 'definition' can therefore be seen to cover everything that is meant by the trust concept. Some points now need to be made, however, about two matters that are, deliberately, omitted from the 'definition'. These are matters that have been suggested as being essential to the trust concept, but that are not.

1.12   THE TRUST AS AN EQUITABLE CONCEPT?

First, it might be said that our description should be refined by recording that the trust is an 'equitable' concept, as opposed to a 'legal' one.

'Equitable' concepts are those that, historically, were developed by the Court of Chancery (whose chief, and for a long time sole, judge was the Chancellor), while 'legal'[28] concepts originated in the common law courts: the King's (or Queen's) Bench, the Common Pleas, and the Exchequer. Trusts originated in the Chancery,[29] and so count as equitable. Noting this fact would certainly add a true detail to our description of trusts. It is, however, questionable whether it adds information of useful significance.

The fact that the English legal system historically had more than one set of courts may have contributed to the emergence of the trust concept. The multiplicity of courts operating along somewhat independent lines probably allowed for a more enterprising exploration of conceptual possibilities than might otherwise have occurred, and trusts may be seen as one of the products of this process. But it would certainly not be impossible to reproduce the trust concept in a legal system that only ever had one set of courts;[30] and indeed, in England itself the different courts have been

---

[28]   When that word is used in contradistinction to 'equitable'. In a broader sense, both equitable and legal concepts are legal, as opposed to, say, merely moral.

[29]   For an account, see A Simpson *A History of the Land Law* 2nd edn (1986) ch 8. For certain periods of their history, however, trusts have been operated by the common law courts as well as by the Chancery; and, more importantly as a challenge to the idea that they originated in the Chancery, it is possible to see them as stemming, at least in part, from the availability of the *common law* action of account as between those whom we would call 'beneficiaries' and 'trustees': see S Stoljar (1964) 80 LQR 203, 210–12; J Getzler in A Burrows and A Rodger (eds) *Mapping the Law: Essays in Honour of Peter Birks* (2006) ch 31.

[30]   For a survey of the occurrence of the trust concept in different countries' legal systems (many of which have never had a separation of courts), see M Lupoi *Trust Laws of the World: A Collection of Original Texts* (1996).

amalgamated for well over a century.[31] So one looks rather for evidence that equitable concepts function differently from legal ones in the contemporary law. It is possible to find such evidence, but its power is open to question.

One piece of evidence is this. We have noted that if trust property is illicitly passed by the trustee to another person, the recipient will commonly, though not always, incur duties attached to the property.[32] The exact circumstances in which transferees are bound by duties attached to property under equitable concepts are slightly different from those in which they are bound by duties attached under legal concepts. To state that trusts are equitable can serve as a shorthand means of saying that they feature one, rather than the other, set of rules in this respect. But there is nothing in the labels 'equitable' and 'legal' to mean that the two sets of rules, and the differences between them, must be as they are. In fact, the modern tendency is to eliminate the differences, and to subject both legal and equitable concepts to a single regime of rules regarding the circumstances in which duties attached to property under them will affect recipients.[33,34]

Another piece of evidence is said to be that equitable concepts are less determinate than legal ones. That is, the law's response to a given set of facts is less easily identified when an equitable concept is in play than when a legal one is. This is because, it is in turn said, equity and the common law define their responses in different ways. Whilst the dictates of legal

---

[31] Ultimately as a result of the Judicature Acts 1873–5, but the assimilation was begun in earlier legislation.   [32] See sections 1.9, 12.1.

[33] Where the property is land, the regime is that contained in the Land Registration Act 2002, to which it is almost irrelevant whether the duties are legal or equitable.

[34] It has been argued (B McFarlane *The Structure of Property Law* (2008) 21–39; B McFarlane and R Stevens (2010) 4 J Eq 1) that there is another difference between the reach of common law and equitable duties: that the latter can affect only someone holding title to the property in question, while the former can apply to outsiders too. It is pointed out that, for example, while the legal owner of some asset can sue someone who steals it (ie the duty to respect the owner's right affects the whole world), the beneficiary of a trust cannot sue one who steals the trust's asset—only the trustee can do so (ie the duty to respect the beneficiary's right affects only those who hold legal title to the asset, and not others such as thieves): see *MCC Proceeds Inc v Lehman Bros International (Europe)* [1998] 4 All ER 675. This is a more or less accurate (though a little over-simplified) statement about the behaviour of the two kinds of duty, but it is hard to see why it should track the fact that the one is legal, the other equitable. Indeed, it is clear that at least some equitable duties have the same sort of reach as legal ones: see especially *Re Nisbet and Potts' Contract* [1905] 1 Ch 391, [1906] 1 Ch 386 (though there seem to be no extant examples of legal duties having the lesser reach of those under trusts). The contrast ought really to be one between *trust* duties, where the whole point is that the trustee is in some sense a cut-out between the beneficiaries and the rest of the world, and others. See further section 12.1.

concepts are (depicted as) generally contained in hard-and-fast rules, which the judge has only to identify and apply, the dictates of equitable concepts are (depicted as) generally established by an exercise of creative judgement—discretion—on the part of a judge.

It is a commonplace that the law as a whole makes use both of relatively determinate rules and of rules requiring a greater degree of discretion. What requires examination is the thesis that discretion, and so the tendency to indeterminacy, is especially characteristic of equity.[35]

One question over the thesis is whether it is factually accurate in the observations it makes about the way in which legal and equitable concepts operate. Presumably the claim is not that discretion is discernible only in equitable doctrines,[36] but that equity uses discretion significantly more than the common law. It is difficult to test this claim. Discretion is not a simple phenomenon;[37] it is straightforward neither to identify nor even to describe, and its use is accordingly hard, if not impossible, to quantify. It is clear, in particular, that propositions that do not explicitly call for judicial discretion may nevertheless do so implicitly. For example, a requirement 'to take reasonable care' does not itself tell us exactly what is required in the circumstances of a particular case: that is established rather by a judge, authoritatively interpreting the requirement. At the same time, it is a mistake to regard a doctrine that (explicitly or implicitly) requires judicial discretion in its implementation as therefore indeterminate. Discretions normally are, and it is thought in legal contexts should be, exercised according to fairly clear patterns. All this needs to be taken into account when attempting to assess a concept's determinacy.

If, despite these problems, one concludes that equitable concepts are as a matter of fact less determinate than legal ones, a second difficulty arises. Is the relative indeterminacy of equitable concepts a necessary facet of their being equitable, or is the link looser than that, or indeed quite illusory? Again, the matter is hard to test, as it is unclear just what it means to say that some characteristic of a doctrine is a 'necessary facet' of its being legal or equitable. But an argument is sometimes made in this vein.

---

[35] For references to literature supporting this thesis, see A Duggan (1997) 113 LQR 601.

[36] There are certainly some common law concepts which rely heavily upon judicial discretion, such as the jurisdiction to quash an administrative action upon judicial review. There are also some highly discretionary jurisdictions which cannot sensibly be ascribed either to the common law or to equity, because in their current forms they substantially post-date the amalgamation of the common law and equity courts; eg the sentencing of criminals, and most jurisdictions concerned with family matters.

[37] See generally K Hawkins (ed) *The Uses of Discretion* (1991) especially Part I.

The argument starts from the proposition that, of its nature, equity is a supplement on the law. That is, equity is the vehicle whereby considerations that deserve attention, but that the law's rules deny that attention, are given effect. This proposition seems to be an accurate description of the way in which equity first developed, in the late Middle Ages.[38] The ordinary legal regime was acknowledged not to do satisfactory justice in all circumstances. Where the Chancellor found that this was likely to be the case, he intervened, making orders calculated to align the outcome better with abstract justice. This is not, however, necessarily to say that equity features, or is special on account of, inherent indeterminacy. To be sure, its interventions against the implications of the common law may have produced indeterminacy, but only in the short term, while the adjustment took hold; thereafter, the new position may have been as determinate as any other.[39] Equity may more properly be seen as special on account of indeterminacy if it is regarded as operating *constantly* to introduce considerations that the law does not otherwise reflect. On this view, it must resort to ideas that are in principle enduringly and necessarily indeterminate, for without this quality they would be unfitted for their work of infinite supplementation.[40] Is there evidence for this version of the account?

It is commonly said that there was a significant degree of indeterminacy about equity as it first developed. In support of this, it is pointed out that the interventions by the early Chancellors were aimed at compelling those involved in the matter in question to follow the implications of 'conscience', in cases when the common law failed to secure this. And the Chancellor's instructions were '*in personam*': ie they consisted not in generalized rules but in individual orders issued to individual people, requiring them to perform, or refrain from, certain acts. In these ways, therefore, equity can certainly be described as having originally operated in some sense ad hoc. It does not, however, follow that it was essentially indeterminate; and careful attention to the history suggests that it was not.

---

[38] For an account of the history of equity, see J Baker *An Introduction to English Legal History* 4th edn (2002) ch 6; and for the issues particularly considered below, see especially M Macnair (2007) 27 OJLS 659.

[39] This vision of equity appeals to eg A Mason (1994) 100 LQR 238, who, whilst celebrating equity's role in facilitating reform, represents any indeterminacy produced thereby only as a short-term price worth paying.

[40] For this version of the argument, see eg M Halliwell *Equity & Good Conscience in a Contemporary Context* (1997).

In particular, the appeal to 'conscience' seems not to have been an invocation of individual, and so potentially idiosyncratic and thus variable, standards of justice. Rather, it meant taking account of facts relevant to the issue in hand, known to the parties (or the court itself) but left out of account by the common law's rules. In the stock example, the common law regarded a sealed bond as incontrovertible evidence of the debt to which it testified; so a debtor who repaid his debt but failed to get the bond itself cancelled remained, so far as the common law was concerned, liable under it. But the Chancellor could establish the fact of the repayment by examining the 'conscience'—ie the knowledge—of the creditor, and, taking cognizance of it, would intervene to prevent such double liability. It should be understood, however, that the common law rules were the product not of wilful obtuseness, but of a concern for what we today would call 'due process'; which concern, however, produced effects that came over time to appear obtuse, eliciting the response of equity.

So although equity's reference to 'conscience' is often relied on as indicating that indeterminacy is of its essence, at any rate the original role of 'conscience' offers no support to this proposition. This observation need not be the end of the story, however. For behind the reference to 'conscience' must lie an understanding of what knowledge (held in conscience) is *relevant*. To revert to the question of repayment of a debt without cancellation of the bond, attending to the bald fact of the repayment presupposes that we are indeed interested in this; that the cancellation of the bond is not substantively crucial. Likewise, a trust will be recognized and enforced only if we *both* attend to the property-owner's knowledge (held in conscience) that he is meant to hold for the object(s), *and* presuppose that this in fact matters. We have no difficulty in sympathizing with such presuppositions, but they are obviously not inevitable. Their roots seem to be less well understood than the idea of 'conscience' itself. In principle, they could be characterized by indeterminacy, and so offer support after all to the idea that equity is essentially indeterminate. In practice, however, they appear not to have been. That is to say, the causes in which the early Chancellors resorted to 'conscience' seem to have been quite systematized, if not necessarily articulated.[41]

---

[41]   There are in fact no records of the earliest Chancellors' activities. This may suggest, contrary to the text, that their operations were rather random, making it profitless to record them. On the other hand, the pleas for their intervention have been preserved. In these, certain kinds of situation are repeatedly referred to in similar terms as meriting attention, prompting the conclusion that there was an expectation, both in principle and in practice, that the Chancellor would operate according to a pattern. From about 1450, however, reports begin to appear which, both in their content and in their very existence, confirm this impression.

It seems however that in Henry VIII's reign, equity could at least sometimes have been, and indeed was, accurately described as indeterminate. But the reasons for this indeterminacy seem not to have been intrinsic to a mission of supplementation. One may have been the personalities or policies of the period's principal Chancellors, Wolsey and More, themselves. Another (possibly linked to the first) may have been the great increase at this time in the volume of the business brought before the Chancellor, which, in the absence of articulated systematization, will have increased the likelihood of inconsistencies. Another again may have been the period's general disturbance of established religious precepts, and so perhaps, if these were (as seems plausible) among their sources, of the 'presuppositions' referred to above as giving late medieval equity its substantive identity; once these precepts and presuppositions were discredited, a space was left as regards their replacements, which the Chancellors' own personal opinions could have helped to fill.

Paradoxically, however, the increase in the volume of the Chancellor's business during this period, increasingly featuring 'ordinary' matters, would have placed a growing premium on determinacy. Predictably, then, it came increasingly to be suggested that the indeterminacy perceived as associated with the Chancellor's activities was unsatisfactory. Whether or not moved by these suggestions, changes in personnel from the 1590s began a trend back towards systematization; perhaps by this time, too, Elizabeth I's state had become more confident in its identity and values than was that of her father. This trend became associated with the more general movement against rule by personal (especially royal) preference in the seventeenth century, other features being the deposition of Charles I and James II; systematization being self-consciously and effectively driven on by Chancellors of this period, above all Lord Nottingham, who—while referring once again to 'conscience', this time meaning the conscience *of the court*—was clear that his task was to operate a system of firm law.[42] A further major contribution in this vein was added by Lord Eldon, in the Georgian period; by this time, there seems to have been no doubt that equity was supposed to be generally no less determinate than

---

[42] D Yale *Nottingham's Chancery Cases* Vol II (1961) Introduction; S Milsom *Historical Foundations of the Common Law* 2nd edn (1981) 88–95. But a republican disquiet continued in the American colonies and (after the Revolution) states, until the 'firm law' vision was pressed and established here too, in the early nineteenth century: see J Story *Commentaries on Equity Jurisprudence, as Administered in England and America* 2nd edn (1839) ch 1 §§ 19–21, ch 2 §§ 56–8; R Pound in P Winfield and A McNair (eds) *Cambridge Legal Essays* (1926) 259, 276.

the common law. Subject to the two qualifications about to be discussed, this vision has broadly persisted to the present day.[43]

The first qualification is that at least some Chancery judges presented equity as inherently indeterminate in the last quarter of the nineteenth century. The context was this. Where a person enters into a contract to buy a piece of land, or to lease it, equity will under certain circumstances regard that person as already the owner or the lessee of the land, even before the legal formalities to that effect are complete.[44] The way in which this doctrine was and is applied assumes that the rights so acquired are reasonably concrete, and this can only be the case if the circumstances in which they are acquired are reasonably determinate. Yet in the last quarter of the nineteenth century, one finds a flurry of judicial statements to the effect that such rights arise only where, if the matter had come before a judge, the judge would have chosen so to order, in the exercise of a discretion. This late outcrop of ostensible affection for indeterminacy was very specific to the area of law in question, however, and it seems to owe nothing to a sense that equity has a peculiar mission of constant supplementation. Rather, it probably sprang from a concern to make the rules of equity difficult to grasp. A recent statutory reform (contained in the Judicature Acts 1873–5) had merged the common law courts with the Chancery, with the aim that the common law and equity should in future be administered by the same personnel. This reform was widely unpopular among Chancery lawyers, and they appear to have played up the indeterminacy and hence impenetrability of this facet of equity as a means of substantiating their claim that equity could never be accessible to common lawyers.[45]

The second qualification is that, from about 1970, a number of judges and commentators (principally in Australia, Canada, and New Zealand, but also in England) have made a point of depicting equity as indeterminate.[46] Much reference has been made to 'conscience', specifically in the form of 'unconscionability'; and although there is nothing about these concepts requiring them to be indeterminate, it is clear that they are so regarded within this movement. It may be possible to ascribe this development too to particular catalysts. One may have been that the equity and common law courts of the dominant Australian jurisdiction, New South Wales, were merged in 1970; like its English counterpart a century earlier, this

---

[43] A non-discretionary view of the implications of the trust concept was, for example, strongly asserted in *Foskett v McKeown* [2001] 1 AC 102, 108–9, 127.

[44] See section 17.6.   [45] S Gardner (1987) 7 OJLS 60, 92–7.

[46] See the literature collected by A Duggan (1997) 113 LQR 601. The approach is undeniably reflected in (the perception of) some equitable phenomena, including the remedial constructive trust and the doctrine of proprietary estoppel: sections 15.3–15.5 and 18.4.

development was opposed by some Chancery lawyers, who may have found a counter-weapon in the depiction of equity as indeterminate. Another may have been the interest in Australia, Canada, and New Zealand, as they and the United Kingdom increasingly diverged politically, in forming distinctive laws of their own, though at the same time continuing for the most part to claim the legitimacy of historical derivation for these laws. The latter end is served by invoking an established concept such as equity, whilst the former is served by claiming that that concept is indeterminate, and so infinitely capable of producing new effects. A third catalyst may have been the movement, in England from the 1980s on, towards barristers losing their virtual monopoly of audience in the higher courts, instead having to share it with solicitors. Indeterminacy in an area of law favours the specialist in that area (ie the barrister), who is in a position to decipher the unwritten patterns, over the non-specialist (the solicitor).[47] A fourth factor may have been the increased academic interest during this period in deconstructionist and post-modernist styles of thought, a trait of which is to emphasize, and to some degree celebrate, the idea of supplementation. Some adherents to these styles of thought see equity as quintessentially the embodiment of that idea.[48] The sustainability of the latter perspective is, of course, the question currently under consideration.

So although equity was at one time marked by indeterminacy, this (though in truth, neither this nor its opposite) should not be seen as crucial to its identity. It remains of course entirely possible to think that somewhere in the law there should be, and perhaps is, a vehicle for constant supplementation, but there is therefore no good reason to think that equity is or has to be that vehicle (indeed, a named institution, such as 'equity', is a rather unlikely candidate for the role); and no other plausible basis has emerged upon which to say that it is special, essentially different from the common law. So although we can accurately add into our description of trusts the point that the obligations in question must be equitable ones, to do so is not to make a significant contribution to that description.

1.13 KNOWLEDGE BY THE TRUSTEE?

The second matter that might be said to be essential to trusts, but that we have omitted from our 'definition', is a requirement that the trustee should *know of* the facts on account of which the law finds a trust.

---

[47] M Galanter (1974) 9 Law and Society Review 95.
[48] eg M Halliwell *Equity & Good Conscience in a Contemporary Context* (1997).

In the example with which we began, there was no reason to suppose that the trustee was unaware of the trust being created. And that will generally be the case, whether the trust is express, where the trustee will know that the settlor is trying to create a trust; or resulting or constructive, where the trustee will know of, because he will have been involved in, the facts that lead the law to impose the trust.

According to Lord Browne-Wilkinson in *Westdeutsche Landesbank Girozentrale v Islington LBC*,[49] such knowledge is essential to a trust. On this view, an express trust cannot arise unless the alleged trustee knows that he is supposed to hold the property on trust, and a resulting or constructive trust cannot arise unless the alleged trustee knows of the facts by reason of which that trust would arise. So if I gratuitously transfer property to you without your knowledge, it is only from the moment of your enlightenment that you hold the property on a resulting trust.[50] Or if I, already a trustee, illicitly transfer trust property to you, you begin to hold it on trust too only when you know of the trust.[51] Lord Browne-Wilkinson concedes however that in the latter of these two situations, but apparently only there, although you do not hold *on trust* until you know of the trust, meanwhile an innominate situation arises in which you may not treat the property as beneficially your own.[52] This means that so long as you retain the property, you can be required to transfer it to the beneficiaries, if they are immediately entitled, or to new trustees; but you have no other responsibilities, so that if you lose the property before attaining the necessary knowledge, you incur no liability to make good the loss. (Though if you give the property to someone else, presumably the same will go for them.)

Lord Browne-Wilkinson's view is widely doubted, however. The commoner opinion is that trusts can arise without the alleged trustee's knowledge,[53] and that is the position taken by our 'definition'. In particular, there seems clear authority that if I gratuitously transfer property to you without your knowledge, you nonetheless hold it on resulting trust.[54]

---

[49] [1996] AC 669, 705–6, 715. Other members of the House of Lords concurred with Lord Browne-Wilkinson: [1996] AC 669, 689, 718, 720. The point was one of several independent reasons which his Lordship gave for the conclusion reached: it is hard to say which, if any, of them should be counted as the *ratio* of the decision.

[50] Section 16.2 describes how resulting trusts arise in cases of gratuitous transfer.

[51] Section 17.2 describes how a recipient of illicitly transferred trust property holds it on trust.   [52] [1996] AC 669, 707.

[53] This view was expressly taken in *Hardoon v Belilios* [1901] AC 118, 123.

[54] *Birch v Blagrave* (1755) 1 Amb 264; *Childers v Childers* (1857) 1 De G & J 482; *Re Vinogradoff* [1935] WN 68.

Lord Browne-Wilkinson based his notion on the idea that trusts, being equitable concepts, can arise only where the alleged trustee's conscience is affected: which, he continues, is only where the alleged trustee knows of the reasons why it should be affected.[55] We saw in section 1.12 that attention to conscience was crucial to early equity, though only from about the seventeenth century did it mean what Lord Browne-Wilkinson must have in mind. But as equitable jurisprudence subsequently underwent the systematization also referred to in section 1.12, its concepts ceased to be defined by direct reference to the dictates of conscience. At the end of that section we noted however that references to conscience have sometimes continued to be made, in the service of other agendas. The view of Lord Browne-Wilkinson under discussion can be regarded in this way. The reference to conscience provides a vehicle, of a historically resonant and contemporarily fashionable kind, for what seems to be a concern to ensure that trusts operate in a practically acceptable way. It is perhaps aimed at one worry in particular. It would be unsatisfactory if someone having no reason to think himself a trustee were liable for breach of a trustee's duty to respect the trust, eg not to use the property as his own. On Lord Browne-Wilkinson's view, he would escape such liability on the ground that he is not a trustee. But the law seems to come to this result anyway. Lord Browne-Wilkinson's opponents assert that whilst someone can be a trustee and so incur the duty whether he knows it or not, he does not *breach* the duty unless he could have known that he held the property in question on trust.[56] This rule is probably the law, though it is little emphasized outside the case of the unwitting recipient of illicitly transferred trust property,[57] as most other trustees do realize their status as such, and would-be claimants against those who do not have probably always recognized the unpromising nature of their claim. If this rule is the law, the practical justification for Lord Browne-Wilkinson's view is removed.

---

[55] [1996] AC 669, 705.

[56] R Chambers *Resulting Trusts* (1997) 201–12; C Harpum in P Birks and F Rose (eds) *Restitution and Equity Volume One, Resulting Trusts and Equitable Compensation* (2000) 165–7.

[57] See section 14.3.

2

Policies Shaping the Express
Trust Concept

In Chapter 1 we identified what we mean by the trust concept. As we saw, the concept involves certain facts being treated in a particular way by the law, above all by the imposition of a legal duty upon the trustee. We did not, however, address the question *why* the law maintains the trust concept, ie treats these facts in this way.

In addressing this question, we need to distinguish between express and constructive trusts. As noted in section 1.3, express trusts arise because a settlor decides to create them, while constructive trusts arise for other reasons (while resulting trusts are aligned with one or the other, opinion differing as to which). In this chapter, we shall consider why such a decision by a settlor elicits the legal response of a trust—that is, an express trust—and whether it should. The reasons for constructive trusts, and the justifiability of the legal significance of these reasons (as well as the position of resulting trusts), will be considered in Chapters 15–18.

2.1 EXPRESS TRUSTS AS FACILITATIVE DEVICES

If we accept that an express trust is one that arises because its settlor wishes it to, have we not thereby answered the question why the law recognizes it? No. There are innumerable situations in which I may wish something to occur, but in which the law does not oblige other people to lend themselves to its occurrence, as it does when it says that they are trustees. Why, then, does the law impose obligations in aid of my wish to create a trust?

One might think of explaining the obligation in express trusts in terms of the trustee's being unjustly enriched at the expense of the settlor. The argument would be that if the trustee did not observe the settlor's instructions, but kept the property for himself or disposed of it however else he wished, he would have been unjustly enriched at the settlor's expense; and that the trustee's duty arises so as to prevent this from occurring.

This suggestion, however, makes no sense in the case where the settlor declares himself trustee of some property that he already holds. Here, no one is unjustly enriched at his expense, because he has not parted with the property. Yet he is still under a duty to implement the terms of the trust. Moreover, the trustee's unjust enrichment at the settlor's expense could always be prevented by requiring the trustee to restore the property to the settlor. So this suggestion does not ultimately provide what we are seeking, namely a reason why the trustee should be under a duty actually to carry out the terms of the trust.

Alternatively, it might be suggested that the obligation arises so as to prevent the trustee's unjust enrichment at the expense of the beneficiary, in the form of his intercepting a benefit that would otherwise have gone to the latter. This suggestion too has problems. What if the object of the trust is not a beneficiary but a purpose? Is it possible to be unjustly enriched at the expense of anything but a (natural or legal) person? Moreover, except in very simple cases where a straightforward gift would have done as well as a trust, it is hard to see how the benefit could have reached the intended beneficiary unless the trust was effective anyway. So in saying that the trustee is enriched by intercepting that which should have gone to the beneficiary, the argument assumes what we need it to prove—namely, again, a reason why the settlor's intention to create the trust should be legally effective.

One seems to get closer to the point if one suggests instead that the settlor's wish to create a trust gives rise to an expectation on the part of the settlor or beneficiary, against the trustee, that the trustee will perform the trust, and that the trustee comes under a duty to fulfil this expectation. But this answer too will not suffice. One cannot realistically identify any such expectation in at least some cases in which a trust is undoubtedly present. For example, a purpose, as opposed to a beneficiary, cannot have expectations. Where the beneficiary has not yet been born, or his identity has not yet been established (eg 'such person as my daughter may in future marry'), he cannot have an expectation. Even where there is an identified living beneficiary, there is no need for him to know about the trust or its terms, so as to form expectations about it. Perhaps a settlor making a trust by will cannot sensibly be said to have expectations either; nor a settlor who makes himself trustee to have expectations against himself. Moreover, this explanation does not suffice even in situations where expectations can meaningfully be said to exist. We wanted to know why the law should translate a wish to create a trust into a legally recognized duty on the trustee to carry out the trust, when it is clear that it does no such thing so far as many wishes are concerned. Speaking in terms of expectations does not answer this question. It merely reformulates it as an inquiry why the law should translate expectations of this particular kind into legally recognized duties.[1]

So all the suggestions considered so far fail to answer the question at which they are purportedly aimed, and would still do so even if their other deficiencies were met or overlooked.

It is striking that all these suggestions envisage the source of the obligation as a natural one, in this sense: they depict the people concerned (especially settlors) as acting in a state of utopian innocence, and then seek to explain, in terms of notions extrinsic to the actions themselves, why their naive actions should have the binding effect that we actually observe. This kind of approach may be appropriate in contexts where the people involved do characteristically act without reference to the question of what their obligations might be: in cases of accidentally causing loss, for example, addressed by the law of tort. The situations in which constructive trusts arise are often of this kind. There, people who acted with no notion of coming under trust-type obligations may have arrived at a position that seems to demand that such obligations be imposed. But our present concern is with express trusts, which arise in principle only where a settlor wants to make one.

This conscious, voluntary quality of express trusts is the key to understanding the obligation that arises in them. It means that the people concerned (settlors, trustees) are characteristically not acting in innocence, with the trust concept coming in from outside to deal with the consequences of what they have done. Instead, they are acting with their eyes already on the concept, and deliberately interacting with it. They can be seen, therefore, as undertaking roles in an activity with preordained rules.

The idea may become clearer if we draw an analogy with the playing of some recognized sport. There is no natural reason whatever why a certain configuration of people on a field ('an offside situation') should lead to one person kicking a ball in a particular fashion ('taking a free kick'). Explaining the connection between them involves referring to the internal arrangements of the game, football, to which the participants submit themselves when they elect to play. So the express trust can be thought of as a defined package in which certain actions have certain specified effects, to which people may choose to subscribe. Deciding to create a

---

[1] In the case of contracts, where the law renders the expectation of performance into a legal obligation to that effect, the answer to the question 'Why?' lies in the presence of consideration. The further questions 'What is the essence of consideration?' and 'Why should it have this effect?' are not without difficulty, however. The outstanding literature includes P Atiyah *The Rise and Fall of Freedom of Contract* (1979) and *Promises, Morals and Law* (1981), and C Fried *Contract as Promise* (1981).

trust gives rise to a duty of giving effect to the trust's terms because that is the convention that one is opting into. There is thus a crucial difference between the question why an obligation should arise where a settlor wishes to bestow certain benefits upon his objects, to which we are hard put to supply a satisfactory answer; and the question why an obligation should arise where a settlor decides to create a trust, to which the answer is, in effect, 'because that is what making a trust means'.[2]

The idea, then, is that society, through the law, maintains the express trust concept as a packaged arrangement of rules about dispositions of property that those who wish to make such dispositions may use in order to do so, in the foreknowledge of what is entailed. As such, the concept is what is known as a 'facilitative' provision: a facility of which people may take advantage if they desire to achieve the results it entails.[3]

2.2 THE BASIS FOR THE FACILITATIVE PROVISION OF A TRUST DEVICE

But this in turn raises the question why this particular facilitative provision should exist. Why should 'deciding to make a trust' mean something more than 'wishing to bestow certain benefits'? The existence of express trusts enables people to make dispositions of their property of a more complicated kind than simply giving it away; why should the law go to the trouble of providing a facility for doing this? There seems to be an assumption that people have a legitimate interest in being able to do so, for which the law should cater by offering the necessary facilitative device. Why should this be?

The answer is rooted in liberalism, especially the liberal vision of the institution of property. Liberalism argues that everyone should be permitted the largest possible degree of autonomy. The autonomy of a property

[2] There is a similarity between trusts and covenants, ie promises made without consideration but in a deed. It is hard to explain why making a covenant should give rise to a legally recognized obligation to perform it (the deed seems to have no 'natural' importance, in the sense used in the text) except in the terms 'Because that is what making a covenant means'.

[3] We can, however, point to no moment when the law first announced 'Henceforth there shall exist the facility to make trusts.' Perhaps there was no such moment. Perhaps the origin of express trusts lies in the constructive trust that arose when an owner of some property transferred it to another, relying as he did so on the latter's promise to hold it in a certain way, as a means of redressing the loss he would suffer if that promise were not kept (see sections 18.1–18.2). Express trusts may have been born when transferors—henceforth, settlors—perceived that they could create such a constructive trust deliberately, so as to engineer their wish for the property to be held in the particular way into a legal obligation on the transferee—henceforth, trustee—to do so. The possibility of creating a trust by declaration, ie by the settlor making himself trustee, obviously post-dates the change, for here there is no transfer with reliance; the basis can only be facilitation. See further S Gardner in C Mitchell (ed) *Constructive and Resulting Trusts* (2010) ch 2, 84–5.

owner is protected if we say that he does not lose his property unless he himself intentionally gives it away; but his autonomy is also maximized if we accord him the greatest possible freedom as to how he may intentionally give it away. If he might wish to dispose of it in some elaborately arranged fashion, he should be able to do so. The law provides the vehicle of the express trust in order to permit this.

But it is not enough to locate the basis of express trusts in liberal theory and leave matters there. Trusts—or at any rate some uses of the trust device—can be seen as serving other useful interests besides the liberty of settlors. Pension provisions and charitable initiatives, for example, may be thought 'good things' for reasons over and above the fact that they represent the fulfilment of someone's wishes. At the same time, while trusts serve the liberty of settlors, they—or, again, some uses to which they are put—may harm other wholesome interests. A trust to finance drug trafficking is harmful, for example, although it is just as much an exercise of its settlor's liberty as any other trust.

Recognizing that the express trust concept has its foundation in liberalism does not, therefore, mean that to point to the settlor's wish is always the only justification for a trust. Nor does this recognition provide a sufficient justification for allowing property owners carte blanche to organize the fate of their property in absolutely any way they may fancy. We should look at the other considerations by which the express trust device may be additionally supported or, on the other hand, according to which it may be problematic.

We shall look at these other considerations under four heads (which are doubtless not exhaustive, nor perhaps mutually absolutely exclusive). The first type is paternalist: preventing a settlor from acting against his own interests. The second is communitarian: taking the point that to concentrate exclusively on the wishes of an individual, the settlor, may be to overlook the interests of groups, which may be affected by those wishes. The third type is utilitarian: considerations as to whether trusts' effects are more beneficial than deleterious. And the fourth focuses upon rights, the concern here being whether trusts vindicate or infringe people's rights. We shall see too how the law to some extent reflects these other considerations, rather than assuming a purely facilitative shape.

2.3 PATERNALISTIC CONSIDERATIONS

Paternalism demands an effort to ensure that people act in accordance with their own interests. So on this view, if it seemed that a settlor was acting against his own interests in making a trust of his property, the law ought not to uphold that trust.

There are, however, different kinds of paternalism. The least controversial simply recognizes the natural limitations of liberalism. It is one thing to leave people to decide for themselves how to behave when they possess the usual collection of faculties and fruits of experience that characterize normal adulthood: then, it can be seen as insulting to them not to leave them to their own devices. But it is another thing to take this attitude if they lack these attributes. So freedoms that are accorded to ordinary adults are often withheld from children and sufferers from mental disorders, because it is thought that such people lack the rationality and experience satisfactorily to make judgements about the exercise of such freedoms. There can be debate about where the lines should be drawn, but the general point is commonplace enough.

Thus, in the trusts context, the facilitative project—the law's provision of the liberty to make trusts—does not extend in its full form to children. A child can make a trust, but is permitted to disavow it at any time up to, and shortly after, reaching majority (the point being that then, as an adult, he is mature enough to be allowed to commit himself).[4] The project likewise does not extend in its full form to persons who persons who 'lack capacity' under the Mental Capacity Act 2005; that is persons who cannot understand the information relevant to the decision whether to make the trust, or retain it, or use or weigh it in the process of making the decision, or communicate the decision once made.[5]

Likewise when a responsible adult is temporarily disabled from exercising his own judgement. Say a person is instructed to do some act at gunpoint, or misunderstands the nature of what he is doing: although he possesses the normal faculties, he is not in a position to give full rein to them, and so it would be wrong to accord his action dispositive effect. In this vein, there are rules that settlors can disavow trusts made under duress, undue influence, and mistake (either a spontaneous misconception by the settlor, or one induced by some other person's misrepresentation).

---

[4] *Edwards v Carter* [1893] AC 360.
[5] Sections 2–3. Strictly speaking, the question of whether a person has the capacity to make a trust is governed not by the Act but by the common law of trusts, the relevant rules receiving a thorough modern discussion in *Re Beaney (Deceased)* [1978] 1 WLR 770. But the common law test is thought to be, and is certainly treated by the courts as, identical with the formula now found in the Act: see *Local Authority X v MM* [2009] 1 FLR 443, [62]–[92], especially [79]–[80]. Under the Act, the Court of Protection, which looks after the interests of such people, may make trusts of their property on their behalf: ss 16, 18(1)(h).

Paternalism moves to another level if it requires effect to be denied to a transaction that, although made by a normal adult in full command of the situation, seems improvident according to some external standard. This is a much more controversial idea, for, unlike the situations we have looked at so far, it cannot be put in terms of the natural limitations of liberalism. However, the law of trusts has some features of this cast, albeit presented in the less controversial terms of incapacity or loss of command. For example, where the settlor makes the trust on the advice of some person who is in a position to sway his judgement, and the trust appears improvident, the trust is *presumed* to have been made under undue influence, and is therefore invalid unless the presumption can be rebutted. At one time, indeed, there seems to have been a presumption that any trust involving a substantial amount of property was made under a misunderstanding as to its effect, so as to make it invalid unless the presumption could be rebutted;[6] but this is not the modern law.[7]

2.4 COMMUNITARIAN CONSIDERATIONS

'Communitarianism' refers to a collection of ideas having, as their common theme, the perception that well-being is better promoted if the potential role, interests and responsibilities of communities are made part of the reckoning. This perception runs counter to liberalism's thesis that well-being is best served by concentrating on the freedom of individuals, and communitarianism can therefore sometimes indicate prescriptions different from liberalism's.[8]

One natural concern of communitarianism is to protect and foster such institutions as the family. Recognition of this concern would entail allowing or indeed encouraging settlors to make trusts whose provisions are aligned with their family obligations. For centuries, in fact, making family provision has been a very important application of the trust device. Indeed, long ago it would probably have made less sense to justify trusts on the ground that they vindicated settlors' freedoms than on the ground that they provided the vehicle for the fulfilment of settlors' family obligations. And a concern that property should not be alienated from families may have underlain the presumption that property gratuitously transferred is held by the transferee on resulting trust.[9] The idea of the 'family'

---

[6] *Hoghton v Hoghton* (1852) 15 Beav 278; *Price v Price* (1852) 1 De GM & G 308.

[7] *Henry v Armstrong* (1881) 18 Ch D 668; *Dutton v Thompson* (1883) 23 Ch D 278.

[8] For a broad perspective, viewing the very idea of (liberal) property as subordinate to the interests of the community, see eg K Gray (1994) 47 CLP 157.

[9] See sections 3.7, 16.2.

behind this point is a rather specialized one, however, having a dynastic quality, or at any rate a dimension of wealth serving more than just basic needs. A more down-to-earth idea of the family can also be served by the trust concept, though, and there is some evidence of the law's reacting to this. In one case, an express trust was found on the basis of less than cogent evidence, so that a portion of a man's property did not pass on his death to his estranged wife, but was held on trust for the woman with whom he had been living for nine years.[10]

A concern to protect and foster institutions such as the family would also entail denying settlors the liberty to make trusts where to do so would have a deleterious effect on those institutions. The law takes this line, in a group of rules prohibiting settlors from attaching conditions to beneficiaries' entitlements of a kind that, broadly, would damage the beneficiaries' natural family relationships. So, for example, conditions tending to promote separation or divorce of married couples (eg 'for Adam, as soon as he leaves his wife'),[11] or tending to separate children from their parents ('for Adam, but only so long as he has no contact with his father'),[12] would probably be disallowed. However, we are asked to distinguish such conditions from apparently similar ones that have been allowed. For example, a trust was permitted to stand when it was viewed as containing arrangements for the aftermath of a couple's separation, as opposed to encouraging the separation or discouraging a reconciliation itself.[13] Some of these distinctions seem more plausible than others. In effect, it seems that different judges take different views on the relative weight they give to this communitarian concern on the one hand, and to liberal considerations on the other. A striking example of liberalism being preferred over communitarianism occurred in one case where the House of Lords, having explicitly discussed the issue in these terms, allowed a trust which forfeited the interest of any beneficiary who became a Roman Catholic, thereby interfering with the upbringing of the infant beneficiaries by their parents.[14] It is possible, however, that this area of the subject will see a change of direction in the wake of the Human Rights Act 1998, whose impact is considered in section 2.6 below.

---

[10] *Paul v Constance* [1977] 1 WLR 527; also *Rowe v Prance* [1999] 2 FLR 787. Certain constructive trusts, too, can arise so as to reflect the moral implications inherent in family relationships: see sections 18.3–18.4.

[11] *Re Caborne* [1943] Ch 224; *Re Johnson's Will Trusts* [1967] Ch 387.

[12] *Re Sandbrook* [1912] 2 Ch 471.   [13] *Re Lovell* [1920] 1 Ch 122.

[14] *Blathwayt v Lord Cawley* [1976] AC 397. Cf *Re Boulter* [1922] 1 Ch 75; *Re Borwick* [1933] Ch 657.

Communitarianism may also ask that we think carefully whether some desired effect is better delivered by legal rules and remedies, or by some other form of prescription. Specifically, the suggestion is that the law's techniques are (necessarily or otherwise) stiff and commonly adversarial; that social techniques marked by these qualities may never be unequivocally desirable, and that there are some contexts, especially those that are or ought to be characterized by more humane values, in which they are certainly out of place.[15] This argument is clearly of potential relevance to the treatment of trusts. In particular, the relationships between the settlor, the trustees, and the beneficiaries of a family trust will commonly be of such a kind that legal enforcement could be thought inappropriate.

First appearances are that the law does not reflect this perception. There is substantial authority to the effect that a trust cannot be valid unless it is capable of being enforced in court.[16] Any inference that the courts necessarily keep trustees on a tight rein would be false, however. In a body of decisions largely taken with reference to family trusts, the judges have shown themselves generally reluctant to intervene against trustees.[17] So long as trustees exercising a discretion take the proper factors and only those factors into account, for example, a court will not interfere with the choice they make, even if the judge disagrees with this choice;[18] moreover, trustees do not generally have to give their beneficiaries access to their papers revealing the reasons behind their choice.[19] And the court will respect a settlor's stipulation that his trustees' duties shall be almost entirely unenforceable against them.[20]

The law's special provision for charitable trusts—broadly, those for the public benefit—can readily be seen in communitarian terms. It may not, however, be correct to conclude that there should therefore be relatively little legal intervention in the case of such trusts. As we shall discover in Chapter 6, the law's treatment of charitable trusts is to a large extent best seen as reflecting a sense that, as well as acts of humanity on

---

[15] This suggestion appears to have been accepted in, especially, the fact that bargains between family members in the family context are often treated as not legally enforceable, as involving no 'intention to create legal relations'.

[16] *Morice v Bishop of Durham* (1804) 9 Ves 399, 404–5, (1805) 10 Ves 522, 539; *Re Astor's Settlement Trusts* [1952] Ch 534, 541–2; *Re Shaw* [1957] 1 WLR 729, 744–5; *Leahy v A-G for New South Wales* [1959] AC 457, 479, 484.

[17] See further section 12.6.

[18] *Gisborne v Gisborne* (1877) 2 App Cas 300; *Tempest v Lord Camoys* (1882) 21 Ch D 571. See sections 12.6, 13.4.

[19] *Re Londonderry's Settlement* [1965] Ch 918; *Schmidt v Rosewood Trust Ltd* [2003] 2 AC 709, [54]. See section 11.9.

[20] *Armitage v Nurse* [1998] Ch 241. See section 10.1.

the part of their settlors, they represent a valuable part of the nation's social provision. If that is so, it follows that there is a public interest in their satisfactory operation, and it is possible to regard this as not less suitable for legal supervision than the satisfactory operation of those aspects of social provision that derive from the government. The latter have in modern times become the subject of a relatively high degree of legal intervention, in the form of judicial review. And indeed, although the actions of charitable trusts are not tightly controlled by the courts,[21] they have increasingly been supervised by a state institution, the Charity Commission.

Communitarian considerations seem at their least relevant, and from this point of view legal intervention therefore seems least contra-indicated, in the case of trusts made in commercial spheres. Unit trusts are of this kind. So may be pension fund trusts,[22] with the demise of the perspective that the provision of a pension is an act of altruism by the employer (which might suggest unenforceability in legal terms) in favour of the perspective that it represents a component of the pay-and-benefits 'package' like any other. The latter description does not fully capture the prevailing perception, however. It misses the points that there is an important social interest in employment conditions (including pension arrangements) satisfactorily reflecting the interests of employees as people; and that the ability of the state to economize on the provision of public pensions depends on the space being filled instead by private (including company) pensions, implying that the latter cannot be significantly less fair or secure.[23] Although these considerations have communitarian resonances, this is an instance where communitarianism might be content to recruit the law, so as to see the considerations satisfactorily vindicated.[24] All in all, therefore, one might expect pension fund trusts to attract a relatively high degree of judicial activity. The picture is ambiguous, however. There is a significant body of modern reported litigation regarding the administration of pension fund trusts, as those aggrieved by actions taken in respect of such trusts have sought judicial relief. But the judicial response has not

---

[21] *Re Beloved Wilkes' Charity* (1851) 3 Mac & G 440.

[22] See further G Moffat (1993) 56 MLR 471.

[23] The importance of private-sector pensions to the state is implicit in the substantial legislative regulation of the area: see the Pensions Act 1995 and Pensions Act 2004.

[24] The considerations may be promoted by other techniques than judicial intervention, however. The Pensions Acts 1995 and 2004 use watchdogs in the shape of the Pensions Regulator and the Pensions Ombudsman, and provide for some of a pension scheme's trustees to be drawn from among its beneficiaries.

always been markedly interventionist.[25] This restraint[26] may, however, be best understood less in terms of communitarianism than in those of a free-market ethic, whereby the parties' bargain is to be respected and not interfered in by the law.[27] A communitarian perspective is once again required, though, when it is realized that the bargains looked to here are collective ones, between the employer and the present and prospective pensioners, and that it was therefore not a foregone conclusion that the latter would have a voice at all.[28] The complexity of the overall picture reflects the point that, in the nature of (our construction of) the human condition, it is routine for communitarian concerns and approaches to be complicatedly entwined with those of other types.

2.5 UTILITARIAN CONSIDERATIONS

Utilitarianism asks that we consider the question whether a trust does more good than harm, and proposes that the settlor be permitted to make it if, but only if, the answer is yes.

It is possible to be selective about the kinds of factors to be included in the calculus of good and harm, but at its widest it involves taking account, on the one side, of the general utility of according rights to private property, the more specific social advantages of the trust device in general, and, more specifically still, the benefits of the particular type of trust or indeed individual trust in question; and, on the other side, of any hurt done to the trust's beneficiaries, to particular other people outside the trust (eg the settlor's creditors), and to society in general.[29]

We cannot here attempt anything like a complete assessment of the kinds of social advantage and disadvantage arising from trusts: the necessary sociological and economic research has never been done, and it would be a very major enterprise. But we can look at some particular matters over which there is, or has been, a live issue.

---

[25] A relatively non-interventionist approach was taken in *Re Courage Group's Pension Schemes* [1987] 1 WLR 495 and *Wilson v Law Debenture Corp plc* [1995] 2 All ER 337; a more interventionist approach in *Cowan v Scargill* [1985] Ch 270, *Mettoy Pension Trustees Ltd v Evans* [1990] 1 WLR 1587, and *Imperial Group Pension Trust Ltd v Imperial Tobacco Ltd* [1991] 1 WLR 589.

[26] Cf the appeal for it in the classic labour law text, K Wedderburn *The Worker and the Law* 3rd edn (1986).

[27] See especially *Re Courage Group's Pension Schemes* [1987] 1 WLR 495. Moreover, the interventionist decision in *Mettoy Pension Trustees Ltd v Evans* [1990] 1 WLR 1587 was overtaken by a collectively bargained compromise pending an appeal.

[28] G Moffat (1993) 56 MLR 471.

[29] For an analysis in economic terms, see A Ogus (1986) 36 U Tor LJ 186.

First, the ways in which trusts may be beneficial. Historically, instances are not difficult to find. In the medieval period, trusts, together with wills, were viewed as a way of ensuring a compliant younger generation: if young people had become absolutely entitled to property, there would have been no check on them, to the detriment of society. Considerations of public order may even have been involved: the withdrawal of the facility of making trusts and wills for a time in the sixteenth century[30] provoked a turbulent reaction, being one of the grievances behind the unpleasantness known as the Pilgrimage of Grace, and the move was soon reversed. For a long time, too, trusts were seen as beneficial because they fostered the existence of the great dynastic families that ruled the nation, by passing their wealth down from one generation of the family to the next, preventing it from being placed at the entire disposal of individuals.[31] Then again, until matters were reformed in the late nineteenth century, the trust device was the only means by which married women could even come close to owning property. In the modern world, factors such as these have disappeared, but trusts continue to facilitate important social benefits. They provide, for example, the vehicle for many kinds of investments, and for private-sector pensions, and the means whereby people (especially couples) can jointly own property (especially their home). And throughout their history, charitable trusts have, at any rate in broad terms, operated to the general good.

So trusts can certainly be beneficial to society. But they can also have bad effects, which may in some cases outweigh the advantages, warranting withdrawal of the facility to make them. Some of these bad effects are narrow, arising from the trust device being put to a particular injurious application; others are more general, common to most or even all trusts.

One instance of trusts being put to a particular injurious application may be their use in the avoidance of tax. The damage, arguably, lies in obliging the government either to reduce its expenditure on objects that would otherwise have benefited the nation; or to levy higher taxes in those quarters where avoidance is most difficult (eg on people's ordinary salaries, taxed by PAYE); or else to borrow more, with the detriment to the economy, and hence people's lives, that that is said to entail. It is sometimes said that it is not for the law to make value judgements about tax

---

[30] By *Lord Dacre's Case* (1535) YB 27 Hen VIII Pasch f 7 pl 22, and the Statute of Uses 1536. The reversal began with the Statute of Wills 1540. See generally A Simpson *A History of the Land Law* 2nd edn (1986) ch 8.

[31] For discussion of the value of trusts from the mid-seventeenth century, and the law's responses, see M Chesterman in G Rubin and D Sugarman (eds) *Law Economy & Society* (1984) ch 1.

avoidance; that if people can manage their affairs so as to escape taxation, they are entitled so to do.[32] But, at any rate if they use the trust device, to argue thus is to overlook the fact that the law itself, by providing this device, is furnishing them with the means to avoid tax. (Indeed,[33] avoiding tax was probably among the main applications to which the device was put in its formative days, meaning that its judicial creators sanctioned it precisely for this purpose.) So the law cannot be neutral on the subject: by maintaining trusts as available for tax avoidance, it abets that avoidance. The law has in fact taken the point, although not consistently. In the early 1980s the judges abandoned their earlier attitude of complaisance,[34] and began to discountenance tax avoidance[35] (though the case law did not arise especially in the trusts context). Later in that decade, albeit with some powerful dissenting voices, their former attitude regained prominence.[36] The more recent picture is mixed.[37]

Another harmful use of the trust device might be so as to injure creditors. Say a trader, fearing that his business might run into difficulties, declared a trust of all his assets for his wife. The plan would be that she should continue to let him use them as his own, so that in practice the couple's life would continue very much as before. But the assets would now be safe, because the creditors' claims are against the trader, not his wife. Allowing people the freedom to make trusts in this way, then, would be injurious to the economic interests of their creditors. There is thus a strong argument that it is socially disadvantageous, and that the availability of trusts should therefore to that extent be curtailed. And in fact, the law does contain a collection of rules proscribing various forms of such trusts.[38]

The position in this area is not entirely consistent, though. Trusts according people interests only until bankruptcy, so that the money in

---

[32] *IRC v Duke of Westminster* [1936] AC 1, 19.

[33] See further J Baker *An Introduction to English Legal History* 4th edn (2002) 252–7.

[34] *IRC v Duke of Westminster* [1936] AC 1; *IRC v Plummer* [1980] AC 896.

[35] *WT Ramsay Ltd v IRC* [1982] AC 300; *IRC v Burmah Oil Co Ltd* [1982] STC 30; *Furniss v Dawson* [1984] AC 474.

[36] *Craven v White* [1989] AC 398.

[37] Cf *Ensign Tankers (Leasing) Ltd v Stokes* [1992] 1 AC 655, *Moodie v IRC* [1993] 1 WLR 266, *IRC v McGuckian* [1997] 1 WLR 991, and *Scottish Provident Institution v IRC* [2004] 1 WLR 3172 (discountenancing tax avoidance) with *Fitzwilliam v IRC* [1993] 1 WLR 1189, *Ingram v IRC* [1999] 1 All ER 297, *MacNiven v Westmoreland Investments* [2003] 1 AC 311, and *Barclays Mercantile Business Finance Ltd v Mawson* [2005] 1 AC 684 (permitting it). The different outcomes may, of course, reflect differences in the cases' individual facts; and there appears to have been some rethinking of the applicable legal analysis itself; but it would be idle to pretend that policy considerations play no part. See further J Freedman (2007) 123 LQR 53.   [38] Insolvency Act 1986 ss 339–42F, 423–5.

question will not go to their creditors,[39] have long been held valid not-withstanding the injury they may do traders by the false appearance of creditworthiness that they create. And in the contemporary law there is confusion in the context of one creditor injuring his rivals by using a trust to establish a prior claim to the available assets. There have been cases in which suppliers of money[40] or materials[41] on credit have set up their right to (re)payment in a trust, so that in the event of the debtor's bankruptcy the money would be regarded as already theirs, giving them a right to all of it, rather than as part of the debtor's assets that they would have to share with the rest of his creditors.[42] Again, this practice gives a false appearance of creditworthiness: the other creditors may have been led to perceive the debtor as a viable concern with adequate resources available to meet its liabilities, when in reality these resources are already bespoken under the trust arrangements. The law's reactions have been mixed. Some judicial decisions[43] have begun and ended with facilitative logic, little or no visible attention being paid to the question whether the arguable injury to other creditors warrants limiting the freedom to make trusts in this respect. Elsewhere,[44] however, judges have refused to give effect to such arrangements.[45] The cases in the former group con-cern money loans, while those in the latter group concern the supply of materials, but it is not easy to see why there should be a bifurcation

---

[39] 'Protective trusts' (see further section 9.2). The essential validity of such trusts was reaf-firmed in *Re Trusts of the Scientific Investment Pension Plan* [1998] 3 All ER 154. In the United States, while 'spendthrift trusts', operating slightly differently but to the same end, are seen as fundamentally valid, there has been some legislative retrenchment of their effectiveness.

[40] eg *Barclay's Bank Ltd v Quistclose Investments Ltd* [1970] AC 567; see further section 12.3.

[41] eg *Aluminium Industrie Vaassen BV v Romalpa Aluminium Ltd* [1976] 1 WLR 676, after which such devices became known as '*Romalpa* clauses'.

[42] See further S Worthington *Proprietary Interests in Commercial Transactions* (1997); cf M Bridge (1997) 17 LS 507.

[43] eg *Barclay's Bank Ltd v Quistclose Investments Ltd* [1970] AC 567; *Re Kayford Ltd* [1975] 1 WLR 279; *Carreras Rothmans Ltd v Freeman Mathews Treasure Ltd* [1985] Ch 207.

[44] eg *Re Bond Worth Ltd* [1980] Ch 228 (which involved a trust), together with eg *Borden UK Ltd v Scottish Timber Products Ltd* [1981] Ch 25; *Re Peachdart Ltd* [1984] Ch 131; *Re Andrabell Ltd* [1984] 3 All ER 407 (which involved other legal devices).

[45] Generally, though, the reasoning has (at least ostensibly) been not that the arrangement came up against the limits of the facilitative project as involving an unacceptable injury to creditors, but instead that the arrangement's terms were not apt to achieve what the parties wanted anyway. Conceding the primacy of the facilitative logic in this way left it possible for equally injurious but better drafted arrangements to succeed in *Clough Mill Ltd v Martin* [1985] 1 WLR 111 and *Hendy Lennox (Industrial Engines) Ltd v Grahame Puttick Ltd* [1984] 1 WLR 485 (again, however, not involving trust arrangements).

on this account. There exists some statutory regulation of this type of arrangement, but its impact is hesitant.[46]

These, then, are examples of the arguably injurious effects of particular uses of trusts. But it is also possible to find social disadvantages in the very nature of the trust situation. Perhaps the most prominent perception in this vein is to the effect that trusts may be injurious to the economy, and hence to the well-being of society. This argument depends upon a free-market economic theory, and runs as follows.

The utilitarian goal of making people as happy as possible is seen as promoted by the generation of as much wealth as possible. And this goal is in turn promoted if assets find their way to those who can afford to offer the highest price for them, because this will be a reflection of the fact that the latter will be able to make the largest profits—extract the greatest wealth—from the assets. In order for this to happen, though, the market needs to be as free and efficient as possible: any clogs upon it, or friction within it, will hinder the process. The absolute owner of a piece of property is able to sell it, and a prospective purchaser is able to buy it from him, without any impediment (this is part of what we mean by 'ownership'): so the market can operate freely, and happiness is maximized. But if property is held on trust, there are likely to be problems with its marketability, and thus with the maximization of happiness; so an argument arises against the trust device.

The most extreme impediment to marketability would be for the settlor to stipulate for the trustee to hold on to the particular piece of property indefinitely, rather than treat it as an investment, to be traded with an eye to the generation of the best return. This might occur, for example, if, as was once common, the settlor holds a great estate and makes a trust providing for it to be kept for succeeding generations of his family. No matter how attractive a price might be offered for the land (by someone who wants to erect a factory on it, for example), the fact that the land is tied up in trust in this way means that it cannot be sold, and so it is withdrawn from the market altogether. Alternatively, say the terms of the trust do allow the trustee to sell the original trust property so as to reinvest the proceeds, but nevertheless impose restrictions on that ability, such as a requirement that

---

[46] In the background is the Companies Act 2006 ss 860–1, under which debts secured on a company's assets by means of a 'charge' must be registered; but valid arrangements of the kinds under discussion are not regarded as 'charges'. (Cf *Re Lehman Brothers International (Europe) (In Administration) (No 2)* [2009] EWCA Civ 1161.) Valid *Romalpa* clauses may not, however, be enforced in the event of the debtor company's insolvency without leave from a court: Insolvency Act 1986 ss 10, 11, 15.

the beneficiaries should consent to the sale, or one insisting that the best possible price be obtained. If a sale in breach of these restrictions were defective, a prospective purchaser would have to spend time and money in checking that they had been complied with. Such expenditure (a form of 'transaction cost') in effect increases the price that the purchaser has to pay for this piece of property above that of a comparable commodity being sold by an absolute owner, and so reduces the wealth that can be extracted from it, perhaps even preventing it from being a profitable proposition at all. Or again, say sale and reinvestment are allowed, but with restrictions on the sorts of assets in which the reinvestment may be made, perhaps out of a natural desire that the beneficiaries' interests should not be jeopardized by risky ventures.[47] The problem here is that these restrictions might disable the money from being spent on whatever new asset would generate the greatest profit.

And most fundamentally and pervasively, even assuming (as is nowadays normal, but has not always been) that the trust property can be invested by the trustees, it may perform less effectively in the economy than equivalent property invested by an absolute owner. For trustees will often, by reason of their consciousness of their position, be more cautious in their approach than an absolute owner would be. After all, their whole *raison d'être* is to serve the interests of the trust's objects, and they may well as a result feel less ready to take risks.

Wherever there is a trust, then, the assets will probably be to some degree less exposed to the market than assets that are owned absolutely. According to free-market theory, this diminishes the amount of wealth, and so happiness, that can be derived from it. So a question arises over the acceptability of all express trusts: that is, over the facilitative project as a whole. The fact that there are such drawbacks, however, does not automatically mean the abandonment of that project. The drawbacks have always to be balanced against the benefits, or against the argument from liberalism itself. In reality, the case for the availability of trusts evidently is accepted, for better or worse, as ultimately compelling. After all, we do still have a law of express trusts. But the facilitative logic does not carry all before it. The law contains a number of rules, comprehensible in utilitarian terms, declining to give effect to settlors' intentions. The relevant rules fall into two broad sets.

The first set consists of rules whose effect is to emphasize the extent to which property held on trust is nevertheless exposed to the market. In

---

[47] Until the Trustee Act 2000 the law itself imposed such restrictions, unless the settlor provided otherwise: see section 7.4.

Chapter 7 we shall examine the rules governing the manner in which the trustees are required to manage and invest the trust property. Broadly, they tend to assimilate the treatment of trust property to the way in which an absolute owner would treat it. But, as we have already noted, even though there is thus no legal constraint on the property's exposure to the market, the trustee's own awareness that he is a trustee and not an absolute owner might still have a sobering effect. The law has, however, experimented with a measure calculated to counteract even this latter effect. In a certain kind of land-holding trust known as a strict settlement (now defunct),[48] the law gave the power to sell the land not to the trustees but to the first beneficiary, the 'tenant for life'.[49] Since the tenant for life received the income from the trust's investments for his lifetime, he had a personal interest in maximizing that income, which in turn meant he would want to sell the land if this was the most profitable thing to do. By placing control over the investment and management of the trust assets not with the trustees, with their natural reticence, but with the tenant for life, with his equally natural self-interest, a closer approach to full marketability should have been achieved.[50] This arrangement had a major drawback: a self-interested tenant for life might have paid attention more to immediate income than to capital growth, to the detriment of the beneficiaries who came after him. But even in market terms, it was not a perfect solution, because a tenant for life might have turned out not to be so self-interested after all. Like the trustees, and even against his own interest, he might have felt a sense of responsibility towards the group of beneficiaries as a whole, or of respect for the settlor's wish that the land should remain in the family. Death duties will commonly have operated to persuade him otherwise in this last respect, however.

Thus although these rules about investment and management go some way to alleviate the economic disadvantages of trusts, they do not remove

---

[48] The possibility of creating a strict settlement was abolished by the Trusts of Land and Appointment of Trustees Act 1996 s 2.

[49] Settled Land Act 1925, replacing the generally similar Settled Land Act 1882. It is known that economic arguments were amongst those supporting the introduction of this legislation: H Perkin in J Butt and I Clarke (eds) *The Victorians and Social Protest* (1973) 177; F Thompson *Transactions of the Royal Historical Society* 5th series vol 15 (1965) 23. There was a high level of concern at the state of the economy in the last quarter of the nineteenth century: F Crouzet *The Victorian Economy* (1982), especially 47–8, 58–63.

[50] Under the Trusts of Land and Appointment of Trustees Act 1996, the place of the strict settlement is taken by the 'trust of land'. The Act allows for the power of sale to be excluded, or subjected to a consent requirement, by the settlor (s 8), and provides for it to lie with the trustees unless they choose to delegate it to a beneficiary (s 9). The trust of land is thus significantly less aligned to free-market considerations than the strict settlement.

them completely. At this point we encounter the second broad set of rules. These are rules limiting the very existence of trusts. So far as presently relevant, they fall into three groups.

The first group comprises some rules tending to ensure that trusts can exist only when they pass capital, or income in cash, to a person. In particular, the 'beneficiary rule', explored in sections 12.2–12.4, asserts (contrary, however, to the actual state of the law) that a trust can be valid only where it operates in this way.

The second group goes further still, promoting the transfer of capital *as opposed to* merely income. At the centre of this group is 'the rule in *Saunders v Vautier*',[51] whereby, under certain (fairly usual) circumstances, beneficiaries can dismantle a trust in their favour and take the capital for themselves as absolute owners. This rule has sometimes been ascribed to the settlor's intentions, but in its developed form it is clear that a settlor's intentions can be simply overridden. Moreover, some kinds of dispositions, which might arguably have been intended to create trusts, are instead read as conferring absolute ownership of the property in question. The details of this phenomenon will be examined in Chapter 3. Once again, it is sometimes expressed in terms of the settlor's intention, but it will be seen that this ascription is dubious. In most of the important decisions on these lines,[52] a man left property to his widow, but apparently on trust so that she should have only the income for her lifetime, with the capital to go thereafter to, say, their son. The courts read the arrangement instead as a bequest of the capital to the widow, she having only a moral obligation to provide in turn for the son.

The third group consists in rules collectively known as the rule against perpetuities. This operates to ensure that a settlor cannot legally provide for assets to remain subject to a trust for longer than legal policy will tolerate: there comes a point at which they must return into absolute ownership, and hence full marketability. In its turn, the rule against perpetuities has three main branches: 'the rule against remoteness of vesting'; 'the rule against inalienability'; and 'the rule against accumulation of income'.[53]

---

[51] (1841) 4 Beav 115, Cr & Ph 240: section 10.4.

[52] eg *Lambe v Eames* (1871) LR 6 Ch App 597; *Re Hutchinson and Tenant* (1878) 8 Ch D 540; *Mussoorie Bank Ltd v Raynor* (1882) 7 App Cas 321; *Re Adams and the Kensington Vestry* (1884) 27 Ch D 394; *Re Williams* [1897] 2 Ch 12.

[53] For a full treatment, see R Maudsley *The Modern Law of Perpetuities* (1979); Law Commission *The Rules Against Perpetuities and Excessive Accumulations* (Law Com No 251, 1998). Connected with the rule against perpetuities was the law on entails. An entail was a special kind of settlement designed so that no one might enjoy an absolute interest, at least for many generations, potentially *ad infinitum*. But for most of its history, the law allowed entails to be overridden—'barred'—by those having the interests, permitting them to gain absolute

The rule against remoteness of vesting stipulates that all the interests conferred by the trust must 'vest' within 'the perpetuity period'. This means that within this time, the details regarding the arrangement of the interests, such as the identity of the people to whom they will belong, must be finalized. In the case of a trust for 'my first-born grandchild', for example, an actual name must emerge. The rule's details have changed over the years, so that they now differ according to whether the trust came into effect before 1964,[54] between 1964 and 2010,[55] or today. In particular, the definition of 'the perpetuity period' has changed. In the most recent version of the rule, it is a period of 125 years from the time when the trust takes effect.[56]

So say a man dies leaving a widow and a son, the latter being then ten years old. The man makes a trust in his will, stipulating for payments first to his widow for her life, then to their son for his life, then to the son's eldest child (ie the eldest child living at the son's death) for its life, then to that child's eldest child for its life. As a newly created trust, the perpetuity period will be 125 years from the time when the trust comes into effect, ie the settlor's death. This trust is certainly valid so far as the provisions in favour of the widow and son are concerned: these entitlements are finalized from the start. The provision for the son's eldest child will very probably be valid too, because if the son has a child at all it will very probably be born within the following 125 years.[57] But the last provision, that for the eldest child's eldest child, is problematic. This child may be born (if at all), and so its entitlement finalized, no later than 125 years after the settlor's death. Probably it will be, and, if it is, this provision will be valid too. But it might not. If the settlor dies around the time of the birth of his son; then that son survives him by say 65 years, and himself has a child at the very end of his life; then that child survives its father by another 65 years; the entitlement of the final

---

ownership of the property in question. Entails may no longer be created: Trusts of Land and Appointment of Trustees Act 1996 Sch 1 para 5. The rules about perpetuities and entails can also be explained in terms of a rights analysis: see section 2.6.

[54] When the Perpetuities and Accumulations Act 1964 came into effect.

[55] When the Perpetuities and Accumulations Act 2009 came into effect.

[56] Perpetuities and Accumulations Act 2009 s 5. By s 2, pension scheme trusts are exempt from the rule, as are provisions whereby one charity succeeds another as a trust's object. These exemptions can be understood on the basis that in such cases, the good outweighs the harm.

[57] 'Very probably', rather than 'certainly', because of such possibilities (present or future) as the freezing of an embryo enabling a child to be born long after its father's death, as well as the elongation of life expectancy itself.

child referred to in the trust will not be finalized[58] until 130 years after the settlor's death, ie five years too late. In this event, then, the trust's final provision would be invalid.

The rule against inalienability (or excessive duration) is simpler. It stipulates that trusts for purposes, rather than beneficiaries, may not last for longer than the duration of a life in existence at the time the trust takes effect plus 21 years. This rule is rather tougher than that against remoteness of vesting. Since it deals with trusts for purposes rather than people, there will very often be no relevant life in existence at the time of the trust coming into effect—especially if it is made in the settlor's will, as many are—and so the limit will be the 21 years alone. And the trust will be invalid unless it is certain from the outset that it must terminate within the permitted period. So a trust providing for the care of a testator's (young-ish) horse will fail, because it will not be certain that its end, on the death of the horse, will occur within 21 years. Apparently, however, such a trust can be saved by the settlor's limiting its duration to the permitted 21 years or less.[59] So a trust for the care of his horse for its life or 21 years, which-ever is the shorter, would be valid, though potentially unfortunate for the horse.

The rule against accumulation of income previously stipulated that a settlor can validly provide for the income upon the trust assets to be accumulated (ie added to the capital, as opposed to being paid out to the objects) only for a limited period. This rule has been abolished for most trusts coming into effect from 2010.[60] The thinking behind this change (it may or may not be well-founded) is that the rule against remoteness of vesting, working on the interests involved, is sufficient to address the concern at stake.[61]

The rule against inalienability overtly limits the time for which capital can be kept out of absolute ownership by being subjected to a trust. In the case of the rule against remoteness of vesting, the point is less obvious. On the face of it, this rule regulates how distantly into the future a settlor's stipulations can come into effect, rather than how long they—and hence

---

[58] It will not be clear who is the 'eldest child' until its predecessor in the trust, the set-tlor's eldest grandchild, dies. For example, the latter's first-born child might predecease its parents.   [59] *Re Hooper* [1932] 1 Ch 38.

[60] Perpetuities and Accumulations Act 2009 s 13. By s 14, the rule survives for charitable trusts, where it is possible to stipulate for accumulation only for a period of up to 21 years: see section 6.1.

[61] *The Rules Against Perpetuities and Excessive Accumulations* (Law Com No 251, 1998) paras 10.12–10.14.

the trust, and the keeping of the property out of absolute ownership—can endure. But the ban on stipulations whose effect remains to be finalized beyond the permitted period has to be seen in combination with the fact of human mortality. A settlor who wants his trust to endure into the future will have to stipulate for new beneficiaries to replace those who die. But once they become too remote, these stipulations will be disallowed by the rule, and so such replacement will become impossible. This combination of mortality with a ban on new stipulations beyond a certain point means that the trust will necessarily come to an end, and, once again, the property will come back into absolute ownership.

Seen thus, therefore, the two principally surviving branches of the rule against perpetuities address two variants of the same phenomenon, the prolonged subjection of property to a trust regime. Their effect is that such subjection will be tolerated so far, but no further, before the property has to be free to come back into absolute ownership, and so marketability. In other words, for the duration of the perpetuity period, the law will accept the degree of damage to social well-being that trusts can entail; but then it draws the line. In terms of the contest of utility, the rule against perpetuities can thus be seen as a compromise (and, when all is said, a fairly arbitrary, rough and ready one), whereby the liberty to make trusts is preserved but its potential for social harm kept within bounds.[62]

2.6 RIGHTS CONSIDERATIONS

To state that some interest of a person constitutes a 'right' is to assert that that interest should be respected, in preference to interests pointing in other directions.

We may discover a right wherever this preferential respect is the product of the law's rules, as for example where my interest in keeping 'my' money is given protection against your interest in taking it for yourself, ie 'stealing' it. This backward-looking, positive, conception is not the idea of 'right' invoked here, however. The latter is, rather, a dialectical device: an

---

[62] For discussion of the rule's value, see Law Commission *The Rules Against Perpetuities and Excessive Accumulations* (Law Com No 251, 1998); this report was the basis for the Perpetuities and Accumulations Act 2009. The Commission was unsure about the balance of economic advantage surrounding the rule, and was instead moved by an argument that the rule achieves maximum happiness by compromising between the desires of different generations for complete freedom with the property in question (see especially paras 1.9, 2.32, 2.37, 7.2, 7.21). For the argument, see L Simes *Public Policy and the Dead Hand* (1955); for criticism, see T Gallanis [2000] CLJ 284. Viewed in the latter way, the rule can also be seen as reflecting rights considerations, as discussed in section 2.6.

argument that my interest *deserves* respect (from the law) when, in relation to it, your interest deserves either no, or less, respect.

There may be various kinds of reasons why my interest might deserve respect. One would be that it is supported by the kinds of consideration we have already considered: for example, that respecting it represents the path of greatest utility. Although an interest that the law requires to be respected for such a reason can satisfactorily be called a 'right' in the positive sense, it is not usually referred to as a 'right' in the dialectical sense. A 'right' in the dialectical sense generally means an interest that (it is asserted) deserves respect on account of its own intrinsic quality; in particular, one which deserves respect because it captures a facet of what it is to be human, and as a result is called a 'human right'. For instance, a person's interest in life—especially, in not being killed—is regarded as a (human) right because life is held to be of the essence of the human condition. There can of course be controversy over whether any given interest fits the template and so qualifies to be seen as a right. And there is also no guarantee that (dialectical) rights will not conflict with one another, requiring some mediating analysis.

It is debatable whether we should acknowledge a human right to property.[63] But if so, the liberty to make express trusts can be seen as founded upon it. His right to enjoy his property entails that a settlor should be able to dispose of it as he wishes. The express trust facility maximizes what is possible in this regard.

On the other hand, the making of a trust—whether itself supported by rights considerations or otherwise—may infringe another person's rights. In this event, there might follow a limitation of the settlor's liberty, so as not to recognize the trust in question. Say a settlor tried to create a trust for the purpose of killing certain people. The proposition that the law should uphold this trust, under facilitative logic, would be assailed by the argument that to do so would involve infringing the right to life. It may be assumed that the law would not uphold such a trust.

In practice, of course, trusts are not commonly found pitted against the right to life. But take trusts that injure creditors, discussed above. Some such trusts operate by contracting the pool of assets from which debtors

---

[63] The right to property is, for example, recognized by the Universal Declaration of Human Rights, the US Constitution, and the European Convention on Human Rights, but not by the Canadian Charter of Rights and Freedoms. For discussion, see J Waldron *The Right to Private Property* (1988). Relevant insights can also be had from other disciplines, such as paleoanthropology. For example, the argument in C Gosden *Prehistory—A Very Short Introduction* (2003) ch 3 may imply that the right to property is, at least in one sense, the most authentically 'human' right of all.

are obliged to pay their debts. By upholding such trusts, the law could be said to infringe any right the creditors may have to the secure enjoyment of their property. Other such trusts accord more favourable treatment to some creditors than to others. So the law, if it upholds these trusts, may contravene a right to equal treatment.[64]

Indeed, trusts may injure the rights of their own beneficiaries. This can occur in two ways. First, if the settlor gives a beneficiary his interest only on specific terms, the terms may violate some right of the beneficiary. For example, a condition that the beneficiary shall forfeit his interest unless he espouses a particular religious faith (eg 'for Adam on condition that he remains a member of the Church of England') may infringe the beneficiary's right to freedom of conscience;[65] and a condition making the beneficiary's interest depend on his family status (eg 'for Adam, once he is divorced from his wife') may infringe his right to a private and family life.[66] Secondly, beneficiaries' rights may be assailed by the very fact that the settlor makes his disposition to them under a trust at all, rather than as an absolute gift. Under a gift, they would have had access to the capital, but under the trust they are confined to the income, and may have to wait for that. This limitation may be seen as violating a right on their part to the full enjoyment of their property.[67]

It might be said that these suggestions cannot be valid, for the following reason. To become a beneficiary under a trust is to be given the certainty or possibility of receiving greater wealth than one already has. If someone does not like the arrangement in question (the restriction on his religious freedom, for example, or the restriction to income, rather than capital), he can decline his interest. In that event, he will merely remain in his existing position, both financially and in terms of his various freedoms. There is nothing about being proposed as the beneficiary of a trust to erode that position, however constricting the trust's terms may be.

But this answer may be too crude. Even if one concedes that a beneficiary who declines the proffered interest loses nothing to which he is actually entitled, one may argue that rights to religious freedom, family life,

---

[64] The European Convention on Human Rights Art 14 requires that the enjoyment of the right to property (First Protocol, Art 1) be 'secured without discrimination on any ground such as . . . property'.

[65] European Convention on Human Rights Art 9.

[66] *Ibid* Art 8.

[67] *Ibid* First Protocol, Art 1. In the United States, withholding capital from the beneficiaries is termed 'the dead hand', and in some minds particularly disfavoured as aristocratic and unrepublican. See G Alexander (1985) 37 Stanford LR 1189.

and the like can be imperilled by a bribe (the offer of a beneficial interest
on the relevant terms) as much as by aggression. Moreover, one might not
wish to make that concession. It is possible to argue that control of property should naturally be vested in those who have a present attachment to
it (the beneficiaries), rather than remaining with someone who has parted
with it and may indeed be dead (the settlor).[68] On this view, a beneficiary
would be essentially entitled to full ownership of the property in question.
To grant him the property in question under a trust, rather than by way of
absolute gift, would be to infringe his right fully to enjoy that entitlement.
The implications of especially the latter perception are profound. The
basis of express trusts is the facilitative thesis, the idea that people's rights
in respect of their property should be vindicated to a maximal degree, by
allowing them to make not only simple but also complex dispositions of it.
This, we now see, can readily conflict with the project of vindicating the
rights of the recipient of the property likewise to a maximal degree. There
are, it is evident, the makings of a struggle here.

In fact, the law of trusts has so far toyed with, but not fully accepted,
the view that particular exceptionable conditions should be disallowed.[69]
There have been many reported cases in which religious conditions have
been involved but have attracted no animadversion from the judges; their
permissibility has occasionally been questioned, but the answer has tended
to be that facilitative logic should prevail.[70] Conditions damaging to family life have been treated more sternly, though still not consistently so.[71]
The more recent enactment of the Human Rights Act 1998 may, however,
require or precipitate a more sceptical view of conditions of these kinds.
Conditions as to race and sex (eg 'for Adam's future wife, so long as she is

---

[68] Note also that, under appropriate (eg dynastic) circumstances, the settlor may be thought
to owe a duty to settle the property in question upon the beneficiaries (cf *Re Brocklehurst's
Estate* [1978] Ch 14, 32). But that duty might be to confer only an entitlement which is itself
subject to a similar duty, rather than absolute ownership.

[69] See further S Grattan in E Cooke (ed) *Modern Studies in Property Law, Volume 1* (2001)
ch 15; M Harding (2011) 31 OJLS (forthcoming).

[70] See eg *Blathwayt v Lord Cawley* [1976] AC 397. However, at any rate conditions removing a beneficiary's entitlement (as opposed to conferring it) have always been subjected to
very strict requirements as to the clarity with which they must be expressed before they will
be accepted as valid. This rule may have been used as a surrogate means of screening them on
policy grounds (see eg *Clayton v Ramsden* [1943] AC 320, striking down in this way a condition
for the forfeiture of an interest if the beneficiary married someone not of Jewish parentage and
faith). But if so, the tide has turned again, in favour of the facilitative logic: modern decisions
have been more easygoing over the degree of clarity required, so that such conditions have
been able to survive (see eg *Blathwayt v Lord Cawley*; *Re Tuck's Settlement Trusts* [1978] Ch 49;
Re Tepper's Will Trusts [1987] Ch 358; though cf *Nathan v Leonard* [2003] 1 WLR 827).

[71] *Re Caborne* [1943] Ch 224; *Re Johnson's Will Trusts* [1967] Ch 387; *Re Sandbrook* [1912]
2 Ch 471; but cf *Re Lovell* [1920] 1 Ch 122.

white', or 'for my first-born female grandchild') have also been accepted without demur, and generally speaking the relevant anti-discrimination legislation (currently the Equality Act 2010) does not touch such stipulations in trusts.[72]

The law seems, however, to have been much more impressed by the idea that a person's rights may be infringed by the very fact of his being placed in the position of a beneficiary, rather than enjoying full dominion over the property in question. This can be seen in the collection of rules, discussed in section 2.5, whereby the scope of the express trust device is itself curtailed. This collection included the rules whereby some kinds of dispositions, which might arguably have been intended to create trusts, are instead read as conferring absolute ownership of the property in question. As a result, for example, an apparent stipulation that a widow should enjoy only the income from her deceased husband's estate for her lifetime, holding the capital for their children, is read as an absolute bequest to the widow, with a moral obligation to provide in turn for the children. The collection included also the rules whereby, under certain (fairly usual) circumstances, beneficiaries can dismantle a trust in their favour and take the capital for themselves as absolute owners.[73] And it included the rule against perpetuities, which ensures that property cannot be subjected to a trust indefinitely, but must at a point prescribed by the law return into absolute ownership.[74] These can all be seen as calculated to vindicate the rights of those in whose favour they operate. Important in this vein too is

---

[72] The Act (ss 193–4 and Sch 14) does have some application to charitable trusts; as does the European Convention on Human Rights, operating via the Human Rights Act 1998 s 6, which requires the Charities Act 2006 to be interpreted as far as possible so as to ensure compliance with the Convention, and s 3, which requires the Charity Commission, as a public body, to abide by the Convention (see further *Catholic Care (Diocese of Leeds) v Charity Commission for England and Wales* [2010] 4 All ER 1041, especially [70]). On the latter basis (*quaere* what would otherwise have been the answer), a purpose of placing children for adoption *only with heterosexual couples* was judged by the Charity Commission not to afford the net 'public benefit' which the Charities Act 2006 s 2(1) demands (see sections 6.4–6.5), and so not to qualify as charitable: see <http://www.charity-commission.gov.uk/library/about_us/catholic_care.pdf>.

[73] *Saunders v Vautier* (1841) 4 Beav 115, Cr & Ph 240; see section 10.4. The case for viewing this provision in terms of rights is especially strong. It *permits* the property to come into absolute ownership, at the option of the beneficiaries, rather than *requiring* it to, as the economic argument would wish; derived from it is a rule enabling beneficiaries merely to modify their trust, if they prefer, rather than dismantle it altogether, in which event there may be no economic gain; and judges have put the matter in rights terms: *Gosling v Gosling* (1859) John 265, 272; *Wharton v Masterman* [1895] AC 186, 192–3.

[74] Although possibly favoured by the Law Commission (*The Rules Against Perpetuities and Excessive Accumulations* (Law Com No 251, 1998) paras 1.9, 2.32, 2.37, 7.2, 7.21), however, a rights analysis does not offer the best account of the rule against perpetuities. The rule gives complete primacy to the settlor's liberty over the liberty of those beneficiaries whose interests

the perception, in some quarters, that a trust can be validly made only if it confers something like ownership upon a beneficiary.[75]

It is perhaps curious that the law should reflect the argument that beneficiaries have a right to dominion over the property in this way, but not concern itself so much over matters of religious, racial, etc discrimination. Perhaps the explanation is that the project of vindicating beneficiaries' dominion over trust property frequently shares goals (above all, finding absolute transfers rather than trusts) with another powerful consideration, the utilitarian economic argument.

---

vest within the perpetuity period, then the reverse in respect of beneficiaries whose interests vest thereafter. There is something here of two wrongs (not) making a right.

[75] See sections 12.2–12.4.

3

Finding Settlors' Intentions

As we have seen, the law recognizes an express trust because a settlor intends to create it. Evidently, this raises a need to say when a settlor has the required intention. This chapter considers how the law goes about that.

3.1 THE NORMAL STANDARD OF PROOF

How certain is it necessary to be as to the required intention,[1] whether regarding the creation of a trust at all or regarding its terms? In civil cases, such as those about trusts, the law normally requires proof on the balance of probabilities. This means accepting whichever view of the facts is more probable than the other. (The onus is on a person asserting a proposition to prove that it is more probable than not, so if the probabilities are even, inertia prevails.) This has been accepted[2] as the standard of proof applicable to the discovery of a settlor's intentions. Following the balance of probabilities in this way can readily be seen as consonant with facilitative thinking. This aims to find an express trust where one is intended and not otherwise, so is neutral as between the two outcomes.

There will often be no difficulty. When a person wants to make a trust, it is in his own interest to make this and the trust's terms clear, so as to

---

[1] The approach to finding the required intention is an objective one; ie the question is whether a reasonable onlooker would discern the intention, rather than whether the settlor genuinely had it: see *Commissioners of Inland Revenue v Raphael* [1935] AC 96, 134–5. Even if the intention can be objectively found, however, a trust will be negated if it is shown that the settlor and trustee(s) actually intended something other than the trust thus indicated, the latter then being a 'sham': *Hitch v Stone* [2001] EWCA Civ 63, [62]–[70]; *Shalson v Russo* [2005] Ch 281, [187]–[190]; *A v A* [2007] EWHC 99 (Fam), [32]–[40]; see further *ibid* [41]–[58], M Conaglen [2008] CLJ 176. A trust found on the basis of an objectively evinced intention will also be negated if the settlor made it under a sufficiently serious mistake (one as to the transaction's 'effect' rather than its 'consequences' or 'advantages'): *Ogilvie v Littleboy* (1897) 13 TLR 399; *Ogilvie v Allen* (1899) 15 TLR 294; *Gibbon v Mitchell* [1990] 1 WLR 1304; *Ogden v Trustees of the RHS Griffiths 2003 Settlement* [2009] Ch 162; *Pitt v Holt* [2010] 1 WLR 1199, [49]–[53].
[2] *Re Snowden* [1979] Ch 528.

avoid the possibilities both of wasteful arguments about what he intended, and of his intentions being frustrated by a false conclusion (and equally, where a trust, or some detail, might be expected but is not intended, to make this clear). To this end, he will probably employ solicitors, who will use a formal document, stating unmistakably what is meant, using words such as 'trust', 'trustee', 'beneficiary', and so on.

Where evidence of that clarity is lacking, a court may find it helpful to address the abstract question of whether a trust was intended in terms of more concrete issues. Two of these have been identified by experience as regularly likely to be useful points to concentrate on.[3] One is whether the alleged settlor intended his wishes to be enforceable by legal sanction. A trust is a legal obligation, and a breach of it will, at any rate in principle, entail legal liability for the trustee. So, for example, if I bequeath all my property to my sister, instructing her to give a quarter of it to charity, we can focus on the question whether the obligation so imposed on her was meant to be a legal one, enforceable in court, or merely a moral one. Finding it to be merely moral tells us that I did not intend to create a trust. Another such indicator is how specific the instructions are. If they are vague, or contradictory, it is generally less likely that they are intended to comprise a trust as opposed to an expression of wishes having at most moral force. Of course, it is not impossible that they were intended to amount to a trust: sometimes one comes across dispositions that are clearly meant to be trusts, but whose terms are poorly expressed. But where the intention to create a trust is questionable, such difficulty does point against it.

3.2 OTHER APPROACHES

Whilst proof on the balance of probabilities is thus the principal tool for discovering settlors' intentions, different approaches are frequently visible. In particular, the judges operate 'rules of construction', requiring that in a certain type of situation, a person shall normally be held to have intended to create a trust; or not, as the case may be. They also follow other, less well crystallized, practices inconsistent with the normal standard of proof.

These rules and practices do not ultimately part company with facilitative logic, as they have effect only in cases where it is not completely clear whether someone intended to create a trust, or what he intended its

---

[3] *Mussoorie Bank Ltd v Raynor* (1882) 7 App Cas 321.

terms to be: where the intention has been made unmistakable, it will be respected, except if it contravenes a rule that avowedly overrides intention, such as that against perpetuities. If our rules and practices rested on an empirical observation that in the kind of situation concerned, people normally do have a certain kind of intention, they could even be ascribed to facilitative logic. But, as we shall see, that is not the case. They instead load the perception of the relevant intentions in a non-naturalistic way, and so conduce to outcomes not justifiable on facilitative grounds. They can therefore usefully be analysed in terms of the kinds of policy considerations noted in the last chapter as cutting across the facilitative project.

We turn now to some of the most prominent of these rules and practices.

3.3 FAMILY PROVISION

The courts appear unusually ready to discover an intention to make a trust where the ensuing trust will make the kind of provision the alleged settlor ought to make for a member of his family.

In *Paul v Constance*,[4] a man had received some money in compensation for an accident that he had suffered, and had started a bank account with it, in his sole name. Later, he and his partner both won small sums at bingo, and these too were paid into the account. There were some vague conversational references to the money as being jointly owned. There was conceivably proof on the balance of probabilities that the man intended to make some sort of provision for his partner, but it is hard to say that there was such proof of an intention to make a trust. The court nevertheless held that the man had declared a trust of all the money in the account for himself and his partner.

The case arose after the man had died intestate. If he had been married to his partner, she would have inherited all his property. Their being unmarried meant that she got none of it,[5] and in fact it went to his estranged wife, from whom he had never been divorced. But the decision meant that his partner was entitled to half the money in the account after all.[6]

A keenness to find a trust in such circumstances is intelligible in terms of a communitarian policy, visible in the law since about the middle of the

[4] [1977] 1 WLR 527.
[5] Except possibly a reasonable amount for her maintenance, under the Inheritance (Provision for Family and Dependants) Act 1975.
[6] See too *Rowe v Prance* [1999] 2 FLR 787, where, on similarly weak evidence, a man was held to have created a trust for a woman with whom he had a lengthy relationship and from whom he had accepted substantial gifts, but whom he now neglected.

twentieth century, seeking to secure family obligations. We shall encounter it again in sections 18.3 and 18.4, as influential in the *constructive* trusts that sometimes arise in family contexts.

Contrast the old case of *Jones v Lock*.[7] There, a man brought home a substantial cheque that he had received, and announced that it was for his baby son, the child of his second marriage. He did so in rather vague terms, which the judge took to mean that he intended to provide for the child in an unspecified way.[8] After the man's death, leaving nothing to the child (but a good deal to the children of his first marriage) in his will, the court held that there was no trust for the baby. The judge insisted on an intention precisely identifiable with a trust on the part of the settlor: 'I think it would be of very dangerous example if loose conversations of this sort, in important transactions of this kind, should have the effect of declarations of trust.'[9] If anything, the approach was in terms of a standard of proof higher than the balance of probabilities. It did nothing to vindicate the duty that the man may be thought to have had to provide for the baby. Inclining against finding a trust, and specifically adding a demand for certainty, it tracks notions of economic utilitarianism. (As we saw section 2.5, trusts are inimical to a free market in themselves, and any uncertainty over whether a piece of property is held on trust will only make matters worse, as clarifying the point will increase the transaction costs.) If the case arose today, we might expect it to proceed more like *Paul v Constance*.[10]

3.4 PRECATORY WORDS

Precatory words are words by which the alleged settlor exhorts the alleged trustee to use the property in a particular way, rather than expressly requiring him to: for instance, where I bequeath property to you 'in the confidence', or 'in the hope', or 'in the belief' that you will use it to take care of my child.

The use of such hortatory language is not necessarily inconsistent with an intention to create a trust. It might have been employed merely out of politeness. But the law presumes that it does not denote such an intention. So where a person transfers property to another and expresses the confidence or similar that the latter will use it in a certain way, a trust, legally obliging the recipient so to use it, does not normally arise. Instead, the transfer is taken to be an absolute gift to the recipient, with at most a moral obligation on him regarding its use.

---

[7] (1865) LR 1 Ch App 25.   [8] *Ibid* 29.   [9] *Ibid* 29.
[10] [1977] 1 WLR 527.

For example, in *Mussoorie Bank Ltd v Raynor*[11] a man's will leaving all his property to his wife 'feeling confident that she will act justly to our children in dividing the same when no longer required by her' was construed as giving her the property absolutely, with merely a reminder of her moral duty to the children, rather than as a trust. On the words of the will and the circumstances of the case, that seems an uncontentious finding of the man's probable true intentions. However, there was more to it than that. The previous attitude of the law had been that such precatory language *did* normally indicate an intention to create a trust.[12] This attitude was displaced in favour of the opposite approach, found in *Mussoorie Bank Ltd v Raynor*[13] and still the law today, by decisions in the nineteenth century.[14]

In terms of the facilitative project, the current position is probably more authentic than that which it replaced: the more natural interpretation of this kind of language probably is that no trust is intended. However, the current position also resonates with arguments of rights and of economic utility.

So far as economic utility is concerned, holding precatory words not to create trusts has two main benefits. First, by producing absolute ownership of the property in question, it promotes the desideratum that property should be freely disposable, rather than tied up by incumbrances restricting its alienation, such as trusts. Secondly, it helps minimize transaction costs, by reducing uncertainty over whether property is held on trust (which a facilitative approach would not especially do).[15] Both effects are to the advantage of a free market.[16]

---

[11] (1882) 7 App Cas 321.

[12] Perhaps this was a reflection of dynastic considerations, favouring the tying up of property so as to keep it within the family: see sections 2.4 and 2.5. Alternatively, the attitude may have arisen in the context of an old rule (against 'mortmain') whereby certain trusts for religious foundations were illegal. To evade this ban, a would-be settlor of such a trust might transfer the property in question to a friend and express the wish that the latter should devote it to the foundation. To vindicate the ban, however, the courts may have been inclined to construe such dispositions—to us, gifts with precatory words—as trusts after all.

[13] (1882) 7 App Cas 321.

[14] *Lambe v Eames* (1871) LR 6 Ch App 597; *Re Hutchinson and Tenant* (1878) 8 Ch D 540; *Mussoorie Bank Ltd v Raynor* (1882) 7 App Cas 321; *Re Adams and the Kensington Vestry* (1884) 27 Ch D 394; *Re Hamilton* [1895] 2 Ch 370; *Re Williams* [1897] 2 Ch 12.

[15] For attention to this, see especially *Re Williams* [1897] 2 Ch 12, 21.

[16] Some of the leading cases on precatory words arose in commercial contexts. Thus in *Mussoorie Bank Ltd v Raynor* (1882) 7 App Cas 321 the widow, treating herself as the absolute owner of the land left to her by her husband, mortgaged it to a bank, which now sought to enforce its rights over it. If she had been a trustee of the land, the mortgage would have been invalid, so the bank would have lost the value of its mortgage. The court decided in favour of

As to rights thinking, a rather specific concordance can be seen. Most of the important decisions establishing this rule involved husbands leaving property in their wills to their widows, on precatory terms as to the upbringing of their children, or some such;[17] and they date from the late nineteenth century. At that period there was a prevalent concern to enlarge married women's property rights, which the common law generally withheld. There emerged a series of statutes, the Married Women's Property Acts, from 1870 onwards.[18] At least at first, however, the approach was not straightforwardly to allow wives to enjoy absolute ownership of property. During their marriage, wives were still disabled from spending their capital, and confined to the income, by a restriction called the 'restraint upon anticipation'. This was acknowledged to be a curtailment of the right of married women to own their own property, but it was regarded as justified in order to protect them against being pressurized by their husbands.[19] But the restraint was lifted, and women became absolute owners of their property, on the termination of their marriage: notably, upon widowhood. And from 1882 the restraint was progressively retracted during marriage itself, giving the basic right still fuller expression.[20] In such a culture, the derogatory effect of trusts restricting widows to a life interest would have been particularly obtrusive. Thus it seems plausible to think of the decisions in which the courts disfavoured such arrangements, and secured that absolute ownership was conferred on the widow instead, as not only aligned with but even directly reflecting a rights perception in this vein.

3.5 PURPOSE TRUSTS

Our next rule of construction concerns purpose trusts: that is, cases where the settlor provides that the money should be spent on achieving some specified purpose, rather than paid out to beneficiaries, who can spend it how they like. The rule is that where achieving the purpose would benefit some person (as opposed, say, to maintaining the testator's cat), such a disposition is normally taken as conferring an absolute entitlement upon

---

the bank by holding that the widow was absolute owner. *Re Hutchinson and Tenant* (1878) 8 Ch D 540 and *Re Adams and the Kensington Vestry* (1884) 27 Ch D 394 are similar.

[17] All the cases cited above are of this kind except *Re Hamilton* [1895] 2 Ch 370.

[18] For an account, see A Dicey *Law and Opinion in England during the Nineteenth Century* (1905) 369–93. For an instance of the Married Women's Property Acts being used to make a political argument outside their actual terms, see *Howes v Bishop* [1909] 2 KB 390, 394.

[19] See J Matthews *The Law Relating to Married Women* (1892) 101–2.

[20] Married Women's Property Act 1882 s 1; Law Reform (Married Women and Tortfeasors) Act 1935 s 2; Married Women (Restraint upon Anticipation) Act 1949 s 1.

that person, with no requirement that the money be spent on the particular purpose after all. The reference to the purpose is regarded as merely an expression of the settlor's motive in making the disposition, rather than as a legally binding stipulation.

For example, in *Re Bowes*[21] a testator's will included this provision: 'I bequeath to my trustees the sum of £5,000 sterling upon trust to expend the same in planting trees for shelter on the Wemmergill estate'. It was physically possible to plant £5,000-worth of trees on the estate, but the owners of the estate did not want them. In their view, not only would the money be better spent on other things, but the land that this number of trees would occupy would be better devoted to other uses. So they sought to have the £5,000 instead of the trees. From the language used by the testator it seems clear that he intended to create a trust to plant the trees, rather than for the owners of the estate absolutely. Nevertheless, the owners' claim to have the money succeeded: the instructions about planting trees were taken as merely the motive with which an absolute entitlement to £5,000 was conferred on them and, as such, were not binding on them.

In cases such as this, the language looks unequivocal enough, evincing an intention to create a purpose trust, but the rule of construction has it otherwise. Although couched in terms of the settlor's intention, the rule thus appears to push fidelity to facilitative ideas to the limit.[22] It does however make sense in terms of rights (regarding the beneficiary as in principle entitled to an absolute interest, from which the settlor would derogate in stipulating the purpose on which the money must be spent)[23] and of economic utility (the way the money is ultimately spent is opened to the market, rather than constrained by the limitations of the settlor's purpose).

These latter perspectives, moreover, illuminate the contrast between *Re Andrew's Trust*[24] and *Re Trusts of the Abbott Fund*.[25] In *Re Andrew's*

---

[21] [1896] 1 Ch 507.

[22] It might be argued that the rule serves a facilitative end in validating trusts which would otherwise fail, in that (non-charitable) purpose trusts are generally invalid: section 12.3. In fact, however, it is only purpose trusts that are not beneficial to people that are generally invalid; those which benefit people are valid under *Re Denley's Trust Deed* [1969] 1 Ch 373. The rule discussed in the text applies (indeed, can by its nature apply) only to purpose trusts that benefit people. So it catches only such trusts as would *not* otherwise fail.

[23] Historically, the rule appears to be connected with that in *Lassence v Tierney* (1849) 1 Mac & G 551, that if a settlor first confers an absolute interest on a beneficiary he cannot then go on to qualify it: which idea seems certainly to revolve around rights. The connection is made in *Re Skinner* (1860) 1 J & H 102.

[24] [1905] 2 Ch 48. *Re Osoba* [1979] 1 WLR 247 is similar.   [25] [1900] 2 Ch 326.

Trust,[26] a fund was set up, and donations made to it, to provide for the education of the children of a deceased clergyman. The children had now reached adulthood, and their formal education was over, but there was still money left. The question was whether the children were absolutely entitled to the money in the fund, so that they should now have the rest of it too; or whether it was strictly for their education, so that the surplus should be returned to the donors. The usual rule of construction was followed, so the trust on which the donations were made was interpreted as one not for the purpose of the children's education but for the children as absolutely entitled beneficiaries. The children were therefore entitled to the surplus.[27]

Re Trusts of the Abbott Fund[28] went the other way. Two sisters, who were deaf and dumb and probably quite elderly, were left without means of support. Friends subscribed to a fund to provide for their maintenance. When in time both ladies died, some money remained in the fund. Again, the question was what was to happen to this money. If the money was treated as put into the fund for the ladies' absolute benefit, it should go to their estates now that they were dead. Whereas if it was treated as given for their maintenance alone, then that purpose came to an end with their deaths, so the remaining money had to be given back to the donors. It was held that the latter was the position. The usual rule whereby purpose trusts are read as conferring absolute entitlements was thus displaced, and at the same time it was assumed that at any rate a purpose trust such as this was valid.

The difference between the two decisions has been explained[29] on the ground that while it is reasonable to recognize an absolute entitlement for the named objects of a fund when they are still alive (as in *Re Andrew's Trust*[30]), it is going too far to deprive the donors of the surplus in favour of whoever is entitled to the objects' estate when they have died (as in *Re Trusts of the Abbott Fund*[31]). This idea is crude. Does the 'true construction' change, for example, if the objects are alive at the time of the hearing at first instance, but then die pending an appeal? There is a better analysis. The effect of the usual rule is that people have full dominion over the money in question, rather than that it is spent on the designated purpose on their behalf. This is attractive in terms both of the rights thesis and of

---

[26] [1905] 2 Ch 48.
[27] The decision was also put on a less general basis: that even if it was a purpose trust for the children's education, education is lifelong and all encompassing, and thus included anything on which they might have wanted to spend the money. This seems far-fetched.
[28] [1900] 2 Ch 326.   [29] *Re Osoba* [1978] 1 WLR 247, 795–6.
[30] [1905] 2 Ch 48.   [31] [1900] 2 Ch 326.

economic utility, as explained above. The attraction holds good, however, only where the people in question are of normal capability. If people of reduced capability are given full dominion over the money, their infirmity may lead to their being exploited. So it is appropriate that the rule should be disapplied, and the purpose trust allowed to stand, in these circumstances. The decision in *Re Trusts of the Abbott Fund*[32] makes good sense in these terms. At first sight, it might seem right to seek the same treatment of trusts for children, such as that in *Re Andrew's Trust:*[33] children too lack full capability and so merit the protection of a trust. But children will eventually become fully capable adults (those in that case had done so by the time it came to court), and in the meantime it is safe to hold them absolutely entitled to the money, since they will still not be able to get their hands on the capital[34] until they reach majority.

3.6 CONTRACTS FOR THIRD PARTIES

If I make a contract with you, in which, say, I undertake to pay you £100, the benefit of that contract—the right to my payment—is a piece of property. As such, you can normally make a trust of it. If you make it clear that that is what you decide to do, there is no difficulty: a trust will arise. But sometimes it may be arguable that a contractual promisee is making a trust of an undertaking in this way without having so expressed himself.

This is the case especially where the contract is itself designed to benefit a third party. Say I make a contract with you in which I promise you that I shall pay £100 to your sister. My contract is with you, ie you are the promisee, but my performing it will mean my paying the money to her. Until it was heavily modified by the Contracts (Rights of Third Parties) Act 1999, the English law of contract maintained a rule, known as 'privity', to the effect that only the promisee can sue on a contract. So despite the fact that I was supposed to perform the contract in favour of your sister, privity prevented her from suing me if I did not. Only you could sue me and, if for any reason you chose not to, there was nothing she could do about it. This state of affairs attracted much criticism. It was widely felt that someone in the position of your sister should be able to sue. So ways round the privity rule were sought. One possibility was a finding that you had made a trust of my promise in your sister's favour, even though you had given no positive indication to this effect. Then, your sister could insist (pointing to your duties to her under the trust) that you sue me if

---

[32] [1900] 2 Ch 326.   [33] [1905] 2 Ch 48.
[34] Under the rule in *Saunders v Vautier* (1841) 4 Beav 115, Cr & Ph 240: see section 10.4.

necessary to enforce my promise, and you would hold the ensuing damages on trust for her.

Such a finding requires discovery of the necessary intention on the promisee's part to make a trust of the contractual right for the third party. A practice of construction is often said to obtain in this area, in the shape of a judicial reluctance to find that intention unless compelled to by clear evidence.

In fact, there are some solid decisions in which trusts of contractual rights were found *without* clear evidence that they were intended. For example, where a partnership agreement provided that if one of the partners died, the other should pay his widow a pension, the court decided that this provision was held on trust for the widow.[35] Where the contract for the hire of a ship contained a promise by the shipowners to the hirers to pay a commission to the broker who had been their intermediary, it was found that the hirers held this promise on trust for the broker.[36] And where a man became a member of Lloyd's, the insurance market, and his father made a contract with the Lloyd's managing committee guaranteeing that he would meet any of his son's unpaid debts to his customers, it was found that the managing committee held this guarantee on trust for the son's customers.[37]

There is also material in support of the alleged practice, however. It is not strong (most of the best-known statements were *obiter*)[38] but it is certainly perceived as establishing that a trust of a contract is not to be found unless there is clear evidence that the promisee intended it. So in many modern cases of this kind, the possibility of a trust for the third party was not even argued.

On the face of it, a reluctance to find trusts in such cases is consonant with the precepts of economic utility. It could be said that free commerce is best promoted by affording contracting parties dominion over their own bargains; that is, by the original privity rule. According rights to outsiders, as such a trust would do, would prevent the parties from dissolving their bargains and renegotiating them and trading their rights in them. But although there is something in this view, it is not entirely satisfactory. Economic utility may be better served by giving a right of enforcement to the third party, as in the three cases mentioned earlier, where trusts

---

[35] *Re Flavell* (1883) 25 Ch D 89.

[36] *Les Affréteurs Réunis SA v Leopold Walford (London) Ltd* [1919] AC 801.

[37] *Lloyd's v Harper* (1880) 16 Ch D 290.

[38] eg *Re Empress Engineering Co* (1880) 16 Ch D 125, 129; *Re Stapleton-Bretherton* [1941] Ch 482, 485; *Re Schebsman* [1944] Ch 83, 89, 104; *Green v Russell* [1959] 2 QB 226, 241.

of promises were found.[39] In all of them, the point seems to have been that the contract envisaged payment to the third party, and so the trust had to be discovered in order to give efficacy to the bargain: a copybook laissez-faire sentiment. Moreover, the discovery of the trust in each of the cases played a positive part in fostering commerce: providing for partners' widows' pensions facilitated the formation of partnerships; providing for shipbrokers' commissions allowed them profitably to provide their service to shippers; and providing for underwriters' guarantees promoted confidence, and hence trade, in the insurance market.

So in fact the opposing approaches are both intelligible in terms of economic utility, the difference between them tracking competing readings of the implications of that policy.[40] Although trusts of contracts impede commerce, by tying the parties' hands, they also promote it by effectuating the bargain as struck. It is quite possible to believe that the latter consideration is of greater force than the former. That view appears to be the foundation of the reform to the privity rule itself, by the Contracts (Rights of Third Parties) Act 1999, as a result of which a contract for the benefit of a third party will often be enforceable against the promisor by the third party.[41] As a result of this reform, it will now rarely be useful to inquire whether a contractual promisee has impliedly declared a trust of the contract's benefit for a third party.

3.7 GRATUITOUS TRANSFERS

Say I transfer property to you (or pay another to do so) *inter vivos*, while you give no consideration for the transfer. In the absence of any further information as to my intentions, the law has traditionally reckoned you to hold the property on 'resulting trust', ie on trust for me.[42] Exceptionally, however, if I am your husband, or your father, or stand *in loco parentis* to you, the law has traditionally applied the 'presumption of advancement' to my transfer, treating me as meaning it to be a gift to you.[43]

---

[39] *Re Flavell* (1883) 25 Ch D 89; *Les Affréteurs Réunis SA v Leopold Walford (London) Ltd* [1919] AC 801; *Lloyd's v Harper* (1880) 16 Ch D 290.

[40] See further P Atiyah *The Rise and Fall of Freedom of Contract* (1979) 412–14.

[41] By s 1(1)(b), a non-party to a contract can enforce it if it 'purports to confer a benefit on him', unless (s 1(2)) 'on a proper construction of the contract it appears that the parties did not intend the term to be enforceable by the third party'.

[42] *Dyer v Dyer* (1788) 2 Cox 92; *The Venture* [1908] P 218.

[43] *Grey v Grey* (1677) 2 Sw 594; *Powys v Mansfield* (1835) 3 Myl & Cr 359; *Kingdon v Bridges* (1688) 2 Vern 67. See further J Glister in C Mitchell (ed) *Constructive and Resulting Trusts* (2010) ch 10. Some Commonwealth jurisdictions apply the presumption also where a mother transfers to her child (eg *Nelson v Nelson* (1995) 184 CLR 538, Australia), but that is

The resulting trust referred to in the previous paragraph is generally referred to as a 'presumed resulting trust'. But it is unclear, and indeed contentious, what is involved. On one view, I am presumed to intend you to hold the property on trust for me, and the trust arises in effectuation of that intention.[44] On another view, what is presumed on my part is the *absence* of any intention that you should take the property for your own benefit (or, we should add, anyone else's), in which case the trust arises not because I intend it, but because that is the consequence of such a transfer.[45] On a third view, no kind of intention or lack thereof on my part is presumed; the important thing is that I transfer the property to you with (in the absence of information as to my intentions) no reason for doing so, and the trust arises, again, as the consequence of this.[46] This third view is preferable to the other two in that, unlike them, it does not involve presuming an implausible intention on the part of the transferor. On the other hand, it achieves this distinction by presuming nothing at all. This makes it hard to see why the trust in question should be labelled, as it is, a 'presumed resulting trust', and, more importantly, leaves this view inconsistent with the currently authoritative judicial treatment of these trusts, which asserts that they arise in reflection of the transferor's (and transferee's) presumed intention, and favours the first of the views just described.[47]

It may, then, be right to see the law as presuming and effectuating an intention on my part that, where I transfer property gratuitously to you, you should hold that property on trust for me. If so, the matter merits discussion in the present chapter. We must then account for the presumptions. They have ancient roots. They probably originated as reflections of the commonest intentions actually held by those making gratuitous transfers of land in the late Middle Ages and for a time afterwards: such transfers being at that period more often aimed at creating a trust for the transferor than at conferring a gift on the transferee, except in the cases caught by the presumption of advancement.[48] So then, the rules were not

not English law (*Bennet v Bennet* (1879) 10 Ch D 474). The Equality Act 2010 s 199 provides for the abolition of the presumption (though cf J Glister (2010) 73 MLR 807), but has not yet been brought into effect.

[44] See W Swadling (2008) 124 LQR 72.

[45] See R Chambers *Resulting Trusts* (1997) ch 1; J Penner in C Mitchell (ed) *Constructive and Resulting Trusts* (2010) ch 8, 241–57.

[46] See R Chambers in C Mitchell (ed) *Constructive and Resulting Trusts* (2010) ch 9, 276–85.

[47] *Westdeutsche Landesbank Girozentrale v Islington LBC* [1996] AC 669, 708: see section 16.3.   [48] A Simpson *A History of the Land Law* 2nd edn (1986) 177–9.

at odds with facilitative logic. But this is surely no longer so. Nowadays, gratuitous transfers are surely normally meant as gifts. Since the presumption of a resulting trust operates as in contradiction of this, as a presumption against a gift, it is counter-facilitative. And on reflection, even the presumption of advancement can be seen as departing from pure facilitative logic in *presuming* a gift, rather than leaving the transferor's intention simply to speak for itself.

This alienation of the presumptions from the facilitative project may be acceptable, however, if they have some other sufficient basis. In this vein, for example, they may be seen as aligned with the dynastic project which endured until, but ended with, the classic period of the great family in the nineteenth century:[49] a resulting trust, tending against the alienation of property, helps ensure that it is passed down between generations of the family, while gifts from father to child are encouraged as setting the next generation up in life. The presumption of a gift from husband to wife tracks the policy that at one time prevailed of promoting the rights of married women, founded on rights considerations. The presumption about gratuitous transfers can also be seen as a paternalistic measure, guarding transferors against easy alienation of their assets. None of these possible justifications for the presumptions can be regarded as convincing today, however.

So if the presumptions are indeed of the transferor's intention to create a trust or not, they affront facilitative logic, and do so to no satisfactory end.[50] It is unsurprising, then, to discover that the courts have generally played them down, holding them rebutted by merely a contrary general impression,[51] and indeed suggesting that they may no longer exist, or are not to be applied in certain contexts.[52]

---

[49] See sections 2.4–2.5.

[50] For an argument that the presumption of advancement is contrary to the European Convention on Human Rights, see G Andrews [2007] Conv 340. See further R Chambers in C Mitchell (ed) *Constructive and Resulting Trusts* (2010) ch 9, 268–76.

[51] *Fowkes v Pascoe* (1875) LR 10 Ch App 343; *Bennet v Bennet* (1879) 10 Ch D 474; *Standing v Bowring* (1885) 31 Ch D 282. But the presumptions can still determine outcomes where the evidence to rebut them cannot be adduced because it involves an illegality: *Tinsley v Milligan* [1994] 1 AC 340; *Tribe v Tribe* [1996] Ch 107. The unhappiness of this effect is the function as much of the illegality rules as of the presumptions, however. See now Law Commission *The Illegality Defence* (Law Com No 320, 2010) Part 2.

[52] *Pettitt v Pettitt* [1970] AC 777, 793, 811, 824, regarding the presumption of advancement between husband and wife; *Tinsley v Milligan* [1994] 1 AC 340, 371 and *Lohia v Lohia* [2001] EWCA Civ 1691, [21]–[26], pointing to the Law of Property Act 1925 s 60(3) (also *Fowkes v Pascoe* (1875) LR 10 Ch App 343, 348), regarding the presumption about gratuitous transfers where the property is land; and *Stack v Dowden* [2007] 2 AC 432, [31], [59]–[60], regarding both the presumption about gratuitous transfers (or at any rate, the resolution of disputes by

But if the presumptions merit discussion in the present chapter at all—in particular, if a presumed resulting trust arises because, in gratuitously transferring property to you, I am presumed to intend you to hold it on trust for me—there is a further difficulty. On this view, the 'presumed resulting trust' emerges as a form of *express* trust. However, the law treats express and resulting trusts as mutually exclusive categories, and handles resulting trusts in a way that makes sense only if the latter do *not* rest on a settlor's intention (exempting resulting trusts from a formality requirement that sometimes applies to express trusts).[53] So it may after all be better to regard 'presumed resulting trusts' in one of the other ways outlined above. Resulting trusts are given further attention in Chapter 16, and the issue of their relationship with intention will be considered further there.

3.8 THE OVERALL PICTURE

We have considered a number of rules and practices whereby the courts, deciding whether to find a settlor's intention in order to determine whether there is an express trust, depart from the ordinary standard of proof. The pattern we have discovered is uneven. Sometimes more than the balance of probabilities is demanded (so that the alleged trust or term is less likely to be found), sometimes less (so that it is more likely to be found). And although it is possible to justify each position taken in terms of one policy or another, there is no consistency in this respect either.

It would not be unreasonable to expect a purer line. The issue centrally at stake is the choice between the claims of the facilitative project, implying that trusts should be found on the basis of intention when, but only when, that intention is genuinely present; and the message of other considerations that allowing people complete, or at the extreme any, liberty to make or not make trusts is undesirable. At least some degree of acceptance of the latter position seems unavoidable. But the better vehicle for it is not the manipulation of the finding of intention, after the fashion of the rules described in this chapter. This is so above all because such rules will always be overridden by a sufficiently definite expression of the genuine intention: and today, when trusts are most often made with professional advice, intentions generally will be given sufficiently definite expression.

---

the use of resulting trusts derived from that presumption) and the presumption of advancement in the context of family homes. But cf *Antoni v Antoni* [2007] UKPC 10, asserting the continued vitality of the presumption of advancement between father and child.

[53] Law of Property Act 1925 s 53(1)(b), (2): see sections 5.4–5.5.

The right vehicle to reflect a non-facilitative consideration is rather a positive rule, overriding any contrary intention: prohibiting a trust where one is not wanted, or generating a constructive trust in the opposite case.

3·9 REPLACEMENT OF FAILED TRANSACTIONS

In the situations we have looked at so far, either outcome—finding or not finding the alleged intention—was possible, though in some cases credulity was strained. We now turn to a different sort of case. Say I try to make a gift to you, but for some reason am frustrated in that. My general plan, however, was certainly to confer a benefit on you, and that would be achieved if I held the property in question on trust for you instead. It is clear that I did not intend to do so: my thoughts were purely about making you a gift. Might the courts nonetheless say that I did?

The point has not arisen in the material that we have considered hitherto in this chapter. There was no issue there of a trust, not intended in itself, being recognized so as to do substitute service in this way for some other concept that was intended. But at first sight, it seems unthinkable that the courts should recognize a trust in such circumstances. We are told that I had no intention to make the trust in question. Finding otherwise would therefore be contrary to the facilitative logic governing the creation of express trusts.

But this view assumes a particular conception of the facilitative project. It is that we should recognize an express trust when the alleged settlor intends to create that trust, but not otherwise. The 'not otherwise' is questionable, however. Perhaps the project is, or should be, not exclusively concerned with whether the alleged settlor had in mind precisely a trust, but prepared also to find a trust, or whatever other legal device may be most appropriate, to give effect to the alleged settlor's broad plan. By this way of thinking, the trust is 'intended', and so should be recognized, not only when the alleged settlor specifically intends to create a trust, but also where it is the best, or best available, legal match for that which he does intend.

On the whole, this wider view of the facilitative project seems preferable to its rival. Otherwise, the law in effect makes the establishment of an express trust depend on the settlor's successful negotiation of a conceptual obstacle course. It is clear that an express trust is created not only when the alleged settlor has that concept in mind by name, but also when he intends a set of arrangements equating with that which the law calls a trust.[54] But 'that which the law calls a trust' is a complicated concept, and

---

[54] *Re Schebsman* [1944] Ch 83, 104.

to insist that the alleged settlor get every detail right is to expect a lot, and in effect to limit the use of the concept to those who are well advised, or perhaps lucky.

Do the courts accept this view? There is evidence both ways. That evidence consists especially of the material in sections 3.10 and 3.11.

3.10 TRANSFERS LACKING REQUIRED FORMALITIES

The degree of formality required for the full legal transfer of a piece of property is sometimes greater than that required to deal with the property in some other way: to make a trust of it, or a contract to transfer it. For example, a deed is usually required to make a full legal transfer of land,[55] while a trust of it, or a contract to transfer it, requires only an ordinary signed written document.[56] So say the owner of some property means to transfer the legal ownership in it to another, but has used insufficient formality to achieve this. So far as formality goes, he may nonetheless have done enough validly to make himself trustee of the property for the intended transferee, or to contract with the intended transferee to pass the property to the latter, thus giving him the right to call for it. Will the would-be transferor be found to have done so? The wider view of the facilitative project suggests that he should; the narrower fastens on the fact that he undoubtedly had no idea of doing anything except make a complete transfer, and says that he should not. What the law actually says apparently depends on which of three kinds of case is in play.

The first kind of case is where the intended transfer was to be a gift but the giver has not taken the correct steps to make it. The law will not readily discover an intention to create a trust in lieu[57] (and there is no question of a contract in lieu, as a contract requires consideration). That is, the courts take the narrower view.[58] The second kind of case is likewise where

---

[55] At one time, a deed alone; nowadays, entry on the official Land Register too. In the future, the latter will probably become the only requirement. The general point remains the same.

[56] For a trust, see Law of Property Act 1925 s 53(1)(b) (see section 5.4); for a contract, Law of Property (Miscellaneous Provisions) Act 1989 s 2.

[57] *Milroy v Lord* (1862) 4 De GF & J 264; *Richards v Delbridge* (1874) LR 18 Eq 11. Cf *T Choithram International SA v Pagarini* [2001] 2 All ER 492, where a purported and ineffective gift to a foundation took effect as a declaration of trust, as the foundation was a trust (so any 'gift to it' would of necessity have taken the form of a transfer to its trustees on its trusts) and the putative donor was one of its trustees (so no *transfer to* its trustees was in fact required).

[58] This might be understood as preventing the avoidance of the formality requirements for a full legal transfer. However, someone consciously wanting to avoid these requirements would have no difficulty in doing so, by deliberately making a trust. The rule in the text prevents only

the intended transfer was to be a gift, but whilst the giver has taken the correct steps, other steps have to be taken by someone else (eg re-registration by a company of gifted shares in the name of the donee) before the transfer is complete. Here, adopting the wider view, the law will discover an intention to make a trust pending the completion of those steps.[59] The third kind of case is where the failed legal transfer was for consideration: that is, broadly, paid for. Here, the law treats the frustrated transferor as intending to contract with the purported transferee to transfer the property to him.[60] By relying on this contract, the putative transferee can claim the property after all. And, generally speaking, the law anticipates his doing so and treats him as if he had already got the property, by regarding the transferor as holding it on a constructive trust for him in the meantime.[61] This manifests the wider view: the intention to contract is no more genuinely to be found in this case than the intention to hold on trust would be in the case of a failed gift.[62]

The pattern of these choices is aligned with economic utilitarian precepts. This policy favours the effectuation of commercial arrangements, ie those where consideration is involved, and so calls for the provision of substitute vehicles, even involving trusts, in their aid. Being generally offended by the creation of trusts, however, this policy is averse to their recognition in place of failed gifts. But there is less difficulty where the fulfilment of the gift is merely delayed, for the offensive trust will soon disappear; and in the meantime a trust will allow the donee to act to an extent as though the property has become his own, which is preferable to the stagnation entailed by obliging him to await the full transfer.

3.11 PAYMENTS TO CLUBS

People frequently want to make payments[63] to clubs and associations, whether by way of membership fee ('subscription'), gift, bequest, or

---

their accidental avoidance in this manner, which seems an improbable aim for the law. On this analysis, too, there is no consistency with the position in the second and third cases, where the law does allow the formal requirements for a full legal transfer to be avoided.

[59] *Re Rose* [1952] Ch 499.   [60] *Parker v Taswell* (1858) 2 De G & J 559.
[61] See section 17.6.

[62] Note that, under appropriate circumstances, the law may alternatively effectuate any kind of intended but as yet ineffective transfer by saying that the transferor holds on *constructive* trust for the transferee: for which no finding of intention to create a trust is required. The constructive trust would most likely arise under the doctrine of proprietary estoppel: see section 18.4. In *Pennington v Waine* [2002] 1 WLR 2075, such a trust was found on the basis of 'unconscionability', but the discussion (at 2090–1) of what constituted the unconscionability, and why, is vestigial.

[63] Or occasionally to transfer some other form of property than money: the issues are the same.

purchase (eg of a raffle ticket). One would expect it to be quite straight-forward to do so. But there is a problem. For the payment to be made, the payee must be capable of receiving it, ie of owning the money given. The law says that people can own property, but that organizations cannot, unless they are 'incorporated'. Trading companies are generally incorporated, and so are some clubs. Payments to these can therefore be validly made. But many clubs are not incorporated, so cannot own property: so no payments can be made to them.

In a clear example of the wider form of facilitative thinking, however, the judges have developed a practice of regarding apparent payments to unincorporated clubs as some other, valid, kind of disposition having an effect similar to the abortive direct payment. They use two principal approaches.

First, the purported gift to the club may be read as a trust for the club's purposes[64] (without this time treating that in turn as a gift to the club's members beneficially).[65] A trust to promote a charitable purpose is valid without more, as explained in Chapter 6; so a purported gift to a club with charitable objects will unproblematically be valid as a trust for those objects, and will always be taken thus.[66] A trust to promote a non-charitable purpose is valid if there are people benefited by, or perhaps otherwise interested in, its performance.[67] Most club members will be benefited by the performance of a trust for their club's purposes, and surely all, even if on the basis of altruism alone, will be interested in the performance of such a trust. Gifts read as trusts for the purposes of non-charitable clubs will thus normally achieve validity too.[68]

Secondly, the purported gift to a non-charitable club may be read as a gift to its members.[69] A gift to the members merely in their personal

---

[64] Some of the payments in *Re West Sussex Constabulary's Widows, Children and Benevolent (1930) Fund Trust* [1971] Ch 1 were treated in this way.

[65] Cf section 3.5. That further step was however taken (and the contractual analysis, below, then applied) in *Re Lipinski's Will Trusts* [1976] Ch 235.

[66] *Re Vernon's Will Trusts* [1972] Ch 300n; *Re Finger's Will Trusts* [1972] Ch 286.

[67] *Re Denley's Trust Deed* [1969] 1 Ch 373: see section 12.3.

[68] Thus in *Re West Sussex Constabulary's Widows, Children and Benevolent (1930) Fund Trust* [1971] Ch 1. Some of the club cases deny the possibility of a purpose trust (eg *Re Recher's Will Trusts* [1972] Ch 526, 540–1), but without adverting to the support to be had from *Re Denley's Trust Deed* [1969] 1 Ch 373. (Similar, though not identical, to the purpose trust approach is the suggestion in *Conservative and Unionist Central Office v Burrell* [1982] 1 WLR 522 that the payment be treated as to the club treasurer, with a mandate to spend it on the club's purposes. The latter analysis has not proved popular, perhaps partly because it is hard to see how it can apply to a purported *bequest* to a club.)

[69] Whether directly, or via a trust of which they are the beneficiaries. A gift to a club with charitable objects could not be read thus without itself becoming a non-charitable trust: conferring the property on the members makes it theirs (even if they have contracted to devote

capacity would be technically unproblematic,[70] but it would not be a close surrogate for the purported gift *to the club*. To achieve a better surrogate, the gift is taken as being to the members 'on behalf of the club'. Between the members of the club there will exist a contract, either express or implied: the club's rules. This contract will, again either expressly or impliedly, govern (amongst other things) the use which the members can make of any money that they own on the club's behalf: essentially, requiring them to spend it (only) on the club's purposes. Income regarded in this way will thus be owned by the members, but be caught by this contractual obligation.[71] This approach is often referred to as 'the contractual analysis'.

Sometimes the judges have no choice between the two approaches. A contract obliging me to make a payment 'to the club' can usually be read only as requiring a payment under the contractual analysis.[72] Say you sell me a £1 ticket for your club's raffle. In technical terms, this occurs under a contract, which obliges me to pay £1 in exchange for the ticket. I will not fulfil this obligation unless I give you the £1 absolutely. Settling £1 on trust for the club's purposes will not do. As the £1 then comes into your absolute ownership, it is caught by the club rules. The same goes for members' subscriptions. The contract under which they are demanded (in return for the benefits of membership) requires them to be paid, say to the treasurer, absolutely; they are then caught by the rules.

But in the case of donations voluntarily made, whether *inter vivos* or by will, the donor can choose the terms on which to make the payment, so both approaches are in principle viable.[73] We, however, are considering what happens if the donor has expressly chosen neither, but has purported

it to charity), and benefiting them is not a charitable purpose (see section 6.5). As the settlor surely intended a charitable disposition, this construction is eschewed in favour of that in the previous paragraph.

[70] Unless for reasons of perpetuity (see section 2.5), if the gift is to members joining indefinitely into the future.

[71] *Re Recher's Will Trusts* [1972] Ch 526. Cases using this approach include *Re St Andrew's Allotment Association* [1969] 1 WLR 229; *Re West Sussex Constabulary's Widows, Children and Benevolent (1930) Fund Trust* [1971] Ch 1; *Re Sick and Funeral Society of St John's Sunday School, Golcar* [1973] Ch 51; *Re Buckinghamshire Constabulary Widows' and Orphans' Fund Friendly Society (No 2)* [1979] 1 WLR 936; *Hanchett-Stamford v A-G* [2009] Ch 173.

[72] Though a contract obliging me to pay money to a charitable club will presumably be taken to require a settlement on the club's trusts, so as not to produce a (non-charitable) payment to the members. Contracts obliging employers and employees to pay into pension schemes likewise require them to place the money on the scheme trusts.

[73] The purpose trust approach is however doubtfully plausible for money placed in a collecting box. The small sum involved and the anonymity of the donor make it more realistic to see him as paying the money absolutely, ie under the contractual analysis. The essence of the point is taken, but its implications not fully absorbed, in *Re West Sussex Constabulary's Widows, Children and Benevolent (1930) Fund Trust* [1971] Ch 1, 11–14.

to make a payment to the club, and the substitute analysis is being con-structed by the court under the wider facilitative logic. It seems right to use the analysis that most closely reflects the failed intended disposition.

Under the purpose trust approach there is a trust obligation to spend the money on the club's purposes. The money in no sense belongs to the mem-bers, and they cannot claim it for themselves or otherwise change the purposes on which it will be spent from those (the club's existing purposes) regarded as designated by the donor.[74] Under the contractual analysis, however, the money belongs to the members. What stops them from taking it home as their own property, or otherwise spending it in a way different from that perhaps envisaged by the donor, is the relevant club rule. But this is a term of a contract made amongst themselves. As the sole parties to this contract, they can change its terms, or even terminate it, by mutual consent, allowing them after all to spend the money as they may wish. This is the main difference between the two approaches.[75] One might see the purpose trust approach's firmer adhesion to the original club purposes as an argument in its favour, as making it more faithful to the donor's intentions. But this is a questionable view. The donor, remember, sought to make a gift to the club. It is strongly arguable that in so doing he meant the members to settle the use of the money thereafter. (Just as if I give you some money as a present, I acknowledge that it is yours to spend, and that you are ultimately entitled to disregard whatever ideas I may have about its use.) And the closer approximation to that is not the purpose trust approach, but the contractual analysis.

In practice, a judge *impelled* to use the contractual analysis regarding part of a club's income (notably the members' subscriptions) may well *choose* to use it also for the rest, for the sake of simplicity.[76] He or she is also likely to be swayed by the relative attractiveness of the results that the rival analyses would throw up in the circumstances that have emerged: often, upon the club's dissolution. If a gift is treated as made on a purpose trust, the failure of that purpose will (unless the giver has provided otherwise)[77]

---

[74] Though if the trustees were willing to misapply the money in some way that the members favoured, the members could bring that about by not enforcing the trust against them (unless the trust can be enforced by its settlor: cf *Carreras Rothmans Ltd v Freeman Mathews Treasure Ltd* [1985] Ch 207): see section 12.3. It would be possible to design a purpose trust whose purposes could validly be varied by the members, but this has apparently not been considered in respect of the purpose trusts that are found in lieu of purported gifts to clubs, as opposed to those made expressly.

[75] Cf *Re Lipinski's Will Trusts* [1976] Ch 235, where the judge did not notice that the two approaches have different consequences and treated them as interchangeable.

[76] See eg *Re Buckinghamshire Constabulary Widows' and Orphans' Fund Friendly Society (No 2)* [1979] 1 WLR 936; but cf *Re West Sussex Constabulary's Widows, Children and Benevolent (1930) Fund Trust* [1971] Ch 1.

[77] By a stipulation in favour of a further object; or, if this be legally possible (assumed so in eg *Re West Sussex Constabulary's Widows, Children and Benevolent (1930) Fund Trust* [1971]

generate a resulting trust, requiring that the surviving amount be repaid to the giver.[78] Where the gift was small, or anonymous, or made some time previously by a person not since connected with the club, effecting such a repayment will be a difficult task. If a gift is treated as made under the contractual analysis, however, upon the club's dissolution it will go in equal shares to the members at the time of the dissolution, unless they agree otherwise.[79] This outcome will normally be easy to effectuate, especially in comparison with a resulting trust solution; it will thus be expedient to have adopted the contractual analysis in the first place.

Ch 1, but doubted by R Chambers *Resulting Trusts* (1997) 58–66), by an intention to leave the property ownerless, and thus, as *bona vacantia*, the property of the Crown. (According to *Air Jamaica Ltd v Charlton* [1999] 1 WLR 1399, 1412, even if it is possible to make the property ownerless an intention to do so cannot prevent a resulting trust from arising; but this both contradicts *Westdeutsche Landesbank Girozentrale v Islington LBC* [1996] AC 669, 708 and is wrong in principle: see section 16.6.)

[78] See section 16.2. In *Re Printers and Transferrers Amalgamated Trades Protection Society* [1899] 2 Ch 184, however, the 'resulting trust' was said to be for the members at the time of dissolution, notwithstanding that they were not the only settlors of the funds. Perhaps the neglected settlors were taken to have transferred their resulting trust interests to the members remaining at dissolution, though there was neither evidence of this nor the written documentation which ought to have been used (Law of Property Act 1925 s 53(1)(c): see section 5.7). Cf *Re Hobourn Aero Components Air Raid Distress Fund* [1946] Ch 86 and *Air Jamaica Ltd v Charlton* [1999] 1 WLR 1399, which use resulting trusts more conventionally.

[79] In *Re Buckinghamshire Constabulary Widows' and Orphans' Fund Friendly Society (No 2)* [1979] 1 WLR 936 and *Re Horley Town Football Club* [2006] EWHC 2386 (Ch), [129], this outcome is attributed to an implied term of the rules contract. In *Hanchett-Stamford v A-G* [2009] Ch 173, however, it is ascribed to the members' very ownership of the club assets, the club's dissolution meaning that they are no longer contractually barred from taking away their individual shares. Both analyses are possible, accordingly as the dissolution does or does not discharge the contract. Many dissolutions will do so (indicating the *Hanchett-Stamford* analysis), but some may not, depending on their particular circumstances. Fortunately the analyses normally yield the same outcome. This is not the case, however, where the club dissolves because its membership dwindles to one. Since the latter is now necessarily *not* a member, an implied term in favour of members will not favour him; instead the remaining property will be ownerless ('*bona vacantia*'), and so go to the Crown. But the *Hanchett-Stamford* analysis, which does not depend on his remaining a member, will leave him sole owner of the remaining property, with no restriction on his ability to take it; this being the outcome, on the facts, in *Hanchett-Stamford v A-G* itself.

4

Promises to Make Trusts

Except for trusts contained in his will, a settlor will generally want the trusts he makes to come into effect immediately. In such cases, he will either transfer the property in question to trustees, or else keep it and declare himself the trustee of it; and from then on it will belong to the trust.

Sometimes, however, it is otherwise. A settlor may plan to make a trust, but, despite being able to do so immediately, decide not actually to do so, perhaps because the circumstances are not quite right. Or he may not yet have the property that he plans to put on trust;[1] for example, he may plan to put on trust an inheritance which he expects to receive upon someone's death in the future. In these cases, until he makes the trust he has done nothing beyond conceive an idea about it in his mind, which has no legal effect. He can change his idea, or abandon it altogether, as he likes. In the case where he does not yet have the property in question, he can please himself whether he goes ahead and makes a trust of it, if and when he receives it.

But a settlor might want to set up something more definite than this. Where he might have made a trust immediately but chose not to because the circumstances were not right, he might want to bind himself to make it if and when things improve. Or, in the case of property that he does not yet have, he might wish to establish a firm arrangement that will produce a trust if and when the property comes to him. This chapter looks at the ways in which settlors might go about making such commitments, and considers the effect that they have.

4.1 REVOCABLE UNDERTAKINGS

One possibility is for the settlor to have a document drawn up containing the terms of his intended trust and saying that the trust is to come into

---

[1] Following upon the idea that a trust must have property (section 1.9), one can only make a trust of property that one actually has: *MacJordan Construction Ltd v Brookmount Erostin Ltd* [1992] BCLC 350.

effect on receipt of the property in question, and then to arrange for the property, when it materializes, to be sent directly to the trustee. Going this far does not bind the settlor. He can still change his mind about making the trust, and revoke the arrangements he has set up. But unless he does something positive to show that he has changed his mind before the property reaches the trustee (such as destroying the document, or cancelling the arrangement for the property to be sent to the trustee), it will generally then be taken that he still intends the trust. And when this presumed continuing intention comes together with the pre-established terms, and with the property now arriving in the trustee's hands under the arrangement, the trust will in fact be made.[2]

The advance that this approach represents over merely intending to make a trust is that instead of the settlor having to bestir himself into making the trust when he receives the property, the trust will automatically come into effect unless he actively prevents it. So it perhaps makes it more likely that the trust will eventually be made. Certainly, it looks more like a commitment than the case of pure intention, and so creates an effect that some people in some circumstances might find useful. Ultimately, however, such an arrangement is no more binding on the settlor than a pure intention.[3]

4.2 CONTRACTS TO MAKE TRUSTS

Sometimes, however, a would-be settlor may want positively to commit himself now to make a trust of property when he gets it in the future. He can in principle do so by making a contract to that effect.

This contract might be of the ordinary kind where both parties give consideration. For example, I might make a deal with my sister whereby she pays me a sum of money now in return for my undertaking to hold any inheritance I may later receive on trust for her children. Her consideration is paying me the money, and mine is the promise to make a trust of the inheritance for her children if and when I receive it. Alternatively, the

---

[2] *Re Bowden* [1936] Ch 71. The trust will not be made, however, if the property reaches the trustees not under an arrangement made by the settlor but adventitiously, eg because the trustee also happens to be the executor of a will under which the property in question is bequeathed to the settlor: *Re Brooks' Settlement Trusts* [1939] Ch 993. That seems right, as maintaining the primacy of the settlor's intention, but the contrary view was taken in *Re Ralli's Will Trusts* [1964] Ch 288, where *Re Brooks' Settlement Trusts* was not cited.

[3] Stipulating for a trust in one's will is a particular instance of this. On death, the property in question will go to the designated trustee and the trust will come into effect; but until then the will is revocable.

contract might be of the special kind known as a covenant, where the settlor uses a deed to make his promise, and there need be no consideration in return. For example, if I want to undertake to give 2 per cent of my net income each year to a charitable trust, I might covenant to the charity's trustees to transfer the sum in question each year to their trust.

In former times, one common use of these contracts to make trusts was found in marriage settlements. These varied in details, but their basic outline was standard. When a woman married, her parents would put some money or other property into a trust, of which she was the beneficiary for her life, then her husband if he survived her, then their children if they had any, but otherwise her next-of-kin (remoter relatives such as nephews and nieces). This was an ordinary immediate trust, of property already in hand. But in addition, the woman signed a deed undertaking to the settlement's trustees that if she received further property during the marriage ('after-acquired property': an inheritance, for example), she would transfer it into this same trust.

This undertaking is clearly a covenant by the woman with the trustees (they did not normally give any consideration). But it is also a contract for consideration between her, on the one side, and on the other side her husband and any children of the marriage. The husband's consideration is the marriage itself, and the law regards this as extending also to their children: they are said to be 'within the marriage consideration'. The next-of-kin, however, are not parties to the covenant, as the trustees are; nor is there a contract between the woman and them in the way that there is between her and her husband and children, because the marriage consideration does not include them and they give no other consideration. Their position is purely that of potential beneficiaries of the trust that the woman has undertaken to make. As people who have given no consideration, they are called 'volunteers'.

4.3 THE ENFORCEABILITY OF CONTRACTS TO MAKE TRUSTS

These contracts to make trusts, whether for consideration or in the form of covenants, might be expected to behave just like contracts to do anything else. In principle they would be binding and enforceable. But in fact, as a result of the decisions that have emerged on the subject, the law about contracts to make trusts has some peculiarities. To see the position, we need to separate three different scenarios.

First: where the beneficiary of the projected trust *has himself given consideration* for the settlor's undertaking to make it. (This is the position of the husband and children in the case of a marriage settlement.) Here, we would expect the contract to be enforceable by the beneficiary, as a party to it. And this is indeed the law.[4]

Secondly: where the beneficiary (such as a next-of-kin) does *not* give consideration, but the settlor makes his covenant not only with the prospective trustees *but also with the beneficiary himself* that he will make the trust, so that the beneficiary is not merely the designated object of the projected trust, but a party to the covenant itself. We would expect that the covenant can be enforced by the covenantees, both the trustees and the beneficiary. Again, this has been accepted in the case law.[5]

Those two positions are normal under the law of contract. Promisees under contracts, whether for consideration or in the form of a covenant, are able to enforce them. So far as these two scenarios are concerned, this goes for contracts to make trusts just as much as any other contract.

The difficulties set in with the third scenario: where the beneficiary (such as a next-of-kin) is a volunteer, ie does *not* give consideration, and the settlor makes a covenant promising the prospective trustees but, this time, *not the beneficiary* that he will make a trust for the beneficiary. Here, the situation is somewhat complex.

In the case of a covenant made before 11 May 2000, the old rules on privity of contract (changed on that date) will prevent the beneficiary from directly enforcing the covenant. Under the ordinary law of contract, however, we should expect the trustees, as covenantees, to be able to enforce. But the cases say that the trustees may not: that a covenant of this kind (one to create a trust in favour of a volunteer) is unenforceable.

In the case of a covenant made since 11 May 2000, the beneficiary is likely to have the benefit of the Contracts (Rights of Third Parties) Act 1999. Under this Act,[6] a contract may be enforced by someone who is not a party to it (a 'third party') but on whom it purports to confer a benefit.[7] Although it is uncertain, the Act may apply to covenants as much as to contracts for consideration.[8] The third party's right to enforce is only, however, as strong as the right of the promisee, our prospective

---

[4] *Pullan v Koe* [1913] 1 Ch 9. Moreover, if the remedy of specific performance is available, then, because 'equity looks upon that as done which ought to be done', the settlor will hold the property on constructive trust pending compliance with the contract (see section 17.6): *ibid*.

[5] *Cannon v Hartley* [1949] Ch 213. There being no consideration, the remedy cannot be specific performance, so (cf n 4 above) there can be no constructive trust pending compliance.

[6] Section 1(1)(b).

[7] Unless on a proper construction of the contract it appears that the parties to it did not intend it to be enforceable by the third party (s 1(2)). A contract is also enforceable by a third party if it contains a term to that effect: s 1(1)(a).

[8] The Act leaves the point unclear, merely using the word 'contract'. The view that it does apply to covenants is suggested by the report proposing the Act: Law Commission *Privity of*

trustees: defences that the promisor can raise against the promisee can also be raised against the third party.[9] And as we have just seen, the law was already that the prospective trustees could not enforce the covenant against the covenantor. Under the 1999 Act, the beneficiary should therefore likewise be unable to enforce it.

Apparently, then, in the third scenario both pre- and post-2000 covenants are unenforceable either by the beneficiary or by the trustees. In the case of a beneficiary seeking to enforce a pre-2000 covenant, this is a result of the then rules regarding privity of contract, and is no surprise. But in the case of the prospective trustees seeking to enforce a pre-2000 covenant, or either the prospective trustees or a beneficiary seeking to enforce a post-2000 covenant, it follows from the cases declaring that covenants to make trusts for volunteers are unenforceable. We need to examine these cases.

4.4 THE UNENFORCEABILITY OF COVENANTS TO MAKE TRUSTS FOR VOLUNTEERS

The main decision holding covenants to make trusts for volunteers to be unenforceable is *Re Pryce*.[10]

The reasoning in the case begins by observing that a covenant of this kind is for the benefit of a volunteer beneficiary. Then it points out that a volunteer, such as this beneficiary, could not claim specific performance of the covenant, because specific performance is an equitable remedy and 'equity will not assist a volunteer'. And, it says, since the Judicature Act 1875, the rules of equity have been superimposed on the common law, so that the law as a whole will not now assist a volunteer: equity's embargo on specific performance for volunteers extends also to common law remedies such as the action to recover money promised under a covenant. Nor, the reasoning continues, will the law allow a volunteer to be assisted indirectly by someone else— the trustees—suing on his behalf. So the covenant is unenforceable.[11]

Contract: Contracts for the Benefit of Third Parties (Law Com No 242, 1996) para 6.4. For the contrary view, see R Stevens (2004) 120 LQR 292, 313.

[9] Contracts (Rights of Third Parties) Act 1999 s 3(2).

[10] [1917] 1 Ch 234. Likewise *Re D'Angibau* (1880) 15 Ch D 228; *Re Plumptre's Marriage Settlement* [1910] 1 Ch 609; *Re Kay's Settlement Trusts* [1939] Ch 329; *Re Adlard* [1954] Ch 29. *Re Cook's Settlement Trusts* [1965] Ch 902 is often said to be similar, but must differ in denying that the covenant is held on trust: as explained below, the other decisions assume the contrary.

[11] It is sometimes pointed out that the question posed to the judge in *Re Pryce* [1917] 1 Ch 234 was 'must the trustees sue the settlor?', and the argument made that his statements to the effect that neither the trustees nor the beneficiaries could sue the settlor were therefore *obiter*

This reasoning, however, is erroneous.[12] Equity certainly withholds its remedy of specific performance from volunteers. Specific performance is a special remedy for the enforcement of contracts. The ordinary remedy is the common law right to monetary relief, either damages or debt. The latter is always available, but specific performance is not. It is given only when the common law remedy fails to do adequate justice to the plaintiff's claim, and in certain situations it will never be given. One of these situations is where the claimant has not given consideration (as with a promisee under a voluntary covenant). But that is as far as it goes. There is no foundation for the further idea that equity has a general antipathy towards volunteers, and that as a consequence not only are equitable remedies such as specific performance withheld from them, but also there is a ban on all other remedies that would benefit them, even common law remedies sought by other people (here, the prospective trustees).

Equity has no general antipathy towards volunteers. It does not even withhold all its own remedies from them. Although it denies them its remedy of specific performance of a contract, it allows, for example, beneficiaries of trusts to have injunctions, an account, and so on even though (as is usually the case) they are volunteers. Again, it certainly does not insist that common law remedies be withheld from volunteers: no more since the Judicature Act 1875 than before.[13] If it did, ordinary covenantees, being volunteers, would be denied not only specific performance of the covenant in their favour, but also any common law remedy; so, there being no remedies at all for their enforcement, covenants would be so much waste paper; which they are plainly not.[14] Nor does equity place an embargo on volunteers being indirectly assisted, by someone else using the remedies to which he is entitled, equitable or legal, on their behalf

(though they were adopted as part of the *ratio* in *Re Kay's Settlement Trusts* [1939] Ch 329). This is incorrect, however. The judge arrived at the answer that the trustees did not have to sue by observing (albeit fallaciously, as we shall see) that they could not sue even if they wanted to.

[12] The issue has provoked much discussion. See especially D Elliott (1960) 76 LQR 100; J Hornby (1962) 78 LQR 228; W Lee (1969) 85 LQR 213; J Barton (1975) 91 LQR 236; R Meagher and J Lehane (1976) 92 LQR 427.

[13] The 1875 Act lays down that equity's line prevails over that of the common law *if they are in conflict*. So if equity did disapprove of volunteers having common law remedies such as debt or damages, its view would prevail and these remedies would indeed be withdrawn. But that has never been equity's position. While withholding its own discretionary remedy of specific performance, it has always been content that volunteers should have the standard common law remedies.

[14] Indeed, in *Cannon v Hartley* [1949] Ch 213, it was decided that a covenant with a volunteer prospective beneficiary was enforceable by him.

(such as trustee–covenantees suing for the sake of a volunteer beneficiary). There is no such embargo even in respect of specific performance, which is where it might be most likely: in a case where one man contracted with another (himself not a volunteer) to pay money to a third party who was a volunteer, the House of Lords granted specific performance to the promisee precisely in order to make the promisor perform this contract in favour of the third party.[15]

It is sometimes suggested that *Re Pryce*[16] can be circumvented, and a volunteer beneficiary enabled to sue after all, if we find that that the right of action—the right to sue the settlor on the covenant—is held by the trustees on trust for the beneficiary. This is incorrect, however. It is certainly possible for the right of action to be held on trust in this way.[17] And it is logical to think that it is indeed held by the trustees for the beneficiary, even without signs of a visible intention that it should be. For otherwise the trustees must either own it for their personal benefit (meaning that they can choose whether to sue, and can keep the resulting damages if they do), or hold it for the settlor (meaning that he has these advantages). In the kind of case under discussion, where the settlor's goal was to confer benefits on the beneficiary, both these alternatives would be absurd, leaving the view that the trustees hold the right of action for the beneficiary as the only tenable possibility.[18] In fact, this view was taken, though not proclaimed, in *Re Pryce*[19] itself. Remember the assumption in the reasoning of the case that, if the trustees were allowed to enforce such a covenant, it would assist the volunteer beneficiary. This was true only if the covenant was held on trust for the latter. If for example the covenant had belonged to the trustees themselves, their enforcement of it would have benefited not the beneficiary but themselves.

The right of action is thus rightly to be seen as held by the trustees for the beneficiary. But ultimately this does not help. For according to *Re Pryce*[20] the right of action is unenforceable: and there is no reason to

---

[15] *Beswick v Beswick* [1968] AC 58.   [16] [1917] 1 Ch 234.

[17] Though in *Re Cook's Settlement Trusts* [1965] Ch 902 it is said that whilst a covenant to settle a pre-determined amount can be held on trust, a covenant to settle an indefinite amount at an indefinite time in the future (as would normally be the case with a covenant to settle after-acquired property) cannot. There is, however, no foundation for this view, which runs counter to the decisions reached in a number of cases, including *Davenport v Bishopp* (1843) 2 Y & CCC 451, 1 Ph 698.

[18] Cf section 3.6, noting that in cases where it would *not* be absurd for the promisee to own the rights personally, clear signs of an intention to place them on trust are required before such a trust will be found.

[19] [1917] 1 Ch 234.   [20] *Ibid*.

think that making an unenforceable right of action the subject matter of a trust renders it enforceable. Contrast some earlier cases,[21] which likewise regarded the right of action on the settlor's covenant as held by the trustees for the volunteer beneficiary, but assumed (correctly: the contrary reasoning in *Re Pryce*[22] being fallacious, as we have seen) that the right was enforceable in the normal way. They concluded that the beneficiaries could enforce the covenant against the settlor, or more exactly could, by pointing to the trust of the right of action, force the trustees to enforce the covenant against the settlor to their benefit.

So the law says (albeit on the basis of fallacious reasoning) that a covenant to place property on trust for a volunteer beneficiary cannot be enforced.[23] It should be noted however that if, despite its unenforceability against him, the settlor complies with the covenant and transfers the property to the trustees, that is nonetheless effective to constitute the trust.[24] There is no inconsistency in this: a promise to make a gift likewise cannot be enforced, but a gift once made is effective. One decision goes further (though another[25] contradicts it), telling us that the trust is also constituted if the trustees acquire the property not from the settlor but in some other way, eg because they are also executors of a will that leaves it to the settlor.[26] This latter position is hard to defend. It attaches legal consequences to mere coincidence, rather than to the settlor's voluntary act, as where the settlor himself complies with the covenant. And it requires all trustees of more than one trust, such as banks, to check whether they hold property under one of their trusts for someone who has undertaken but cannot be forced to transfer it to them under another: an unrealistic expectation.

---

[21] *Davenport v Bishopp* (1843) 2 Y & CCC 451, 1 Ph 698; *Fletcher v Fletcher* (1844) 4 Hare 67.   [22] [1917] 1 Ch 234.

[23] Although the reasoning is readily demonstrated as fallacious to modern eyes, as the text has shown, it has historical roots. It can be identified with an earlier and enduring struggle as to the enforceability of voluntary trusts, in the course of which a number of conceptual positions were essayed. In its essentials, that to be found in *Re Pryce* [1917] 1 Ch 234 does not come across as simply freakish, or to be justified only outlandishly, in the way that modern commentators tend to regard it. See especially *Kekewich v Manning* (1851) 1 De GM & G 176; J Anderson in W Cornish et al *The Oxford History of the Laws of England, Volume XII: 1820–1914 Private Law* (2010) Part One VI, 253–60.

[24] *Re Adlard* [1954] Ch 29.   [25] *Re Brooks' Settlement Trusts* [1939] 1 Ch 993.

[26] *Re Ralli's Will Trusts* [1964] Ch 288. *Re Brooks' Settlement Trusts* [1939] 1 Ch 993 was not cited.

4.5 THE POLICY PERSPECTIVE

It is essential to notice that the substantive context of decisions such as
Re Pryce[27] is the making of a marriage settlement, as explained in section 4.2; the settlor–covenantor being the wife. And what is therefore
at stake in them is whether the wife should have to place property she
acquires after the marriage into the settlement trust, not only while she
has a husband and children (for they count as having given consideration,
ie not volunteers, so that her covenant can be enforced by them or on their
behalf), but also once she finds herself a childless widow (when the only
other persons interested under the settlement are the volunteer next-of-
kin). If she does have to place such property into the trust, ie if (contrary
to *Re Pryce*[28]) her covenant can be enforced against her, she does not lose
out entirely: under the trust's terms, she has the income from it for her
life, before it goes absolutely to the next-of-kin thereafter. But if she does
not have to place the property into the trust, ie if (following *Re Pryce*[29]) her
covenant cannot be enforced against her, she simply retains the property
in question as her own capital. So although such decisions are reasoned
(albeit fallaciously, as we have seen) in terms of 'equity not assisting a volunteer', their concrete crux is whether a childless widow should be allowed
to keep incoming property straightforwardly for herself, or required to
hand it over to trustees and enjoy only the income.

It is not difficult to appreciate the attraction of the former outcome.
The latter was clumsy and demeaning, and for a long time even before
Re Pryce[30] it had usually been avoided, treating the covenant as impliedly
effective only for the duration of the marriage.[31] Eventually, this interpretation was discarded as over-strained,[32] but substantially the same
pattern of outcome was immediately restored via the reasoning that was
in due course adopted in *Re Pryce*.[33] By this time, indeed, there was a

---

[27] [1917] 1 Ch 234.   [28] *Ibid.*   [29] *Ibid.*   [30] *Ibid.*

[31] *Howell* v. *Howell* (1835) 4 LJ Ch 242; *Dickinson v Dillwyn* (1869) 8 Eq 546; *Carter v Carter* (1869) 8 Eq 551; *Re Edwards* (1873) 9 Ch App 97; *Re Campbell's Policies* (1877) 16 Ch D 686. Note that interpreting the covenant in this way meant that not even the children could enforce it against their mother, despite their not being volunteers.

[32] *Re Ellis's Settlement* [1909] 1 Ch 618.

[33] [1917] 1 Ch 234: see *Re Plumptre's Settlement* [1910] 1 Ch 609. On this approach, which excludes only volunteers, the children—being within the marriage consideration—could of course sue their mother; though a decision giving an early sight of this analysis, *Re D'Angibau* (1880) 15 Ch D 228, 242, introduces a grain of doubt as to that. On all these developments, see J Anderson in W Cornish et al *The Oxford History of the Laws of England, Volume XII: 1820–1914 Private Law* (2010) Part One VI, 260–1.

resonance with a more specific policy perspective. Towards the end of the nineteenth century, perceptions about economic utility and married women's property rights became especially prominent considerations. Marriage settlements were problematic on both counts. By preventing a wife from getting her hands on her capital, and restricting her to the income, they tied the capital up, took it out of circulation in the market; and they infringed her right to control her own affairs. During the joint lives of the woman and her husband, and probably also if they had children, there were countervailing considerations. But if she were left a childless widow (the situation in which, as we have seen, her covenant to settle after-acquired property on trust for her volunteer next-of-kin becomes relevant), the economic and rights arguments for restoring her absolute ownership of the capital possessed substantial power. By their decisions, the courts gave her that absolute ownership.

From this point of view, there is an interesting contrast between two decisions of 1880: on the one hand *Re D'Angibau*,[34] which was a precursor to *Re Pryce*,[35] and on the other hand *Lloyd's v Harper*.[36] The latter too involved a contract to pay money to volunteer third parties, but the context was this time not a marriage settlement, but trade. A father had given an undertaking to the managing committee of Lloyd's, the insurance market, to guarantee his son's debts when the latter became a member of the market. This undertaking was for the benefit of the son's creditors, who were third party volunteers.[37] In terms of the law as it began to emerge in *Re D'Angibau*[38] and was later confirmed in *Re Pryce*,[39] this should have been fatal. But the court took the opposite view of the law, and held that the managing committee held the father's undertaking on trust for the creditors, who could insist on its enforcement. In this context there was nothing corresponding to the argument about married women's rights, and in terms of economic utility the arrangement was positively advantageous, for such guarantees were necessary to establish confidence, and so promote trade, in the insurance market. In these terms, then, it is quite consistent that this contract should have been held enforceable while those in marriage settlements were not.

But although the views taken in the cases were thus consistent with the dominant policy positions of the period in which they emerged, they

---

[34] (1880) 15 Ch D 228.   [35] [1917] 1 Ch 234.   [36] (1880) 16 Ch D 290.
[37] They did of course give consideration to the son (ie their premiums), but were volunteers so far as the father's undertaking was concerned. But although their bargain with the son was thus analytically an entirely separate matter, it rendered the context one of trade, which makes all the difference to the policy significance of the case.
[38] (1880) 15 Ch D 228.   [39] [1917] 1 Ch 234.

strike few chords today. Confronted with the kind of arrangement under discussion, we should find it hard to find external policy reasons for wanting to see it enforced or otherwise. We should probably think simply that a covenant to make a trust ought (in the absence of the usual vitiating factors such as duress or misrepresentation) to be enforced, on the internal ground that that is what entering into a covenant means and demands.

We noted above that whilst the Contracts (Rights of Third Parties) Act 1999 allows a third party to enforce a contract, this will make no difference to this area of the law. The third party's action is made subject to the same defences as apply to an action brought by the promisee,[40] and as the law stands *Re Pryce*[41] tells us that the promisee has no action, since a covenant to make a trust for a volunteer is unenforceable.[42] Nevertheless, the advent of the 1999 Act may provide the occasion for bringing this area of the law once more before the courts. Given that (as just suggested) to modern eyes there is little at stake in this kind of case beyond the normal impulse to uphold the covenant, the opportunity may well then be taken to leave behind the reasoning in *Re Pryce*,[43] whether expressly or by applying the Act, skating over the difficulties of this course.

There would in fact be problems about expressly overruling *Re Pryce*[44] in favour of a position that covenants to make trusts for volunteers are enforceable. Overruling a case declares that it always was wrong, and that the newly stated position has always has been the correct one. As explained in section 4.4, there is no doubt that the prospective trustees hold the right of action under the covenant on trust for the beneficiary. If that right of action is enforceable, they are therefore under a duty to the beneficiary to use it. If *Re Pryce*[45] is overruled and the right of action declared enforceable, trustees who had relied on that case and not sought to enforce would therefore find themselves to have been, all along, in breach of their duty to the beneficiary.[46]

---

[40] Contracts (Rights of Third Parties) Act 1999 s 3(2).   [41] [1917] 1 Ch 234.

[42] To argue the contrary, ie that the Act does allow both the designated beneficiary and indeed the trustee (so dealing with s 3(2)) to enforce the covenant, one might observe that the reasoning in *Re Pryce* [1917] 1 Ch 234 involves reference to privity, and then contend that the Act aims to disallow such reference. The principal difficulty is with the latter contention, which involves an imaginable, but decidedly broad-brush, reading of the Act's actual terms.

[43] [1917] 1 Ch 234.   [44] *Ibid.*   [45] *Ibid.*

[46] Though relief might be available under the Trustee Act 1925 s 61: see section 10.2.

5

Formalities

In this chapter we shall look at the degree of formality that the law demands in the creation of trusts, and also in dealings with beneficial interests.

The law frequently requires that transactions that manipulate property interests should be marked with some formality: above all, it requires that the transaction should be embodied in a permanent form, such as writing. Traditionally, for example, changes of ownership of land had to be made by deed. Today, the important step is the recording of them in a government register; another kind of formality.

So far as making trusts is concerned, however, the basic rule is that no formalities are required. But there are two exceptions to this. First, when the trust is to come into effect on the settlor's death, it will be made through the medium of his will: and wills must be in writing, signed by the testator, and attested by two witnesses.[1] Secondly, where the subject matter of the trust is land, then even if it is to come into effect in the settlor's lifetime ('*inter vivos*'), it must be put in writing and signed by the settlor.[2] There are no formality requirements in respect of resulting or constructive trusts, however.[3]

There is a further formality rule in the trusts area, which concerns not the making of them but dispositions of the beneficial interests existing under them; in particular, where a beneficiary transfers his interest to someone else. Such a disposition must be made in writing, and signed by the person making it.[4]

We must assess these rules, both to understand them and to consider their sustainability. In particular, they engage Art 1 of the First Protocol to the European Convention on Human Rights, protecting the right to property, and so require justification as proportionate means of promoting a legitimate end.[5] Our assessment will begin with a look at the function of formality requirements in general.

---

[1] Wills Act 1837 s 9, as amended by Administration of Justice Act 1982 s 17.
[2] Law of Property Act 1925 s 53(1)(b).   [3] *Ibid* s 53(2).   [4] *Ibid* s 53(1)(c).
[5] For the application of the Convention (via the Human Rights Act 1998) to formality requirements—though regarding contracts rather than trusts—see *Wilson v First County Trust Ltd (No 2)* [2004] 1 AC 816.

5.1 THE FUNCTION OF FORMALITY REQUIREMENTS

The principal function[6] of formality requirements is to maximize certainty about the fact that a transaction took place at all, and about what it comprised.

This happens in two ways. One is obvious: having the fact that the transaction was made, and its details (eg exactly what was being transferred, and to whom, and on what terms), embodied in a permanent form makes them much less controvertible than if they had been left oral. The other is that if people making a transaction have to write it down, they will probably give closer attention to it than if they were making it orally: so they are more likely to shape it fully and coherently, rather than leaving gaps and loose ends. They will probably also consider more deeply whether they want to make the transaction at all, giving the formality requirement an additional 'cooling-off' effect.

Making transactions as certain as possible is valuable at several levels. Most obviously, it is useful for the people actually involved in the transaction. It enables them to ensure that the transaction does what they want it to. In this respect, then, formality serves the facilitative logic underpinning express trusts.

Beyond the people involved in the transaction itself, certainty is also important for others with whom they in turn deal. Say I sell you a house. Later, you want to sell it to someone else, or to lease it to a tenant, or to offer it to your bank as security for a loan. You will need to establish that you really do own it; otherwise, these dispositions would all be ineffective. To do so, you need to point to the transaction by which you acquired it from me, and to that by which I myself acquired it before that, and so on. The ease with which you can do this, and so the marketability of your property, is a function of certainty, and that is promoted by formality.

The certainty provided by formality also allows transactions to be observed by state agencies, because it makes them more visible. This in turn allows the government to regulate both the transactions themselves and the state of affairs that results from them. A familiar illustration is registration of the ownership of motor vehicles, which enables taxes to be collected and traffic offenders to be traced. Similarly, traders are required to keep records so that their liability for value added tax can be checked. Another tax, stamp duty, has a particularly close relationship

---

[6] For extended treatments of the functions of formality requirements, see eg L Fuller (1941) 41 Columbia LR 799, 800–6; J Perillo (1974) 43 Fordham LR 39, 43–71; together with further writings there cited.

with formality rules. Stamp duty is levied on certain transfers of property, at a rate varying with the property's value. It is levied not on the transaction, with the formality just making matters more visible to the collectors, but on the formality, the written instrument embodying the transaction, itself. If the same transaction could be made without an instrument, the tax would not be payable. So the formality rules, determining when a transaction must be put in writing, *ipso facto* establish its susceptibility to stamp duty.

These, then, are some of the major advantages of maintaining formality rules in a general way. But there are also disadvantages. In particular, if the law disallows a transaction because it was made informally, it will fail to give effect to the intentions of the people involved in the transaction. That is disadvantageous in terms of facilitative thinking, the policy of allowing people to make whatever dispositions they like. Where, for example, someone has expressed himself perfectly clearly and fully about what is to happen to his property after his death, but has failed to observe the formalities that the law requires for a will, facilitative policy will be affronted if the law says that no effect is to be given to his wishes. So in fact facilitative logic is ambivalent on the subject of formality requirements. They can both help, through getting people to make clear and satisfactory dispositions, and hinder, by disallowing dispositions which are clear and satisfactory but that lack the prescribed formality.

So when the law imposes a formality requirement, with the rider that non-compliance undermines the transaction in some way, it is not necessarily an unqualifiedly good idea to do so. The point is rather that the arguments in favour of requiring formality outweigh those against. Deciding whether to require formality involves assessing the advantages and disadvantages either way, and comparing them, to see where the greater benefit lies. So, for example, in having the rule that any attempt to dispose of property on death other than by using the ordained formalities is ineffective, the law takes it that the balance lies in favour of such insistence; that the potential ineffectiveness of attempted informal dispositions is an acceptable price to pay for the advantages of minimizing uncertainty.

5.2 THE GENERAL POSITION IN TRUSTS

In principle, then, the question whether or not formalities should be required in the making of trusts involves a choice between two positions. One is to procure certainty (etc) by having a formality requirement, but at the expense of disallowing dispositions where the settlor omits to comply with it. The other is the converse: to accept as a valid trust every disposition that was meant as one, at the expense of having to accept uncertainty (etc) in at least some cases. In fact, the basic rule is along the latter lines: that no formality is required to make a trust. Ultimately, therefore, the desire not to frustrate settlors in the making of informal trusts is given precedence over the advantages of a converse rule.

But the absence of a formality rule does not mean that trusts are in practice often made informally. They are mostly made in circumstances where a degree of formality will naturally tend to be present, even though the law does not require it. People who consciously make trusts will generally want to put beyond doubt that they have done so, and exactly what they have effected: and the natural way of doing this is to embody the transaction in a formal written document.

Not all settlors are as well organized as this, however. Some are quite vague about what they want, and do not use professional advice. The likelihood of informality is obviously greater in such cases. As we saw in section 3.1 however, the law is generally reluctant to recognize these vaguer dispositions as trusts anyway. In fact, in having as one of its bases (as we saw) the desire to avoid uncertainty over entitlements, this approach to recognition operates as a kind of surrogate for a formality requirement.

So these factors shaping the circumstances in which trusts are created, or are recognized by the law as created, mean that the absence of a general requirement of formality involves sacrificing such a requirement's attractions to a smaller extent than might at first sight appear. But there can still be cases in which trusts do arise without formality. Evidently, the feeling is that the balance of advantage is in favour of accepting them as valid, in order to further the facilitative project, albeit at some cost in terms of convenience.

If this is so, however, why should there be the two exceptions to the basic absence of a formality requirement for the making of trusts, whereby testamentary trusts and *inter vivos* trusts of land must be made formally? Let us look at these in turn.

5.3 TESTAMENTARY TRUSTS

The rule for testamentary trusts is that they must be made in the form prescribed by the Wills Act: in writing, signed, and witnessed.[7] This is a general formalities rule for wills, rather than directed particularly at trusts within them, and so the perspective on the balance

---

[7] Wills Act 1837 s 9, as amended by Administration of Justice Act 1982 s 17.

between the advantages and disadvantages of the rule must be this more general one.

The advantages and disadvantages are the usual ones. The testator is served by knowing that effect will be given to the dispositions contained in his last will made in the proper form, and to these alone. The recipients and non-recipients of his property will know where they stand without contest. Title to the property in question is assured, easing subsequent trade in it. And having the dispositions encompassed in a single document that must be given official recognition (called 'probate') before it can be put into effect gives the revenue authorities a straight run at them for the collection of the relevant taxes. On the other hand, the rule will frustrate the wishes of anyone who attempts to dispose of his property on his death without using the proper form.

By requiring formalities for wills, the law takes it that the balance lies in favour of the advantages. This seems to be right. We all know that we are going to die; we have surely all heard of the idea of 'making a will', have some notion of what it means, and consider the possibility of doing so; almost all of us have also heard that the law imposes some formality requirements on the making of a will, even though we may not know exactly what they are; and we enjoy a literate and stable society in which finding out what the requirements are, and complying with them, is reasonably easy.[8] So in this context, the problem of frustrating settlors ignorant of a certainty requirement is negligible, leaving very little to be said against the obvious advantages of imposing such a requirement: as the law does. There seems no difficulty, then, in regarding this rule as compatible with the European Convention on Human Rights.

5.4 TRUSTS OF LAND

The other formality requirement in the making of trusts is that *inter vivos* trusts whose subject matter is land must be put in[9] writing and signed by the settlor. This rule is contained in the Law of Property Act 1925 s 53(1)(b).

Why should trusts of land be singled out in this way as the only *inter vivos* trusts for which formality is required?

---

[8] Understandably therefore, given the contrasting context, the testamentary dispositions of military personnel on actual military service, and of mariners at sea, are exempted from the usual formality requirements: Wills Act 1837 s 11; Wills (Soldiers and Sailors) Act 1918.

[9] Strictly, not 'put in' but 'manifested and proved by'.

Trusts of land are particularly likely to be made formally in practice. People making dispositions of land are especially likely to perceive that they are doing something significant, and will almost certainly use professional advisers, who will always want to put important matters down on paper. So, as with wills, the danger of a requirement of formality frustrating settlors' intentions is slight, allowing the balance of advantage to come down in favour of its imposition.

Another consideration may be the protection of those who buy land from trusts. Someone buying property from a trust will want to acquire it as absolute owner, free from the trust obligations. If the trustees act properly in selling, that will be the result; the trust obligations are 'overreached'.[10] If they act improperly, however, the purchaser may find himself bound by the trust obligations. It will help him to guard against this outcome if he has the information that the sellers are trustees. Formality in the original making of the trust can provide this information. And trusts of land are especially pressing cases in this respect because of a rule, applying to them alone, that the sale will be improper unless the purchase money is paid not simply to one trustee, but to at least two.[11]

As with the provisions regarding wills, therefore, it seems possible to regard this rule as compatible with the European Convention on Human Rights. Though to the extent that the case for this rests on the need to service another rule, in the manner identified in the previous paragraph, perhaps the pair of rules merits consideration in the round. Our conclusion then might not be so sanguine, as the rule requiring purchase money for trust land to be paid to two trustees is not so easy to justify.[12]

---

[10] See section 12.1.

[11] Law of Property Act 1925 s 27(2) (unless the trust has a corporate trustee, such as a bank, when payment to one suffices). Many cases reveal the adverse effect on a purchaser who does not comply with this rule, most notably *Williams & Glyn's Bank Ltd v Boland* [1981] AC 487. (The rule may have been altered in the case of registered land by Land Registration Act 2002 s 26, but commentators generally doubt this: S Gardner *An Introduction to Land Law* 2nd edn (2009) 303–6.)

[12] The 'two-trustee' rule is generally understood as a 'compromise' between the previous treatment of some land trusts, whereby the obligations arising under them could not be overreached at all; and the rule applying to non-land trusts, whereby the obligations under them would be overreached upon payment simply to one trustee. (See *City of London Building Society v Flegg* [1988] AC 54, 73–4.) It is, however, a very odd compromise. From the point of view of a beneficiary who does not wish the land to be sold, it has no merit at all. It may offer more security for the payment in the hands of the trustees than a rule requiring receipt by only one trustee, but the rule permitting the latter has not proved unacceptable in trusts generally.

5.5 RESULTING AND CONSTRUCTIVE TRUSTS OF LAND

There is, however, an exception to this formality requirement regarding trusts whose subject matter is land. By the Law of Property Act 1925 s 53(2), resulting and constructive trusts of land need not be put in writing.[13]

Purchasers of trust land are required to pay two trustees just as much where the trust is a resulting or constructive trust as where it is express, so it would be convenient for such purchasers if the formality requirement applied here too. But resulting and constructive trusts can arise without anyone giving any thought to the matter,[14] and so if formality were to be required for them to be valid, they would generally never come into existence at all. And that would frustrate the aims of the rules generating them in the first place.

Probably the commonest instance of a resulting or constructive trust of land is that where a family home is owned in the name of only one member of a couple, but the attendant circumstances require it to be shared between them. This topic is considered in detail in section 18.3. There are two features of it that concern us here. First, the fact that there is a trust will not be recorded in writing, or even, quite possibly, known to the couple themselves: the whole point is to deal with the situation where the couple themselves have not been organized enough to formally settle their own rights. So a purchaser will not have the usual warning that the house is trust property and that he therefore has to deal with two trustees. Secondly, there will in fact only be one trustee (ie the person in whose sole name the house is owned).[15] So the purchaser will necessarily be dealing with only one trustee rather than two, and, as we have seen, that places him in jeopardy. There is quite a lot that he can do to protect himself—such as look to see who lives in the house, or require that all its residents

---

[13] Strictly, the provision exempts 'resulting, implied or constructive trusts'. But 'implied' here seems to mean not 'express but not explicit', but 'imposed by the law for some other reason than to effectuate a settlor's wish', making it synonymous with 'constructive'. See further however P Matthews in C Mitchell (ed) *Constructive and Resulting Trusts* (2010) ch 1, 14–17.

[14] In the case of resulting trusts this statement rejects the position taken by Lord Browne-Wilkinson in *Westdeutsche Landesbank Girozentrale v Islington LBC* [1996] AC 669, 708. The argument for doing so is advanced in sections 16.3–16.4.

[15] The same rule operates where the house is owned in both parties' names, but without a declaration of their respective beneficial interests. This scenario will be less common, however, for where a transfer is made into joint names, the parties' lawyer will normally ensure that their beneficial interests *are* declared, and in writing: in which event there will be an express trust, made with proper formality.

sign a disclaimer—but, at the lowest, this kind of situation is one where the sale and purchase of trust property is not as streamlined as the law would normally want it to be. The trap of the rule requiring payment to two trustees exists without the formality requirement to signpost it. But to impose a formality requirement would mean that virtually all of these trusts would be destroyed. So if they are to exist at all, it can only be on the basis that they are valid despite informality. Evidently, since the law does uphold them, it takes the view that the reasons for doing so outweigh the consequent difficulties.[16]

5.6 NON-COMPLIANCE WITH THE WILLS ACT AND SECTION 53(1)(b)

So we have looked at the two formality rules applicable to the making of express trusts: one, that express *inter vivos* trusts whose subject matter is land must be in writing, and the other, that all express trusts stipulated to take effect on the settlor's death must be in the form required by the Wills Act. Sometimes, of course, cases arise in which a settlor has not complied with the relevant rule. We should expect the result to be, quite simply, that no effective trust arises. That is indeed sometimes the outcome, but not always. In some cases, an effective trust, embodying the settlor's wishes, arises after all. This will occur if the settlor has consulted the intended trustee and obtained his agreement to, or at least acquiescence in, the projected trust before transferring the property in question to him.[17,18]

In the testamentary context, trusts arising in the latter manner are called 'secret trusts'. There are two kinds of secret trusts. The first is where the

---

[16] However, the overall tenor of the cases concerning this area in fact shows considerable solicitude for the purchaser who is caught unawares by such a trust. He is often held not bound, on a number of other grounds. See S Gardner *An Introduction to Land Law* 2nd edn (2009) 308–14.

[17] *Blackwell v Blackwell* [1929] AC 318, 334. Contrast the ordinary rule for express trusts. A person cannot be made to act as trustee of an express trust against his will, but there is no requirement that his consent be sought in advance in this way: he may hear of his nomination as trustee only as he comes to receive the property, and is then at liberty to decline to act if he so wishes. See section 11.1.

[18] In half-secret trusts, described below, the English authorities say the consultation etc must occur earlier—before or contemporaneously with the settlor's making of the will (the transfer itself takes place on the settlor's death): *Re Keen* [1937] Ch 236; *Re Bateman's Will Trusts* [1970] 1 WLR 1436. This complication may well be misconceived. It is explicable in terms of a misplaced analogy with another doctrine, incorporation by reference, and rejected in *Re Browne* [1944] Ir R 90, Ireland, and *Ledgerwood v Perpetual Trustee* (1997) 41 NSWLR 532, Australia.

settlor makes a will leaving the property to the trustee and stipulating that the latter shall hold it on trust, but fixes the terms of the trust not in the will but in a private communication with the trustee. Notwithstanding the failure to comply with the Wills Act, the arrangement takes effect as a trust. This trust is called a 'half-secret' trust, because the will does disclose that the legatee takes the property as trustee, but withholds the details of the trust. The second kind of secret trust is found where the settlor makes a will leaving the property to the trustee, as before, but this time without stipulating at all in the will that the property is given on trust, and settles both the fact that it is given on trust, and the terms of that trust, by private communication with the trustee. Again, notwithstanding the failure to comply with the Wills Act, the arrangement takes effect as a trust. This time the trust is called a 'fully secret' trust, because the will omits not only the terms of the trust but also any mention of its very existence: it suggests that the legatee takes the property as absolute owner, for his own benefit.

Likewise in the *inter vivos* context. If the owner of some land transfers it to someone else without stipulating in writing that the latter shall hold it on a trust (as s 53(1)(b) would require), but previously makes an oral arrangement with the transferee that he shall do so, the law gives effect to this arrangement as a trust too.[19]

Why should the law recognize secret trusts and their *inter vivos* counterparts in this way? Various arguments can be found, in the cases and in the writings of commentators.

According to one argument,[20] secret trusts are express trusts, but are not afflicted by their failure to comply with the Wills Act because (runs the argument) they take effect from the time of the agreement, which is necessarily before the testator's death.[21] They are thus *inter vivos*, so the Wills Act simply does not apply to them: they operate, it is said, 'outside—or *dehors*—the will'. The crux of this argument is the idea that, although the transfer of the property by the settlor's will constitutes the trust, the earlier agreement amounts to a 'declaration' of it. That is a reasonable thing to say, if the word 'declaration' is being used in a non-technical sense. Unfortunately, in order to prove that the trust takes

---

[19] *Rochefoucauld v Boustead* [1897] 1 Ch 196; *Bannister v Bannister* [1948] 2 All ER 133; *Hodgson v Marks* [1971] Ch 892.

[20] See especially J Martin *Hanbury and Martin Modern Equity* 18th edn (2008) 170–5.

[21] It is possible to some extent to communicate the terms of the trust after the required moment (by means of a sealed letter, placed in the trustee's hands, to be opened later), so long as the trustee has by the required time agreed to be bound by them no matter what they turn out to be. See *Re Boyes* (1884) 26 Ch D 531; *Re Keen* [1937] Ch 236.

effect at the time of the agreement, the word must be used in its technical sense, as meaning 'creation' (normally, in the case where the settlor makes himself trustee).[22] The argument is then revealed as unsustainable. As we saw in section 1.9, there cannot be a trust without property. Until the property reaches the trustee's hands upon the settlor's death, the admittedly earlier agreement between the settlor and the trustee therefore cannot generate a trust.[23] It is possible that the agreement generates some other kind of obligation,[24] but it is clear that the entity for which we are trying to account here is indeed a trust. Although in part dependent upon the prior agreement, then, the trust takes effect at the time of the settlor's death. The argument thus fails. And although it is hard to find an application of it to *inter vivos* trusts of land, it must fail here too. It would require us once again to see the agreement, preceding the transfer of the land, as a 'declaration' of the intended trust. Even were this tenable in itself, however, s 53(1)(b) actually requires a 'declaration' of a trust of land to be put in writing.

According to a second argument, by contrast, the secret trust, or its *inter vivos* counterpart, is the very express trust which the settlor originally sought to create, neglecting to use the required formality—saved from ineffectiveness because the formality rule is disapplied. The latter step is taken on the basis that 'equity will not permit a statute [the Wills Act, or s 53(1)(b)] to be used as an instrument of fraud'.[25] And, it is said, this would occur if the settlor's intended express trust were held ineffective when he has transferred the property in question to the trustee after securing the trustee's agreement to hold it on the trust, as the law demands for the trusts under discussion.

---

[22] See section 1.4.

[23] In *Re Gardner (No 2)* [1923] 2 Ch 230, however, it was held that the effect of a secret trust does pre-date the testator's death. The decision cannot be correct, for the reason given in the text.

[24] Possibly a contract, under which the settlor transfers the property in consideration for the transferee's promise to hold it on the agreed trusts. Under the Contracts (Rights of Third Parties) Act 1999, the beneficiaries could normally enforce such a contract, but this only gives them contractual rights against the trustee personally, not (as given by the rules under discussion) a beneficial entitlement arising from the moment the property reaches the trustee's hands. Such a beneficial entitlement would arise, however, if the beneficiaries' contractual rights allowed them to claim specific performance against the trustee of his obligation to hold the bequeathed property on trust; by the doctrine 'equity looks upon that as done which ought to be done' a constructive trust would be generated anticipating the trustee's compliance with this: see section 17.6.

[25] This appears to be the approach taken in *Rochefoucauld v Boustead* [1897] 1 Ch 196, 206–7; and see further the authorities cited there, and in *Re Duke of Marlborough* [1894] 2 Ch 133.

If the latter set of circumstances is to be seen as amounting to 'fraud', so as to allow this justification for the trusts under discussion, it has to be acknowledged that the usage of 'fraud' has certain unusual features. First, it does not necessarily imply deceit, as in other contexts. A trust can arise under this principle as much where the trustee agrees in good faith to hold it on the proposed trust as where he only pretends to agree. Second, it does not necessarily imply that the trustee himself will gain, if he is not held to his agreement. This can be seen from half-secret trusts. In their case, unlike in fully secret trusts, there is no question of the trustee keeping the property for himself. The will itself establishes that the bequest is made on trust, so if the trustee does not hold it on the intended trust, he will certainly hold it on resulting trust for the testator's estate. Third, there is no necessary implication that the trustee actively wants to break his agreement with the settlor. He may be content or keen to comply with the agreement, but encounter objections from other quarters to his doing so. Say, for example, that the trustee of a fully secret trust has become bankrupt. He wishes to operate the trust, but his creditors maintain that it is ineffective for lack of formality, so that the property has come to him under the terms of the will alone: then, it would belong to him absolutely, and they could take it to pay off his debts to them. Or say that the trustee of a half-secret trust is willing to carry out the trust as agreed with the settlor, but the person entitled to the residue of the testator's estate argues that the agreement is ineffective for lack of formality, leaving only the terms of the will, with the result that the property would be held on resulting trust, and so added to the residue. Secret trusts arise in these cases just as much as they do where the trustee personally seeks to resile from the agreement. Finally, the 'fraud' here need not consist in behaviour that has already occurred: it can consist in a state of affairs that would be objectionable, if it were to occur in the future. The trusts under discussion arise not merely from the time that the trustee seeks to resile from his agreement with the settlor, but from the earlier time when he acquires the property, on the basis of the agreed terms. In other words, there need never be any attempt to resile.

In short, if we are to account for these trusts via the idea that 'equity will not permit a statute to be used as an instrument of fraud', 'fraud' needs to be seen as the possibility of your resiling from an agreement you made with me, prior to my transferring the property to you, to hold it on trust. Certainly, such circumstances do constitute a basis for legal reaction, as they involve my relying to my detriment on your promise; and 'fraud' is not an impossible label for this basis, if we can understand it to mean simply 'against conscience'. However, although the idea that equity will

disapply a formality statute so as not to allow 'fraud' may be historically authentic, it is not, today, constitutionally supportable. 'Equity' means the judges, principally of the Chancery Division. The judges have no general power to disapply an Act of Parliament on the ground that it does or allows imperfect inter-personal justice ('fraud') in individual cases.[26]

Neither of the two arguments considered so far appears acceptable, therefore. But there is a more plausible way of explaining these trusts. It once again focuses on the 'fraud' just described, though this time, it is the make-up of that notion, rather than its label, that matters. Under this argument, the 'fraud' requires not the disapplication of the statutory formality rule from the settlor's original express trust, but the generation of a new obligation—a constructive trust—calculated to correct the 'fraud'. The secret trust, or its *inter vivos* counterpart, is that constructive trust.[27]

The ideas involved here are considered further, and their implications developed, in sections 18.1–18.2,[28] but the essential point is this. If I transfer property to you in reliance on your promise to hold it on the trust terms I propose, but you are able to resile from that promise, I suffer detriment, in the shape of the loss of my opportunity to achieve my object in some better way. To correct that detriment, the law must hold you to your promise, ie impose my trust on you. Arising in this way, the emergent trust is obviously not an express trust (ie one aimed simply at vindicating a settlor's intention to create it), but a constructive trust[29] (ie one arising for some other reason). It is then easy to see why it should be unaffected by the formality requirements. The operation of s 53(1)(b) is explicitly confined to express trusts: as we have seen, s 53(2) excludes constructive trusts from its ambit. The Wills Act is in effect so confined as well, applying as it does to testamentary dispositions. Although the Act does not

---

[26] It is sometimes asserted that the judges have a power to disapply a purported Act of Parliament that is unconstitutional, ie exceeds the powers accorded to Parliament by the common law: see eg J Laws [1995] PL 72; *R (Jackson) v A-G* [2006] 1 AC 262, [102]. Even if accepted, however (for it is controversial in itself, of course), this view does not come close to permitting judges to disapply a formality rule which perpetrates or permits 'fraud'.

[27] See *McCormick v Grogan* (1869) LR 4 HL 82, 97; *Blackwell v Blackwell* [1929] AC 318, 329, 334–5, 342; *Bannister v Bannister* [1948] 2 All ER 133, 136.

[28] More fully still in S Gardner in C Mitchell (ed) *Constructive and Resulting Trusts* (2010) ch 2.

[29] This is the view taken in *Bannister v Bannister* [1948] 2 All ER 133, 136. It is unclear whether the same can be said of the earlier decision in *Rochefoucauld v Boustead* [1897] 1 Ch 196. The court's reasoning at 206–7, noted and criticized in the text following n 23 above, may suggest a view of the trust enforced there as express. But a passage at 208 seems to portray it as constructive, assimilated to an express trust only for limitation purposes, within the thinking developed in *Soar v Ashwell* [1893] 2 QB 390. See further W Swadling in C Mitchell (ed) *Constructive and Resulting Trusts* (2010) ch 3.

define these, they appear to equate with the transfers that a testator asks the law to effectuate upon his death. When the law imposes a constructive trust on the legatee in the manner just described, however, it is correcting the testator's detrimental reliance, rather than effectuating his requested transfer. (Properly speaking, in fact, it is in this way that a secret trust can be said to be unaffected by the Wills Act—to arise 'outside the will'.[30] And that the judges prevent the statutory formality requirements, rendering the settlor's original express trust ineffective, from operating as 'an instrument of fraud'.[31])

In principle, then, secret trusts, and their *inter vivos* counterparts, arise so as to correct reliance loss (which is proper), and not so as to effectuate the settlor's intention for its own sake (which, that intention being expressed without the required formality, would be improper). In reality, however, it is impossible to make such a clean distinction between the two projects. The practical distance between them is minimal. Remember that these constructive trusts arise when the trustee agrees to the settlor's terms and, on the faith of that, the settlor transfers the property to the trustee. The only difference between this state of affairs and that required for the establishment of an express trust is the need for the settlor to secure the trustee's prior agreement to the proposed trust. And that is not much of a difference at all: to secure such agreement would in any event be no more than good manners, as well as prudent from the settlor's own point of view, so as not to nominate a trustee who might turn out to be unwilling to act. Moreover, the necessary conditions for such a constructive trust can easily be deliberately engineered by a well-advised settlor. The upshot is that people are able easily to use these constructive trusts to, in effect, opt out of the formality requirements for express testamentary trusts and *inter vivos* trusts of land.[32]

Is this acceptable? Very possibly not. As we saw earlier, there is a strong case for having the formality requirements. It seems however that in practice people do not exploit the loophole much. So far as one can judge from the reported case law, the deliberate engineering of these construc-

---

[30] The analysis is put thus by Viscount Sumner in *Blackwell v Blackwell* [1929] AC 318, 334, 340.

[31] The analysis is put thus by Lord Westbury in *McCormick v Grogan* (1869) LR 4 HL 82, 97.

[32] But cf S Gardner in C Mitchell (ed) *Constructive and Resulting Trusts* (2010) ch 2, 85–7, for a contrary argument, to the effect that a settlor who deliberately engineers the requisite situation in this way does not, as he must, rely on the trustee's agreement: that he relies instead on the law. If this is correct, these constructive trusts can arise only in case of innocent accident.

tive trusts is limited to the testamentary context,[33] and, there, more or less confined to two particular kinds of situation.[34] Our judgement about the justifiability of upholding such trusts depends on our feelings about these usages.

The first situation is where a testator wants to keep a bequest secret from the outside world. The main instance of this seems to be where a man wants to provide for his mistress or illegitimate child.[35] He would have no problem about complying with a formality requirement in itself, but probate (the process of having a will officially recognized as valid) involves placing the will in the Public Record Office, where it can be looked at by anyone who so wishes. It is this publicity that the testator seeks to avoid.[36] So he leaves money in his will to someone to whom he might plausibly make a bequest—a close friend, say, or a brother— and privately gets the latter to hold it for the mistress or child. This arrangement then takes effect as a secret trust. (There is no corresponding difficulty if the testator wants surreptitiously to put land on trust for a mistress or illegitimate child during his lifetime, since instruments written in compliance with s 53(1)(b) do not become public documents in the way that wills do: they should in fact remain private.) So in effectuating these secret trusts, the law seems in practical terms to take it that the balance of advantage lies in favour of suspending the usual formality rule so as to permit people to make provision for their mistresses and illegitimate children in this way.

There might have been a case for this view in the past. But nowadays it seems implausible. A trust is really only apt for the posthumous preservation of the position of dependency in which the testator's illicit family would have existed in former times.[37] That position is surely not normally characteristic of mistresses and illegitimate children today. To the extent that mistresses and illegitimate children continue to feature in society

[33] The decisions concerning *inter vivos* trusts of land (*Rochefoucauld v Boustead* [1897] 1 Ch 196; *Bannister v Bannister* [1948] 2 All ER 133; *Hodgson v Marks* [1971] Ch 892) all appear to concern accidental failures to comply with the formality rule.

[34] But see R Meager [2003] Conv 203 for other possible applications.

[35] See eg *Re Boyes* (1884) 26 Ch D 531; *Blackwell v Blackwell* [1929] AC 318; *Re Keen* [1937] Ch 236.

[36] The point is presumably as much to spare one's widow the embarrassment of a public declaration of one's infidelity, as to keep that infidelity a secret from her even after death; many wives surely know of their husbands' mistresses and illegitimate children.

[37] During the testator's lifetime, indeed, his mistress and illegitimate children were dependent to the extent of having no legal rights against him at all. This state of affairs would be preserved after his death if he left property to (say) his brother absolutely, but with a *moral* obligation to care for his dependants. By adopting the trust device instead, with its *legal* rights, he in fact strengthened their position.

(and developments in divorce and contraception have surely reduced that extent), they are likely to be financially less dependent on the man's bounty than previously, as a result of factors such as widespread women's employment, maintenance obligations, and social security. So even if a man nowadays does want to make secret provision for his mistress or illegitimate child, it would be not only simpler but more in keeping with the nature of their relationship to do so not by establishing a (secret) trust but by for example setting up a bank account in their name while he is still alive. It is therefore far from clear that there continues to be a public interest in favour of allowing the formality rule to be sidestepped. If there is such an interest, however, then doubt must arise as to the rule's supportability, and acceptability under the European Convention on Human Rights, in the first place.

The other main reason why people in the reported cases seem to want to avoid the formality rules is that they want to remain free to change their minds frequently about how to dispose of their property.[38] This again seems only to occur in the testamentary context. Since wills do not come into effect at the time we make them, but wait until our death, there is the opportunity for vacillation over their content; *inter vivos* dispositions are generally made so as to be immediately binding. Testators prone to vacillation could make a new will every time they had a new thought, but that would be tiresome, and expensive in solicitors' fees. So they make a will leaving some property to someone they are in close touch with, and then informally settle with the latter how they actually want the property disposed of, altering their instructions every time they have a new idea: and these arrangements will then be enforced despite their informality, as secret trusts.

We are talking here about people who are decisive but mercurial, rather than just vague. There will be plenty of the latter, but their thoughts will probably not be sufficiently organized to amount to trusts anyway; remember that incoherence in a disposition weighs against a conclusion that it was meant to be legally binding.[39] The decisive but mercurial testator is probably rather uncommon. Most people err on the side of infrequency in making provision for their own demise. So the point of in effect dispensing with the usual Wills Act formalities in this type of context would be to save the occasional testator of this kind the additional trouble and expense involved in making a series of wills to keep pace with his

---

[38] See eg *Re Snowden* [1979] Ch 528.
[39] See section 3.1; and *Re Snowden* [1979] Ch 528. *Ottaway v Norman* [1972] Ch 698 seems similar, though the point was not taken.

series of different ideas. It seems very hard to believe that this amounts to a sufficient justification. Once again, however, if the contrary is true, doubt must arise as to the supportability of the rule itself, and its acceptability under the European Convention on Human Rights as a proportionate means of achieving a legitimate end.

5.7 DISPOSITIONS OF SUBSISTING BENEFICIAL INTERESTS

There is one further rule about formalities in the area of trusts that we need to look at. Unlike the rules that we have been looking at up to now, which concern the making of trusts, this one concerns dealings with trusts that already exist. By s 53(1)(c) of the Law of Property Act 1925, a disposition of a subsisting—ie already existing—beneficial[40] interest must be made in writing, and signed by the person making it (or, if it is to take effect on his death, placed in a valid will). This rule applies to trusts of any subject matter. So although no formality is needed to make an *inter vivos* trust of anything other than land, formality is required to make a disposition of a beneficial interest arising under it, whether land is involved or not. The rule also applies, apparently, whether the beneficial interest in question arises under an express trust, or a resulting or constructive trust.

The idea of a 'disposition of'—that is, a transfer of, or some other dealing with—'an existing beneficial interest' is apparently simple. But experience has shown that it requires elucidation. Two questions need attention. First, as we are about to see, I can bring about such a disposition not only directly but also in certain indirect ways. Does the rule apply to these too? Conversely, secondly, I can find myself disposing of a beneficial interest not only as a self-contained exercise, but also as part of some transaction with other elements (eg a simultaneous transfer of the legal title). Is the rule applicable under such circumstances? For help with these questions we need to look not only at the statutory wording but also at the decided cases.[41]

---

[40] The Act actually speaks of 'a disposition of an equitable interest or trust'. *Quaere* what a 'disposition of . . . [a] trust' would look like; what concerns us is the disposition of an 'equitable interest'. The set of 'equitable' interests wholly contains (see section 1.12), but goes wider than, that of 'beneficial' interests; ie all beneficial interests are equitable interests, but there are some equitable interests (eg equitable easements) that are not beneficial interests (see section 1.10). Given this book's focus on trusts, however, the discussion in the text concentrates on the latter.

[41] See further B Green (1984) 47 MLR 385.

The first of our two questions was at issue in *Grey v IRC*.[42] Here, a beneficiary under a trust wanted to transfer his interest to his grandchildren. If he had done so directly, the transfer would clearly have been a 'disposition' and so would have needed to be made in writing, because of s 53(1)(c). But under the relevant tax legislation, that would have meant paying substantial stamp duty. He therefore decided to make the transfer instead by a roundabout route, which did not require a written instrument and so would not attract the tax. So he gave his trustees an oral instruction to hold in future for his grandchildren rather than himself. Giving such an instruction was accepted as being, upon some unspecified analysis, in principle an effective way of achieving the same result as transferring his interest to the grandchildren directly. But the question was whether it was likewise a 'disposition' of a subsisting beneficial interest within s 53(1)(c), and had therefore to be done in writing. The court decided that, whatever the analysis upon which it was in principle effective, the manoeuvre amounted in reality to such a 'disposition'. And that, the court decided, concluded the matter. In other words, s 53(1)(c) catches not only direct transfers of (or other dealings with) beneficial interests but also other transactions which, regardless of the means employed, produce the same result.

To say that *every effectual transfer* (etc) of a beneficial interest is therefore caught by s 53(1)(c) would be over-inclusive, however. In the terms of the provision, the transfer has always to be the product of a 'disposition'. 'Disposition' suggests the transferor having *set out to* make the transfer (hence the word 'transactions' at the end of the previous paragraph). So if the transfer occurs for reasons not connected with the transferor's wishes, it is not the product of a 'disposition', and is not caught by the provision. Which is as it should be, for in this case the transferor cannot be expected to comply with the writing requirement. Say I own a beneficial interest and come under a constructive trust of it in your favour. Since you thereby gain an absolute right to the interest, it is arguably (though as we shall see below, not everyone agrees) effectually transferred to you. But this transfer is not the result of a 'disposition' on my part, for, as sections 1.3 and 15.1 explain, constructive trusts arise for reasons other than to vindicate a settlor's intention (and this is why they too are exempt from any formality requirement:[43] there being no need for a constitutive intention, it cannot be expected that such a requirement would be complied with). In *Neville v Wilson*,[44] then, people had contracted to transfer beneficial

---

[42] [1960] AC 1.   [43] Law of Property Act 1925 s 53(2); see section 5.5.
[44] [1997] Ch 144.

interests one to another, and, the contracts being specifically enforceable, the law regarded the sellers as holding the interests on constructive trust for the buyers.[45] The interests were taken to have been thereby effectually transferred, but it was held that this transfer did not involve a 'disposition' to which s 53(1)(c) would apply.

So long as the imposition of a constructive trust and the idea of a 'disposition' are mutually exclusive in this way, there is no difficulty. But this is not necessarily the case. Say the owner of a beneficial interest deliberately engineers a constructive trust so as effectually to transfer his interest; and take it, again, that a transfer is indeed the result. He has deliberately contrived the transfer of his interest, and so, by the above argument about the proper meaning of 'disposition', should be seen as having made a 'disposition' of it. Exempting such a transfer from s 53(1)(c) would leave the requirement under-inclusive.

Oughtred v IRC[46] involved a situation of this kind. That is, its pattern of facts was essentially the same as that in *Neville v Wilson*,[47] except in the respect that is crucial under our hypothesis: that, so far as we know, it was only in *Oughtred v IRC*[48] that the parties deliberately engineered the facts generating the constructive trust, and so used the constructive trust to make a 'disposition'. They hoped, by using the constructive trust to transfer the interest without writing, to save the stamp duty payable if the transfer were made in writing. They failed.

In fact, none of the reasoning directly addresses our hypothesis, that a transfer of a beneficial interest via a deliberately engineered constructive trust should count as a 'disposition' within *Grey v IRC*,[49] and so be caught by s 53(1)(c). The *ratio decidendi* focuses on the rules about stamp duty themselves. But some of the judgements have a bearing on our hypothesis, by rejecting its key assumption that the constructive trust effects a transfer of the interest at all.[50] According to them, saying that *I hold my interest on trust for you* means only that you can demand the interest's transfer from

---

[45] See section 17.6 for the principle generating constructive trusts in this way.
[46] [1960] AC 206.   [47] [1997] Ch 144.   [48] [1960] AC 206.
[49] [1960] AC 1.
[50] [1960] AC 206, 230, 233, Lords Cohen and Denning, and also 220–1, argument of counsel (but see too 227–8, Lord Radcliffe, taking the contrary position adopted in *Neville v Wilson* [1997] Ch 144, above). Also adopting the view favoured by Lords Cohen and Denning, or something like it, is *Nelson v Greening & Sykes (Builders) Ltd* [2007] EWCA 1358, [49]–[58]. There, instead of a constructive trust as discussed in the text, the relevant trust appears to have been either a declared express trust (as discussed in *Grey v IRC* [1958] Ch 690, 715) or a resulting trust (the interest in the hands of the trustee having been paid for by the beneficiary). But that should make no difference: either way, it was, like a constructive trust, a bare trust, under which the beneficiary could demand immediate transfer of the interest.

me; not, as was assumed in our hypothesis and also in *Neville v Wilson*,[51] that *it has already been transferred to you*.[52]

If the trust therefore does not itself effect a transfer, it produces nothing that could count as a 'disposition', and as such attract the operation of s 53(1)(c). And this is as true where the interest's owner deliberately engineers the constructive trust as where he does not. If the interest's transfer is not effected by the constructive trust, however, it will need to be made—if it is to occur at all—in the trust's wake, ie in vindication of the right that, on this view, the trust gives you to demand the interest's transfer from me. The transfer will then, inevitably, constitute a 'disposition' of the interest, which will need to comply with s 53(1)(c). And this will be so as much where the constructive trust arises innocently as where it is engineered. Although it invalidates the result reached in *Neville v Wilson*[53] (that the interests had been effectively transferred without writing) however, this position should not in principle give cause for concern. The point is only that the provision cannot and should not apply to a transfer that the transferor does not set out to make: and a transfer in the wake of even an innocently arising trust is one that the transferor does set out to make. If it is inappropriate to make a person innocently having a constructive trust right to a beneficial interest therefore pay stamp duty on gathering it in, that is really a problem for the stamp duty rules themselves.

The second of our two questions was whether s 53(1)(c) applies to transfers of beneficial interests effected by transactions *that also have other effects*. This question was addressed in *Vandervell v IRC*.[54] Mr Vandervell was the beneficiary of a trust of some shares, the trustee being a bank. He decided to donate these shares to the Royal College of Surgeons. On his instructions, the bank transferred the legal title in the shares to the college. But he made no written transfer of his beneficial interest to the college. The court decided that he had nonetheless succeeded in giving the shares to the college (so that he did not on this account[55] have to continue paying income tax on the dividends on them). The ground for the decision seems to be that a beneficiary's transfer of his interest does not have

---

[51] [1997] Ch 144.

[52] This is an intelligible position, but not an inevitable one. It broadly corresponds with the view taken by the minority in *Baker v Archer-Shee* [1927] AC 844: see section 12.3. The majority view there is closer to, though still perhaps not identical with, the idea that a bare trust effects a transfer of the asset concerned. For further resonances, see the discussion between J Mee and J Penner in C Mitchell (ed) *Constructive and Resulting Trusts* (2010) chs 7, 8.

[53] [1997] Ch 144.   [54] [1967] 2 AC 291.

[55] Though his retention of a beneficial interest in an option to repurchase the shares from the college made him liable to tax after all. See the discussion of *Re Vandervell's Trusts (No 2)* [1974] Ch 269 below.

to comply with s 53(1)(c) unless the transferee becomes the beneficiary of a trust: Mr Vandervell's scheme was not merely to install the college in his place as the beneficiary of the trust, but to terminate the trust by passing both the beneficial interest and the legal title to the college.

The case decides, then, that to count as a disposition of a subsisting beneficial interest and so attract the application of s 53(1)(c), a transaction *must substitute the transferee for the transferor as the beneficiary of a trust*. Lord Upjohn offered a reason why the provision's scope should be limited in this way.[56] According to him, it is vital for a trustee to know who his beneficiaries are; if beneficial interests could be transferred—ie new beneficiaries substituted—without formality, the trustees might not get to know about it, or might not be sure what had been done; and s 53(1)(c) is aimed at preventing this difficulty. So the provision has application only where there is a (continuing) trustee who might otherwise be deceived: that is, where the transaction is aimed at replacing the transferee for the transferor as the trustee's beneficiary.[57]

Putting everything together, then, the ambit, and thus also the purpose, of s 53(1)(c) can be seen as: providing for trustees to be informed of all manner of deliberately-made changes in the identities of their beneficiaries. There are two reasons, however, why this may not be a satisfactory mission for the section. First, there is nothing in the provision (or indeed elsewhere)[58] to say that the required writing should be brought to the trustee's attention. Secondly, the boon of informing trustees may not be so important as to merit a statutory requirement of formality, non-compliance with which makes a transaction ineffective. Compare the position as regards the establishment of a trust: an *inter vivos* trust of anything except land may be made informally. That too seems to create the possibility of mistakes about the identity of the beneficiaries (amongst other things, including whether there is a trust at all), but evidently the potential difficulties are accepted as tolerable. It is hard to see why the problem should be more widespread, or more serious, in the case of people acquiring interests under existing trusts than in the establishment of new trusts. For these reasons, then, s 53(1)(c) may be regarded as introducing into the law a rule that generates litigation and can defeat unobjectionable

---

[56] [1967] 2 AC 291, 311.

[57] Though not quite always then. Accordingly to *Re Holt's Settlement* [1969] 1 Ch 590, s 53(1)(c) does not apply to transfers of beneficial interests made in the context of a variation of a trust under the Variation of Trusts Act 1958 (see section 10.5). But such a variation is necessarily recorded in a court order, which provides the trustee with all necessary information.

[58] *Donaldson v Donaldson* (1854) Kay 711 holds that notice to the trustee is not required for the transfer itself to be effective.

6

Charitable Trusts

Among the rules noted so far, we have seen that trusts are invalid if they infringe the rule against perpetuities,[1] or, in the view of some, if they do not have a legal person as beneficiary.[2] One type of trust is, however, treated differently, being exempt from any requirement of a beneficiary and from most aspects of the rule against perpetuities. This is a trust for a charitable purpose.

Trusts for charitable purposes attract certain other forms of special treatment. Some of these are unusual rules within the law of trusts, while others are not restricted to trusts, applying equally to other vehicles by which charitable purposes are promoted, especially charitable companies and Charitable Incorporated Organisations.[3]

A purpose is charitable if it is for the public benefit, in one of a long list of ways identified by the law. The kinds of purposes listed are, broadly speaking, not unfamiliar: most of them are catered to by the bodies that seek funds through public collecting boxes.

This chapter describes the special treatment, and explains which trusts qualify for it.

6.1 THE SPECIAL TREATMENT

There are four main aspects to the special treatment of charities.

First, special provision is made towards ensuring that charities are properly run. On top of the usual factors that tend to promote good performance on the part of trustees, which we shall look at in Chapter 11, for charities a body known as the Charity Commission, provided by the state

---

[1] See section 2.5.

[2] See section 1.5. The alleged need for a beneficiary, precluding trusts for purposes (other than charitable purposes) is examined further in sections 12.2–12.4.

[3] See further Charities Act 1993 Parts VII, VIII, and VIIIA. J Warburton [1999] Conv 20 argues that charities should no longer be thought of in conjunction with the ordinary law of trusts at all.

at public expense,[4] gives general guidance (especially through its website)[5] and individual advice to trustees.[6] The state also offers help with the safeguarding and investment of charities' assets, via an Official Custodian for Charities and pooled investment and deposit funds.[7]

Secondly, special provision is also made for bringing problems with charities to court, if that seems to be called for. The normal way in which trustees' duties are enforced is by their being sued by some person interested in seeing the trust carried out, usually a beneficiary. But charities are exempt from any requirement of a beneficiary; indeed, as a necessary corollary of the fundamental idea that they exist for the benefit of the public, they *cannot* have beneficiaries.[8] This diffusion of benefit means, in turn, that very often no individual will be sufficiently moved to undergo all the trouble and expense involved in suing. So a substitute system for enforcement against charitable trustees is provided, again by the state, at public expense. Trustees who may have broken their duties can be brought to court by the Charity Commission.[9] So that the Commission can know when to intervene in this way, charities are required to register with it,[10] and to submit annual reports and accounts to it;[11] and the Commission may inquire into their affairs.[12] In some matters, moreover, the Commission can act in lieu of the court,[13] and it also has powers on its own initiative to change charities' trustees and freeze their assets.[14]

Thirdly, many taxes that would otherwise apply are wholly or partially lifted from charities. Broadly speaking, they are not liable to income tax, corporation tax, capital gains tax, and stamp duty, and they receive favourable treatment in respect of value added tax and the rates payable on their premises. Gifts to charities are also given tax breaks, in particular via 'GiftAid'.

Finally, there is a group of rules whereby charitable trusts enjoy greater endurance than others. The fundamental idea that such trusts are

---

[4] Though the Commission does charge for certain items of work: Charities Act 1993 s 85.

[5] <http://www.charity-commission.gov.uk>.   [6] Charities Act 1993 s 29.

[7] *Ibid* ss 2, 21–5.

[8] Those to whom the benefits of charitable trusts are distributed are therefore merely recipients, not beneficiaries (though they are sometimes inaccurately so called, eg in the publications of the Charity Commission). See *A-G v Cocke* [1988] Ch 414, 419–20; *Catholic Care (Diocese of Leeds) v Charity Commission for England and Wales* [2010] 4 All ER 1041, [62]–[63].

[9] Charities Act 1993 ss 1C, 32: alternatively, the proceedings may be brought by the Attorney General or, exceptionally (s 33), by private individuals acting with the Commission's authority.

[10] Charities Act 1993 s 3A.   [11] *Ibid* ss 41–9A.   [12] *Ibid* ss 8–9.

[13] *Ibid* s 16.   [14] *Ibid* s 18.

beneficial to society is taken to mean that if possible they should not be
lost to it.

These rules begin with one whereby a trust which is evidently intended
to be charitable, but whose purpose is not clearly defined in the way that
would otherwise be required for its validity,[15] is accepted as valid anyway,
with a purpose settled by the Charity Commission.[16] They continue with
the exemption of charitable trusts from certain aspects of the rule against
perpetuities, described in section 2.5. The branch of the rule known
as 'the rule against remoteness of vesting' applies in the normal way to
the initial commencement of a charitable trust: so any delay must be not
longer than (under the new regime) 125 years. As we saw in section 2.5,
this rule helps limit the duration of trusts for beneficiaries, by making it
impossible to replace dying beneficiaries beyond the perpetuity period;
but because charitable trusts have no beneficiaries, they are immune from
this effect. Moreover, an arrangement whereby one charitable trust succeeds another is unaffected by the rule.[17] And while non-charitable purpose trusts are subject to 'the rule against inalienability', restricting their
duration to (commonly) 21 years, charitable trusts are exempted from
this.[18] The result is that, in principle, trusts for charitable purposes can
endure forever.[19]

This is not, however, to say that charitable trusts are by their nature
necessarily immortal. They are prone to fail too, though in ways different
from trusts for beneficiaries. For example, a charitable trust could simply
run out of money, in the sense of no longer being able to afford to carry
out its designated purpose. Or its purpose could become impossible or
obsolete. Or it could be linked to some institution that ceases to exist, such
as a trust in support of a particular orphanage, which closes down. So in
pursuit of its desire to see charitable trusts endure, the law goes beyond
exempting them from artificial termination through the perpetuity rules,
and positively helps them to survive at least some of these more natural
limits on their existence. It does this in two main ways.

---

[15] See Chapters 8 and 9.   [16] *Moggridge v Thackwell* (1816) 1 Ves Jun Supp 186.
[17] Perpetuities and Accumulations Act 2009 s 2(2).
[18] *Chamberlayne v Brockett* (1872) LR 8 Ch App 206, 211.
[19] The rule against accumulations, otherwise abolished by the Perpetuities and
Accumulations Act 2009 s 13, is however preserved for charities, preventing them from accu-
mulating income for more than 21 years (s 14). But this does not impinge on the point made in
the text, that in principle they can endure forever. Indeed, the rule has been preserved in the
case of charities *precisely because*, unlike other trusts, they can endure forever, making lengthy
accumulation a more realistic concern. See Law Commission *The Rules Against Perpetuities
and Excessive Accumulations* (Law Com No 251, 1998) paras 10.19–10.20.

The first concerns trusts that are attached to a particular institution, such as the trust in support of an orphanage instanced above. It might be thought that if the institution disappears, the trust must fail. But the view is often taken that the institution is not essential to the trust, but is merely a dispensable mechanism for carrying the purpose out: so when it disappears, it has only to be replaced by other mechanism, the trust itself carrying on. In one case,[20] for example, a trust for the Sheffield Boys' Working Home was read as a trust for the purpose carried on at the Home, ie the care of poor boys in Sheffield. So the disappearance of the Home did not mean that the trust failed (there were still poor boys in Sheffield to be cared for); it merely necessitated a new mechanism to carry out the trust in the Home's place. This approach yields, however, if the institution was intended to be crucial to the trust—if, say, the settlor in this example had wanted only the Sheffield Boys' Working Home to carry out his trust; then, although the trust remains one for the institution's purposes, the institution is *essential* mechanism, meaning that the trust must fail with its disappearance, even if the purposes themselves are still viable.[21] In practice, it is usually unclear which interpretation is right on the facts of a particular case, and the choice depends on judicial attitude. To judge from the case law, at any rate some judges are evidently eager to see charitable trusts kept alive in this way.[22]

The second means of preserving charitable trusts from natural termination is a rule that, if they do fail,[23] the money does not go on a resulting trust, as would normally be the case, but is 'applied cy près',[24] ie allocated to some other charitable object, close to the original one. For example, if a trust is for an animal sanctuary, which closes down, the funds might be

---

[20] *Re Roberts* [1963] 1 WLR 406; see too *Re Finger's Will Trusts* [1972] Ch 286.

[21] *Re Rymer* [1895] 1 Ch 19; *Re Spence* [1979] Ch 483. A line of cases including *Re Faraker* [1912] 2 Ch 488 takes a slightly different approach, treating the money as on trust for the purposes pursued by the institution, or any successor to it, *as time goes on*. On this construction too, if the institution were to disappear—without a successor—the trust should fail, for there would no longer be a means of identifying its purposes.

[22] This is especially visible in the judgment in *Re Roberts* [1963] 1 WLR 406.

[23] The text focuses on 'failure' in its more or less literal meaning, ie instances where the original trust cannot realistically continue to function. The concept of 'failure' has however been extended, to embrace situations where the original trust could continue to function, but it would be sub-optimal to allow it to do so (Charities Act 1993 s 13(1)(e)(iii)). This extension represents less the kind of loss identified in the text as the characteristic of the 'special treatment' of charities; more an expedient whereby the state can get better value for that special treatment. It is thus a form of modification, and as such is discussed further in section 10.6.

[24] Pronounced 'see pray'; literally, 'near to it'. Originally, the new object had to be close to the original one. By the Charities Act 1993 s 14B(3)(c), however, the choice of the new object has also to reflect 'the need for the relevant charity to have purposes which are suitable and effective in the light of current social and economic circumstances'.

given over to another such sanctuary. If the failure occurs after the original trust has come into effect ('subsequent failure'), application cy près follows automatically. However, if the failure prevents the trust from ever coming into effect ('initial failure'), application cy près follows only if the settlor had a 'general charitable intent': that is, if his overriding wish was to give money to charity, rather than exclusively to the particular object that he named. It is often unclear whether a settlor had such a general charitable intent, so again the matter becomes largely one of judicial attitude. The strength of the desire, in at least some quarters, to prolong the endurance of charitable trusts is revealed in some decisions making cy près applications on the strength of unlikely findings of such intent.[25]

6.2 THE BASIS OF THE SPECIAL TREATMENT

All this special treatment has one factor in common. It is given at the expense of the state or the nation. Sometimes this is obvious, as with the provision of the Charity Commission and the tax relief. If less obvious, it is also true of the provisions extending the endurance of charitable trusts. As we saw in section 2.5, in non-charitable trusts the rule against perpetuities ensures that after a while the assets come into the hands of an absolute owner, and so become fully exposed to market forces, thereby playing their part in a process whereby (it is said) everyone becomes richer and happier. The provisions for prolonging the endurance of charitable trusts entail that the assets committed to such trusts may be at least partially withdrawn from the market indefinitely, and so will not participate so fully in this process. The withdrawal does not amount to complete isolation: normally, the capital will be invested, and the income expended on the trusts' purposes. But the income will only be spent on the commodities required to effectuate the purposes, such as schooling or building; sometimes it will take the form of cash payments to people, usually the poor, but this has a similar effect, since by definition the poor will only spend the money on a limited range of commodities, the necessities of life. And the capital will be invested more conservatively than absolutely owned assets might be: as we shall see in section 7.5, trust money is generally invested less adventurously than non-trust money; and trustees of small charities are probably amongst the least adventurous investors. Overall, then, while the withdrawal of a charitable trust's assets from the market is certainly not total, it is substantial, and it may

---

[25] eg *Re Lysaght* [1966] Ch 191; *Re Woodhams* [1981] 1 WLR 493.

be prolonged indefinitely by the provisions for increasing such trusts' endurance, just considered.

Why should charitable trusts be given special treatment at the expense of the state or nation in this way? It cannot be in order to assist the settlor's aims, for the treatment of non-charitable trusts has that aim, but does not possess the features under discussion. The latter seem to be explained rather by pointing to utilitarian and/or communitarian considerations[26] especially identifiable with charitable initiatives, ie those for the public benefit. In broad terms (we shall look at the rules explicating 'public benefit' in a moment), initiatives for the public benefit are by definition calculated to bring the nation a pronounced degree of good; and the altruism of their movers (settlors) can be seen as valuable in communitarian terms. It is the appeal of charitable initiatives to these considerations that is taken to justify the expense that the state or nation suffers in treating them as it does—though of course, one could reasonably conclude that it falls short of doing so.

6.3 CHARITABLE PURPOSES

What trusts count as charitable, so as to receive this special treatment? Broadly, charitable trusts are those whose object[27] is to provide benefit to the public, rather than to particular people. An instance of a straightforward non-charitable trust might be '£100,000 for Adam': it benefits exclusively Adam. '£100,000 to assist the work of the National Health Service' would be a charitable trust: its benefit extends to the population at large.

Whether a trust or other putative charity qualifies as a charity is not, however, decided simply by an ad hoc judgement of its usefulness to the public. Instead, the question is separated into its two aspects (what is required in terms of 'benefit', and how widely the benefit must extend), and each of these is addressed via certain rules. An element of ad hoc judgement necessarily remains in the application of those rules, however.

---

[26] See sections 2.4–2.5.

[27] A trust with mixed charitable and non-charitable objects does not qualify as charitable (*Chichester Diocesan Fund and Board of Finance v Simpson* [1944] AC 341; *IRC v Baddeley* [1955] AC 572; Charities Act 2006 s 1(1)(a))...unless the two elements can be separated and treated as distinct trusts, the charitable of which alone will receive the special treatment (*Salusbury v Denton* (1857) 3 K & J 529); or the non-charitable element can be suppressed (*Re White* [1893] 2 Ch 41; Charitable Trusts (Validation) Act 1954), or regarded as mere mechanism (*Re Coxen* [1948] Ch 747).

6.4 'BENEFIT'

The law maintains a catalogue of the kinds of benefit that count as charitable. This catalogue used to be embedded in judicial decisions,[28] so there
was no definitive articulation of it. Now, however, it is for the most part[29]
set out in s 2(2) of the Charities Act 2006.

The kinds of benefit listed in s 2(2) are:

(a) the prevention or relief of poverty;
(b) the advancement of education;
(c) the advancement of religion;
(d) the advancement of health or the saving of lives;
(e) the advancement of citizenship or community development;
(f) the advancement of the arts, culture, heritage or science;
(g) the advancement of amateur sport;
(h) the advancement of human rights, conflict resolution or reconciliation or
     the promotion of religious or racial harmony or equality and diversity;
(i) the advancement of environmental protection or improvement;
(j) the relief of those in need by reason of youth, age, ill-health, disability,
     financial hardship or other disadvantage;
(k) the advancement of animal welfare;
(l) the promotion of the efficiency of the armed forces of the Crown, or of the
     efficiency of the police, fire and rescue services or ambulance services.

The move to this statutory articulation has, however, made little difference to the catalogue's contents. The catalogue to be discovered in
the previous case law could have been expressed in very similar terms.[30]
Moreover, the Charity Commission, rightly or wrongly, assumes that
the various terms used in the catalogue have the same meaning as they

---

[28] The principal statement was by Lord Macnaghten in *Income Tax Special Commissioners v
Pemsel* [1891] AC 531, 581, referring to three specific categories of charitable benefits—the
relief of poverty, the advancement of education, and the advancement of religion—and then
a fourth, 'other purposes beneficial to the community not falling under any of the preceding
heads'. On the face of it, this suggested that beyond the first three categories the idea of 'benefit' was at large, rather than defined by law. But subsequent judicial statements (*Williams'
Trustees v IRC* [1947] AC 447; *Scottish Burial Reform and Cremation Society v Glasgow Corp*
[1968] AC 138) established that, on the contrary, other purposes were charitable only if established as such by the case law or by statute.

[29] But any kind of benefit that used to count as charitable but was omitted from the statutory list is included in the catalogue too: s 2(4)(a). Moreover, purposes 'that may reasonably be
regarded as analogous to' those in the catalogue are themselves added to it: s 2(4)(b)–(c).

[30] Possible innovations, by way of their addition to the catalogue, are 'the advancement of
amateur sport', 'the advancement of animal welfare', and the inclusion within 'the advancement of religion' of the advancement of 'a religion which does not involve belief in a god'
(s 2(3)(a)).

had in the previous case law. For example, the Commission's account of 'the advancement of religion' is based on a very extensive analysis of the pre-2006 authorities.[31] There was, and on this view therefore still is, a considerable quantity of further law defining most of the terms. There is insufficient space to go into detail about this further law here; reference should be made to specialist books.

Before 2006, a purpose falling within the catalogue was presumed on that account to meet the underlying requirement of delivering a 'benefit'. That is to say, if a purpose counted as—for example—the advancement of education, it was taken to be beneficial, unless proved otherwise. It was sometimes said[32] that this presumption only applied to the relief of poverty or the advancement of education or religion, leaving the benefit of other kinds of purposes to be proved as a matter of fact from case to case; but in reality, all inquiry after factual benefit was rare, and not visibly commoner as regards other kinds of purpose than as regards those three.[33] It occasionally occurred, however.[34] It involved an evaluation not only of the trust's purpose itself, but also of its consequential effects, for good or ill.[35] So, for example, a purpose to provide private hospital care was held charitable because, inter alia, this relieved pressure on and supported the work of the neighbouring public hospital;[36] while a purpose to suppress the practice of vivisection was held non-charitable because, while it offered benefit in the way of countering the human tendency to

---

[31] Charity Commission *The Advancement of Religion for the Public Benefit* (2008), <http://www.charity-commission.gov.uk/Charity_requirements_guidance/Charity_essentials/Public_benefit/pbreligion.aspx>; *Analysis of the Law Underpinning 'The Advancement of Religion for the Public Benefit'* (2008), <http://www.charity-commission.gov.uk/Library/guidance/lawrel1208.pdf>. Cf A Iwobi (2009) 29 LS 619, 621–30.

[32] The source of this view seems to have been a remark by Lord Simonds in *National Anti-Vivisection Society v IRC* [1948] AC 31, 65–6, which does not however quite state it.

[33] In *Funnell v Stewart* [1996] 1 WLR 288, moreover, the presumption was explicitly extended beyond the three categories (to apply also to the promotion of faith-healing).

[34] See eg *Royal Choral Society v IRC* [1943] 2 All ER 101, *Re Delius* [1957] Ch 299, and *Re Pinion* [1965] Ch 85, considering whether various artistic works were of sufficient merit that their (educational) promulgation was charitable; *Gilmour v Coats* [1949] AC 426 and *Re Hummeltenberg* [1923] 1 Ch 237, whether (religious) provisions for intercessory prayer and for educating people to become spiritualist mediums generated provable benefits. (J Hackney (2008) 124 LQR 347 argues that, once a purpose was recognized as within the catalogue, there never followed an inquiry as to benefit. That argument seems to overlook such decisions.)

[35] *Incorporated Council of Law Reporting for England and Wales v A-G* [1972] Ch 73, 99.

[36] *Re Resch's Will Trusts* [1969] 1 AC 514 (though cf *Re Compton* [1945] Ch 123, where a similar argument was rejected). See too *Neville Estates Ltd v Madden* [1962] Ch 832 and *Re Hetherington* [1990] Ch 1, in both of which a religious purpose was accepted as charitable after account was taken of its wider impact.

cruelty, this was outweighed by the detriment it would entail to medical research and so health.[37]

But the Charities Act 2006, while continuing to require a purpose not only to fall within the catalogue but also to be beneficial,[38] abolished the previous presumption linking the two requirements.[39] In principle, therefore, the current law demands an inquiry by the Charity Commission after factual benefit in each and every case.[40] It is clear, however, that such an inquiry will not always be made. According to the Commission,

> In some cases an organisation's aims may be so clearly beneficial to the public that there will be no need for the organisation to provide evidence to demonstrate that there is a benefit...In other cases, the element of benefit to the public may be more debatable, or may depend on the circumstances, and will need to be shown by evidence.[41]

Although the Commission describes the latter type of case as preponderant,[42] it seems likely that in practice the Commission will usually regard the answer as obvious, so returning us to something very like the old law.

This assertion is made not because the answer will in fact be obvious, but because the Commission will have little alternative but to treat it so. There are three reasons for this. First, while the Commission, very properly, thus proposes to base its assessments upon evidence, the relevant evidence will commonly be difficult or impossible to assemble. In particular, the benefits and detriments may be far downstream, and difficult to measure; and their connection with the purpose controversial.[43] Second, a decision whether a purpose offers a net benefit will commonly, or indeed always, require a value-judgment, which the Commission is not constitutionally equipped to make. Consider for example a trust to provide special

---

[37] *National Anti-Vivisection Society v IRC* [1948] AC 31.   [38] Section 2(1).

[39] Section 3(2).

[40] In the conduct of this inquiry, the idea of 'benefit', being statutory (Charities Act 2006 s 2(1)), must be interpreted as far as possible so as to ensure compliance with the European Convention on Human Rights (Human Rights Act 1998 s 6), and the Commission, as a public body, must abide by the Convention (*ibid* s 3). See *Catholic Care (Diocese of Leeds) v Charity Commission for England and Wales* [2010] 4 All ER 1041; <http://www.charity-commission.gov.uk/library/about_us/catholic_care.pdf>.

[41] Charity Commission *Charities and Public Benefit* (2008), <http://www.charity-commission.gov.uk/Charity_requirements_guidance/Charity_essentials/Public_benefit/public_benefit.aspx>, para E2.

[42] *Ibid* para D7.

[43] Cf *Gilmour v Coats* [1949] AC 426. The purpose was to support a community of strictly cloistered nuns. It was argued that this carried benefit in the form of edification to outsiders, resulting from the nuns' example. This was discounted as too 'indirect, remote, imponderable and...controversial' (*ibid* 447).

education to an intellectual elite. This might be said to entail benefit to those receiving the education, but damaging consequences for other students. Deciding on the balance of advantage requires prices to be set, in comparable terms (it is no use expressing one in terms of apples, the other in terms of pears), on the two effects. There is room for a variety of views on the setting of these prices. There is no reason to give primacy to such view as may happen to prevail in the Charity Commission. The matter is an essentially political one.[44]

The third reason why the Commission will find it difficult to assess benefit is that sometimes such an assessment cannot be made in an evidence-based way, or indeed otherwise rationally, at all. This is most obviously so in the case of religious purposes.[45] Subject to the above reservations about *their* assessment, the downstream secular consequences may carry the day[46] (though a rigorous evaluation of them, taking account of possible negative as well as positive effects, has yet to be undertaken). But to assess a purpose on the basis of its collateral effects alone, necessarily omitting any evaluation of the purpose itself,[47] can hardly be thought a satisfactory

[44] The issue becomes especially exciting if the negative consequences to be taken into account include (and why would they not?) the costs of the special treatment the trust will receive if determined to be charitable—the tax advantages and so on (section 6.1). To assess these costs, they will need to be translated into more concrete terms, such as the number of extra hospital beds, teachers, nuclear submarines, or whatever that would otherwise be purchased by the tax foregone (an impossible inquiry in itself); and the latter weighed up against the benefits to be had from the trust. Once again, that exercise would be a political one, which the Charity Commission is not constituted to undertake. The prospect of such an inquiry was viewed with apparent equanimity by Lord Cross in *Dingle v Turner* [1972] AC 601, 624–5, but with alarm by Lords Dilhorne, MacDermott, and Hodson, *ibid* 614.

[45] The Charity Commission in effect acknowledges this, though not the depth of the resulting difficulty: *The Advancement of Religion for the Public Benefit* (2008), < http://www.charity-commission.gov.uk/Charity_requirements_guidance/Charity_essentials/Public_benefit/pbreligion.aspx>, para D2: 'if it is not possible to demonstrate a benefit, then the law cannot take account of it in assessing public benefit. The benefits to the public should be capable of being recognized, identified, defined or described but that does not mean that they also have to be capable of being quantified. Benefits that can be quantified and measured may be easier to identify but we also take non-quantifiable benefits into consideration, provided it is clear what the benefits are. The benefits may or may not be physically experienced. We realise that often in the case of charities whose aims include advancing religion some of the benefits are not tangible and could be potentially difficult to identify. However, this is not to say that a public benefit assessment would only take account of tangible, practical benefits.'

[46] Charity Commission *Analysis of the Law Underpinning 'The Advancement of Religion for the Public Benefit'* (2008), <http://www.charity-commission.gov.uk/Library/guidance/law-rel1208.pdf>, para 3.8. In its decision to accept the Druid Network as charitable (<http://www.charity-commission.gov.uk/library/about_us/druiddec.pdf>), the Commission asserted (at para 32) 'English law does not enquire into the nature, worth or value of religious belief', before (at paras 57–61) finding public benefit on the basis of downstream effects.

[47] In *Gilmour v Coats* [1949] AC 426, the trust was for a community of nuns who were strictly cloistered. As a result, no downstream secular consequences could be found, and the

way of deciding whether it is beneficial.[48] The necessary irrational decision, too, can only be made (if at all) politically.

So the insistence of the Charities Act 2006 on an inquiry as to benefit
in each and every case cannot be expected to translate into reality. Instead,
the fact that a purpose falls within the law's catalogue of possible charitable purposes will normally be determinative, just as it was before 2006.
And that is as it should be. The inclusion of a type of purpose within
the catalogue must be a proxy for a judgement that its effectuation will,
unless there are unusual damaging side-effects in the individual case,[49]
be beneficial. As we have seen, that judgement often cannot satisfactorily
be made ad hoc, and certainly cannot be made apolitically. It is therefore a judgement that must be made by Parliament,[50] and embedded in a
rule—the inclusion of that type of purpose in the catalogue—for application by the Charity Commission. By the same token, if (despite these
objections) there is to be an ad hoc assessment of benefit, as the 2006 Act
demands, there is no sense in requiring putative charitable purposes *also*
to fall within a catalogue: if the catalogue makes a difference at all, this
can only be to exclude from charitable status some purposes (those that
do not appear within it) that, so far as raw benefit is concerned, deserve
that status.

In one particular context, the Charity Commission has itself noticed
the impossibility of the Act's structure. Before 2006, it was clear that a
'political' purpose[51] could not be charitable. This was put principally on
the ground that the judges, who at that time were responsible for deciding on charitable status, were constitutionally incapable of assessing the
value of such purposes.[52] In the context of the pre-2006 law, with its presumption that a purpose within the charitable catalogue was beneficial,

decision had to depend solely on an assessment of the value of religion itself, which was found
incapable of proof. As a result, the required benefit was not found.

[48]   See further M Harding (2008) 71 MLR 159; A Iwobi (2009) 29 LS 619, 630–43.

[49]   'Unusual', because universal negatives—notably the costs of the special treatment—
would be factored into the decision whether to include the type of purpose in the catalogue
at all.

[50]   The pre-2006 catalogue was largely judge-made, though originating in the preamble to
the Charitable Uses Act 1601. Although its longevity made it less acutely controversial, it was
on that account ultimately unsatisfactory.

[51]   A purpose counted as 'political' if it supported a particular political party or sought a
change in the law or executive practice (*Bowman v Secular Society Ltd* [1917] AC 406; *National
Anti-Vivisection Society v IRC* [1948] AC 31; *McGovern v A-G* [1982] Ch 321), or a cause
regarded by the court as politicized, eg socialized medicine (*Re Bushnell* [1975] 1 WLR 1596),
pacifism (*Southwood v A-G* (2000) 80 P & CR D34).

[52]   *Bowman v Secular Society Ltd* [1917] AC 406, 442. See further G Santow (1999) 52
CLP 255.

that was perhaps not a necessary position: if, notwithstanding its political overtones, a purpose fell within the catalogue,[53] the presumption meant that the judges had no inevitable need to assess its value. The abolition of the presumption by the 2006 Act, however, removes that possible refuge, leaving the judges' position the only safe one. The Charity Commission, which nowadays has to decide on charitable status, recognizes that it is no more capable than the judges of making the necessary assessment of such purposes, but claims that the old rule against political charities has survived the Act, saving it from having to do so.[54] But there is nothing in the Act to support this view: on the contrary, it rules that a purpose is charitable only if it falls within the catalogue, and is found, on an ad hoc assessment, to be beneficial.[55] Properly speaking, then, the Commission has no option but to judge whether political purposes are beneficial; something which, by its own admission, it cannot satisfactorily do—for the same reason as it cannot satisfactorily make any of the other such judgements that the Act requires of it. The Act has thus succeeded in building a mare's nest, albeit that this will doubtless be for the most part conveniently ignored.

6.5 'PUBLIC'

Given that the purpose in question is one recognized as generating a 'benefit', there is then the further requirement that the benefit must be to the 'public'.[56] For example, a trust to provide for medical treatment for one's own child would certainly fall within the catalogue[57] and confer a benefit, but only on the child, not on the public.[58] Further rules deal with this

---

[53] Some did not, meaning that the difficulty never arose: in particular, a purpose to further the interests of a particular political party (*Re Hopkinson* [1949] 1 All ER 346).

[54] Charity Commission *Charities and Public Benefit* (2008), <http://www.charity-commission.gov.uk/Charity_requirements_guidance/Charity_essentials/Public_benefit/public_benefit.aspx>, para E2. See too *Hanchett-Stanford v A-G* [2009] Ch 173, [15]–[17]. For reflection on the place of charities within the political scene, see A Dunn (2008) 71 MLR 247; *Charity, Law and Politics* (2009).

[55] Section 2(1).   [56] Charities Act 2006 s 2(1)(b).

[57] *Ibid* s 2(2)(d).

[58] Two of the catalogue's items, '(i) the advancement of environmental protection or improvement' and '(k) the advancement of animal welfare', need particularly careful attention in this respect. Unlike those covered by the remainder of the catalogue, purposes of these kinds are not necessarily aimed at providing human benefit at all. They can thus qualify as charitable only via any consequential benefits that they generate for humans. In the case of item (i), such downstream benefits will not usually be hard to discern; but in the case of item (k), they are likely to be tangential, as 'to promote public morality by checking the innate [human] tendency to cruelty' (*Re Wedgwood* [1915] 1 Ch 113, 117).

point, defining how widely a purpose's benefit needs to extend before it is regarded as charitable. The Charities Act 2006 carries forward the rules which obtained under the previous law.[59]

There is a single rule for the majority of the catalogue's types of purpose, but special (less demanding) rules for its first two items: the prevention or relief of poverty, and the advancement of education.

Where the usual rule applies, the purpose's benefit must be open to anyone who is equipped and wants to take advantage of it. This rule does not mean that the proffered facilities must be equally useful or attractive to everyone: the provision of a public recreation ground will be acceptable, despite many people making no use of it. The rule means that no one who might want to use the facility in question may be *artificially* debarred, by limitations not inherent in the purpose itself.[60] So the provision of a children's playground is acceptable, despite the exclusion of adults. The provision of facilities only to the inhabitants of a particular locality is likewise acceptable, so long as the restriction makes sense in terms of the nature of the facilities:[61] it would not be charitable to provide an Olympic-standard swimming pool to be used only by the inhabitants of a particular village. But a trust to provide social and recreational facilities specifically for Methodists does not qualify,[62] because Methodists have no special need for such facilities and non-Methodists, who might want to use them just as much as Methodists, would be barred. (The fact that some selection is involved is not a problem so long as the competition is open in this way to all who could benefit. So a trust for the trustees to send, say, 12 disadvantaged children on holiday will qualify.)

It appears that the usual rule applies to trusts for the advancement of religion, meaning that such trusts too will be charitable so long as their benefits are available to any suitable person who wishes to take advantage of them. So it should not be problematic that a trust's benefits are in practice available only to those of a religious disposition; nor that the trust is confined to an individual religion or denomination, to which only some people will in practice be drawn, so long as the religion or denomination

---

[59] Section 3(3).

[60] The Charity Commission puts it thus: 'any restrictions on who can benefit must be "reasonable". That means the restrictions are legitimate, proportionate, rational and justifiable given the nature of the organisation's charitable aims. It is not charitable to restrict who can benefit by reference to criteria that are unrelated to the charitable aims to be carried out' (*Charities and Public Benefit* (2008), <http://www.charity-commission.gov.uk/Charity_requirements_guidance/Charity_essentials/Public_benefit/public_benefit.aspx>, para F3).

[61] *Ibid* para F4.   [62] *IRC v Baddeley* [1955] AC 572.

is open to all who wish to join it (and does not, for example, admit only persons born to a mother who was herself a member of the sect). The cases are not entirely consonant with this picture, however. In particular, in *Gilmour v Coats*[63] a trust for the purposes of a cloistered order of Roman Catholic nuns was not accepted as charitable, despite the fact that in principle any woman might join the order. Viewed in terms of the usual rule, just explained, this seems a doubtful decision; it was arrived at[64] so as not to disturb earlier authority dealing with similar trusts in the same way.[65] Such problem as there may be, however, is removed if the recipients also mix with the rest of the population, so that the benefit of their religiosity becomes diffused amongst the public at large.[66] So a trust for an open, rather than cloistered, order should be accepted as charitable.

In the area of poverty, however, artificial restrictions have traditionally been tolerated: that is, trusts aimed at relieving poverty have been accepted as charitable even though the benefits under them are confined to a narrower class than all who are capable of taking advantage of them and wish to do so. So, before 2006, trusts to relieve poverty among members of a particular family,[67] or among employees of a certain company,[68] qualified as charitable; one to relieve poverty among Methodists would presumably have qualified too. It is not clear that the position remains the same since 2006. The 2006 Act preserves the rules about 'public benefit' that obtained under the previous law,[69] but it does insist that there be such a benefit.[70] So the traditional treatment of poverty trusts will have survived if it embodied a special reading of the 'public benefit' requirement, but not if it treated such trusts as exempt from that requirement. It is hard to know which of these is the case. It is certainly arguable that such trusts do offer a public benefit, in the sense that relieving any class of the poor, however restricted, benefits the public: perhaps by lifting the burden of doing so from the public generally, or by alleviating the social ills associated

---

[63] [1949] AC 426.   [64] *Ibid* 448-9.

[65] *Cocks v Manners* (1871) LR 12 Eq 574; *Re White* [1893] 2 Ch 41; *Dunne v Byrne* [1912] AC 407. For suggestions that this position reflects a utilitarian or Protestant bias, see H Cohen (1983) 36 CLP 241 and M Blakeney (1981) 2 *Journal of Legal History* 207; cf C Rickett [1990] Conv 34.

[66] *Neville Estates Ltd v Madden* [1962] Ch 832. It was assumed, following *Gilmour v Coats* [1949] AC 426, that a trust would not be charitable if it benefited only the closed membership of a particular synagogue. The trust was, however, held charitable on the ground that the members mixed with, and so passed the benefits on to, the public at large.

[67] *Re Scarisbrick* [1951] Ch 622. Such trusts need to be distinguished from trusts for the benefit of particular individuals, who happen to be poor. Charity tends to be found where the persons to be befitted are designated in an open-ended way, eg 'the settlor's poor relations and their descendants in perpetuity' (*A-G v Price* (1810) 7 Ves Jun 371).

[68] *Dingle v Turner* [1972] AC 601.   [69] Section 3(3).   [70] Section 2(1)(b).

with poverty, again to the benefit of the general community.[71] If this is right, the traditional position continues to obtain post-2006.

The traditional rule for education was a variation on that for poverty. Some artificial restrictions were once more tolerated: so trusts providing scholarships for children defined by reference to their religion, nationality, or parents' occupation, qualified as charitable.[72] Again, this can be seen as expressing rather than rejecting a need for public benefit, in that the provision of education even to a limited group is beneficial to the nation generally; if this view is taken, the position remains the same post-2006. But here, unlike in the case of poverty, the traditional rule went on to say that availability could *not* be restricted by reference to a relationship with a particular family[73] or employer.[74] This difference was justified on the ground that, whatever their benefits to the nation generally, the educational provisions of families and companies should not receive public subsidy, especially tax exemption; there being no such aversion to families' and companies' provisions against poverty.[75] Assuming the rule expresses rather than rejects a need for public benefit generally, this detail is preserved by the provision in the 2006 Act,[76] which carries forward the precise rules about public benefit that obtained previously.

Benefits are sometimes made available only at a cost to the user. The obvious case is that of the educational benefits offered by fee-paying schools, but there are many other examples.[77] That users are charged in this way may mean that the benefit does not count as available to the

---

[71] *Re Compton* [1945] Ch 123, 139.

[72] Cf Charity Commission *Charities and Public Benefit* (2008), <http://www.charity-commission.gov.uk/Charity_requirements_guidance/Charity_essentials/Public_benefit/public_benefit.aspx>, para F6, which records the rule against restrictions based on family or employer, noted below, but overlooks the acceptability of other artificial limitations.

[73] *Re Compton* [1945] Ch 123.

[74] *Oppenheim v Tobacco Securities Trust Co Ltd* [1951] AC 297. Lord MacDermott, dissenting, preferred to address the question whether an educational benefit extended sufficiently widely not via the rule described in the text, but as one of degree, to be decided rather impressionistically. Taking that approach, he would have accorded charitable status to the purpose in that case, which was to educate the children of the (over 110,000) present and former employees of a certain company, and as such was held by the majority not to qualify as charitable. Lord MacDermott's general approach was supported by Lord Cross in *Dingle v Turner* [1972] AC 601, 623–4, but Lord Cross, applying it, would have reached the same conclusion as the majority in *Oppenheim v Tobacco Securities Trust Co Ltd*, on account of tax considerations ([1972] AC 601, 624–5)—thus emphasizing the approach's impressionistic quality.

[75] *Dingle v Turner* [1972] AC 601, 624–5, Lord Cross.   [76] Section 3(3).

[77] eg *Scottish Burial Reform and Cremation Society Ltd v Glasgow Corp* [1968] AC 138, where those seeking the cremation services provided by the society were charged for them. The society was held charitable nonetheless.

'public': to be charitable, a purpose need not be limited to the poor,[78] but it must not exclude the poor.[79] Where benefits are extended on a fee-charging basis, then, care will have to be taken over the level of the fee, and/or expedients adopted aimed at ensuring accessibility by the poor notwithstanding the level of the fee (eg, in the case of schools, the availability of scholarships).[80]

---

[78] *Income Tax Special Commissioners v Pemsel* [1891] 1 AC 531.

[79] *Re Macduff* [1896] 2 Ch 451, 464.

[80] Charity Commission *Charities and Public Benefit* (2008), <http://www.charity-commission.gov.uk/Charity_requirements_guidance/Charity_essentials/Public_benefit/public_benefit.aspx>, para C3; *Public Benefit and Fee-charging* (2008), <http://www.charity-commission.gov.uk/Charity_requirements_guidance/Charity_essentials/Public_benefit/pbfeecha.aspx>, sec C.

7

Stewardship

We turn now to look at trustees' duties: ie what is actually required of trustees.

7.1 TRUSTEES' DUTIES GENERALLY

In recent years, it has become fashionable, resurrecting an older tradition that had to some extent faded, to discuss the duties of trustees in terms of their obligation to 'account' to the trust objects for the state of the trust fund.[1] This obligation is considered in more detail in Chapter 13. It is mentioned here because it is sometimes depicted as meaning that, in at least some circumstances, a trustee's liabilities to make good deficiencies in the trust assets are to be assessed *without asking whether he has breached one of his duties*. If this were right, it would be inapt for us to inquire after those duties, as this and the following two chapters set out to do. As is explained in section 13.4, however, the analysis making no reference to trustees' duties, while historically accurate (and indeed understandable, as part of a response to an old principal–agent problem),[2] is neither satisfactory in principle nor supportable within a sympathetic understanding of the modern law. What follows will, therefore, be put in terms of trustees' duties after all.

The most basic duty on a trustee is to respect the fact that the property is not beneficially his own. Where the trust has beneficiaries, then, he must respect the beneficiaries' entitlements. The exact content of this duty is a little speculative, however, perhaps because it is commonly overlain by the more specific and demanding duties considered below. Probably it

---

[1] See eg P Millett (1998) 114 LQR 214 (and *passim* in this author's judicial utterances); R Chambers in P Birks and A Pretto (eds) *Breach of Trust* (2002) ch 1; S Elliott *Compensation Claims against Trustees* (2002, unpublished Oxford DPhil thesis); S Elliott and C Mitchell (2004) 67 MLR 16, 23–33; S Elliott and J Edelman (2004) 18 TLI 116; D Hayton in S Degeling and J Edelman (eds) *Equity in Commercial Law* (2005) ch 11; C Mitchell (2006) 59 *Current Legal Problems* 267; J Penner *The Law of Trusts* 7th edn (2010) 320–32; C Mitchell and S Watterson in C Mitchell (ed) *Constructive and Resulting Trusts* (2010) ch 4.

[2] See section 13.7. For the principal–agent problem, see section 1.10.

consists only in a requirement that, if the trustee still has the trust property, he shall transfer it, if asked to do so, to the beneficiaries if they have immediate rights to it, or to fresh trustees. This duty is found in all trust situations;[3] it is in fact the very essence of a trust, indeed another way of expressing the idea 'trust'.

Express trusts, however, generally ask more of their trustees, in two main ways. They normally call for the payment out of money (to the beneficiaries, or towards the—usually charitable—purpose), not as a simple immediate transfer but in a more complex manner. Complex duties of payment are examined in Chapters 8 and 9. They also normally require the safe-keeping, and usually the management, of the trust property pending payment out. This interim stewardship is needed because settlors do not generally stipulate that the entire trust property should be immediately paid out, but instead provide for the trust to endure for a time; there would generally be little point in establishing a trust to do the work of a simple gift. This duty of stewardship is the topic of the present chapter.

These various calls on express trustees can be onerous, and their satisfactory performance cannot be taken for granted. Chapter 11 is devoted to the range of techniques—some of them involving further, adjectival, duties—calculated to promote such performance. Allowing settlors to demand so much also poses problems when essentially well-meaning trustees fall short of what is required, or when the settlor's scheme offends the beneficiaries' desires, or otherwise over time comes to appear ill conceived. The law accordingly has rules allowing for trustees' duties to be modified. That is the topic of Chapter 10.

The duties upon trustees of resulting and constructive trusts are not well documented. They will receive attention in section 18.5, after we have examined the nature of the trusts in question.

7.2 SAFEGUARDING THE TRUST PROPERTY

If trust property does not survive, it cannot be transferred to the objects. Trustees of express trusts accordingly have duties to safeguard it. One of these requires them, if the trust property is not already in their own hands, to seek without delay to have it vested in themselves[4] or in their nominees

---

[3] And Lord Browne-Wilkinson in *Westdeutsche Landesbank Girozentrale v Islington LBC* [1996] AC 669, 705–7, accepts its application to the situation, generally regarded as but not in his view a 'trust' (see section 1.13), where someone unwittingly holds property illicitly transferred to him by true trustees (see section 17.2).

[4] *Wyman v Paterson* [1900] AC 271.

or custodians.[5] Once there, a further duty requires them to endeavour to keep it safe.[6] In the case of a piece of land, for example, that might mean providing sensible security, and taking steps against any trespassers. They must not place the property in the hands of anyone not authorized to have it,[7] though of course they may—and indeed often should—entrust it to suitable agents and others of that ilk, such as bankers.[8] They must also not mix it with other property, the danger being that it will prove impossible to retrieve from the mixture.

A trustee is not required to safeguard the property come what may.[9] He will be liable for failing to do so only if he knows, or should know, the property to be trust property. If he loses the trust property before realizing it to be trust property, he thus commits no wrong. And he is required not to guarantee the property's safety, but to exercise a degree of diligence and expertise in looking after it (though he is under a strict duty not voluntarily to pass it to someone not authorized to have it).

The Trustee Act 2000 introduced a new formulation of the degree of diligence and expertise required of trustees in respect of certain of their duties. Subject to exclusion by the settlor,[10] a trustee

> must exercise such care and skill as is reasonable in the circumstances, having regard in particular—
>
> (a) to any special knowledge or experience that he has or holds himself out as having, and
>
> (b) if he acts as trustee in the course of a business or profession, to any special knowledge or experience that it is reasonable to expect of a person acting in the course of that kind of business or profession.[11]

---

[5] Trustee Act 2000 ss 16, 17.   [6] *Speight v Gaunt* (1883) 9 App Cas 1.

[7] So, for example, in *Clough v Bond* (1838) 3 My & Cr 490, a trustee's estate was liable for breach of this duty when he banked the trust assets in a joint account with his co-trustee, and, upon his death, the latter withdrew and absconded with them. He ought to have used an arrangement whereby they could not have come into the sole hands of one who was supposed to be a co-trustee in this way.   [8] *Speight v Gaunt* (1883) 9 App Cas 1.

[9] The contrary seems to be assumed in *Westdeutsche Landesbank Girozentrale v Islington LBC* [1996] AC 669, 690, 703. But note the insistence there that the holder of the property cannot be a trustee at all, and incur duties as such, until he knows of the facts generating the trust. This view, which is not widely held, is best seen as a proxy for the rule stated in the text. That is, the property-holder is a trustee even before he knows of the facts generating the trust, and so incurs a trustee's duties, but cannot breach the latter until he knows of those facts. See R Chambers *Resulting Trusts* (1997) 201–12; C Harpum in P Birks and F Rose (eds) *Restitution and Equity Volume One, Resulting Trusts and Equitable Compensation* (2000) 165–7; see further section 1.13.   [10] Trustee Act 2000 Sch 1 para 7.

[11] *Ibid* s 1(1).

(Arguably, 'the circumstances' include a particular trustee's *lack of* professed knowledge or experience, meaning that only a reduced level of care and skill can be demanded of him; though the contrary is more usually assumed.) This formulation is however applied only to those trustees' functions listed in the 2000 Act,[12] and these do not include the duty to take care of the trust property. The latter, therefore, seems still to be governed by the old—judicially articulated—formulation, namely that (again, subject to exclusion by the settlor)[13] a trustee should emulate an ordinary prudent man of business looking after the interests of others,[14] it being less clear than in the new formulation that the standard rises for professionals[15] (and, perhaps, drops for avowed amateurs).

One would think that the general duty of keeping the property safe would normally entail a duty to insure it. Curiously, this has never been authoritatively confirmed in England,[16] though it is clear that trustees can spend trust funds on doing so.[17] In respect of details such as the choice of policy, trustees must use reasonable care and skill, as formulated in the 2000 Act.[18]

7.3 GENERAL MANAGEMENT

Pending the ultimate transfer of the trust property, especially where substantial time is to elapse before this, trustees also have a number of more active management functions. One of them, the investment of the trust assets, is singled out and dealt with separately in section 7.4. Some others are considered here. They are, broadly, matters of housekeeping. They might include setting up, and where appropriate changing, bank accounts; deciding whether to employ an accountant, and if so choosing one; deciding whether and how to try to recoup from a solicitor loss caused

---

[12] Schedule 1.   [13] *Armitage v Nurse* [1998] Ch 241, 253.

[14] *Re Whiteley* (1886) 33 Ch D 347, *Learoyd v Whiteley* (1887) 12 App Cas 727. These decisions were in turn based on *Speight v Gaunt* (1883) 22 Ch D 727, 9 App Cas 1, where however the standard was put as that of an ordinary prudent man of business *acting for himself*; for the significance of this difference, see at n 68 below. And see generally J Getzler in P Birks and A Pretto (eds) *Breach of Trust* (2002) ch 2.

[15] It was said to do so in *Re Waterman's Will Trusts* [1952] 2 All ER 1054, 1055, and *Bartlett v Barclay's Bank Trust Co Ltd (Nos 1 and 2)* [1980] Ch 515, 534; but no such statement was made, where it would have been relevant, in *Nestle v National Westminster Bank plc* [1993] 1 WLR 1260.

[16] Indeed, the old case *Bailey v Gould* (1840) 4 Y & C Ex 221 denied any duty; but one was accepted in *Pateman v Heyen* (1993) 33 NSWLR 188, Australia.

[17] Trustee Act 1925 s 19, substituted by Trustee Act 2000 s 34.

[18] Schedule 1 para 5.

to the trust by his bad advice, and implementing the decision taken; and so on, down to buying the postage stamps needed to communicate with the beneficiaries.

In respect of these matters, the law does not require trustees to take what hindsight reveals to be, or a judge might later think, the 'right' course.[19] So turning down an out-of-court settlement and instead suing the solicitor for his bad advice, only to lose the case completely, will not necessarily be a breach of their duty. Instead, the law leaves trustees[20] to exercise judgement as to whether something should be done, and if so what. It does, however, require them, in the way they exercise their judgement, to pursue the correct end; and to apply a proper philosophy, and also an appropriate level of diligence and expertise, in selecting and then carrying out a particular course of action so as to achieve that end.

The end at which trustees must aim is the promotion of the interests of the trust's objects (beneficiaries or purposes), to the exclusion of all else.[21] Although in principle distinct, the questions of the proper philosophy and of the appropriate level of diligence and expertise are governed by a single formula. Before the Trustee Act 2000, the requirement was (subject to exclusion by the settlor)[22] to act as an ordinary prudent man of business looking after the interests of others.[23] By way of philosophy, this meant seeing the objects' interest as better promoted by caution than by risk-taking, that being the prudent way of looking after the interests of others; and by way of diligence and expertise, it meant being no less careful and skilful than a prudent businessman ordinarily would. Under the 2000 Act, in respect of those functions to which the latter applies[24]—the old formulation continuing to apply to other functions—the requirement is (subject to exclusion by the settlor)[25] to exercise such care and skill as is reasonable in the circumstances.[26] This is less revealing than the old formulation, with the latter's more pregnant term 'prudent', but it is generally assumed

---

[19] *Tempest v Lord Camoys* (1882) 21 Ch D 571.

[20] A settlor can stipulate for the trustees' choices to be subject to veto by some other person, or entrust such choices to such other person. The other person is nowadays often termed a 'protector', and may well be introduced into the trust to represent a particular interest, especially that of a particular beneficiary or the settlor. In that event, the protector (and hence the administration of the trust) may be free from the duties described in the following text. See D Waters in A Oakley (ed) *Trends in Contemporary Trust Law* (1996) ch 4.

[21] *Cowan v Scargill* [1985] Ch 270, 286. See further section 7.5. This requirement cannot be excluded: *Armitage v Nurse* [1998] Ch 241, 253–4; though cf *Hayim v Citibank NA* [1987] AC 730—see further section 10.1.

[22] *Armitage v Nurse* [1998] Ch 241, 253.

[23] *Re Whiteley* (1886) 33 Ch D 347, *Learoyd v Whiteley* (1887) 12 App Cas 727.

[24] Schedule 1.   [25] *Ibid* para 7.   [26] Section 1: see at n 11 above.

to mean the same. As regards the quarrel with the trust's solicitor, therefore, the trustees should aim at looking after the trust's interests, rather than, say, at venting personal spite; they should be responsible rather than gung-ho in deciding whether to pursue litigation, or accept an out-of-court settlement, or indeed cut the trust's losses by admitting defeat; and they should display reasonable care and skill in identifying the course of action that best meets these criteria, and in then pursuing it.

Much of the general management of a trust is not naturally attended to by the trustees themselves, but is given over to professional agents: clerks, bankers, solicitors, stockbrokers, and so on (unless the trustee is a trust corporation, such as a bank, when everything might be done under its own umbrella). Subject to certain safeguards regarding what functions are entrusted to whom and how, the law allows trustees to use agents and other kinds of representatives in this way.[27] Subject to exclusion by the settlor, the accustomed position follows. In deciding whether to use an agent, the trustees must follow the usual aim of acting in the trust's interests, and interpret this as requiring caution. If one of the trustees' functions is normally performed only by someone with specialist expertise, and they lack that expertise, this is likely to mean that they should recruit someone who has it. If they do decide to delegate, they must exercise reasonable care and skill in implementing that decision,[28] ie in selecting an agent, agreeing his terms of engagement, etc. And they must review any delegation's continuing satisfactoriness in the same way.[29]

7.4 INVESTMENT

The idea of investment is to produce a periodic return, or to preserve or increase the real value of the capital sum, or both. So investing trust property will help provide for the payments out to the objects. Say that a settlor settles £100,000, and stipulates for the income to be paid to you for your life, and then the capital to me. If the £100,000 were left in a non-interest-bearing bank account, there would be no income to pay to you; and the capital would still be £100,000 when, on your death, it had to be paid over to me, which would be displeasing if the worth of £100,000 had meanwhile been eroded by inflation. By investing the money, however, it should be possible to do better. A return can be produced for payment to you. Everyday investments like bank deposit accounts and building

---

[27] Trustee Act 2000 Part IV. The facility can however be limited or excluded by the settlor: s 26.
[28] *Ibid* s 1(1) (see at n 11 above); this function being one to which the Act applies: Sch 1 para 3.   [29] *Ibid* ss 21, 22.

society accounts provide this; company shares generally do too, by way of dividends, but there is no guarantee: how much, if anything, they yield depends on how well the company is doing. It should also be possible to increase the value of the capital. Bank deposit accounts and building society accounts do not have this feature of capital appreciation, but company shares potentially do, because their value is a reflection of the actual worth of the undertaking, which in favourable circumstances will rise; though again, there is no guarantee: the company could fade and then its shares will lose value. Land, too, can produce both an income return (eg if it is rented out) and capital appreciation (as either the price of land in general, or the value of the particular site, rises).

Unsurprisingly, therefore, trustees[30] normally have the power[31] to invest the trust property (and to change investments from time to time). Even if there is no express duty to invest, as there often is (notably in unit trusts, of which it is the whole point), the general duty to act in the objects' interests will normally require investment, so as to get the best financial return for them.[32] The trustees in the example above could hardly, given this requirement, receive the £100,000 and keep it as cash, providing no income for you and only £100,000, devalued by inflation, for me. But investing so as to seek the best financial return for the objects is not necessarily a simple matter. Before even approaching the selection of a particular investment—or, indeed, its retention, for there is also a duty periodically to review the trust's portfolio against the same yardsticks[33]—trustees seeking such a return must deal with two dilemmas of principle.

First, an investment's possible gains have to be weighed against its risks. More speculative investments have the greater potential for large gains, but also for heavy losses (eg shares in a new company intending to prospect for gold, which might either make a fortune or fail completely). On

---

[30] Trustees may (Trustee Act 2000 s 11), and commonly will, delegate their investment function to an agent. The agent may be appointed on its own terms (s 14); only where this is 'reasonably necessary', but market conditions mean that it often will be. Subject to that, the agent must (s 13) broadly speaking follow the same precepts as to the conduct of the function as would have applied to the trustee. The settlor may also introduce a protector, see n 20 above, in respect of investment.

[31] Individual settlors may impose an express duty, as does the law itself in certain cases (eg Trustee Act 1925 s 31: where income that would otherwise be payable to an infant beneficiary is instead retained and added to the trust capital, it must be invested).

[32] *Cowan v Scargill* [1985] Ch 270, 286. See section 7.5 for the question whether the law should take a different approach, together with discussion of an instance (where the trust property is land) where it appears to do so.   [33] Trustee Act 2000 s 4(2).

the other hand excessively cautious investments can equally result in loss, albeit by attrition rather than collapse (eg a basic savings account, which maintains its nominal capital value while inflation erodes its actual worth). Seeking the 'best' financial return involves striking a balance. Secondly, different types of investment will affect different beneficiaries in different ways. There is an economic trade-off between maximizing income and preserving or increasing capital value. Investments that are good for one are relatively poor for the other. So an investment that is advantageous for objects entitled in the present (like you in the example above) would be disadvantageous for those entitled in the future (like me), and vice versa. Again, a balance has to be struck. The law controls the way in which trustees strike these balances, and the choices of investments that they then go on to make.

To control the balances struck, the law uses the familiar technique of a requirement as to philosophy. The Trustee Act 2000 requires trustees to appraise investments in terms of their 'suitability to the trust'.[34] The more explicit traditional formulations may continue to give guidance. So as regards the balance between risk and caution, the philosophy should be the familiar one of an ordinary prudent businessman acting on behalf of others.[35] As regards the balance between income (for present beneficiaries) and capital (for future beneficiaries), the requirement used to be termed one of even-handedness,[36] but has been more recently expressed as one of fairness.[37] Especially operating together, these ideas point to a relatively conservative approach to investment. A prudent businessman investing on behalf of others and trying to be fair as amongst them would, in particular, not wish to place the capital at significant risk.[38]

---

[34] Section 4(3)(a). This duty is apparently not excludable by a settlor.

[35] *Re Whiteley* (1886) 33 Ch D 347, *Learoyd v Whiteley* (1887) 12 App Cas 727.

[36] *Raby v Ridehalgh* (1855) 7 De GM & G 104. As regards certain scenarios, the law translates this requirement into detailed rules, especially that in *Howe v Earl of Dartmouth* (1802) 7 Ves 137. The complexity and patchiness of these rules is problematic, however, and their abolition (leaving the more abstract requirement of even-handedness) has been recommended: Law Reform Committee 23rd Report *The powers and duties of trustees* Cmnd 8733 (1982) Part III.

[37] *Nestle v National Westminster Bank plc* [1993] 1 WLR 1260. The change may be one of substance: trustees are now said (*ibid* 1279) to be permitted, for example, to seek income at the expense of capital value so as to favour a poor beneficiary over a rich one, or a close relative of the settlor over a distant one. Presumably this conversion of the discretion from administrative to dispositive (cf section 9.1) is ascribable to the settlor's intentions.

[38] *Nestle v National Westminster Bank plc* [1993] 1 WLR 1260, 1284–5. As the unreported first instance judgment in the case asserted, however, the correct approach is not to view each investment in isolation, but to consider the exposure of the portfolio as a whole.

The trustees must then decide, as amongst the universe of 'suitable' investments, whether or not to acquire or retain a particular investment.[39] In so doing, they must, unless the settlor negates this, exercise reasonable care and skill.[40] In the present context, this standard requirement is partly explicated by rules that trustees must have regard to the need for diversity among the trust's investments, so far as is appropriate to its circumstances;[41] and that they must obtain and consider the advice of a person qualified to give it, unless they reasonably consider it unnecessary in the circumstances to do so.[42] Although phrases such as 'have regard to' and 'obtain and consider', and the possibility of not seeking advice at all, make these latter rules rather loose, the desirability of staying clearly within them nevertheless exerts a degree of pressure. Oddly, whilst the requirement to exercise reasonable care and skill can be negated by the settlor,[43] these latter rules apparently cannot.

Investment choices complying with these requirements as to philosophy and diligence and expertise will not be interfered with on the basis that a judge thinks them nonetheless inappropriate.[44] It is, however, possible to deny trustees certain choices altogether. Rules to this effect were once a feature of the law.[45] Before 1961, they forbade trustees from investing in company shares ('equities'), restricting them to assets such as government securities and real property interests. Prior to the late nineteenth century, this was a predictable position. Equities were not then a credible form of responsible investment. The law regulating companies' conduct was comparatively primitive, and, following such earlier debacles as the South Sea Bubble, from 1825 to 1866 there was a series of roughly decennial financial catastrophes. People were still lured into such investments, but there was a clear sense that they were foolish.[46] From the

---

[39] They may consult the beneficiaries as to their wishes, so long as they do not surrender their own ultimate discretion: *Fraser v Murdoch* (1881) 6 App Cas 855, Scotland. According to *X v A* [2000] 1 All ER 490, they *must* so consult, but this is unlikely, if only for impracticability. Where the trust is of land, however, they must (unless the settlor ordains otherwise) consult the beneficiaries and give effect to their majority wish, 'so far as consistent with the general interest of the trust': Trusts of Land and Appointment of Trustees Act 1996 s 11.

[40] Trustee Act 2000 s 1 (see at n 11 above), Sch 1 paras 1, 7.

[41] *Ibid* s 4(3)(b).

[42] *Ibid* s 5. The exception could apply to very small trusts and to trustees (including corporate trustees) who are themselves qualified to give the advice.

[43] *Ibid* Sch 1 para 7.   [44] *Tempest v Lord Camoys* (1882) 21 Ch D 571.

[45] For developments and their background during the important formative period of the nineteenth century, see J Anderson in W Cornish et al *The Oxford History of the Laws of England, Volume XII: 1820–1914 Private Law* (2010) Part One VI, 278–87.

[46] See Charles Dickens's *Little Dorrit* (1855–7), where Mr Clennam invests partnership (ie trust) money in Mr Merdle's undertakings, and is mortified as they then collapse. For

late nineteenth century on, the modern, more favourable, view of equity investment emerged, but the law did not fully reflect this shift until the Trustee Investments Act 1961 allowed trustees to invest in shares. This new facility extended only to half of the trust's property, however, and was subject to certain other restrictions. These limitations too were soon found unduly restrictive. They were removed by the Trustee Act 2000, which allows trustees to invest trust property in any way that would be open to them if they were its absolute owners,[47] and controls their decisions only in the manner described above.[48]

The investment of the assets of pension fund trusts and unit trusts is generally not subject to the regime of the 2000 Act.[49] Pension fund trusts are, however, in this respect governed by some essentially similar provisions of the Pensions Act 1995,[50] while the investment arrangements of unit trusts are governed by those trusts' own defining instruments, backed by financial services regulations.[51]

7.5 THE PRIMACY OF THE OBJECTS' (FINANCIAL) INTERESTS

It was stated above that trustees must act in the trust's best interests.[52] Various court rulings have assumed that this obliges trustees to seek the *best financial return* for the objects, both in the matter of investment and in managing the trust generally. For example, trustees selling trust property must allow gazumping, ie must renege on an informal agreement to accept a certain price if they later receive a higher offer.[53] They must take possession of the property that the settlor has placed in trust, even if it is in the hands of the beneficiaries' relatives and retrieving it from the latter will damage family relationships.[54] And they must choose investments with an eye to financial return rather than to the moral or political positions held

---

the background, see Dickens's 1857 Preface, and N Russell *The Novelist and Mammon* (1986).

[47] Section 3. The range of permitted investments can however be limited by the settlor: s 6. A settlor might for example insist on investment only in ethical funds.

[48] For an account and critique of these developments, see J Getzler (2009) 3 J Eq 219.

[49] Trustee Act 2000 ss 36, 37.

[50] Sections 34–6. The duty of care and skill (which remains defined by the traditional formulation) cannot be excluded: s 33.

[51] Again, the duty of care and skill cannot be excluded: Financial Services and Markets Act 2000 s 253.

[52] *Cowan v Scargill* [1985] Ch 270, 286.   [53] *Buttle v Saunders* [1950] 2 All ER 193.

[54] *Re Brogden* (1888) 38 Ch D 546.

by some of their beneficiaries, or argued, unverifiably, to be implicit in their charitable purposes.[55]

This equation between a duty to promote the objects' interests and one to maximize the financial benefit to them is not inevitable, however. Whilst the former cannot be excluded,[56] the latter certainly can be. An express or implied stipulation by the settlor can achieve this: as where say paintings, furniture, or jewellery are placed on trust for use as such, rather than to be sold and the proceeds invested for a yield;[57] or where a potential investment (eg in a tobacco company) would be indisputably antagonistic to the trust's purposes (prevention of heart disease).[58] Likewise an express or implied preference on the part of the beneficiaries themselves: a position held by all a trust's beneficiaries (say, against the drinking of alcohol) takes precedence over contradictory financial considerations (indicating, say, investment in a brewery).[59] If a sufficiently uncontroversial alternative conception of benefit could be identified, it might also in principle be possible for trustees to take a non-financial view of their beneficiaries' benefit, unless the settlor insisted otherwise. But in our culture it is questionable whether such a conception can be identified, though in another context the courts have found benefit for beneficiaries, outweighing financial loss, in various kinds of family well-being.[60]

Is it possible to go further, and suggest that trustees need not necessarily act in their objects' best (financial or non-financial) interests at all? The duty to do so has been said to be fundamental to the very idea of a trust,[61] and, as already noted, therefore not excludable even by the settlor,[62] though beneficiaries could presumably condone a breach of it.[63] Derived from this duty is the rule that trustees must not promote their own values over the objects' interests, where the two conflict.[64] (The argument that particular people or institutions are appointed trustees for their individual qualities, and so should not be required to disregard their own values,[65]

---

[55] *Cowan v Scargill* [1985] Ch 270; *Harries v Church Commissioners for England* [1992] 1 WLR 1241.   [56] See n 21 above.

[57] A very familiar instance is the holding of stately homes and their contents by charities such as the National Trust, but provisions for use by beneficiaries are also common in family trusts.

[58] *Harries v Church Commissioners for England* [1992] 1 WLR 1241, 1246–7.

[59] *Cowan v Scargill* [1985] Ch 270, 288.

[60] *Re T* [1964] Ch 158; *Re Weston's Settlements* [1969] 1 Ch 223; *Re CL* [1969] 1 Ch 587; *Re Remnant's Settlement Trusts* [1970] Ch 560: all dealing with the variation of trusts (section 10.5).   [61] *Armitage v Nurse* [1998] Ch 241, 253–4.

[62] See n 21 above.   [63] See section 10.3.

[64] *Cowan v Scargill* [1985] Ch 270, 286–8: see further section 11.10 for rules requiring trustees to avoid entering upon situations which might involve such a conflict.

[65] Cf sections 1.6, 11.8, 12.6.

is not detectable in the material on trustees' management duties.) So long as the effect is not to exclude all obligation to serve the objects, however, the law itself can instruct trustees to give priority to some competing goal of public policy. Various goals might be promoted at the expense of the objects' interests in this way. Given the vast amount of wealth that is tied up in trusts, a prominent concern might be the good of the economy. As we saw in section 2.5, economic liberalism is chary of trusts, because (at the lowest)[66] the caution associated with serving the interests of others militates against full exposure of the trust property to the market and so the maximization of wealth and happiness. To counteract that, trustees would need, in managing their trusts, to forget that they are trustees. At one point, the law briefly experimented with a rule ordering them to do so. Before it came to refer to the prudent businessman looking after the interests of others,[67] the formulation of the required philosophy instructed trustees to emulate an ordinary prudent man of business *acting on his own behalf*.[68] This approach was dropped presumably because it was felt to go too far in subordinating the objects' interests; indeed, it contradicts the idea that trustees always, as essential to the very trust concept, have a duty of acting honestly in the objects' best interests. Another impediment to the maximization of wealth is sometimes said to be the phenomenon of 'short-termism', whereby money is invested so as to produce an advantageous return in the short term, rather than for the long-term benefit of the economy. During the 1980s there was accordingly a proposal that the law should conscript a proportion of the assets of institutional investors, including large trusts, away from the service of their objects' interests to the financing of a national investment bank, whose remit would be the promotion of domestic industrial development; but this proposal was never implemented.[69]

At first sight, the fundamental necessity for trustees to serve their objects' interests seems to conflict with some rules whereby trustees may

---

[66] The ability to make any kind of investment available to an absolute owner (Trustee Act 2000 s 3(1)) now means that the problem is no worse than that; previously the law itself placed some forms of investment to some extent out of bounds for trusts. See section 7.4.

[67] *Re Whiteley* (1886) 33 Ch D 347, *Learoyd v Whiteley* (1887) 12 App Cas 727.

[68] *Speight v Gaunt* (1883) 22 Ch D 727, 739–40; 9 App Cas 1, 19.

[69] The idea was a minority recommendation in the *Report of the Committee to Review the Functioning of Financial Institutions* Cmnd 7937 (1980) ch 20, and was Labour Party policy for the 1983 and 1987 elections. An attempt by the National Union of Mineworkers to have the National Coal Board's pension fund invested along such lines (ahead of legislation) was the background to *Cowan v Scargill* [1985] Ch 270, which reaffirmed trustees' duty to secure the best financial return for their beneficiaries.

buy land for a beneficiary's occupation or 'for any other reason',[70] and that a beneficiary may, under certain circumstances, claim trust land for his occupation.[71] The occupying beneficiary can be regarded as choosing to enjoy his interest in a non-financial form. But as the assets concerned are in no way used for the benefit of the non-occupying beneficiaries,[72] the rules appear to exclude the duty to serve their interests. Perhaps, however, the idea is that trustees are given a discretion, to the extent of these rules, to suspend or destroy beneficiaries' interests: in which case those interests would not exist to be served. (Discretions to adjust beneficial interests are considered in Chapter 9.) But if all the beneficiaries' interests were destroyed in this way for the sake of 'any other reason', no trust would remain. The rules may not be fully supportable, therefore.

---

[70] Trustee Act 2000 s 8(1). The power can be excluded by the settlor: s 9(b). In addition (s 4(1)), the trustees of an express trust of land have a non-excludable power to retain the land, and are 'not liable in any way' for exercising this power, meaning that they can neglect the usual imperatives to benefit the trust objects, and to do so even-handedly.

[71] Trusts of Land and Appointment of Trustees Act 1996 ss 12, 13.

[72] The occupying beneficiary may (but not must) be charged rent (s 13(6)), but this is paid only to other beneficiaries who might have occupied the same land, and thus does not equate to an investment return for all the other beneficiaries to whom such a return would otherwise have been payable. See S Gardner *An Introduction to Land Law* 2nd edn (2009) 291–4.

8

Fixed Trusts

The point of an express trust is to confer benefits upon its objects. Sometimes this will be by the transfer of some or all of the capital; more often, at least for a period, the capital is held and invested to produce an income, as we saw in Chapter 7, and this income is paid to the objects. The essence of the operation, payment out according to the settlor's stipulations, is the same either way. In this chapter and Chapter 9 we shall look at what this operation involves.

On the face of it, payment out would seem a straightforward exercise. If the trust provides for the money to go to such-and-such a person, that seems to be the long and short of it: the trustees have to pay that person, no more and no less. There seem to be none of the questions of judgement that we found as regards management. In some trusts, in fact, matters are not so simple, because the settlor leaves the trustees to decide such questions as who shall be paid, how much, and when: this is the case in discretionary trusts, and in trusts equipped with powers of appointment, maintenance, and advancement. Here the actual business of payment is preceded by these discretionary activities on the part of the trustees, and the law's attitude to the conduct of the latter is a matter of interest in its own right. We shall look at that in Chapter 9. In the present chapter, we shall confine ourselves to the kind of trust, known as a 'fixed trust', where there is no such complication: the beneficiaries' entitlements are established by the settlor.

So, for example, trusts to pay '£1,000 to Adam', '£2,000 each to Adam and Briony', '£3,000 to be divided equally between Adam, Briony, and Caitlin' are all fixed trusts. But a trust providing for '£4,000 to be divided as my trustees think right between Adam, Briony, and Caitlin' would be a discretionary trust, which we are leaving for the moment.

8.1 DISTRIBUTION IN FIXED TRUSTS

The duty to pay the trust's objects is known as the 'duty to distribute'. The trustees must pay the correct amount to the designated object(s), and refrain from paying anyone else.

In some cases, the trustees have simply to follow the settlor's stipulation. In a trust to pay '£1,000 to Adam', for example, they have to pay Adam his £1,000, and not pay it to anyone other than Adam. Similarly with '£2,000 each to Adam and Briony': they have to pay Adam and Briony, and no one else, their £2,000 each. In cases of this kind the payment to each individual beneficiary is independent, and carrying it out requires no reference to any surrounding dispositions. In the case of '£1,000 to Adam' this is obvious: Adam is the only beneficiary. '£2,000 each to Adam and Briony' takes a moment's thought, but the point is that it consists of two dispositions, each of £2,000, one to Adam and one to Briony: it could equally well be expressed in the form '£2,000 to Adam; £2,000 to Briony'. A problem with one of the dispositions need have no repercussions on the other. So if there is no such person as Briony, it makes no difference to the position regarding Adam: he still gets his £2,000, no more and no less.

In other cases, there is an additional stage. Before the trustees come to make the actual payment, they need to calculate each beneficiary's entitlement. '£3,000 to be divided equally between Adam, Briony, and Caitlin' is a case of this kind. To know how much they have to pay each object, the trustees have to divide the total amount available (£3,000) by the number of objects (three). Such a trust is still fixed: the amounts of the beneficiaries' entitlements do not depend on the trustees' discretion. But its terms stipulate not the actual amount to be paid to each individual beneficiary, as in the cases covered in the last paragraph, but the arithmetical formula by which that amount is to be calculated. The trustees have to perform the calculation in order to arrive at a concrete figure. And in contrast to the cases covered in the last paragraph, the figure arrived at will vary with the circumstances. We saw a moment ago how, in the case of a trust to pay '£2,000 each to Adam and Briony', the non-existence of Briony made no difference to Adam: he still got his own £2,000, no more and no less. But in '£3,000 to be divided equally between Adam, Briony, and Caitlin', if there is no such person as Caitlin (say she has already died), Adam and Briony will each get £1,500 from the £3,000 that was to have been divided equally between the three, but now only two, of them.

8.2 THE NEED FOR CERTAINTY

According to the law's classical position (examined further in section 12.6), a disposition can be accepted as a valid trust only if it is guaranteed to be capable of enforcement.[1] That is, the trustees' duties—such as those

---

[1] *Morice v Bishop of Durham* (1804) 9 Ves 399, (1805) 10 Ves 522.

just described—must be capable of performance by them, and this performance must be susceptible to judicial scrutiny and if necessary intervention. This requirement can be seen as stemming from the provision of trusts as facilitative devices: in offering them to settlors as vehicles for giving effect to their wishes, the law has to ensure that they can be relied upon to do just that.

So say a settlor required his trustees 'to pay most of the income to my nicest grandchild, the rest to the others'. This instruction would be invalid, because the trustees and the court could not say how much (what is 'most'?) should be paid to whom (who is the 'nicest' grandchild?). The example shows how imprecision in the instructions to the trustees can entail the invalidity of the trust, because it can mean that the trustees' duties cannot be performed or supervised in the required way. Precision sufficient to the duty in question is needed—and in the example is lacking—both as to the amount of money to be paid ('certainty of subject matter') and as to the identity of the person to whom, or purpose upon which, it must be paid ('certainty of object').

8.3 CERTAINTY OF SUBJECT MATTER

As noted in section 1.9, a trust must have some property as its subject matter. So, whatever else it might be, an obligation not relating to the use of property could not be a trust. Likewise, a purported trust of 'the contents of my deposit account', when I have no deposit account, would have no effect.[2] Our present concern is with the further requirement, that the subject matter be well enough identified that the trustees and the court can know what it is.[3] This requirement applies both to the trust as a whole and, where different provisions are made for different objects of the trust, to the property dedicated to each provision.

References to particular assets, such as 'my house', will normally be sufficiently precise, unless there is a difficulty such as ambiguity (eg if I have two houses). But a problem seems to arise if the reference is to *an unseparated part of* an asset or collection of assets.[4] Say I declare a trust (ie create a trust with myself as trustee) of £1,000 out of the £20,000 that I in fact have, or of 100 of my 1,000 shares in X Co, in your favour, without ear-marking a particular £1,000 or 100 shares. How are we to know which £1,000 out of the £20,000, or which 100 of the 1,000 shares, are

---

[2] *MacJordan Construction Ltd v Brookmount Erostin Ltd (in receivership)* [1992] BCLC 350.

[3] See further P Parkinson [2002] CLJ 657, 663–76.

[4] See S Worthington [1999] JBL 1.

the subject matter of the trust, to be distributed to you? We might need to know this if, for example, I subsequently gamble away £10,000 of the £20,000 or 500 of the 1,000 shares. Do my losses include the £1,000 or 100 shares of which I declared myself trustee for you, or do they extend only to the assets that I retained as my own?

The courts have not allowed this problem to invalidate such trusts.[5] If the trust is valid, I (as trustee) incur duties to safeguard the trust property; notably, the duty to separate it, and keep it separate, from any other assets I may hold.[6] If I perform this duty, the £1,000 or 100 shares that will belong to the trust will thenceforth be separately identified, and it will be possible to say whether a later transaction on my part, such as a gambling loss, affects them or only my own property. If on the other hand I do not perform this duty, so that the £1,000 or 100 shares remain unseparated from my own assets, I have in effect wrongfully mixed them with the latter. In section 17.5, we shall encounter some rules—known as 'tracing' rules—which, among other things, allocate rights over the assets remaining in or emerging from mixtures that a trustee wrongfully makes between his trust property and his personal property. These rules will say, therefore, whether my gambling losses comprise the trust assets as well as my own. By this reasoning, the problem we initially identified falls away, and there remains no difficulty about regarding such dispositions as valid trusts.

But since this approach relies on the trustee to separate the trust assets out from the surrounding pool, or reacts to his failure to do so, there is a further difficulty if the assets in the pool are not all the same. Each £1 in my £20,000 is the same as any other, and all my shares in X Co are (let us say) of the same kind. So it does not matter which £1,000, or which 100 shares, go to the trust. But if I purport to declare myself trustee of, say, '10 hectares of my land', it does matter, because some of my land may be different from (more valuable than) the rest. Similarly with '20 cases from my stock of [some particular wine]', if we accept that the various bottles in my stock of that wine may likewise vary in quality. Unsurprisingly, then, it has been held that an unseparated part of a collection of heterogeneous assets cannot validly be placed on trust.[7]

---

[5] *Hunter v Moss* [1994] 1 WLR 452; *Re Harvard Securities Ltd (in liquidation)* [1998] BCC 567.   [6] See section 7.2.

[7] *Re London Wine Co (Shippers) Ltd* [1986] PCC 121. But in *Re Goldcorp Exchange Ltd (in receivership)* [1995] 1 AC 74, it was again held that no trust arose, even though the assets were gold bullion, ie homogeneous. To reflect this position, it is sometimes said that the trust can be valid only where the assets in question are *both* homogeneous *and* intangible (as shares are, and money, if in the form of the balance in a bank account, but not bullion). But this limitation

Even in the case of unseparated heterogeneous assets, however, it is not impossible to establish a valid trust. There is no uncertainty if the settlor places the entire set of assets—all his land, or all his stock of the particular wine—on trust for his intended object and himself. He might do this in one of two ways: first, by a discretionary trust,[8] leaving the trustee to choose which of the assets should go to the object, and which to the settlor; or, alternatively, by making his object and himself co-beneficiaries ('joint tenants', or 'tenants in common'), neither being allocated any particular part of the set of assets, which instead remain a single entity, held for the settlor and the object together, in proportion to their shares. Although straightforward in themselves, such constructions have not been much used by the courts to rescue otherwise unpromising trusts of unseparated assets, perhaps because they usually appear strained interpretations of the settlor's language. (While my declaration in your favour of a trust of 'half of my land' can fairly easily be read as making us co-beneficiaries, for example, it is harder to see one of '10 hectares of my land', when I in fact possess 20 hectares, in the same way.) Arguably, however, the courts ought to be readier to salvage such dispositions in these ways, by analogy with the devices they have adopted regarding certainty of objects and discussed in section 8.5.[9]

Finally, contrast expressions such as '£1,000', or '100 of my 1,000 shares in X Co', or '10 hectares of my land', or '20 cases from my stock of wine' with others such as 'most of my land', or 'the bulk of my money'. The latter suffer from yet a further difficulty. As well as not saying *which* among the relevant collection of assets shall be held on the trust, the settlor has not even said *how much* of it shall be. The courts have accordingly held trusts of this latter kind invalid.[10] But an apparently imprecise expression will be acceptable if the identification is supplied in some other way. 'Income' sounds vague, in that the income from an asset can vary over time, as for example interest rates change. But a trust to hold £1,000 on trust and pay the income as it arises to Adam will be valid, as by the time the trustee has to pay each instalment of income to Adam, the amount of that instalment

---

to intangible assets is unprincipled; the 'tracing' reasoning, yielding validity in the case of homogeneous assets, works as well where those assets are tangible as where they are intangible. The point is rather that the 'tracing' reasoning was simply not considered. The decision may nonetheless be accepted, however, on the ground that, on the particular facts, the parties could not realistically have intended a trust of the bullion at all, for other reasons.

[8] See Ch 9.

[9] The co-beneficiary technique has been statutorily introduced as the default position regarding sales of a particular quantity from a bulk: Sale of Goods Act 1979 s 20A.

[10] *Sprange v Barnard* (1789) 2 Bro CC 585; *Palmer v Simmonds* (1854) 2 Drew 221.

will necessarily have been established. Likewise, it is common for a testator to leave the 'residue' of his estate on trust: that is, the property left in his estate after the payment of particular legacies. 'Residue' sounds vague, but when the testator dies and his estate is reckoned up, which is the time from which the trust will come into effect, it will necessarily be possible to say precisely what constitutes the residue. So such a trust will be valid. A trust to pay a beneficiary 'a reasonable income' has also been held valid on the basis that 'a reasonable income' can be objectively determined,[11] but this may be thought optimistic. Beyond such cases, too, it should once again sometimes be possible to read a trust of this kind as requiring the trustee to decide how much of the property in question the designated object shall have, ie as a valid discretionary trust.

8.4 CERTAINTY OF OBJECTS

The trust's beneficiaries,[12] too, must be identified well enough for the performance of the duty to distribute.

Consider a perfect distribution, ie one in which the designated objects are correctly paid, period. Consider then its implications in terms of the identification of the beneficiaries. (In a moment we shall see that the law, deterred by the difficulty of the latter, does not in fact demand a perfect distribution, but this theoretically ideal position is the best place to start.) To avoid paying the wrong people, the trustees need to be able to tell whether any given person is or is not a beneficiary. But to go further and actually pay the right people, they need to know who the beneficiaries are, and be able to locate them. When the trust involves the further operation of quantifying the beneficiaries' entitlements, they also need to know how many beneficiaries there are, because this information will always figure in the calculation. Remember our example of '£3,000 to be divided equally between Adam, Briony, and Caitlin'. To know whether Adam should be paid £1,000 or £1,500 or £3,000, they need to know whether the £3,000 has to be shared equally with two other people (Briony and Caitlin), or one (Briony or Caitlin), or none.

There are in fact four different kinds of information involved in all this, and it will be helpful to separate them.[13]

---

[11] *Re Golay* [1965] 1 WLR 969.
[12] Or purposes: essentially the same considerations will apply.
[13] See generally C Emery (1982) 98 LQR 551.

To be able to know who is a beneficiary and who is not, so as not to pay the wrong people, would require two kinds. First, that the description of beneficiaries used in the trust should be precise enough that one could say in principle (ie assuming that the facts are clear) whether someone matched it or not. This quality is called 'conceptual[14] certainty'. So something like 'Adam Smith, of [his address]', or 'my husband', will normally be valid. But 'my old friends', for example, will not. We might have no doubt about people's relations with the settlor, but not know whether or not they fitted the description because we are unsure what kind, degree, or duration of amity the description requires. Secondly, given conceptual certainty, it would need to be possible to determine whether someone matched the description on the facts. This requirement is called 'evidential[15] certainty'. For example, the description might be 'the former employees of X Co'. As a description, this seems perfectly clear, but if the company's premises have been burnt down and some of the former employees have lost their old payslips and so on, it might be impossible for the trustees to know whether they fit it or not.

Thirdly, in those cases where quantification is needed as a prelude to distribution, the trustees would need to be able to know the total number of beneficiaries. Conceptual and evidential certainty alone, equipping the trustees to say whether people are beneficiaries *when they claim*, would not suffice for this.[16] To perform the calculations required to quantify the beneficiaries' shares, the trustees would need to enumerate—know the number of—the beneficiaries: and to do so even if the beneficiaries do not come forward to claim. In the instance '£3,000 to be divided equally between Adam, Briony, and Caitlin', for example, in order to know whether to pay Adam £1,000, or £1,500, or £3,000, the trustees would need to know whether Adam is the only extant beneficiary or whether he has to share the £3,000 with one or with two others, ie whether Briony and Caitlin exist: and they must be able to know this even if no one claiming to be Briony or Caitlin presents herself. (As in this example, the usual way of knowing the number is to identify—though not necessarily locate—those entitled, and so the requirement is often referred to as one for a 'complete list' of beneficiaries. But in principle the crucial information is the number.)

---

[14] Or 'semantic', or 'linguistic', or 'definitional'.   [15] Or 'factual'.

[16] Some accounts use the expression 'evidential certainty' to refer, without distinction, to the two issues which the text insists on separating, namely (reactive) evidential certainty and (proactive) enumerability.

A description that might be deficient in this respect is 'all the descendants of Y'. If a settlor created a trust to divide £10,000 between 'all the descendants of Y', there might be no conceptual or (given DNA testing) evidential uncertainty, ie no obstacle to deciding on the entitlement of anyone who claimed; but the trustees might well not be able to discover the total number involved, so as to put a figure on the individual entitlements.

Fourthly, a perfect performance of the duty to distribute would involve not just knowing who are the right people and who are not, and sometimes working out the size of the right people's entitlements, *but also actually paying them*. To do this, the trustees would need to be able to find them. This goes further even than the requirement that we have just discussed. That did not involve the trustees actually being able to find the beneficiaries; just being able to know how many they were, so as to calculate their shares. Physically to pay money over to someone, it is necessary to locate them.

In short, then, for a perfect performance of the duty to distribute in a fixed trust, there would need to be conceptual and evidential certainty as to the identity of the beneficiaries, and knowledge of their whereabouts. In cases where the trustees have to quantify the beneficiaries' shares, they would also need to be able to know of the beneficiaries' existence; but in fact this does not demand anything extra, because it is subsumed within the ability to locate them.

If it represented the law, this position would be extremely exigent. The possibility, for example, that the trustees might not be able to perform their duty actually to pay out to the beneficiaries would apparently invalidate a purported trust. Such a possibility would be almost inevitable, for a beneficiary might disappear at any moment. The implication is that valid trusts would be more or less unknown. To put it mildly, that would pose a problem for the facilitative project. Trusts are supposed to offer a legal facility by which people can make certain kinds of dispositions. There would be little point in offering such a facility if people had to meet such impossible certainty requirements in order to take advantage of it.

The problem arises from the nature of the operations that appear to be required of trustees. As we have seen, a perfect distribution requires trustees to clear a number of practical hurdles, and the certainty requirements have to anticipate the difficulties inherent in these. To enable the certainty requirements to be relaxed, so allowing sensible access to the facility after all, therefore, the law does not in fact seek a perfect distribution. There are several rules that require less of trustees.

8.5 DILUTING THE REQUIRED DISTRIBUTION

These rules exist in relation to each of the four aspects of certainty that we considered above.

Take first the need to be able to locate the beneficiaries, so as to pay them their entitlements.

The problem is that a beneficiary might disappear at any time, making it impossible to guarantee that this duty can be performed. The law's solution has been to allow trustees to discharge their duty to pay out the money without it necessarily reaching the hands of the designated objects. If a beneficiary cannot be found, his share can be paid into court, whence he can claim it if and when he turns up. Moreover, in certain relatively safe cases a missing beneficiary's share can be paid to other beneficiaries instead. If either there is evidence that a beneficiary is dead, or he is presumed to be, as having disappeared for seven years, or if he has failed to respond to advertisements placed in newspapers, the trustees can[17] obtain a court order permitting them to administer the trust in disregard of his claim.[18] Thus, if he is an object of a trust requiring money to be shared between a number of objects, the trustees can divide his share amongst the other objects. Relaxing the duty to pay out to the designated objects in these ways, then, means that there is no need to be able to locate them after all: so this requirement is in effect removed.

The difficulty of knowing the total number of beneficiaries, so as to quantify their shares in trusts where that is necessary, has been eased by placing special meanings on some of the most frequently used descriptions, so as to confine them to groups whose numbers are likely to be easily discoverable. 'My relatives', for example, could be troublesome.

---

[17] Arguably, not 'can' but 'should'. Since trustees' options must be exercised in the best interests of all their beneficiaries, and since a decision to leave missing beneficiaries out of account would evidently contravene that rule, as palpably not in those beneficiaries' interests, the facility surely cannot viably exist as an *option*. Whereas a *duty* to exclude could comprise a recognition that the facility sacrifices the interests of missing beneficiaries, together with a judgement on the law's part that it is right to do so.

[18] *Re Benjamin* [1902] 1 Ch 723; Trustee Act 1925 s 27 (though the latter does not apply to all kinds of trust). These devices do not immediately destroy the unpaid beneficiary's entitlement. If, up to six years later, he turns up after all, he can reclaim his share from those to whom it has been paid over. But they absolve the trustees from the breach of their duty to pay the beneficiary which they would otherwise have committed, and for which they would have been obliged to compensate him. A different approach is for the trustees to accept the risk of being in breach, but to buy (at the trust's expense) 'missing beneficiary insurance' to cover their liability if the missing beneficiary reappears and claims against them.

Meaning all those connected with the settlor by blood, it is conceptually certain, and let us assume that there is no problem with evidential certainty, but trustees might well find it hard to know the number of such people off their own bat. So the law presumes that 'my relatives' means instead only the settlor's statutory next-of-kin, which is likely to be a much tighter class, with a much better prospect of enumerability.[19] This device is obviously, however, useful only in certain cases, rather than across the board. A more generalized palliative seems not to have been devised.[20]

Evidential certainty is in principle necessary so as to distribute to the true beneficiaries, and to no one else. It is the ability to know whether, on the facts, any given person is or is not entitled to payment. The problem is that there is always at least a strong chance that the answer might be unclear. This time the response is to say that it is up to the putative beneficiary to prove, on a balance of probabilities, that he fits the trust's description of its beneficiaries. If he cannot prove that he does, then it is taken that he does not.[21] So as far as evidential matters are concerned, then, the trustees' apparent duty to pay the right people and not the wrong people becomes instead one of paying those, but only those, who can prove themselves entitled. The requirement of evidential certainty is thus virtually eliminated: so long as the description used is of a nature that it is not

---

[19] This presumption operates only as a palliative to difficulties of enumerability; in cases where such difficulties do not arise, 'relatives' is given its more natural wider meaning of all blood relations: *Re Poulton's Will Trusts* [1987] 1 WLR 795. In the discretionary trust case *Re Baden's Deed Trusts (No 2)* [1973] Ch 9, Stamp LJ (at 27–9), in a minority on this point, used the device so as to allow the listing of beneficiaries (if not complete, then close to it) which he wrongly thought to be required in that context.

[20] It may however be suggested that a generalized device could be found, by extension of existing 'class-closing rules'. Where trustees are to distribute to a class which at the moment is open ended, eg 'my grandchildren' (some of whom may not yet have been born), these rules allow the class to be closed off to those members who already exist. The calculations and distribution are then made solely on this basis: a future-born grandchild cannot claim a share back from those thus paid. The idea is that the settlor's intention for his existing grandchildren to have some money is higher than his wish to benefit all his grandchildren. As it stands, this device does not help in the case where, amongst the beneficiaries who already exist, there may be some whom the trustees do not know about. But could not a similar approach be used to allow the trustees to divide the fund only between those beneficiaries who are known to them? It would mean attributing to the settlor the higher intention of saving his trust from invalidity; which seems no less plausible than the higher intention that supports the present form of the class-closing rules, or than the special meaning given, where helpful, to the word 'relatives'.

[21] *Re Baden's Deed Trusts (No 2)* [1973] Ch 9, 19–20, Sachs LJ; the remaining judges do not address the issue. The case deals with discretionary trusts, but it should apply equally to the fixed trusts under discussion here, as the relevant duty—paying (only) objects—is the same in both.

impossible for people to show that they fit it, which is hardly likely, potential evidential difficulties will not be a reason for invalidity.

The same technique is also used to reduce difficulties of conceptual certainty. Again, it is up to the claimant to show on a balance of probabilities that he is within the description—but this time in the sense that the meaning of the description used is such as to embrace him. So a description will be sufficiently certain so long as it is possible for a claimant to do that: that is, so long as the description is not devoid of any clear meaning at all. Take the description 'my old friends'. Although this has a large grey area in which it is hard to say whether a person qualifies, it also has a recognizable core meaning (we could think of at least one 'old friend', even if only hypothetically). So the description is valid in itself; and actual claimants are then left to show that it covers someone like them. This approach was originally taken in *Re Allen*.[22] In *Re Gulbenkian's Settlement Trusts*,[23] however, it was disapproved in favour of the purist view, deduced in section 8.4, whereby the terms of the description must allow one to say definitely whether or not any given person fits it. This decision concerned powers of appointment rather than fixed trusts, but the requirement of conceptual certainty is aimed at the duty of not paying the wrong people, which is common to all types of disposition, and so ought to be the same across the board. However, in the context of fixed trusts *Re Gulbenkian's Settlement Trusts*[24] has not been followed: the more lenient approach in *Re Allen*[25] was taken up again in *Re Barlow's Will Trusts*,[26] and that is the present position.

8.6 DUTIES, CERTAINTY, AND THE FACILITATIVE PROJECT

In short, then, the theoretically ideal notion of distribution under a fixed trust is that payment should be made to all those, and only those, designated by the settlor. But a trust has to be guaranteed operable in order to be valid, and a duty to distribute in this form would demand so much in the way of certainty that in all probability no trust would ever be valid. In reality, the certainty requirements for fixed trusts are less daunting.

We have examined the devices used to produce these lower certainty requirements. They are various in their juridical nature. Some, for

---

[22] [1953] Ch 810.
[23] [1970] AC 508; followed for discretionary trusts in *McPhail v Doulton* [1971] AC 424.
[24] [1970] AC 508.   [25] [1953] Ch 810.   [26] [1979] 1 WLR 278.

example, are put in terms of an interpretation of the words used, others in terms of burdens of proof. But essentially, they all address what is required of the trustees by way of distribution. In place of the ideal of paying all those, and only those, designated by the settlor, with all the difficulties we have found that to entail, they imply a qualified duty, which demands less certainty. Trustees must pay people who can show on a balance of probabilities that they fit the settlor's description, conceptually and evidentially, and not those who cannot; and if they cannot find a particular person whom they are supposed to pay, they can generally administer the trust in disregard of his entitlement, or pay the money into court. Where trustees need first to quantify the beneficiaries' shares, and so need to know the entire number of beneficiaries, they are commonly instructed to take a specially narrow view of who the beneficiaries are.

At first sight, such dilution of what is required in respect of distribution arguably means that the law fails to respect the settlor's wishes, and so loses sight of its facilitative mission. The settlor might well want payment to all those, and only those, whom he has designated. He might say, for example, that by the expression 'my relatives' he really does mean all his blood relatives, and not just his statutory next-of-kin.

But when we introduce the consideration of certainty requirements, it seems likely that the settlor would change his view. Distribution in accordance with the ideal can never take place because the law, seeking only to offer the trust facility where it can ensure performance,[27] and realizing that it cannot do so if the performance has to be in accordance with the ideal, will not allow the trust to come into effect. For the settlor to persist in demanding the ideal would then be quixotic. He would probably accept the diluted arrangements for distribution, for the sake of their more easily satisfied certainty requirements, and so the possibility of making a valid trust at all. It is plausible, then, that the package deal that the law has devised, involving a qualified form of the duty of distribution and a lower certainty requirement, is the best compromise: the most convincing overall representation of what settlors want, and so, in fact, facilitatively the best response after all.

As well as being explained above, the resultant rules about certainty of objects are summarized—along with those relevant to discretionary trusts and powers of appointment—in section 9.8.

---

[27] *Morice v Bishop of Durham* (1804) 9 Ves 399, (1805) 10 Ves 522.

9

Dispositive Discretions

In Chapter 8 we looked principally at fixed trusts, ie those in which the settlor tells the trustees whom to pay, how much, and when. Sometimes, however, a settlor will give his trustees the task or option of deciding such matters for themselves. Such a task or option is a 'dispositive discretion'. In the present chapter, we look at the questions that arise when trustees are given a dispositive discretion.

9.1 FIXED STIPULATIONS AND ADMINISTRATIVE AND DISPOSITIVE DISCRETIONS

The characteristic of a fixed trust, as we noted in Chapter 8, is that the settlor stipulates the objects of the trust and their entitlements (either concretely, or by laying down an arithmetical formula for arriving at a concrete result). We have seen[1] how the law in fact replaces the settlor's specification with a more subtle and qualified one calculated to make the trustees' task more practicable. But this substitute is still essentially fixed. The trustees have to use their judgement at certain points. For example, they have to decide whether a putative claimant has demonstrated on a balance of probabilities that he is entitled. This is a matter for their judgement in the sense that there will sometimes be no clear answer. But they are supposed to approach it in an objective spirit. They are not asked or entitled to make active choices whether or not to pay somebody some money.

But the law also allows settlors to provide that their trustees should make such active choices: that is, to exercise discretion. Settlors very commonly avail themselves of this option. It is a valuable one at several levels. At the lowest, it would be inefficient for a settlor to stipulate in fixed terms every step his trustees must take: as regards many matters, there

[1] See section 8.5.

will be little danger in leaving trustees to work things out for themselves, and it will be a waste of time to give them detailed instructions. It would be absurd, for example, for a settlor to prescribe the brand of stationery his trustees should buy. Then, a settlor who stipulates everything in fixed terms, according to what seems advisable at the time of creating the trust, will leave his trust vulnerable to changes in circumstances over the time of its existence, which can be long. He can solve the problem by giving the trustees discretion to decide how to proceed. For instance, a settlor who prescribed the exact investments his trustees were to make would very likely prevent them from using more appropriate alternatives at some stage, even if not at the outset. Especially the latter point is true not only as regards matters of management but also of the trust's very beneficial interests (or purposes). A settlor, realizing that his original configuration of those interests may turn out to be inappropriate—as, for instance, if a beneficiary proves in an unforeseen way unworthy of his beneficence— can give his trustees discretion to alter that configuration, by deciding afresh whom to pay, and/or how much, and/or when. Such a discretion is especially used to deal with foreseeably but unpredictably changing needs, such as the requirements of growing children or elderly persons. Indeed, the settlor can even leave the trustees to configure the beneficial interests from the outset (with or without the option of changing them thereafter), which is especially helpful if the interests are not to come into effect immediately, or as a means of effectuating a wish that beneficial interests shall reflect degrees of need or desert.

Trustees' discretions are commonly sorted into two types, 'administrative' and 'dispositive'. Dispositive discretions are intended to allow a structuring or restructuring of the beneficiaries' interests, whilst administrative discretions are not. The significance of the distinction[2] is that (it follows) trustees with an administrative discretion must exercise it even-handedly as between the beneficiaries:[3] whereas trustees given a dispositive discretion are on the contrary expected to make the sort of choices, which will often involve favouring one possible object at the expense of another, that a settlor would otherwise make.[4]

Discretions in which trustees are explicitly or implicitly asked to make choices of the latter kind are thus inevitably classed as dispositive. Discretions in which they are told not to make such choices can only be

---

[2] *Pearson v IRC* [1981] AC 753, 785.
[3] *Raby v Ridehalgh* (1855) 7 De GM & G 104; *Re Whiteley* (1886) 33 Ch D 347; *Learoyd v Whiteley* (1887) 12 App Cas 727.
[4] *Edge v Pensions Ombudsman* [2000] Ch 602, 618–21, 627.

administrative. Some, however, neither require nor rule out such choices. A discretion of this kind could fall into either class: in principle it is for the settlor, though in practice usually for the judges, to say whether or not the trustees are to act even-handedly in exercising it. Traditionally, the discretions found in the management of trusts (described in Chapter 7) were normally taken as administrative. In particular, the discretion to select investments for the trust assets was regarded thus, meaning that choices had to be made that did not, in particular, favour capital growth (and so future beneficiaries) at the expense of current income (and so present beneficiaries), or vice versa.[5] But recently, and perhaps controversially, this discretion has been redefined as dispositive, permitting trustees to angle their choices so as, say, to favour a poor beneficiary over a rich one, or a close relative of the settlor over a distant one.[6]

Can allowing trustees the option of creating especially dispositive discretions be understood in terms of facilitative logic? Certainly, in recognizing such discretions, the law goes beyond the idea of 'giving effect to a settlor's wishes' in the sense required to explain the recognition of fixed trusts. Instead, it fulfils the wishes of those settlors who choose to operate by leaving the crystallization of their project to at least some extent to others. This extension can be understood in terms of the thinking developed in section 2.2, where the facilitative thesis was rooted in the liberal argument that people should be accorded the largest possible degree of autonomy regarding their actions. According (therefore) the owner of some property the greatest possible freedom as to how he deals with it means effectuating not only his fixed stipulations regarding it, but also such arrangements as he may wish to make whereby it is controlled by the decisions of others.[7] It should also be noted, although it is not essential to this argument, that trustees operating such discretions are commonly, and it seems properly,[8] guided by what they understand of the settlor's own views regarding the issue, or kind of issue, facing them.

We looked at the operation of the principal administrative discretions regarding management in Chapter 7. The remainder of this chapter

---

[5]   *Raby v Ridehalgh* (1855) 7 De GM & G 104; *Re Whiteley* (1886) 33 Ch D 347; *Learoyd v Whiteley* (1887) 12 App Cas 727.

[6]   *Nestle v National Westminster Bank plc* [1993] 1 WLR 1260, 1279. See further section 7.4.

[7]   *Re Beatty* [1990] 1 WLR 1503 explicitly considers whether dispositive discretions can be reconciled with the facilitative nature of testamentary trusts in particular, and answers in the affirmative.

[8]   *Breadner v Granville-Grossman* [2001] Ch 523, [20]–[22]. Trustees given a discretion must not however cede judgement entirely to the settlor, or indeed anyone else: *Turner v Turner* [1984] Ch 100 (see section 9.5).

concerns the nature of, and the problems presented by, the main instances of dispositive discretion.

9.2 VARIETIES OF DISPOSITIVE DISCRETIONS

We shall look particularly at five of the most important types of dispositive discretion: discretionary trusts; powers of appointment; powers of accumulation; powers of maintenance; and powers of advancement.

In a *discretionary trust*,[9] the settlor defines a class of people—such as the members of a family, or the employees of a company—and stipulates that the available property has to be distributed to members of this class, but leaves it to the trustees to decide what, if (normally) anything,[10] each particular individual in the class will receive. Dispositions such as '£10,000 to be divided as my trustees shall decide amongst my children' and '£50,000 to be divided as my trustees think best among the employees of X Co' would be discretionary trusts.

Discretionary trusts were at one time commonly used in family contexts to avoid certain tax liabilities. The fact that the beneficiaries' entitlements lay in the trustees' discretion left them insufficiently concrete to attract the fiscal rules as these were then framed.[11] Also in family contexts, and more enduringly, the discretion provides the flexibility to respond to changing circumstances: the needs of the children, for example, as their lives take shape and move in one direction or another, or those of an elderly person who may begin to find difficulty in managing his own affairs and meeting the expense of special medical or residential requirements. A particular instance of this is the 'protective trust',[12] where a beneficiary is given a fixed interest until (broadly) such time as he goes bankrupt, whereupon he loses that interest and instead becomes one of a number of beneficiaries of a discretionary trust. This device enables his entitlement to be kept out of the hands of his creditors (it may be thought surprising that the law should permit, indeed support, this),[13] while allowing him to continue in practice to be provided for.

---

[9] Or 'trust power', though that expression is, confusingly, also used with other meanings.

[10] Though trustees might, for example, be asked to decide which of two beneficiaries shall enjoy each of two houses.

[11] For the lack of concreteness of interests under a discretionary trust generally, see *Gartside v IRC* [1968] AC 553 (see section 12.3).

[12] A standard form is provided in the Trustee Act 1925 s 33.   [13] Cf section 2.5.

Discretionary trusts are also extensively used to confer benefits on deserving cases amongst large constituencies, in much the same way as charitable trusts, but without the charitable status. For example, such trusts often provide for payments amongst the employees of a company or their dependants. A trust for such a constituency will not normally be charitable;[14] providing essentially private fringe benefits to the employees rather than a public benefit, it does not merit the special treatment (especially tax exemption) given to charities, as explained in sections 6.1–6.2. But just as might occur in a similar charitable trust, a discretion is given so as to avoid the difficulty of defining 'a deserving case' in advance; and so as to allow the amount paid to reflect the degree of desert, for which it would be hard to stipulate in a fixed formula.

Powers of appointment are quite similar to discretionary trusts. Again, there is provision for assets to be distributed to members of a class, the selection of the actual recipients and the fixing of the amounts they are each to receive being left to the trustees. (Or sometimes these are left to other 'appointors',[15] though the trust within which the power is located continues to be in trustees' hands.)[16] The difference is that whereas in discretionary trusts the trustees are required to pay out all the available property to members of the class, in powers of appointment they are not. Any property that they do not pay to members of the class—which might even be all of it—goes instead to people known as the 'takers in default of appointment' (because they take the property if the trustees do not exercise their power to 'appoint' it to members of the class). So an example of a power of appointment would be '£10,000 for my children so far as my trustees may think fit, but otherwise to my widow absolutely'. The children are the objects of the power; the widow is the taker in default.[17]

---

[14] See section 6.5; *Oppenheim v Tobacco Securities Trust Co Ltd* [1951] AC 297; cf *Dingle v Turner* [1972] AC 601.

[15] Especially in off-shore jurisdictions, a non-trustee appointor may be referred to as a 'protector', particularly where his role is to introduce the settlor's thinking into the operation of the power. See D Waters in A Oakley (ed) *Trends in Contemporary Trust Law* (1996) ch 4.

[16] Appointors can be potential recipients themselves: eg a trust of two houses, 'one to be chosen by Adam for himself, the other for Briony' (cf *Boyce v Boyce* (1849) 16 Sim 476). This may be the best way to understand cases in which a trust applied only to such property as remained in the trustee's hands at his death: *Birmingham v Renfrew* (1937) 57 CLR 666, Australia; *Ottaway v Norman* [1972] Ch 698; *Re Cleaver (deceased)* [1981] 1 WLR 939; *Re Goodchild (deceased)* [1996] 1 WLR 694. Writing such an arrangement into a *fiduciary* power may be awkward, however, given the duties of such a power's appointor (see text below), which may jar with the necessary toleration of self-interest; but cf n 44.

[17] Two types of power arrangement may be confusing at first sight. First, the objects of the power and the takers in default may be the same people: eg '£10,000 for my children so far as my trustees may think fit, but otherwise to be divided between my children equally'. Secondly,

Traditionally, such dispositions were seen as primarily trusts for the takers in default, but with an option for the trustees to give the property to other people, the objects of the power, if they felt it right to do so.[18] On this view, the objects of the power were 'Cinderellas', the passive recipients of fortuitous bounty if the trustees happened to exercise the power in their favour, rather than having any real entitlement: that was the monopoly of the takers in default.[19] So although the legal effect is the same either way, the real flavour is better sensed if the wording of the example is reversed: if instead of '£10,000 for my children so far as my trustees may think fit, but otherwise to my widow absolutely', we put it in the form '£10,000 for my widow absolutely, except to the extent (if any) that my trustees think fit to appoint to my children instead'. This perception reflects the traditional use of such arrangements in family contexts, their primary provision being a fixed stipulation for the taker(s) in default, the power to appoint differently being inserted so as to allow for the unforeseen.

At one point, powers of appointment came to be used in order to minimize tax liability. This usage traded on the idea, just explained, that the interests of a power's objects were not entitlements but merely hopes of having the power exercised in one's favour. But whilst that idea genuinely reflected the conception of powers of appointment as traditionally used, it did not correspond to the reality of these arrangements aimed at avoiding tax. In the latter, it was understood that in practice the money would be paid to at least some objects of the power (generally members of the settlor's family), and not left for the takers in default. So (certain of) the objects of the power were the true centre of attention; the takers in default were decoys. In time, this new conception of the realities of powers of

where the terms make it clear that (unlike in a discretionary trust) the trustees do not have to pay all the available money out to the members of the class, but do not specify who is the taker in default; the answer being the settlor himself, under a resulting trust: eg '£10,000 from which my trustees may, if they think fit, make payments to my children'.

[18] *Re Somes* [1896] 1 Ch 250, 255; *Vatcher v Paull* [1915] AC 372, 379; *Re Greaves* [1954] Ch 434, 446.

[19] It seems to follow that, unlike objects of trusts, objects of powers of appointment were not required to be people at all; since they had no rights even if they were, they could just as well be animals or non-charitable purposes. *Re Douglas* (1887) 35 Ch D 472, sometimes cited in support, does not deal explicitly with the issue, and is equivocal in what it appears to assume about it. But the thesis may be accepted in *Re Harpur's Will Trusts* [1962] Ch 78, 91, and is assumed correct by the Ontario Perpetuities Act 1966 s 16 and similar statutory provisions, reconstructing failed purpose trusts as valid purpose powers. *Barclays Bank Ltd v Quistclose Investments Ltd* [1970] AC 567 and analogous cases are said to feature a purpose power (*Twinsectra Ltd v Yardley* [2002] 2 AC 164, [13], cf [77]–[100]), but always to date one for the benefit of a certain person or persons, and so analogous to the type of purpose trust validated by *Re Denley's Trust Deed* [1969] 1 Ch 373 (see section 12.3).

appointment was reflected in a new construction of their legal nature, which obtains today under the name of a 'fiduciary power'.[20] Although the development may not be quite complete,[21] the essential idea is that appointing under the power and allowing the money to go over in default are equipollent options, the trustees having an even choice as between them, and the objects of the power having rights as powerful as those of the takers in default. (The old conception continues to apply to 'non-fiduciary' powers.[22] But a judge commonly has scope to characterize a power either way, and the burgeoning of the fiduciary category reveals the current attraction of the latter. It is sometimes said that a non-fiduciary power may be more readily found in a family trust,[23] but the cases in which fiduciary powers have been developed do not obviously bear this out. There may, however, be a tendency against finding a power to be fiduciary where the appointor is not otherwise a trustee.)

A *power of accumulation* is like a power of appointment in involving a trust, for the taker(s) in default of accumulation, which the trustees may override by choosing to exercise their power. Here, the overriding takes the form of keeping back income from the trust's investments, which would otherwise be payable to the taker(s) in default, and (unless the terms stipulate otherwise) adding it to the assets invested—that is, turning it into capital. Trustees exercising the power will thus benefit beneficiaries entitled in the future, as the latter will receive more (whether the enlarged capital itself or the increased income flowing from the enlarged capital), at the expense of those entitled in the present.[24] Like powers of appointment, powers of accumulation came to be used in an attempt to minimize tax liability, as the theoretical emphasis remained on the trust in default of accumulation while the real expectation was that there would

---

[20] The development is visible especially in *Re Gestetner Settlement* [1953] Ch 672, 688; *Re Gulbenkian's Settlement Trusts* [1970] AC 508, 518 (but cf 521, 524–5); *McPhail v Doulton* [1971] AC 424, 449; *Re Manisty's Settlement* [1974] Ch 17, 25–6; *Re Hay's Settlement Trusts* [1982] 1 WLR 202, 209–10; *Mettoy Pension Trustees Ltd v Evans* [1990] 1 WLR 1587, 1614, 1617–18; *Breadner v Granville-Grossman* [2001] Ch 523, [49]. It is reviewed with apparent approval in *Schmidt v Rosewood Trust Ltd* [2003] 2 AC 709, [56]–[64].

[21] There remains no remedy if trustees wrongfully fail to consider exercising a fiduciary power within the time allowed: *Re Allen-Meyrick's Will Trusts* [1966] 1 WLR 499, 505; *Breadner v Granville-Grossman* [2001] Ch 523, [52]–[53].

[22] *Mettoy Pension Trustees Ltd v Evans* [1990] 1 WLR 1587, 1613–14.

[23] *Imperial Group Pension Trust Ltd v Imperial Tobacco Ltd* [1991] 1 WLR 589, 597; *Mettoy Pension Trustees Ltd v Evans* [1990] 1 WLR 1587, 1618.

[24] Contrast a *duty* to accumulate, ie a situation where the settlor stipulates that the trustees must (subject to any powers to do otherwise) add income as it arises to the trust's capital. Here, there is no otherwise-entitled beneficiary whose interests are harmed by the accumulation in the way that there is in the case of a *power* to accumulate.

be an accumulation. But, also in parallel with the story regarding fiduciary powers of appointment, just noted, the courts came to realign their
perception of the theoretical with the practical, regarding the possibility
of accumulation and the trust in default of it as options of equal validity,
between which trustees have an even choice.[25]

A *power of maintenance* allows trustees to pay out trust income for an
infant beneficiary's upbringing, schooling, etc, when otherwise they would
have to accumulate it. A paternalistically cautious regime normally gov-
erns the position of beneficiaries who are children. They are not generally
trusted simply to receive the trust income as cash in the way that they
would if they were adults. The income that would otherwise have been
payable to them is accumulated into the capital. But a power of maintenance enables trustees to devote some or all of the income to (what adults
regard as) their infant beneficiaries' proper expenses. The usual version of
this power, which is set out in s 31 of the Trustee Act 1925, gives trustees
discretion to apply the available income for an infant beneficiary's 'maintenance, education or benefit'. Unless the settlor stipulates otherwise,[26] the
section automatically implies this provision for accumulation and maintenance into all trusts where income would otherwise have been payable
to an infant beneficiary. A power of maintenance is much narrower than a
discretionary trust or power of advancement or accumulation. It merely
provides for the accelerated expenditure on the beneficiary in question of
money that was ultimately to go to him anyway. That money is not taken
from other beneficiaries.[27]

A *power of advancement* applies where a beneficiary is due to become
entitled to trust capital—not just income—at some time in the future,
and allows the trustees to anticipate his entitlement by paying him some
or all of the capital to which he will eventually succeed. Just as it may be a
good idea to spend income to provide for children's education and so on
ahead of their unfettered entitlement to it, it is felt sensible sometimes also
to be able to pay over capital to a beneficiary early: say, if he needs to buy
a house. Section 32 of the Trustee Act 1925 gives the standard version of

---

[25] *Pearson v IRC* [1981] AC 753, deciding that a beneficiary under the trust in default of
accumulation does not have an 'interest in possession': given the possibility of deprivation by
accumulation, his interest is too unstable to be so described. The result was that tax was payable which would otherwise have been avoided.   [26] Trustee Act 1925 s 69(2).

[27] Other rules commonly found in association with the power of maintenance can have the
latter effect, however. By these rules, income is sometimes treated as payable to a beneficiary
(and so, if he is a child, accumulated into a beneficiary's capital and/or applied to his maintenance) even if his interest lies in the future, and therefore is uncertain ever to come into effect:
eg if he is to gain an interest only if and when he reaches the age of 18, or marries. Details of
these rules, which are complex, may be found in specialist works.

the power, which is again implied unless the settlor indicates otherwise:[28] it allows for such anticipatory payments for the beneficiary's 'advancement or benefit'. But note that trustees, making such an advancement, are not simply paying the beneficiary money that is ultimately certain to be his. Unlike a power of maintenance, a power of advancement can affect other beneficiaries too, in two ways. First, since the advanced beneficiary's normal entitlement lies in the future, he may never arrive at it, if for no other reason because he may die first. In that case, the money advanced to him would have been payable to someone else: and the latter will now have lost it. (It cannot be reclaimed from the advanced beneficiary's estate: otherwise the advanced beneficiary would be unable safely to spend it, so defeating the usefulness of the advancement.) As a partial safeguard, s 32 provides that not more than half the anticipated entitlement can be advanced, though settlors sometimes override this and allow for advancement of the whole sum. Exercise of the power on especially the latter terms amounts to a substantial adjustment by the trustees of the trust's beneficial interests. Secondly, the money to be advanced may be capital from which another beneficiary currently derives income. Section 32 stipulates that in these circumstances the advancement requires the latter's consent.

9.3 DUTIES AND CERTAINTY REQUIREMENTS IN TRUSTS INVOLVING DISPOSITIVE DISCRETIONS

These, then, are the principal kinds of dispositive discretions. Now we need to think about what duties arise in performing trusts involving such discretions. There are two main ones. The first is basic, and shared with fixed trusts: remaining within the terms of the disposition as laid down by the settlor (above all, paying only the right people). The other, though, is distinctive to discretionary dispositions: handling the exercise of the discretion in a proper way. We shall look at these in turn.

Then there is the question of certainty. We saw in Chapter 8 how a need for certainty arises from the principle that a trust must be capable of performance by its trustees, and if necessary, supervision and performance by the court.[29] As we look at each of the duties, therefore, we shall

---

[28] Trustee Act 1925 s 69(2).
[29] *Morice v Bishop of Durham* (1804) 9 Ves 399, (1805) 10 Ves 522.

also need to think about what it requires in this respect. Our conclusions will be summarized, along with the corresponding rules regarding fixed trusts, in section 9.8.

9.4 REMAINING WITHIN THE TERMS OF THE DISPOSITION

First, then, we look at the duty to remain within the terms of the disposition as laid down by the settlor.

Any action that the trustees, in their discretion, decide to take must be an action that is authorized by the terms of the trust. For example, trustees do not validly exercise a power of accumulation if they embezzle the money in question for themselves, or a power of maintenance or advancement if they spend the money on something not beneficial to the relevant beneficiary.[30] Most especially, if they decide to pay out money to someone as a beneficiary, that person must indeed be a beneficiary. In the case of a power of maintenance or advancement, this person is fixed by the settlor himself; as we have seen, the discretion is to accelerate the payment that the beneficiary should ultimately receive. In discretionary trusts and powers of appointment, on the other hand, the trustees choose whom to pay. But they may make a choice only within the range defined by the settlor. So in a discretionary trust '£50,000 to be divided as my trustees think best among the employees of X Co' they can choose and pay no one other than such employees. And in a power of appointment '£10,000 for my children so far as my trustees may think fit, but otherwise to my widow absolutely', they can select and pay only the settlor's children (and in default, must pay the settlor's widow).

This duty is the same as the duty not to pay anyone other than the designated objects in fixed trusts, examined in section 8.1. So we should expect that in this context too, the duty would be diluted to one of paying only people who seem on a balance of probabilities to fit the stipulation. Just as with fixed trusts, this would dispense with the apparent need for conceptual and evidential certainty—ie for it to be possible to say definitely whether any given person is or is not an object—and would instead demand merely that the settlor's designation must not be meaningless.

---

[30] The words 'maintenance', 'education', and 'advancement' alone read even more restrictively, but as regards both kinds of power the Trustee Act 1925 (ss 31 and 32) adds 'or benefit'. Even this wider formulation has limits, however, some of which are examined in *Pilkington v IRC* [1964] AC 612; and see *X v A* [2006] 1 WLR 741.

As regards powers of maintenance and advancement, where the people in whose favour the power can be exercised are fixed by the settlor anyway, there is no reason to doubt that this is the rule. However, as to discretionary trusts and powers of appointment the courts have decided that the position developed in the fixed trust context is only partially applicable. It obtains so far as evidential considerations are concerned.[31] But on the conceptual side, the duty remains the full one of paying only someone who is definitely within the stipulation, and the certainty requirement is correspondingly that of being able to say whether any given person is or is not within it.[32] So while, as we have seen, a fixed trust '£10 to each of my old friends' would be valid,[33] a discretionary trust '£1,000 to be divided as my trustees think best among my old friends' would not. It cannot be said whether *any given person* is or is not an 'old friend' (although it can be said one way or the other of *some* people), because this description has a grey area in which the answer could be unclear. This discrepancy between fixed trusts and discretionary trusts and powers of appointment is unsatisfactory. Not paying the wrong people is the same operation in discretionary trusts and powers of appointment as it is in fixed trusts, so the legal duty and concomitant certainty requirement should also be the same. And there is a strong case[34] that it should be at the lower level, currently confined to fixed trusts; as we saw in section 8.6, this may well offer the better reading of the facilitative thesis.

Once the trustees have decided to exercise a discretion in a certain way (in favour of certain objects of a discretionary trust, for example), the money has to be paid over accordingly. In the context of fixed trusts, we saw how in principle this could create difficulties, because the trustees might seem to be under a duty to pay someone who had disappeared, but that these difficulties are dispelled by measures such

---

[31] *Re Baden's Deed Trusts (No 2)* [1973] Ch 9, 19–20, Sachs LJ (the issue is not addressed by the remaining members of the court).

[32] *Re Gulbenkian's Settlement Trusts* [1970] AC 508 (powers of appointment); *McPhail v Doulton* [1971] AC 424 (discretionary trusts).

[33] *Re Barlow's Will Trusts* [1979] 1 WLR 278: see section 8.5. A trust '£1,000 to be divided equally between my old friends', however, would fail, because the fact that it requires the trustees to quantify the beneficiaries' entitlements makes it additionally necessary to be able to know the overall number of beneficiaries; and this description is too vague for that.

[34] Some judges have indeed taken this position. See *Re Gibbard's Will Trusts* [1967] 1 WLR 42, and the Court of Appeal in *Re Gulbenkian's Settlement Trusts* [1968] Ch 126: both overruled in favour of the 'is or is not' test by the House of Lords, [1970] AC 508. A variant on the suggested position was also advocated by Megaw LJ in *Re Baden's Deed Trusts (No 2)* [1973] Ch 9, 24, requiring it to be possible to think of a 'substantial number' of people who definitely fit the description, rather than just one.

as payment into court. It is improbable that this question would arise in the present context, because trustees are unlikely to exercise their discretion in favour of an object of whose whereabouts or existence they are unsure. But if it did, it would presumably be dealt with by the same measures.

A discretionary payment will be within the terms of a particular disposition only if it consists of the money (or other property) that the trust permits to be distributed in this way. In the case of a discretionary trust, indeed, the discretionary payments must distribute all the assets available for them. The money (or other property) available for distribution under the discretion must therefore be sufficiently defined: ie there must be appropriate certainty of subject matter. This issue was discussed in section 8.3, in the context of fixed trusts. *Mutatis mutandis*, what was said there applies here too. Remember however that a problem of uncertain subject matter in a fixed trust can sometimes be solved if the trust is instead regarded as discretionary. So an invalid fixed trust of '20 cases of my wine' in your favour could, for example, be a valid trust of all my wine, the trustee having the duty to choose 20 cases and allocate them to you, while holding the remainder for me.

9.5 THE CONDUCT OF THE DISCRETION

The trustees' other kind of duty in respect of dispositive discretions concerns the exercise of the discretion itself. If there were no requirements as to the trustees' behaviour in this regard, they would be left to make decisions as arbitrarily and whimsically as they liked. In fact, the law demands certain standards of them.

Trustees' duties in this respect are probably essentially the same for each of the five principal types of dispositive discretion described above, though the implications may differ from one type to another. Distinct from this are non-fiduciary powers of appointment, which adhere to the old conception of the power as primarily a trust for the takers in default, the trustees having an option to divert money to the objects of the power instead, but the latter having no rights in the matter. Those holding such a power have duties to behave properly only so far as a failure to do so will injure the takers in default. There is thus no such thing as a wrongful non-exercise of such a power,[35] because that would injure only the objects of the power.

---

[35] *Re Somes* [1896] 1 Ch 250; *Re Greaves* [1954] Ch 434.

Put shortly, the law requires that trustees should give proper consideration to their discretion, and neither exercise it nor refrain from exercising
it without such proper consideration. Most basically in this, trustees are
required to think about whether to exercise their discretion at all. So they
are at fault if they refrain from making an advancement, say, without even
thinking about whether they should; or, conversely, if they do make it,
without thinking about whether they should not.[36] For example, there
is a failure in this respect if the trustees merely follow instructions that
they receive from the settlor, without exercising any judgement of their
own;[37] or indeed if they simply do not realize, or forget, that they have a
discretion to exercise, and do nothing about it. This requirement seems
to make no demands in the way of certainty; it does not need the settlor to
supply any information for the trustees to be able to know that they have
to think.

But the law requires trustees not simply to think, but also to think
properly: to take all relevant matters into account, and leave irrelevant
ones out of account. Some old authorities required trustees merely to be
appropriately intentioned; that is, to act in good faith,[38] and only for a, or
the, purpose for which the discretion is given[39]—a failure to do so being
known as a 'fraud on a power', though there is no requirement of dishonesty.[40] The formulation used here is intended to include these rules,
but also a further requirement, asserted principally in more recent cases
and generally known as 'the rule in *Re Hastings-Bass*',[41] that the trustees'
thinking should in addition be appropriately informed.[42] In so linking the
rules, the formulation is unusual, for they are more commonly depicted as
distinct, but it is not clear why.[43]

---

[36] *Wilson v Turner* (1883) 22 Ch D 521.

[37] *Re Locker's Settlement Trusts* [1977] 1 WLR 1323; *Turner v Turner* [1984] Ch 100. On
the other hand, the trustees must not simply ignore the settlor's wishes: *Breadner v Granville-
Grossman* [2001] Ch 523, [20]–[22]; *Breakspear v Ackland* [2009] Ch 32, [8].

[38] See eg *Gisborne v Gisborne* (1877) 2 App Cas 300, 305.

[39] See eg *Duke of Portland v Lady Topham* (1864) 11 HLC 32, 54, 55–6.

[40] *Vatcher v Paull* [1915] AC 372, 378.

[41] [1975] Ch 25. There are however earlier signs of the same, or a similar, idea, including *Re
Beloved Wilkes' Charity* (1851) 3 Mac & G 440, 448; *Re Vestey's Settlement* [1951] Ch 209, 216,
220, 221; *Re Abrahams' Will Trusts* [1969] 1 Ch 463, 483, 485.

[42] See especially *Re Hastings-Bass* [1975] Ch 25, 36, 41; *Mettoy Pension Trustees Ltd v Evans*
[1990] 1 WLR 1587, 1621–6; *Sieff v Fox* [2005] 1 WLR 3811; R Walker (2002) 13 King's
College LJ 173; C Mitchell (2006) 122 LQR 35; M Ashdown (2010) 16 T & T 826. See further
section 13.4, especially regarding what constitutes a breach of this duty.

[43] They are however linked in *Sieff v Fox* [2005] 1 WLR 3811, [76], and *Futter v Futter*
[2010] EWHC 449 (Ch), [34]. See generally R Nolan [2009] CLJ 293.

There are two aspects to the duty to think properly. The first concerns the bases on which trustees should make their decisions: the kinds of considerations that should and should not influence them. The second concerns the lengths to which they need to go in providing themselves with information relevant to those considerations before making their decision. We shall take these two aspects in turn.

9.6 THE PROPER BASES FOR A DECISION

There are some matters to which trustees must not attend. For example, it will not normally be right for a trustee to take account of his own personal interests.[44] So it will be wrong, say, for a trustee having a power of appointment, of which he himself is not an object, to exercise it in a particular person's favour in return for a percentage of the sum appointed.[45] Again, the trustee's unreasoned feelings about the beneficiary ought not to come into the matter. So refusing to make an advancement out of personal dislike of the beneficiary would be wrong.[46] The objection, however, is to a reliance on mere prejudice, not to the formation of a personal but reasonable opinion: the trustee's very role is to bring such an opinion to bear on the discretion, and commonly he will have been appointed trustee because the settlor likes (among other things) his set of values.[47]

Beyond such basic matters, what factors are relevant and irrelevant depends on the particular discretion, or at any rate kind of discretion, involved. As regards a power of maintenance under the statutory formula, for instance, the objective has to be the child's 'maintenance, education or benefit'; and for the corresponding power of advancement it must be the beneficiary's 'advancement or benefit'. These formulae are broad, but they nevertheless set limits to the bases upon which the trustees may act. Maintenance, for example, must not be given in order to benefit the child's

---

[44] Problems evidently arise if the persons in whose favour the discretion can be exercised are expressed to include the trustee. This often occurs in pension fund trusts, where the trustees will include representatives of the pensioners, employees, and employer, all of whom may be benefited by the discretions ordinarily given. After earlier misgivings, the courts came to accept self-interested decisions by such trustees as not *ipso facto* invalid (*Re Drexel Burnham Lambert UK Pension Plan* [1995] 1 WLR 32), and to regard the overall balance of the board of trustees (*Edge v Pensions Ombudsman* [2000] Ch 602, 630, 633) and the employer's duty of good faith towards its employees (*British Coal Corp v British Coal Staff Superannuation Scheme Trustees Ltd* [1995] 1 All ER 912, 923–8) as substitute guarantees of fairness. A statutory provision (Pensions Act 1995 s 39) covers some of the same ground.

[45] *Vatcher v Paull* [1915] AC 372, 378.   [46] *Klug v Klug* [1918] 2 Ch 67.

[47] *Edge v Pensions Ombudsman* [2000] Ch 602, 630.

father[48] (though it is recognized that benefiting children will usually their parents too), nor withheld out of disapproval of him.[49]

For discretionary trusts and powers of appointment and accumulation, there is no such standard formula, and the proper bases for the exercise of the discretion will vary from one trust to the next.[50] In theory, settlors could write into the terms of the trust itself a catalogue of the matters to which their trustees should attend. In practice, they rarely do so explicitly, though they may give implicit pointers. (They may and often do give guidance to the trustees outside the terms of the trust, either alongside making the trust or as time goes by, but such guidance cannot be binding on the trustees.)[51] There is some confusion as to whether such a lack of direction presents a problem.

The leading case on discretionary trusts asserts that the potential objects of a discretionary trust must amount to 'something like a class'.[52] 'All the residents of Greater London' was said to be objectionable in this regard, and discretionary trusts for the inhabitants of West Yorkshire,[53] and for the whole world except a few specified people,[54] have subsequently been regarded as objectionable on this score. The assertion has puzzled commentators.[55] But from the surrounding context it seems to have been intended as a certainty requirement: a demand that, for a discretionary trust to be valid, the information needed to secure its 'administrative workability',[56] ie to perform it and to control that performance, must be present. In these terms, a discretionary trust for 'all the residents of Greater London', without more, is apparently bad because there is nothing in its terms to provide information about the proper bases for the exercise of the discretion. (The requirement has

---

[48] *Wilson v Turner* (1883) 22 Ch D 521: the trustees paid all the available money over to the father, without considering whether it was actually needed for the child's maintenance.

[49] *Re Lofthouse* (1885) 29 Ch D 921, 925–6: the trustees withheld maintenance apparently from disapproval of the child's father having become a town councillor (for the wrong party?); the judge at first instance found a breach, but the case was compromised on appeal.

[50] They will, however, normally include the tax consequences of adopting one course of action rather than another, as impacting on the benefit to the objects. Trustees' decisions overlooking or misjudging this consideration have been frequently impugned under the rule in *Re Hastings-Bass* [1975] Ch 25: see eg *Abacus Trust Co (Isle of Man) Ltd v NSPCC* [2001] STC 1344; *Burrell v Burrell* [2005] STC 569; *Sieff v Fox* [2005] 1 WLR 3811, [86]–[90], [119]. The tax authorities have now begun to challenge the propriety of this, but so far unsuccessfully: *Pitt v Holt* [2010] 1 WLR 1199, [40]–[43].

[51] *Turner v Turner* [1984] Ch 100.   [52] *McPhail v Doulton* [1971] AC 424, 457.

[53] *R v District Auditor, ex p West Yorkshire Metropolitan County Council* [1986] RVR 24.

[54] *Re Hay's Settlement Trusts* [1982] 1 WLR 202, 213–14.

[55] See eg L McKay (1974) 38 Conv 269; Y Grbich (1974) 37 MLR 643; I Hardcastle [1990] Conv 24.

[56] *McPhail v Doulton* [1971] AC 424, 457.

been said not to apply to powers of appointment,[57] though this may be less because they are relevantly different[58] than because of a reluctance to disturb a traditional understanding that powers can be made in favour of such classes.)

However, it is more usually thought that the bases for the exercise of discretion need not be indicated by the settlor, but can be left to be devised by the trustees themselves. (So long as they do not relinquish their own discretion, they can, though they need not,[59] invite suggestions from others, notably the settlor and beneficiaries.)[60] The trustees are required only to avoid acting 'capriciously', as one judge put it, discussing a power of appointment: on the basis of factors that are 'irrational, perverse or irrelevant to any sensible expectation of the settlor; for example, if they chose a beneficiary by height or complexion or by the irrelevant fact that he was a resident of Greater London'.[61] Take, say, a discretionary trust in favour of the employees of a company. The trustees might adopt criteria such as loyalty, need, contribution to the firm; they could not look at matters such as race or religion. This approach of leaving trustees to establish their own bases, so long as these are not capricious, demands little in the way of certainty. It implies that a trust or power will be valid so long as it is not impossible for its trustees themselves to arrive at a reasonable notion of a basis upon which to exercise it: which should not normally be any problem at all. In one case[62] it was suggested that a power to appoint amongst 'the residents of Greater London' would fail because such a designation would be inconsistent with the adoption of sensible criteria by the trustees in this way. But that suggestion is hard to accept in principle, and indeed the same case went

---

[57] *Re Manisty's Settlement* [1974] Ch 17; *Re Hay's Settlement Trusts* [1982] 1 WLR 202. The same is assumed in *Re Beatty* [1990] 1 WLR 1503.

[58] One suggested explanation for the requirement of a 'class', however, is that 'the residents of Greater London' are too multitudinous to be permitted to enforce against the trustees the rights to a proper exercise of discretion enjoyed by potential objects of a discretionary trust (I Hardingham and R Baxt *Discretionary Trusts* 2nd edn (1984) 37–41). If that is right (which it may not be), the different rule in powers might be explained on the ground that the potential objects of powers traditionally had no rights against the trustees (*Re Hay's Settlement Trusts* [1982] 1 WLR 202, 213–14). Nowadays, however, the rights of potential objects in this respect are the same in powers as in discretionary trusts (*Mettoy Pension Trustees Ltd v Evans* [1990] 1 WLR 1587), suggesting that the 'class' requirement should apply to powers too.

[59] Except perhaps where they are contemplating a change of approach such as to cut off a beneficiary whom they have hitherto favoured: *Scott v National Trust for Places of Historic Interest or Natural Beauty* [1998] 2 All ER 705, 718.

[60] *Hartigan Nominees Pty Ltd v Rydge* (1992) 29 NSWLR 405, 431, Australia.

[61] *Re Manisty's Settlement* [1974] Ch 17, 26.   [62] *Ibid* 27.

on to hold a power in favour of the entire world, minus a few specified people, to be valid.[63]

9.7 ASSEMBLING INFORMATION

The other issue regarding the duty to take relevant and not irrelevant matters into account concerns the depth of information with which trustees are required to equip themselves before making their decision. Given some suitable criterion, to what lengths should trustees go in acquainting themselves with the claims of potential objects in terms of it?

Trustees who, on the basis of some criterion, are minded to exercise a discretion in favour of a particular person must of course take steps to check that that person is indeed deserving in terms of the criterion. For example, they would be wrong to exercise a power of advancement on the ground that the beneficiary to be advanced needed the money to buy a house without at least asking the beneficiary to provide some substantiation of this assertion.[64]

Must trustees also take stock of the standing, relative to their criteria, of those whom they propose *not* to benefit? They need not invite representations from any beneficiary,[65] though they may do so, and they must listen to any they do receive.[66] But before making their selection, they must themselves to some extent consider the claims in respect of their chosen criteria of all the potential objects of the discretion.

The latter requirement, however, takes the form of a duty to make only such a survey of potential recipients as seems sensible in regard to the size of the class in question. In the case of a discretion as between the settlor's living children, for example, the trustees probably have to think about the claims of each child individually; there is no difficulty about their doing so.[67] At the other extreme, in the case of a discretion amongst a very large class, such as a company's employees, the trustees are not expected to give

[63] Likewise *Re Hay's Settlement Trusts* [1982] 1 WLR 202.

[64] *Nestle v National Westminster Bank plc* [1993] 1 WLR 1260, 1279 (duty to check whether a beneficiary is poor before setting the trust's investment policy so as especially to benefit him on that ground).

[65] *Karger v Paul* [1984] VR 161, Australia. The position appears to be different in pension fund trusts, where the trustees must ensure that they have all relevant information before taking a decision: D Hayton [2005] Conv 229, 235.

[66] *Re Manisty's Settlement* [1974] Ch 17, 26. The courts will assist a beneficiary with a potentially strong case to make such a representation, by if necessary ordering disclosure of the trustees' names and addresses: *Re Murphy's Settlements* [1999] 1 WLR 282.

[67] According to the decision on the facts in *Karger v Paul* [1984] VR 161, Australia, but questionably, a very superficial appreciation of the different individuals' claims is enough.

individual consideration to every member of the class. The requirement here is known, rather opaquely, as 'inquiry or ascertainment'. With the criteria for the exercise of the discretion in mind, the trustees are expected to examine the field, by class and category; possibly to make diligent and careful inquiries, depending on the amount of money and the means available, as to the composition and needs of particular categories and of individuals within them; to decide on priorities or proportions, and then to select actual individuals to receive the money.[68] So in a discretionary trust for company employees, for instance, where they have adopted criteria of need and/or loyalty, they might decide to look primarily at those on low salaries, those who have recently taken maternity leave, those approaching retirement, and those who have served the firm for upwards of ten years, and then perhaps work on some sort of points system to arrive at a provisional allocation, before doing a final detailed check on the circumstances of the individuals arrived at and finally paying out.

Once again, for the disposition to be valid, any information necessary for this exercise must be present. Where trustees have to inform themselves about one or more specific individuals, therefore, they must be able to identify who those individuals are. Identifying the person in whose favour a power of maintenance or advancement might be exercised should require only such information as is already required by the duty ultimately to pay him anyway. In the case of a discretionary trust or power of appointment, in order to identify the members of a small class (such as the settlor's children) so as to think about them all individually, it must be possible to compile a complete list of the members. As regards a large class such as the employees of a substantial company, however, the business of 'inquiry or ascertainment' does not require a complete list, nor obviously involve any requirements in the way of information. The ability to devise categories, for example, seems to need imagination rather than information; and the eventual narrow field of actual individuals will supply itself, rather than needing to be defined from the start. One proposed explanation for the demand (discussed in section 9.6) that the potential objects of a discretionary trust amount to 'something like a class' suggests that the trustees might not be able satisfactorily to make 'inquiry or ascertainment' across a group the size of 'the residents of Greater London'.[69] But given what has just been said, there seems no foundation for this view.

---

[68] *McPhail v Doulton* [1971] AC 424 (discretionary trusts); *Re Hay's Settlement Trusts* [1982] 1 WLR 202 (powers of appointment).
[69] *Re Hay's Settlement Trusts* [1982] 1 WLR 202, 213, adding that powers of appointment are exempt from the requirement because the duty of inquiry or ascertainment is less stringent

9.8 CERTAINTY OF OBJECTS: A SUMMARY

It may be helpful to summarize the rules about certainty of objects that we have noted in this and the previous chapter. Given that certain other potential requirements have in practice been sidelined, as explained in section 8.5, we are left with the following.

Both fixed trusts and those involving a dispositive discretion have a requirement of conceptual certainty, ie certainty in the description of the object(s). Classically, this requirement demands that the language used in the description should be sufficiently precise that one can say whether any given person (or purpose) is or is not within it—that is, to say 'don't know' means that the description is invalid. And this is indeed the rule so far as discretionary trusts[70] and powers of appointment[71] are concerned. So far as fixed trusts are concerned, however, it has been replaced by a more lenient rule. This replacement came about via the re-interpretation of facilitative logic explained in section 8.6, and in principle just as viable in the case of discretionary trusts and powers of appointment, but, as explained in section 9.4, not in fact adopted there. This more lenient rule requires us only to be able to identify one (even hypothetical) person as clearly within the description, tolerating the answer 'don't know' in all cases beyond that.[72] That is to say, in this context, the possibility of 'don't knows' does not invalidate the description: individual putative objects have to argue why the description should be read as including people like them, and those who succeed will qualify, while those who fail—including those about whom the answer remains 'don't know'—will not. So consider, for example, a description 'my friends'. It is obviously possible to think of at least one (even if hypothetical) person who could certainly be termed a 'friend', but at the same time many others about whom we would have to say 'don't know—it depends just what you mean by friend'. This description would therefore be certain enough for use in a fixed trust, but not in a discretionary trust or power of appointment. But a description such as 'my descendants' would be certain enough for the latter (as well as the former, of course): it is in principle possible to say whether any given person can be termed one of my descendants.

in them (itself a questionable view, assuming that the set of potential objects is the same in both: any difference in duty should be less a question of trust or power than a reflection of the size of that set).

[70] *McPhail v Doulton* [1971] AC 424.
[71] *Re Gulbenkian's Settlement Trusts* [1970] AC 508.
[72] *Re Allen* [1953] Ch 810; *Re Barlow's Will Trusts* [1979] 1 WLR 278.

Although in the current law it thus takes two forms, the requirement of conceptual certainty is needed for all trusts: its concern is with the information that the trustees (and potentially the court) have to have in order to pay the right people and not the wrong people, which is a duty found in all trusts. Beyond this, different kinds of trusts have different further duties, giving rise to different additional requirements by way of certainty of objects. Three in particular should be noted.

First, the performance of some trusts requires knowledge of the number of entitled objects. This is the case where a global sum of money has to be divided in some pre-ordained way—most commonly, equally—between them (rather than as determined by a discretionary decision). This is the case, then, for fixed trusts in favour of a group, and also perhaps (it certainly was once so) for discretionary trusts in favour of a small, close class, where, if the trustees failed to exercise a discretion, the court would find it uncomfortable to do so, and would therefore resort to equal distribution after all: maybe a class such as 'my children'. In trusts of these kinds, there is therefore a requirement that the number of entitled objects be discoverable.[73] 'My friends' would obviously not meet this requirement: as noted above, we cannot even say whether any given person is or is not a friend, let alone enumerate the entire class of friends. Nor however would 'my descendants' necessarily meet it: although we can say whether any given person is or is not within it, we might find it hard to enumerate all those who do.

Second, in discretionary trusts, in order to achieve 'administrative workability', the objects are required to comprise 'something like a class'.[74] As section 9.6 explains, this is a puzzling requirement in principle, but in practice is taken to rule out very large groups, such as the residents of Greater London,[75] the inhabitants of West Yorkshire,[76] or the whole world except a few specified people;[77] though a class comprising

---

[73] This requirement is sometimes said to demand a 'complete list' of the objects. That is not completely accurate: what is needed is not a list of the names, but simply the number. However, a common way of establishing the number will often be to draw up a list of the relevant names, and count them. So with 'my children', for example. Note also that there is a genuine 'complete list' requirement in another context, as explained in the text below.

[74] *McPhail v Doulton* [1971] AC 424, 457. For powers of appointment, there is a requirement that the power must not be 'capricious': *Re Manisty's Settlement* [1974] Ch 17, 26–7; but this means only that it must not be capable of exercise only on the basis of factors which are 'irrational, perverse or irrelevant to any sensible expectation of the settlor; for example, if they chose a beneficiary by height or complexion or by the irrelevant fact that he was a resident of Greater London'. [75] *McPhail v Doulton* [1971] AC 424, 457.

[76] *R v District Auditor, ex p West Yorkshire Metropolitan County Council* [1986] RVR 24.

[77] *Re Hay's Settlement Trusts* [1982] 1 WLR 202, 213–14.

the current and former employees of a particular company and their relatives and dependants appears to be acceptable, even if it runs into some thousands.[78]

Third, a discretionary trust in favour of a small class of objects may perhaps be valid only if it is possible to compile a complete list of those objects. This rule follows if we believe that, in the case of such a trust, the trustees must prepare their decision whom to pay by thinking about the claims of each and every potential recipient: a complete list of the latter being essential in order to do so. Such a preparatory survey is certainly not required in the case of a discretionary trust in favour of a large class of objects, or a power of appointment, however. There, the preparatory exercise is one of 'inquiry or ascertainment', which means that, with the criteria for the exercise of the discretion in mind, the trustees must examine the field, by class and category; possibly make diligent and careful inquiries, depending on the amount of money and the means available, as to the composition and needs of particular categories and of individuals within them; decide on priorities or proportions, and then select actual individuals to receive the money.[79] In a discretionary trust for a large class of objects, or a power of appointment, then, there is no need to think about all the potential recipients, so there is no requirement of a list of them—indeed, no specific rule about their identifiability at all (though presumably, if for some reason they were quite unidentifiable, the description would have to fail). The requirement of a full survey, and so complete list, in the case of a discretionary trust for a small class of objects, stems from the idea that a settlor of such a trust would expect as much from his trustees, precisely because of the trust's small scale; and the more relaxed position in the case of other discretionary trusts and of powers of appointment stems from the idea that a settlor of such a trust would expect so much less from his trustees, precisely because of the disposition's larger scale.

The net effect of all this is as follows. A fixed trust in favour of an individual object[80] cannot be valid unless it is possible to identify one, even hypothetical, person as clearly within the description used (ie beyond this one, the answer 'don't know' is tolerated). A fixed trust in favour of a group of objects, on the other hand, cannot be valid unless the objects can be enumerated. A power of appointment cannot be valid unless it is

---

[78] *McPhail v Doulton* [1971] AC 424.

[79] *Ibid* (discretionary trusts); *Re Hay's Settlement Trusts* [1982] 1 WLR 202 (powers of appointment).

[80] One sometimes encounters clusters of such trusts: eg '£1,000 to each of my children'. The same rule applies.

possible, in terms of the language used, to say whether any given person is or is not covered by the settlor's designation of the objects (ie the answer 'don't know' is *not* tolerated). A discretionary trust shares that requirement, but also has one whereby the objects must amount to 'something like a class' ... unless it is in favour of only a small class of objects, in which case it may be valid only if a complete list of the objects can be compiled (and also their number known, but that demand would be eclipsed by the need for a complete list).

Modification

We have spent the last three chapters looking at some of the main duties that trustees have in regard to the performance of express trusts. One point we noticed, especially when we were dealing with fixed trusts in Chapter 8, was that these duties are sometimes not what one might at first expect: they are more qualified. For example, the trustees' apparent absolute duty of paying a beneficiary his entitlement is replaced by a more dilute, and thus more practicable, duty. So instead of having to pay the designated objects, and no one else, and to do this come what may, the trustees are required to try to pay the people who can show that they are probably the designated objects, and not anyone who cannot, and if they cannot find them to pay the money in some circumstances to certain other people, and otherwise into court.[1]

With these dilutions, the idea is not that the duties were once absolute but are then relaxed, or that an imperfect performance of them is tolerated. It is their very definition that is diluted. Say, for example, a claimant showed that he was probably, though not definitely, the designated beneficiary, but the trustees still refused to pay him. He could sue the trustees, because they would be in breach of their duty to pay the money over to him. There never was any absolute duty only to pay genuinely designated beneficiaries: it was a theoretical mirage, which turns out to be this more tractable duty when properly examined.

Thus diluted or otherwise, however, the forms of the duties we have examined are default configurations. The law maintains a number of rules whereby these default configurations can be modified. This chapter sets out to consider the main such rules.[2]

---

[1] See section 8.5.
[2] For others, see *Re New* [1901] 2 Ch 534; *Chapman v Chapman* [1954] AC 429; Trustee Act 1925 s 57; Settled Land Act 1925 s 64. See also the Trusts of Land and Appointment of Trustees Act 1996 s 14, which may (it is unclear) allow the court to order trusts of land to be operated in ways not open to the trustees: see S Gardner *An Introduction to Land Law* 2nd edn (2009) 286, 294-5.

10.1 MODIFICATION BY THE SETTLOR

Express trustees' duties are in practice often modified by the terms on which the settlor establishes the trust. Depending on its particular wording, such a modification can operate either to adjust the duty itself, or, leaving the duty itself unchanged, to adjust the liability that the trustees would otherwise incur upon breaching the duty. In theory, a settlor could adjust his trustees' duties so as to make them more, rather than less, demanding, but this is infrequently encountered.

Such modifications are very commonly used, but have received relatively little attention from the courts. The probable reason for this, and also the dominant consideration when the courts have become involved, is an acceptance of facilitative logic: the idea that settlors should be able to configure their trusts as they like. So the courts[3] have allowed the exclusion of liability in respect of all duties, except the 'core' duty of honestly acting in the objects' best interests[4,5]—the point being that in the absence of liability for breach of this core duty, there would simply be no trust at all.[6] In fact, the rule would be put better by saying that liability can be excluded even in respect of the duty to act honestly in the objects' best interests, but that the result would be a moral arrangement rather than a trust (and if the remaining terms suggested that a trust *was* intended,

---

[3] *Armitage v Nurse* [1998] Ch 241; interpreted in *Walker v Stones* [2001] QB 902, 939, as requiring (though perhaps of only specially qualified trustees) a performance *reasonably perceivable as* in the beneficiaries' best interests. The duty of care and skill regarding investment cannot be excluded in unit trusts or pension fund trusts: Financial Services and Markets Act 2000 s 253, Pensions Act 1995 s 33.

[4] *Armitage v Nurse* [1998] Ch 241 contains an ambiguity. At 254, the judgment states that a trustee who relies on the presence of even the widest permitted exemption clause to justify what he proposes to do will thereby lose its protection, presumably as being dishonest. But at 251, the judgment states that a trustee who breaches his trust, even deliberately, in the objects' best interests—eg makes an unauthorized but advantageous investment—acts honestly (a reading of 'honestly' also visible in *Perrins v Bellamy* [1899] 1 Ch 797: n 24 below), and so has the benefit of the clause. The trustee in the latter case does not necessarily 'rely on' the exemption clause, but commonly will: and where he does, the two statements conflict.

[5] Millett LJ, who gave the judgment in *Armitage v Nurse* [1998] Ch 241, elsewhere (*Bristol and West Building Society v Mothew* [1998] Ch 1, 18) describes trustees as having a 'core' obligation comprising, apparently, *all* their fiduciary duties, meaning not only the duty to act honestly in the objects' best interests, but also the anti-distraction duties considered in section 11.10 (the 'no conflict' rule, etc). If he intends the word 'core' to carry the same meaning in both judgments, Millett LJ emerges as asserting that liability for breach of the anti-distraction duties cannot be excluded. This is unlikely to be correct, especially as it is quite clearly possible to exclude such duties themselves: *Sargeant v National Westminster Bank plc* (1991) 61 P & CR 518.

[6] The argument assumes that a duty is effective only if there is liability in respect of a breach of it. For a suggestion to the contrary, see section 12.6.

the court would have the difficulty of deciding which reading should have precedence). No firm judicial statement seems to have been made about the limits, if any, to a settlor's ability to adjust his trustees' duties themselves. But in principle, such duties ought likewise to be reducible in any way except one that requires or allows the trustees not to act honestly in the beneficiaries' best interests: again, reducing them beyond that point would produce something that is not a trust at all.[7]

It can however be asked whether this position is too generous in the exclusions it tolerates in respect of trustees' duties and liabilities; English law controls exclusion clauses in contracts and 'notices',[8] and many common law jurisdictions control them also in trusts.[9] The Law Commission has considered the question, and concluded that there should be no change in English law, though encouraging professional and regulatory bodies (for example, the Law Society, which regulates solicitors) to require paid trustees to ensure that settlors are aware of, and understand, any provisions excluding or limiting their liability for negligence.[10]

This position leaves the emphasis on settlors' freedom, indeed seeming to enhance the latter by ensuring that settlors are better apprised regarding the provisions they are setting their name to. It is also calculated to maintain the supply of trustees, and to keep their fees down (without the exclusion, trustees might decline to act, and/or raise their fees to meet the cost of insurance cover); thus helping to secure the satisfactory performance of trusts, in the way explained in section 11.2. As such, the position is

---

[7] In *Sargeant v National Westminster Bank plc* (1991) 61 P & CR 518, the trust permitted its trustees to act despite a conflict of interest. As explained in section 11.10, the default duty to the contrary aims to promote compliance with the duty to serve the objects' best interests; but the latter can certainly exist without it. *Hayim v Citibank NA* [1987] AC 730 is more challenging to the position taken in the text. The trust permitted its trustees to disregard the objects' interests, albeit temporarily, and in respect of only one item of the trust property; but this difficulty received no attention from the court. In *Citibank NA v MBIA Assurance SA* [2007] 1 All ER (Comm) 475, [82], it appears to be assumed that negation of the 'core' duty would prevent the arrangement from being a trust.

[8] Unfair Contract Terms Act 1977; Unfair Terms in Consumer Contract Regulations 1999 SI No 2083. *Baker v J E Clark & Co (Transport) UK Ltd* [2006] EWCA Civ 464, [18]–[21] holds that a trust is neither a contract, nor the kind of 'notice' envisaged by the legislation.

[9] Cf eg *Robertson v Howden* (1892) 10 NZLR 609, New Zealand; *Re Poche* (1984) 6 DLR (4th) 40, Canada; Trusts (Jersey) Law 1984 Art 26(9). The general tendency is to allow exclusion of liability for ordinary negligence, but not for anything worse.

[10] Law Commission *Trustee Exemption Clauses* (Law Com No 301, 2006). (Note the assumption that a trust will be valid even though its settlor does *not* understand its terms.) The Report's recommendation was accepted by the Government on 14 September 2010, and the necessary rules are being promulgated.

certainly supportable.[11] But there are arguments against it.[12] Settlors may in practice have little option but to accept an extensive exclusion; awareness and understanding may be necessary conditions for a free choice, but they are not sufficient. And losses will fall upon objects, who will have virtually no way of passing them on; probably a less satisfactory outcome than their falling upon trustees, but met from insurance—so long as insurance is available, which cannot however be necessarily assumed.[13]

10.2 TRUSTEE ACT 1925 SECTION 61

Section 61 of the Trustee Act 1925[14] provides that where trustees have breached their duty, but in doing so they acted honestly and reasonably, the court can negative their liability (entirely or partially) if it thinks it fair to do so. Many of the cases in which this provision has been applied have involved a misunderstanding by the trustees of their duty (eg by misinterpreting the terms of the trust),[15] though it can also be used where trustees make no mistake about what they are supposed to do, but fall down in actually doing it.

Discussion of this provision by the courts usually centres on the requirement that the misunderstanding or default must have been a reasonable one. When the duty breached is one to use care and skill in the management of the trust, there might be thought no scope to find the breach 'reasonable', for such a duty demands no more than reasonable behaviour in any event;[16] though it would be rash to be too dogmatic about

---

[11] Law Commission *Trustee Exemption Clauses* (Consultation Paper No 171, 2003), preceding Report No 301, had been more aggressive, provisionally proposing to ban provisions excluding or restricting professional trustees' liability for negligence. This position was abandoned by the Report as undesirable in various ways, most especially as damaging the interests identified in the text.

[12] For a further consideration, that the extant law conflicts with (what in this book is called) the interest thesis, see J Penner in P Birks and A Pretto (eds) *Breach of Trust* (2002) ch 8. This may not be a serious objection, since the status of the interest thesis is itself questionable. See further section 12.3.

[13] See Law Commission *Trustee Exemption Clauses* (Law Com No 301, 2006) Appendix B.

[14] L Sheridan (1955) 19 Conv 420; J Lowry and R Edmunds in P Birks and A Pretto (eds) *Breach of Trust* (2002) ch 9. Section 61 was originally enacted as the Judicial Trustees Act 1896 s 3, and many of the reported cases concern the latter. The Charities Act 1993 s 73D makes analogous provision for charitable trusts, the dispensing power here being given to the Charity Commission.

[15] Expressly recognized as a proper case for the section's application in *Re Allsop* [1914] 1 Ch 1.

[16] In respect of such duties, trustees are required to 'exercise such care and skill as is reasonable in the circumstances': Trustee Act 2000 s 1(1). (Previously, and in certain contexts still, to emulate an ordinary prudent man of business looking after the interests of others: *Re Whiteley*

this, for 'reasonable' could have at least slightly different connotations in the two contexts. The inquiry whether a breach is reasonable really comes into its own, however, in respect of duties with which a strict compliance is on the face of things demanded, as especially the duty to act in accordance with the terms of the trust. Many kinds of factors could come into the reckoning in this inquiry, but in practice two are especially important. One is whether the trustees misunderstood their duty in a way with which the court can sympathize.[17] The other is whether the trustees have taken what the court regards as appropriate procedural steps in an effort to perform the trust properly.[18] In particular, their error will not be regarded as reasonable if they should have sought instructions from the court (a consideration mentioned by the section itself), or consulted a lawyer or some other appropriate professional, but did not.[19] Trustees who act confidently upon a pardonable misunderstanding, however, cannot be blamed for failure to seek advice; and where they remain expected to do so, they are not required to go to the same lengths in every case: what reasonableness demands varies with the amount of money at stake.[20] Only in case of substantial amounts are the trustees likely to be expected to incur the expense of going to court or taking counsel's opinion (ie the advice of a barrister specializing in the field) in order to be said to have acted reasonably; in matters of more moderate dimensions, they will probably have acted reasonably if they consulted their normal solicitors; and in the smallest ones, it may well be reasonable for them not to have taken professional advice at all.

When giving relief under s 61, the law appears not to say (as it does when it dilutes an apparently absolute duty into a more practicable one, or allows the trustees' duty itself to be modified) that it was actually correct for the trustees to act as they did.[21] In the cases to which the section applies, the trustees were still supposed to perform their duty in its unmodified form, but the law thinks it right to exonerate them when, in pardonable circumstances, they did not. This idea is a familiar one in the criminal law, in its division of defences into 'justifications' (where the behaviour is regarded as desirable: eg use of reasonable force in prevention of crime)

(1886) 33 Ch D 347, *Learoyd v Whiteley* (1887) 12 App Cas 727.) See section 7.3. The point in the text is made in *Re Stuart* [1897] 2 Ch 583, 590–1.

[17] *Re Grindey* [1898] 2 Ch 593; *Re Allsop* [1914] 1 Ch 1.
[18] *Re Windsor Steam Coal Co (1901) Ltd* [1929] 1 Ch 151.   [19] See section 11.6.
[20] *Re Grindey* [1898] 2 Ch 593, 602–3; *Re Allsop* [1914] 1 Ch 1, 13, 21; *Marsden v Regan* [1954] 1 WLR 423, 435. See too *Perrins v Bellamy* [1899] 1 Ch 797, 800–1: the trustees need not come to court if it would be futile to do so.
[21] *Re Stuart* [1897] 2 Ch 583, 590.

and 'excuses' (where the behaviour is regarded as undesirable, but pardonable: eg stealing under duress). Using this terminology, the defence provided by s 61 is an excuse, rather than a justification. This characterization is the effect of three of its features.

The first is the fact that the section applies only to breaches that have already occurred, and does not provide for the court to authorize them in advance.[22] The second is the requirement that the trustees should have acted honestly, as well as reasonably. This seems usually to be taken to mean that they should have been trying to observe their duty, and not doing something, however reasonable, deliberately contrary to it. And the third is statements by the courts that relief under the section will depend on all the circumstances of the individual case.[23] These statements seem to be principally aimed at preventing the judges' hands from becoming tied by precedent, but they also prevent other trustees from interpreting the grant of relief in a previous case as the green light for them to commit a similar breach (though since the judges exercise the jurisdiction in a regular rather than capricious fashion, trustees may not be taken in by this, especially if they take professional advice).

Some treatments of the section, however, take it as justificatory: that is, as allowing trustees not to be counted as in breach of trust at all if they act reasonably and honestly, in the different sense of 'for the objects' benefit'. The principal judicial statements in this vein are those of Lindley MR in *Perrins v Bellamy*.[24] As Lindley LJ, he had previously advocated a provision on these lines in his evidence to the House of Commons Select Committee whose report led to the section's enactment.[25] It seems clear, however, that on that occasion, he—obviously correctly—envisaged that a provision on these lines should enable trustees to seek court approval for their actions *before* committing them, rather than afterwards, which is all the section permits. The section as enacted thus does not lend itself entirely well to the work that Lindley MR later sought to extract from it.

There is, however, a fundamental difficulty about providing an excusatory defence in a civil law context. A trustee's liability for breach is not

---

[22] *Re Tollemache* [1903] 1 Ch 457; *Re Rosenthal* [1972] 1 WLR 1273.

[23] *Re Turner* [1897] 1 Ch 536, 542; *Re Kay* [1897] 2 Ch 518, 524.

[24] [1899] 1 Ch 797, 798 ('the main duty of a trustee is to commit judicious breaches of trust'), 801 ('I have not the slightest doubt that it was a most judicious breach of trust . . . ; and there is not one trustee in a thousand, or one business man in a thousand, who would not have done likewise').

[25] House of Commons Select Committee on the Administration of Trusts, *Report* (1895 HC 248), *Minutes of Evidence* qq 457–61, 463, 532–2.

like criminal liability. Excusing a transgressor in the criminal context has no repercussions for anyone else (or only remotely, in terms of its effect on the law's future deterrence). By contrast, in our context the liability is to compensate the beneficiaries for the damage that the breach has done them: so relief of the trustee means non-compensation of the beneficiaries, a two-sided matter that does not arise in the criminal law.

Section 61 seeks to absorb this difficulty by leaving it to the court to decide in the individual case whether, on top of the breach being honest and reasonable, it is 'fair' to give relief. But in many of the decisions under the section, the court has missed the significance of this element, and gone straight from finding honesty and reasonableness to granting relief. The point is sometimes taken, however. In one case, the court decided that there was no unfairness in leaving a trust corporation, which acted for payment, to bear its own liability.[26] The argument cannot be that a higher standard of performance is expected of such a trustee,[27] for that would tell us that the breach was not a 'reasonable' one, rather than that the breach was reasonable but the trustee ought not fairly to bear it. It is perhaps that a commercial entity such as the trust corporation was better placed to bear and spread the loss than private individual trustees would have been, and certainly than the beneficiaries were.[28]

The jurisdiction in s 61 is referred to much less frequently nowadays than it was in the first years after its original enactment at the end of the nineteenth century.[29] This decline matches a similar decline, over the same period, in the number of reported cases of possible breach of trust. (For a quick if unscientific measure, compare the two, occasionally three, volumes per year in the 'Chancery' series of the Law Reports towards 1900 with the generally one volume today.) One explanation might be that trustees' standards of performance have risen, especially as professional trustees have become more common and the creation of small family trusts with lay trustees has declined. Another suggestion might be that the standards required of trustees have fallen. Formally, the law has remained much the same over the period, but its de facto implications may have moderated; there is certainly evidence of such a movement

---

[26] *National Trustees Co of Australasia Ltd v General Finance Co of Australasia Ltd* [1905] AC 373; see too *Re Windsor Steam Coal Co (1901) Ltd* [1929] 1 Ch 151.

[27] Though that is true, at any rate in today's law: Trustee Act 2000 s 1(1)(b).

[28] The fairness requirement also received attention in *Re Evans* [1999] 2 All ER 777, but the reasoning concentrates on keeping the trustee from bearing too much of the loss (given her position) rather than on why it was right to make the beneficiary suffer any of it.

[29] As the Judicial Trustees Act 1896 s 3.

from just before the section's enactment, and indeed the two were avowedly linked, indeed depicted as a composite project.[30] A third, certainly plausible, is that cases of unsatisfactory performance have come to be dealt with in some other way, especially by the invocation of an exclusion clause (as discussed in section 10.1) so as to negative the breach or its consequences—the increased use of such clauses being itself associated with the increased use of professional trustees, who commonly insist upon them.

10.3 THE CONSENT PRINCIPLE

Trustees incur no liability for breach of trust if they act with their beneficiaries' consent.[31]

Beneficiaries who consent to a breach and continue to approve of it will of course not wish to sue anyway. The consent principle attains practical importance where consenting beneficiaries subsequently regret doing so. So, for example, if the beneficiaries agree to an investment outside the terms of the trust, thinking it advantageous, but in the event it fails, the trustees commit no breach and so cannot be sued for the loss.

'Consent'[32] can involve instigating the trustees to commit the breach, or expressly concurring in their proposal to do so, or tacitly acquiescing in it; and can be given before the breach, or after it. The beneficiary's consent can count as such despite at any rate some degree of misunderstanding of what is afoot, including a failure to realize that a breach is involved (eg agreeing to a particular investment, assuming it to be authorized, when in fact it is unauthorized). That is not to say, however, that consent will be found in every case falling within the terms of this pattern. It will be found only if the overall nature of the circumstances makes it 'fair and equitable' that the trustee should not be liable. So consent might well not be found, and the trustee would remain liable, if, say, the beneficiary learns of the breach only as a fait accompli, does not fully understand what has occurred, and concurs only to the

---

[30] The evidence consists in *Speight v Gaunt* (1883) 22 Ch D 727, 9 App Cas 1, where the appeal succeeded because the trial judge had taken a view regarding the behaviour of the 'ordinary prudent man of business' which the Court of Appeal and House of Lords saw as too demanding. For the link (with s 61's predecessor, the Judicial Trustees Act 1896 s 3), see House of Commons Select Committee on the Administration of Trusts, *Report* (1895 HC 248) iv, and *Minutes of Evidence* q 462; see too qq 422, 552–4.

[31] J Payne in P Birks and A Pretto (eds) *Breach of Trust* (2002) ch 10.

[32] *Walker v Symonds* (1818) 3 Swans 1, 64; *Re Pauling's Settlement Trusts* [1962] 1 WLR 86, 106–8 (not discussed on appeal, [1964] Ch 303).

extent of not objecting. There is no consent if the beneficiary acts under undue influence,[33] or is under 18 or disqualified on grounds of mental infirmity.

The effect of the beneficiary's consent under this principle is not to require, or justify, or even excuse,[34] the trustees' breach. Rather, the trustees continue to be in breach, but the consenting beneficiary is not allowed to blow hot and cold by suing them for it.[35] The trustees' duties are thus modified only in this very limited sense; there is no real challenge to the primacy of the settlor's instructions. So configured, however, the principle disregards the beneficiaries' claim, explored in section 2.6, to enjoy the trust property as they themselves wish. Accepting the latter claim would mean treating the breach as not merely non-actionable, but rightful and indeed exigible, so that the trustees *must* comply with the beneficiaries' wishes, the trustees' original duties being modified in the full sense: replaced by those preferred by the beneficiaries. Although this is not the extant conception of the consent principle, however, it is central to a narrower rule based on the beneficiaries' consent, to which we now turn: the rule in *Saunders v Vautier*.[36]

10.4 *SAUNDERS v VAUTIER*

According to the rule in *Saunders v Vautier*,[37] if a trust has only one beneficiary, and he is an adult and of unimpaired legal capacity, he can wind the trust up entirely. That is, he can require the trustees to transfer him the trust property, so that he becomes no longer beneficiary of a trust of it, but straightforwardly its owner.[38] Equally, if a trust has multiple beneficiaries, and they are all adults and of unimpaired legal capacity and agree to do so, they can proceed in the same way.

Despite the focus of both on the beneficiaries' wishes, this rule operates in a manner quite different from the consent principle, just

---

[33] The central instance of undue influence is pressure, but it extends more widely, especially to cases where there is a prima facie possibility that pressure might have been exerted and the contrary is not proved: see generally *Royal Bank of Scotland plc v Etridge (No 2)* [2002] 2 AC 773.

[34] Though the Trustee Act 1925 s 61 (section 10.2) may be invoked to that effect, especially where the beneficiary has positively pressed the trustees to commit the breach.

[35] See especially *Re Pauling's Settlement Trusts* [1962] 1 WLR 86, [1964] Ch 303.

[36] (1841) 4 Beav 115, Cr & Ph 240.   [37] *Ibid.*

[38] If the beneficiary wants to modify rather than dismantle his trust, he can do so by settling the capital again on whatever new terms he pleases—and even use the same trustees, if the latter are amenable. So proceeding can have bad tax consequences, however.

discussed. The beneficiaries are not merely prevented from suing the trustees if the latter do as the beneficiaries ask. Rather, the trustees are positively required to do as the beneficiaries ask, their duties changing accordingly.

The techniques of diluting trustees' prima facie duties that we examined in section 8.5 and alluded to at the start of this chapter are at least reconcilable with the aim of effectuating the settlor's intentions, and, as explained in section 8.6, may in fact offer the best available way of promoting that aim: for they allow trusts to go forward in a looser but more practicable form, when they would otherwise fail for potential impossibility. The jurisdiction to excuse a breach in s 61 of the Trustee Act 1925 allows trustees to depart from the settlor's terms without liability, but as we saw it is calculated not to encourage departure. The consent principle too emphasizes the trustees' duty to adhere to the terms of the trust. In these terms, however, *Saunders v Vautier*[39] crosses the Rubicon. Under it, the beneficiaries' wishes are given precedence over the settlor's. It thus reflects the thesis, described in section 2.6, that the beneficiaries, as recipients of the property, should be able to enjoy the property absolutely, rather than on the settlor's terms.[40]

One facet of the rule is especially revealing in this vein. Where a beneficiary is given an absolute interest, but only upon some condition such as his reaching a certain age—eg 'for Adam once he reaches the age of 25'—the condition can be disregarded. So Adam can invoke the rule, and take the property, as soon as he is 18, despite the fact that the trust appears to stipulate that he shall have no interest at all until seven years later. It is said that in giving him an absolute interest but delaying it until he is 25, the trust contradicts itself: so the contradiction is removed by dispensing with the age requirement.[41] But there is only a contradiction if we assume his interest is absolute in the first place: which, given the condition of his reaching 25, it is not. The assumption, then, seems to be tendentious,

---

[39] (1841) 4 Beav 115, Cr & Ph 240.

[40] In fact, applications of *Saunders v Vautier* (1841) 4 Beav 115, Cr & Ph 240—or its derivative, the Variation of Trusts Act 1958, which we come to in a moment—are often aimed at reducing tax liabilities, and in these cases it is often unreal to think in terms of the settlor's wishes being overridden. Many settlors have tax avoidance as one of their main concerns in making their trust, and will be happy to see the beneficiaries further streamlining it. In these cases, *Saunders v Vautier* is better seen and judged as a part of the facility which the law offers the settlor: a device by which he can have his disposition fine-tuned as circumstances develop.

[41] *Gosling v Gosling* (1859) John 265, 272 (adopted as the classic exposition of the doctrine in *Wharton v Masterman* [1895] AC 186, 192–3).

based less on the settlor's actual disposition than on the objectives of the rights argument itself.[42]

10.5 THE VARIATION OF TRUSTS ACT 1958

The rule in *Saunders v Vautier*[43] allows the trust to be dismantled only if all the beneficiaries are adult and not affected by incapacity, and agree to the initiative. The rule is therefore unavailable in many cases. For example, the beneficiaries may include children, or people not yet born, or adult beneficiaries who are incapacitated by mental illness or who cannot be found. But the law goes on, in the Variation of Trusts Act 1958,[44] to provide that in various cases of this kind, trusts may be modified or dissolved, on the strength of a judge's supplying such people's agreement on their behalf.[45]

The Act details the kinds of people for whom a judge can give consent in this way.[46] They are those under 18 (including the unborn), those incapacitated, (roughly speaking) those who might become beneficiaries in the future,[47] and the beneficiaries under the discretionary element of a protective trust,[48] where that element has not yet come into effect. There is thus no power under the Act to supply the consent of a beneficiary simply on the grounds that his whereabouts are not known, or that, however inconveniently, he refuses to consent to what is proposed. In most trusts, there is a mixture of people covered by the Act and others. A modification can then occur only if the judge supplies consent on behalf of the former, and the rest give their own consent.[49]

---

[42] The rule was rejected for the United States in *Claflin v Claflin* 149 Mass 19 (1889) and following cases, allowing what is there termed the settlor's 'dead hand' to prevail over what the English rule treats as the beneficiary's right to unencumbered enjoyment. See G Alexander (1985) 37 Stanford LR 1189. J Getzler (2009) 10 *Theoretical Inquiries in Law* 355 opens up the apparent political paradoxes in the contrast between the two positions.

[43] (1841) 4 Beav 115, Cr & Ph 240.   [44] See J Harris *Variation of Trusts* (1975).

[45] Alternatively, and avoiding the need to go to court, the settlor may have given one or more people the power to reconfigure the trust's beneficial arrangements. These might be the trustees, or some or all of the adult beneficiaries of full capacity, or an outsider; the latter two categories being perhaps referred to as 'protector(s)'. See D Waters in A Oakley (ed) *Trends in Contemporary Trust Law* (1996) ch 4.

[46] Section 1(1).

[47] Section 1(1)(b): eg the person a beneficiary may at some time marry, or the people who will be a beneficiary's next-of-kin when he dies: *Knocker v Youle* [1986] 1 WLR 934.

[48] See section 9.2.

[49] There is an inelegancy here. The Act allows consent to be supplied in the cause of 'varying or revoking' the trust (s 1(1)), which has been held to exclude the complete restructuring of it (*Re T's Settlement Trusts* [1964] Ch 158, 162; *Re Holt's Settlement* [1969] 1 Ch 100). *Saunders v Vautier* (1841) 4 Beav 115, Cr & Ph 240 however allows only the revocation of the trust, after

The Act is not designed simply to remove obstacles from the path of those who are able to consent for themselves. A judge can normally supply consent on a person's behalf only if the proposed variation is to that person's benefit.[50] In most cases, the proposed variation will bring financial gain to that person, and the judge has no difficulty in seeing this as the necessary benefit. (Sometimes chances are involved, but the judge will then take an actuarial approach to finding financial gain.)[51] But the Act requires benefit as a proxy for a more nebulous, but essentially correct, inquiry whether the person in question would have wanted the modification to which his consent is being supplied, if he had been adult, of full capacity, etc.[52] In one case the judge, posing himself the latter question, found benefit to an elderly, mentally incapacitated beneficiary in a variation that deprived her of a small amount of income that she did not need, but that saved large sums in tax for her presumable heirs.[53] Other decisions too have departed from a strictly financial view of benefit, but in a way that seems less about a wider view of benefit than about the imposition of the judge's own values. Thus judges have perceived benefit in a proposed variation that, though likely to be financially detrimental to infant beneficiaries, was calculated to secure family amity;[54] and in a variation postponing from 21 to 30 the age at which infant beneficiaries would come into their interests, on the basis that this would improve their moral fibre.[55] Conversely, and most strikingly of all, they have found a proposed variation *not* to children's benefit when, although to their financial advantage, it would have involved their moving to Jersey.[56]

---

which there can be a resettlement amounting either to a varying or a complete restructuring of the original trust. There is thus a mismatch in what can be achieved, and the procedure to be used for achieving it, as between those relying on *Saunders v Vautier* and those for whom the Act is invoked.

[50] Section 1(1). Benefit is not required in the case of a beneficiary under the discretionary element of a protective trust that has not yet come into effect: perhaps because such a person's role in the trust is viewed (cynically, but correctly) as to lend colour to a device aimed at protecting the principal beneficiary's entitlement against the effects of bankruptcy (see section 9.2).

[51] *Re Cohen's Will Trusts* [1959] 1 WLR 865; *Re Holt's Settlement* [1969] 1 Ch 100, 122; *Goulding v James* [1997] 2 All ER 239, 242.

[52] *Re Van Gruisen's Will Trusts* [1964] 1 WLR 449.   [53] *Re CL* [1969] 1 Ch 587.

[54] *Re Remnant's Settlement Trusts* [1970] Ch 560. But in *Re Tinker's Settlement* [1960] 1 WLR 1011, on similar facts, the judge refused to find benefit.

[55] *Re Holt's Settlement* [1969] 1 Ch 100.

[56] *Re Weston's Settlements* [1969] 1 Ch 223. Although the judgment lauds an upbringing in England, the objection was perhaps less to an upbringing in Jersey as such, than to a life organized around financial considerations. General adoption of the latter perspective would of course be fatal to large numbers of proposals for variation which are in fact accepted.

The Act provides that, given benefit in the cases where it is required, the court 'may if it thinks fit' supply consent 'on behalf of' a person who cannot give it for himself.[57] These words introduce an element of discretion. They allow the judge, asking the familiar question 'would a beneficiary able to consent for himself agree to this?', to consent on a beneficiary's behalf only if he thinks the proposed modification offers the beneficiary *enough* benefit.[58] They also allow the judge to refuse consent on a beneficiary's behalf if that question deserves a negative answer on grounds other than the beneficiary's self-interest. But given a positive answer to the question, the judge should use the discretion against giving consent only if to consent would involve the court in an illegality.[59] By contrast, involvement in legal tax avoidance is not regarded as a problem,[60] and indeed this is the nature of most applications under the Act. Nor is there an objection to departure from the settlor's wishes: the rule in *Saunders v Vautier*[61] allows departure on the part of beneficiaries who are able to consent for themselves, and the Act operates to extend that rule to those not able to consent for themselves.[62]

10.6 CHARITABLE TRUSTS

Finally, the law has some rules allowing specifically for modifications in the duties of charity trustees.

Foremost among these is the cy près jurisdiction, already referred to in section 6.1. Where a trust to promote a charitable object fails, it must be restructured into a new form in which it can carry on—ie its trustees must be given new duties—by 'application cy près'.[63] Traditionally, the idea of

---

[57] Section 1(1).

[58] *Re Van Gruisen's Will Trusts* [1964] 1 WLR 449. A beneficiary able to consent for himself might not consent to a proposed modification giving him some benefit if he can hold out for more: the discretion enables the judge to do the same on behalf of a beneficiary not able to consent for himself.

[59] Such as a fraud on a power (*Re Robertson's Will Trusts* [1960] 1 WLR 1050), or, presumably, the creation of new provisions impermissible under the law of trusts (eg on grounds of perpetuity).

[60] *Re Sainsbury's Settlement* [1967] 1 WLR 476; *Fitzwilliam v IRC* [1993] 1 WLR 1189, 1197 (but cf 1222, and *Re Weston's Settlements* [1969] 1 Ch 223, n 56 above).

[61] (1841) 4 Beav 115, Cr & Ph 240.

[62] This view has not always been taken. In *Re Steed's Will Trusts* [1960] Ch 407, the settlor had designed the trust precisely so that it should not take the form proposed, and consent was for that reason refused. But more recently, in *Goulding v James* [1997] 2 All ER 239, the court preferred the approach described in the text.

[63] The law proceeds directly from failure to application cy près in this way where the failure is 'subsequent', ie occurs after the trust has taken effect. If the failure is 'initial', ie the circumstances are such that the trust fails immediately upon taking effect, there is application cy près

'failure' was limited to the case where the original trust could not realistically continue to function (more or less the same understanding as leads
to a resulting trust where the cy près doctrine does not apply); and the
new form of the trust had to be as close as practicable to the original. Now,
however, there is also a 'failure' where the original trust could continue to
function, but it would be sub-optimal to allow it to do so;[64] and (whether
after a failure of the new or the old variety) the new form of the trust must
reflect not only the original angle of the trust, but also 'the need for the
relevant charity to have purposes which are suitable and effective in the
light of current social and economic circumstances'.[65]

Both old and new versions of the cy près jurisdiction promote utilitarian goals. The old version does so only by preventing the property in
question from being lost to charity (ie the public benefit), as it otherwise
would be. The new version does so more assertively, by increasing the
amount of public benefit flowing from the trust. Both versions have the
potential to conflict with the settlor's intentions, but to differing extents.
Again, the new version is more assertive, allowing restructuring where the
settlor's original plans can be bettered, and allowing the restructured trust
to lie further from those plans. It is certainly possible to see the law here as
breaching faith with settlors: inducing them, facilitatively, to think they
can safely entrust it with the effectuation of their intentions, before in
fact putting their money to ends of its own. Even in the jurisdiction's own
utilitarian terms, indeed, especially the new version of the jurisdiction
may prove counter-productive: it would be no surprise if, given the extent
to which the law is ready to override their intentions, settlors became less
willing to create charitable trusts.

The cy près jurisdiction applies only where there is a 'failure', but
in that event the trust must be modified.[66] The law also contains a rule
whereby the duties of charitable trustees may be modified even without
failure. Where some course of action is not otherwise permitted to the
trustees, but appears to the Charity Commission to be 'expedient in the

only if it is possible to find a 'general charitable intention' on the part of the settlor—that is, his
overriding wish was to give money to charity, rather than exclusively to the particular object
which he named. The cases show a readiness to find such intent despite unpromising facts: see
eg *Re Lysaght* [1966] Ch 191; *Re Woodhams* [1981] 1 WLR 493.

[64] Charities Act 1993 s 13(1)(e)(iii), whereby failure occurs where the trust's original purposes have 'ceased . . . to provide a suitable and effective method of using the property available
by virtue of the gift, regard being had to . . . (on the one hand) the spirit of the gift concerned,
and . . . (on the other) the social and economic circumstances prevailing at the time of the proposed alteration of the original purposes' (s 13(1A)).

[65] Charities Act 1993 s 14B(3)(c).

[66] Save where the failure is initial, and there is no general charitable intent: see n 63.

interests of the charity', the Commission may authorize it.[67] This rule too seems utilitarian (getting the most out of charities) in its inspiration, though in requiring the action to be expedient in the interests of the *charity*, rather than more generally, it may go less far in that direction than the prevailing form of the cy près jurisdiction.

---

[67] Charities Act 1993 s 26(1). The action must be 'in the administration of' the charity, but in the context this may not limit the rule to administrative actions, as opposed to dispositive ones (cf section 9.1). The rule applies 'whether or not [the action] would otherwise be within the powers exercisable by the...trustees'; if it would, the matter is one of elucidation rather than modification (cf section 11.6). By s 26(2), the authorization can apply either to a single action, or to all actions of a designated type. Section 27 allows the Commission to authorize charitable trustees to use the trust property to make payments or waive entitlements *ex gratia*, where they regard themselves as under a moral obligation to do so but would not otherwise be permitted to.

11

Securing Performance

The law advertises the express trust device as a means by which settlors can achieve their intentions. But the mere fact of making a trust—placing the property with trustees, and putting them under a legal obligation to carry out those intentions—does not guarantee that outcome. There exist, however, a number of mechanisms that help to ensure its delivery.[1] This chapter reviews some of them.

First we shall look at mechanisms calculated to ensure that trusts are performed *at all*. Then we shall look at mechanisms calculated to see that they are performed *properly*.

11.1 THE PRESENCE OF TRUSTEES

We saw in section 1.6 that a trustee is essential to the concept of a trust, because a trust consists in duties to handle the trust property in a certain way, and duties are propositions about what people ought to do. The point can also be put more pragmatically. A trust stipulating for property to rest undisturbed for all eternity, if not pointless, would certainly be illegal.[2] Valid and realistic trusts require certain acts to be done: above all, money to be invested and paid out to objects. These things cannot do themselves: someone is required to do them. Ensuring the presence of such a some-one, ie a trustee, is the most fundamentally useful way in which the law can promote the performance of trusts.

The settlor will normally name people as trustees; if he does not, the court will make the appointment.[3] But it cannot be taken for granted that a person nominated as a trustee will be available, either initially or for the trust's duration. He might die or disappear. Or he might be unwilling to act. In the latter case it would be unwise to insist that he does, because of the consequent danger of his doing so badly. So the law allows people to

---

[1] On the relationship between extra-legal ideas of 'trust' and the law's visions regarding the satisfactory performance of its 'trusts', see R Cotterrell (1993) CLP 75.

[2] See section 2.5.   [3] *Dodkin v Brunt* (1868) LR 6 Eq 580.

opt out of being trustees, either by disclaiming a trusteeship for which they have been named before they have embarked on it, or, later, by retiring from it.[4] All this would be a source of vulnerability for trusts if it were not for rules allowing for the appointment of new trustees.[5] The details of these rules are complex, and left to larger works. The effect of all these provisions is encapsulated in the idea that 'a trust will not (be allowed to) fail for want of a trustee'.

11.2 ENSURING THE SUPPLY OF TRUSTEES

But such provisions are not a panacea for ensuring that there are trustees to operate trusts. There must also be an adequate supply of people willing to serve as trustees.

By and large, it seems that the law does not need to do anything positive to induce people to act as trustees. People are generally willing in principle to serve as trustees, out of family loyalty, friendship, and the like, to oblige the settlor and/or the prospective objects, to whom or which they are in some way devoted. And the supply is augmented by the existence of those offering to serve as trustees on a commercial basis, in return for payment: such as solicitors, accountants, banks. So human goodwill and the profit motive between them can be relied upon to produce a supply of people prima facie willing to be trustees. What the law needs to do is essentially conservative: to see that these people are not put off when they find out more about what trusteeship involves: that the position of a trustee is not so unattractive as to make them think better of their original preparedness to act.

In particular, the law needs to ensure that the demands made of trustees—their duties—are kept within tolerable bounds. In our survey of the main kinds of trustees' duties, in Chapters 7–9, we noticed how the law does this. We saw in section 8.5, for example, how instead of the apparent duty in a fixed trust to pay the money to the true designated object, and to no one else, come what may, the trustees are actually required to try to pay the person who shows that he is probably the true designated object (and not anyone who does not), and failing that to pay the money in some circumstances to certain other people, or otherwise into court: which is much more practicable. And we saw

---

[4] Especially under the Trustee Act 1925 s 39.
[5] Particularly the Trustee Act 1925 ss 36 and 41. A settlor can however stipulate that the original trustee shall not be replaced, or that only persons with particular characteristics shall be trustees: *Re Rymer* [1895] 1 Ch 19. If a replacement is required and is blocked by such stipulations, the trust will fail.

in sections 7.2–7.4 that the general requirement in regard to managing the trust and investing its assets is only to exercise such care and
skill as is reasonable in the circumstances,[6] not to ensure success come
what may. So the demands made of trustees are much less off-putting
than might have been the case.[7] The trend has not been unqualified,
however. There remain some stringent, and so off-putting, duties: especially those aimed at keeping trustees from distraction from the trust's
interests, described in section 11.10. As noted there, and unsurprisingly
in view of our present preoccupation, the strictness of these duties has
been criticized by both judges and commentators.

Further in this vein of ensuring that trusteeship is not too unattractive,
the law also maintains a safety-net provision whereby, when trustees have
in fact broken their duty but acted honestly and reasonably in doing so,
the courts have discretion to relieve them from liability. This is s 61 of the
Trustee Act 1925, which we looked at in section 10.2. This provision was
originally enacted in 1896,[8] upon the recommendation of the House of
Commons Select Committee on the Administration of Trusts. Members
of the committee, and its witnesses, felt that there was a shortage of people
willing to be trustees, and ascribed this to the excessive onerousness of
trustees' duties. So the committee recommended reducing the duties to a
more reasonable level, via this jurisdiction to exonerate trustees who had
broken their duty but acted pardonably.[9] In fact, as section 10.2 explains,
this provision has not been especially successful in reassuring trustees that
nothing unreasonable is expected of them, because it makes no promises
as to the kinds of situations in which relief will be given, and the courts
have tended to avoid making any in applying it; but the case law does contain some more positive elements.[10]

The law also allows for the attenuation of the trustees' duties and the
exclusion of their liabilities by the terms of the trust itself, and this is

---

[6] Trustee Act 2000 s 1(1). The original icon of this rule, before it was given statutory form,
was *Speight v Gaunt* (1883) 22 Ch D 727, 9 App Cas 1 (see too *Re Whiteley* (1886) 33 Ch D
347, *Learoyd v Whiteley* (1887) 12 App Cas 727). The desirability of maintaining the supply
of trustees is specifically adverted to: (1883) 22 Ch D 727, 740, 762. See too *Barnes v Addy*
(1874) 9 Ch App 244, 251–2, 254, 256, concerning the desirability of maintaining the supply
of trustees' professional agents: banks, accountants, etc.

[7] See further section 11.11, explaining how trustees' legal liability has been progressively
curtailed, to the same effect.   [8] Judicial Trustees Act 1896 s 3.

[9] House of Commons Select Committee on the Administration of Trusts, *Report* (1895 HC
248) iv. For the links between this reform, the view that the traditional rules about trustees'
liability were off-putting, and *Speight v Gaunt* (1883) 22 Ch D 727, 9 App Cas 1, n 6 above as
an earlier reaction to the latter problem, see *Report* iv, and *Minutes of Evidence* q 462; see too
qq 422, 552–4.   [10] Especially *Perrins v Bellamy* [1899] 1 Ch 797.

frequently found.[11] Those otherwise prepared to serve as trustees may be unwilling to do so without such an attenuation or exclusion, and to that extent the practice makes a contribution to keeping up the supply of trustees. In practice, however, the mechanism is probably subtler than that. Attenuations and exclusions allow professional and corporate trustees, in particular, to keep down their costs, by removing or reducing the need for insurance and expert advice; such trustees' costs work through into their charges; and the lower their charges, the more likely settlors and beneficiaries are to employ them.

The law's main efforts in the direction of ensuring the supply of trustees thus take the form of ensuring that the demands of trusteeship are not too off-putting. But there is a longstop, in the form of a corporate trustee provided by the state: the Public Trustee. This facility, established by the Public Trustee Act 1906, also flowed from the 1895 Select Committee report. Nowadays, the need for such a longstop is quantitatively much less than it was perceived to be then. This is especially because of the rise of the commercial corporate trustees (banks, etc, whose undertaking of trust work was eased by a change in the law in 1920),[12] and because trusts are nowadays much less commonly made in family situations than they were a century or more ago. The number of trusts in the office's hands climbed sharply in the decade or so immediately after its establishment, and continued rising to peak at over 20,000 in the 1940s, but fell away thereafter. The need for such a longstop is not just quantitative, however: despite the small numbers involved, the Trustee is still apparently regarded as a worthwhile provision for those few cases where, for one reason or another, settlors cannot find ordinary trustees that suit them.

11.3 SECURING AN ACCEPTABLE PERFORMANCE

So far, we have been thinking about the basic, though essential, matter of seeing that trusts are performed at all, by ensuring that they have trustees to perform them. Now, we shall progress to a higher level matter: ensuring that the performance rendered is acceptably good.

It is important for the law's facilitative objective that trustees should achieve at least reasonably good standards of performance. Moreover, it is more desirable that trustees should perform their trusts satisfactorily in the first place than that they should fail but then have to pay compensation.

---

[11] See section 10.1.   [12] Administration of Justice Act 1920 s 17.

This is self-evident so far as the trustees themselves are concerned, but it is also true from the objects' point of view, because recovering such compensation involves time, effort, expense, and unpleasantness, and may ultimately not succeed anyway, if the trustee is a private individual whose own resources do not cover the amounts for which he is responsible (though it is common nowadays for trustees to be covered by insurance).

The remainder of this chapter will be devoted to the mechanisms that help secure a successful performance. First, we shall look at some relatively direct measures, which operate by pointing trustees in the right direction. Then we shall go on to other factors, which work more indirectly, by establishing a culture in which trustees can normally be relied upon to do their job satisfactorily. Finally we shall encounter a further factor: exclusions apart, the legal liability facing trustees who fail in their duties.

11.4 THE STANDARDS REQUIRED OF TRUSTEES

The first of these mechanisms is the most obvious: the standards that the law sets for trustees. On the face of it, it might seem that the higher they are, the better. But that would be wrong.

If the duties were too stringent, trustees, seeking to avoid liability, would err on the side of caution: making for a less satisfactory performance than if they were left more room to manoeuvre. For example, if there were an absolute duty to pay the persons designated by the settlor, the trustees would spend time and (trust) money making as sure as possible of the identity and whereabouts of these persons before paying out. And if they were required never to allow the trust's capital to diminish in value, they would confine themselves to the sorts of ultra-safe financial products that in practice would probably serve the beneficiaries less well than somewhat more adventurous ones. So the setting of trustees' duties at more practicable levels also serves this objective of achieving a decent performance. Because the need for such defensive measures is reduced or eliminated, the trust can be performed, perhaps not perfectly, but at least acceptably, and certainly more expeditiously.

Clauses excluding trustees' liability can be viewed in the same light. It has been held permissible to remove all duties, and to exclude liability in respect of them, except that of honestly acting in the beneficiaries' best interests.[13]

---

[13] See section 10.1. (Though as will be seen there, the position as regards the exclusion of the duties themselves is not completely clear.)

Provisions on these lines are common, either from a desire by settlors to remove the worry of legal liability from the relatives and friends whom they appoint as trustees, or because professional or corporate trustees refuse to act without such an exclusion. Such provisions likewise mean that the trustees need not spend excessive time and money watching their step. But do they go too far? As regards levels of performance in practice, probably not. It is true that, although some attenuations of duties actually specify the settlor's preferred course of action, other attenuations, and certainly exclusions of liability, operate instead to cut the trustees some slack; and that they often permit not only acceptable and expeditious, but also positively poor, performance. But they do not promote the latter: trustees normally want to perform satisfactorily, for reasons considered below. As explained in section 10.1, however, such provisions may be more problematic from other perspectives.

11.5 THE LAW'S ACCOUNTS OF TRUSTEES' DUTIES

A statement, for example, that trustees should in relation to their management duties 'exercise such care and skill as is reasonable in the circumstances'[14] is less conducive to a good performance than a statement telling trustees more exactly what is expected of them. Faced with the uncertainty inherent in the more abstract statement, trustees might err on the side of caution, impeding their performance of the trust as much as if perfection were demanded. Or they might underestimate what is required of them, and fail to provide an acceptable performance.

To some extent the law addresses this problem. It sometimes translates abstract standards such as these into more concrete terms, spelling out what they mean in practice. So, for example, the management duty just referred to is explicated into such specific measures as the diversification of investments and the taking of appropriate advice.[15] Similarly, in the business of payment under a fixed trust, the law stipulates such measures as the placing of advertisements, after which, if the beneficiary does not appear, the trustees should deal with his money on the basis that he is dead.[16] Especially in regard to management duties, however, the law has over time trended away from such explication. In particular, after at one time proscribing most forms of investment altogether from use by

---

[14] Trustee Act 2000 s 1(1): see section 7.2.   [15] Trustee Act 2000 ss 4(3)(b), 5.
[16] See section 8.5.

trustees, the law progressively gave wider scope, the current rule allowing a trustee to 'make any kind of investment that he could make if he were absolutely entitled to the assets of the trust'.[17] From today's perspective, the greater transparency of the previous approach cost too much in terms of substantive restrictiveness.

The Charity Commission publishes (at public expense) semi-authoritative explications of duties that are relevant to charitable trustees.[18]

11.6 ELUCIDATION OF TRUSTEES' DUTIES IN INDIVIDUAL CASES

As the law thus tends not to explicate its general statements of trustees' duties, situations can arise in which trustees remain unsure what is required of them. They can commonly obtain the necessary guidance from their solicitors and other professional advisers. As well as a good understanding of trustees' duties in the abstract, these advisers will have access to information about specific precedents: similar situations that have arisen in the past, where one course of action or another was taken, which a court either approved or disapproved on subsequent litigation.

The law provides a further means of elucidating, and thus helping to secure the good performance of, trustees' duties. Trustees can go to court[19] (at the trust's expense) and have a judge tell them what would be a proper course for them to follow. They can use this procedure, for example, if they are unsure whether a putative beneficiary fits the settlor's definition. For instance, in the case of a trust 'for Adam, on condition that he is a practising Christian', when Adam holds Christian beliefs but attends church only for the annual carol service, they can ask the court to say definitively whether he is entitled.

There are strong incentives for trustees to take advice in these ways. Doing so will almost certainly bring them within the terms of any exclusion they may have: reckless indifference to the beneficiaries' interests is not covered by a term limiting liability to 'dishonesty',[20] and might be shown by failure to take advice. Even where there is no such exclusion,

---

[17] Trustee Act 2000 s 3(1). See section 7.4.

[18] Charities Act 1993 s 29(4), (5); <http://www.charity-commission.gov.uk/publications_and_guidance.asp>.

[19] Or in the case of a charity, to the Charity Commission: Charities Act 1993 ss 26, 29. Section 26 allows the Commission to authorize an action 'whether or not it would otherwise be within the powers exercisable by the charity trustees', so going beyond elucidation into overt modification (see section 10.6).   [20] *Armitage v Nurse* [1998] Ch 241, 250.

moreover, trustees who take advice are likely to be safe from liability. This is certainly the case when the advice is that of a judge: this counts as a definitive statement of the trustees' duty, so they are completely protected when they act upon it.[21] Taking appropriate professional advice about investment, and other management matters, may be the best way of showing that they have taken the required degree of care. And trustees who have broken their duty on the strength of professional advice are much more likely to be relieved from liability under s 61 of the Trustee Act 1925[22] than those who acted in a similar way on their own initiative.[23] To have taken advice is thus in trustees' interests if the advice turns out to be bad: but more usually it will be good, so encouraging trustees to take it again helps towards securing a satisfactory performance from them.

11.7 BACKGROUND FACTORS PROMOTING SATISFACTORY PERFORMANCE

Now we move to factors lying more in the background, which operate by establishing a culture in which satisfactory performance is more likely than it would otherwise be. Here we shall look at three of the most important: the characteristics of those made trustees in the first place; the ability of beneficiaries to scrutinize the trustees' activities, and so criticize them; and a rule, or set of rules, whereby trustees must not allow themselves to be distracted by factors that might lead them to neglect their duty to serve the trust.

11.8 TRUSTEES' CHARACTERISTICS

Perhaps the most important of all the factors promoting the successful performance of trusts is the nature of those who are trustees.[24]

Children cannot be appointed trustees.[25] People convicted of crimes of dishonesty, bankrupts, or deemed unsuitable for certain other reasons, cannot normally be trustees of charities,[26] and are liable to be removed

---

[21] Charity trustees taking a formal view from the Charity Commission are similarly protected: Charities Act 1993 ss 26(1), 29(2).

[22] See section 10.2.   [23] *Re Allsop* [1914] 1 Ch 1, 13.

[24] For recognition of the relationship between this factor and the judicial approach to the maintenance of standards, see *Edge v Pensions Ombudsman* [2000] Ch 602, 630, 633.

[25] Law of Property Act 1925 s 20. Children may, of course, find themselves trustees of constructive and (some) resulting trusts, which do not involve their appointment as such.

[26] Charities Act 1993 s 72. The lack of ongoing scrutiny by charitable settlors, and the absence of particular beneficiaries, increases the risk of malversation.

from other trusts.[27] Those incapacitated by illness are liable to be removed, and a trustee who remains out of the United Kingdom for more than a year may also be removed.[28]

Beyond that, the choice of trustees is a matter for settlors themselves, though there is further provision for removing trustees who turn out to neglect the trust's interests[29] or who the beneficiaries wish to see removed[30] or who prove unsuitable to administer a charity.[31] A settlor will generally choose people in whom he has confidence, and who seem to him suitable for the kind of trust in question. Assuming that settlors' judgement is mostly good (sometimes, of course, it is unfortunately not), those whom they select can generally be relied upon to make a decent job of their task.[32]

There are some specific characteristics that those chosen as trustees are likely to have, which also affect the prospects of a satisfactory performance. Two main types of trustee are commonly used, and they have different kinds of motivation towards performing their trust well, and different strengths and weaknesses affecting their likelihood of doing so.

One type of person frequently appointed trustee is someone closely connected with the settlor himself and/or the objects of the trust. In a family trust, for example, it might be a relative or friend or colleague of the settlor. In a trust for company employees, representatives of the workforce and the board would probably feature largely. The motivation of trustees of this kind towards performing the trust well arises from a sense of loyalty to the settlor and/or the objects.

The alternative is a professional trustee: a person or entity prepared to act as a trustee as part of their work. A professional trustee may be an individual, eg a solicitor or accountant, or a corporation, commonly a bank (which of course in practice operates through individual officers). Professional trustees' services will normally have to be paid for. Their principal motivation to perform the trust well is a desire to do a good job, but they are also encouraged by commercial and professional factors.

The commercial encouragement comes from competition with other professional trustees (and with lay trustees too, for that matter), settlors

---

[27] Trustee Act 1925 s 36(1).   [28] *Ibid* s 36(1).

[29] *Letterstedt v Broers* (1884) 9 App Cas 371; *Clarke v Heathfield (No 2)* [1985] ICR 606.

[30] Trusts of Land and Appointment of Trustees Act 1996 s 19.

[31] Charities Act 1993 s 18.

[32] Where a new trustee is appointed (the relevant—complicated—rules vest this power, or allow it to be vested, in a variety of persons, as well as in the courts), the same considerations will apply.

seeking the best buy amongst them. This is not a complete recipe for securing a good performance from them, however, because the market is an imperfect one. Although their prices can be compared, from their published tariffs, it is more difficult to judge their quality. In particular, people who appoint trustees at all must rarely do so more than once in their lifetime, and so are ill placed to make comparisons about performance. The deficiency is, however, to an extent made up by such trustees' professional standards. Banks, for example, have training, rule books, and procedures for their staff, calculated to ensure a good performance. They are also subject to the control of the Financial Services Authority,[33] with its systems of authorization, training, and discipline, and the Financial Ombudsman Service.[34] There are parallel regulatory arrangements for solicitors, accountants, and so on.

The strength of lay trustees such as family friends is their intimate understanding of the settlor's wishes and the objects' situations, which makes especially for a less cumbersome[35] and more refined handling of a trust's dispositive discretions. On the other hand lay trustees are likely to be relatively weak on matters such as investment, and their closeness to the settlor and objects may also make them susceptible to pressure, so that they go wrong: for example, they may be persuaded into exercising a power of maintenance or advancement not for the benefit of the child, but so as to help its parents out of some financial difficulties. The strengths and weaknesses of professional trustees are generally the reverse of these. They should be adept at the managerial aspects of the trust. Being more remote, they will lack the intimate understandings shown by their lay counterparts, but this should make them better able to resist improper pressures.[36] So the two types of trustees are complementary to one another, and the best approach is often to combine the two: to have at least one trustee of each kind.

It is wrong to view the ideal performance as that given by a trustee uninfluenced by settlor or objects: trustees may consult and attend to input

---

[33] <http://www.fsa.gov.uk>.   [34] <http://www.financial-ombudsman.org.uk>.

[35] In particular, trustees who know the beneficiaries personally can dispense with the level of proof of identity, etc, that a professional trustee would need to demand: see House of Commons Select Committee on the Administration of Trusts, *Report* (1895 HC 248), *Minutes of Evidence* qq 434, 488–90.

[36] But note *Nestle v National Westminster Bank plc* [1993] 1 WLR 1260 and *Re Pauling's Settlement Trusts* [1964] Ch 303, notorious cases where bank trustees fell short of such expectations.

from both,[37] so long as they do not allow themselves to be dictated to.[38] Trustees are often selected precisely because of their likely receptiveness to such input. They may indeed be selected because they can supply the input themselves, usually through being also settlor or beneficiary. The appointment of such 'stakeholder' trustees is common. In pension fund trusts some of the trustees must be drawn from the scheme's members,[39] and others will usually represent the employer: the overall mix being explicitly seen as a factor promoting appropriate performance.[40] Charity trustees often include 'consumers' of the charity's activities.[41] In certain private (especially family) trusts of land, the law used to give the principal beneficiary (the 'tenant for life') most of the trustees' powers,[42] and it remains common for such a person to be a trustee or to be delegated trustees' powers.[43]

While the trustees' characteristics are a factor promoting good performance, they can however be a source of weakness. The law contains some provisions calculated to check that possibility. In case the appointed trustees lack the professional expertise needed to carry out the trust's administrative functions, they can employ appropriate professional assistance,[44] and indeed delegate such functions altogether.[45] (But they cannot delegate their dispositive functions:[46] this would be a case of failure to exercise their own discretion.) Against the possibility of ineptitude or dishonesty,

---

[37] *Fraser v Murdoch* (1881) 6 App Cas 855, Scotland; *Re Manisty's Settlement* [1974] Ch 17, 26; *Hartigan Nominees Pty Ltd v Rydge* (1992) 29 NSWLR 405, Australia; *Breadner v Granville-Grossman* [2001] Ch 523, [20]–[22]. (Sometimes they *must* consult, and in this case give effect to their majority wish, 'so far as consistent with the general interest of the trust': Trusts of Land and Appointment of Trustees Act 1996 s 11. See too *X v A* [2000] 1 All ER 490.)

[38] *Re Pauling's Settlement Trusts* [1964] Ch 303; *Re Locker's Settlement Trusts* [1977] 1 WLR 1323; *Turner v Turner* [1984] Ch 100.   [39] Pensions Act 2004 ss 241–3.

[40] *Edge v Pensions Ombudsman* [2000] Ch 602, 630, 633. Having representation from one constituency but not the other, however, can cause distortion: M Milner [1997] Conv 89.

[41] Charity Commission *Users on board: users who become trustees* (2000), <http://www.charity-commission.gov.uk/publications/cc24.asp>.

[42] Settled Land Act 1925 Part II.

[43] Trusts of Land and Appointment of Trustees Act 1996 s 9.

[44] *Speight v Gaunt* (1883) 22 Ch D 727, 9 App Cas 1; and see *Barnes v Addy* (1874) 9 Ch App 244, 251–2, 254, 256, and section 14.1 generally, for rules calculated to ensure that such assistants are not frightened off by the prospect of over-stringent liability if things go wrong.

[45] Trustee Act 2000 s 11, and Part IV generally. The rules for charities are slightly different: *ibid*. In choosing a delegate, etc, trustees are required to 'exercise such care and skill as is reasonable in the circumstances' (Sch 1 para 3). The decision whether to delegate at all seems to be controlled by the traditional requirement to act as a prudent businessman looking after others' interests.

[46] Except to some extent in charitable trusts, where (Trustee Act 2000 s 11(3)) they may delegate the 'carrying out' of decisions they have taken—something that may presumably involve the taking of further, smaller scale, decisions.

the settlor, court, Charity Commission (in case of charity),[47] or trustees themselves[48] can appoint a custodian, ie a bank or similar whose sole function is to hold the trust assets safely; and trustees must act in not less than a pair to receive purchase money when selling land[49] (though it is unclear why that should be a case of special danger). Presumably as a corrective to idiosyncrasy,[50] except in charities[51] and pension trusts[52] (the justification for these exceptions probably lying in the larger number of trustees such trusts often have) they must be unanimous in choosing their courses of action.[53]

A settlor may not be content to rely on his trustees' characteristics. Especially in 'off-shore' jurisdictions, he is increasingly likely to introduce a 'protector' into the trust arrangements. The protector is a person, or group of people, given power to veto the trustees' proposed actions, or indeed to instruct the trustees to take a particular course, whether in administrative or dispositive matters; and possibly having few or no legal responsibilities.[54] The settlor will choose as protector a person likely to represent his own thinking regarding the operation of the trust; or that of a particular beneficiary or class of beneficiaries whom he wishes especially to protect.[55] The use of a protector, thus selected for his characteristics, will conduce to a good performance of the trust from the perspective of the person or people represented. Evidently, however, there may be a price to be paid from other perspectives.

11.9 DISCLOSURE AND SCRUTINY OF TRUSTEES' ACTIVITIES

The second of our background factors is the visibility of trustees' activities to those interested. Even if such scrutiny were not the prelude to suing or prosecuting the trustees, it would disclose anything questionable in their

---

[47] Charities Act 1993 s 18.

[48] Trustee Act 2000 s 19; Part IV generally, and Sch 1 para 3.

[49] Law of Property Act 1925 s 27(2).   [50] J Jaconelli [1991] Conv 30.

[51] *Re Whiteley* [1910] 1 Ch 600, 608.   [52] Pensions Act 1995 s 32.

[53] *Luke v South Kensington Hotel* (1879) 11 Ch D 121, 125. The rule in default of a choice to do otherwise can thus be important, and if inappropriate can produce odd results: *Re Mayo* [1943] Ch 302.

[54] D Waters in A Oakley (ed) *Trends in Contemporary Trust Law* (1996) ch 4.

[55] The protector may indeed be the favoured beneficiary or beneficiaries; possibly even the settlor, though in this case the settlor's lack of detachment from the trust assets may leave him enduringly liable to tax upon them, normally a prohibitive consideration.

operation of the trust, and so create a source of pressure and assistance towards a good performance.

It used to be thought that some beneficiaries have a firm right to some trust documents, as an aspect of their beneficial entitlement,[56] though the scope of this right was never very clear.[57] A different approach has now been adopted, however, whereby all beneficiaries—and indeed objects of fiduciary powers of appointment[58]—are recognized as having a right to an account from their trustees,[59] and this right is in turn recognized as entitling them to a certain level of information about the constitution and running of the trust (presumably, whether that information takes the form of extant documents or otherwise).[60] The content of this level of information is also unclear, however; it has to be fixed by a discretionary judicial decision,[61] taken in the circumstances of the individual case.[62] This decision needs to reflect, on the one hand, the likely practical usefulness of the particular information in question to the particular beneficiary in question (so those who are merely make-weight members of very wide discretionary classes can expect little, certainly less than those with fixed entitlements); and on the other hand, any proper reasons for *not* requiring disclosure, in particular the interests in privacy and confidentiality of the various beneficiaries, the trustees themselves, and relevant outsiders. The discretion also allows disclosure to be ordered in some limited way, such as in a redacted form, or to the beneficiary's professional advisers alone.

It is historically accurate, and plausible in principle, to see a beneficiary's claim to information as springing from his right to an account: indeed, the latter without the former would be meaningless. But this basis in the right to an account makes it surprising that the claim to information should be discretionary. The supposition is that the 'right' to an account is the 'right' to have a court supervise, and if necessary to intervene in, the

---

[56] *O'Rourke v Darbishire* [1920] AC 581.

[57] See especially the confused judgments in *Re Londonderry's Settlement* [1965] Ch 918.

[58] For the assimilation of such powers with discretionary trusts (especially by *McPhail v Doulton* [1970] AC 508 and *Mettoy Pension Trustees Ltd v Evans* [1990] 1 WLR 1587), see section 9.2.   [59] For account generally, see sections 13.2–13.8.

[60] *Schmidt v Rosewood Trust Ltd* [2003] 2 AC 709.

[61] *Breakspear v Ackland* [2009] Ch 32, [66]–[71], [96], however, presents the discretion as primarily that of the trustees themselves, the court interfering only to the limited extent that it does with trustees' discretionary decisions generally (see section 13.4, referring to *Gisborne v Gisborne* (1877) 2 App Cas 300; *Tabor v Brooks* (1878) 10 Ch D 273; *Tempest v Lord Camoys* (1882) 21 Ch D 571; *Edge v Pensions Ombudsman* [2000] Ch 602, 630). *Quaere* whether this is a true reading of the thrust of *Schmidt v Rosewood Trust Ltd* [2003] 2 AC 709.

[62] *Schmidt v Rosewood Trust Ltd* [2003] 2 AC 709, [54], [67].

administration of one's trust—as the court itself sees fit.[63] If taken literally, this view would mean that beneficiaries ultimately have no entitlements against their trustees at all, even to be paid the sums stipulated by the settlor in a fixed trust: for the trustees' obligation to make these payments is an aspect of their duty to account, which, we are now told, means whatever a court holds it to mean. This is an unfamiliar vision.[64]

Looked at in its own right, however, investing the claim to information with a discretionary quality seems a reasonable response to the difficulties of balancing the various considerations that may be relevant. But it is not problem-free. It is Kafkaesque that beneficiaries should have to go to court in order to discover whether they can even have the means to find out about a wrong they suspect they may have suffered. And it will be practically difficult for trustees and beneficiaries to know, without the trouble and expense of litigation, how to negotiate issues of disclosure.[65] However, the courts' previous praxis is apparently meant to remain broadly valid.[66] So, apparently, a beneficiary will normally be able to see the documents constituting the trust,[67] and also, unless he has only a remote chance of being favoured under a discretion, to know the names and addresses of the trustees.[68] He can also see the account books that trustees must keep,[69] recording both the state of the trust's investments and the payments out to the objects; and can insist that the accounts be audited.[70] But he will not normally be able to see any letter that the settlor may have given the trustees alongside the trust, letting them know how he would like them to exercise their discretion;[71] nor the agendas and minutes of the trustees' meetings, nor their correspondence with different beneficiaries, in which might be revealed, say, the thinking leading up to their exercise of a power of appointment or suchlike—why, for instance, they decided to give a sister a larger amount of money than her brother.[72] The latter position has even been taken in the context of a charitable trust,[73] notwithstanding the

---

[63] *Ibid* [51]–[54], [66]–[67].
[64] Though it resonates with the statement in *Nestle v National Westminster Bank plc* [1993] 1 WLR 1260, 1279, that trustees should administer trusts in such a way as to produce 'fairness' among the different beneficiaries. See sections 7.4, 9.1.
[65] See *Breakspear v Ackland* [2009] Ch 32, [9]–[10].
[66] *Schmidt v Rosewood Trust Ltd* [2003] 2 AC 709, [54].
[67] *Re Londonderry's Settlement* [1965] Ch 918.
[68] *Re Murphy's Settlements* [1999] 1 WLR 282.
[69] *Pearse v Green* (1819) 1 Jac & W 135, 140.
[70] Public Trustee Act 1906 s 13. This statutory rule is presumably non-discretionary.
[71] *Breakspear v Ackland* [2009] Ch 32.
[72] *Re Londonderry's Settlement* [1965] Ch 918; *Breakspear v Ackland* [2009] Ch 32.
[73] *Re Beloved Wilkes' Charity* (1851) 3 Mac & G 440.

public interest in charities; and of a pension fund trust,[74] notwithstanding
the argument that the members of the pension scheme deserve greater
access because of their contractual rights in it. There is however extensive
provision for the disclosure of more formal kinds of information about
such trusts,[75] and in the case of pension schemes the mandatory presence
of scheme members among the trustees[76] may make it likely that trustees
will agree to wider disclosure.

Perhaps above all else, the reluctance to order disclosure of trustees'
discretionary thinking seems likely to provoke challenge; even in well-run
trusts, discretionary decisions can easily attract dissatisfaction. At one
time, this reluctance could be justified[77] on the ground that trustees have
no duty to think, or to abstain from thinking, in a particular way (other
than in good faith, which is assumed unless clearly disproved)—making
information as to their thoughts irrelevant. Now, however, it is clear that
trustees must take account of proper considerations and not of improper
ones,[78] and information as to their thoughts seems fully relevant to the
question whether they have done so. A refusal to order disclosure of such
information might still be defended, however.[79] It has been suggested that
the questioning and disputation consequent upon revealing their thinking might render the trustees' role so invidious as to deter people from
agreeing to undertake it in the first place, so endangering the supply of
trustees: the preoccupation with which we began this chapter.[80] Another
suggestion is that having to disclose their thinking might lead trustees
to exercise their discretion one way rather than another with an eye to
minimizing the ensuing dissension, rather than according to what they
see as the real merits: so that preserving confidentiality actually conduces
to a more satisfactory performance of their function. A third suggestion
is that to compel disclosure would be to injure the private quality that

---

[74] *Wilson v Law Debenture Trust Corp plc* [1995] 2 All ER 337. Cf D Hayton [2005] Conv
229, 234–7, suggesting that, on the contrary, disclosure of discretionary thinking is required
of pension fund trustees, for the reason given in the text.

[75] Charities Act 1993 Part VI (trustees of charities must make their accounts available to
the public, and, where their charity's annual turnover exceeds a specified sum, must each year
submit accounts and a report to the Charity Commission); Occupational Pension Schemes
(Disclosure of Information) Regulations 1996 SI No 1655.

[76] Pensions Act 2004 ss 241–3.

[77] As in *Re Londonderry's Settlement* [1965] Ch 918, 936–7.

[78] See sections 9.5–9.6. This development makes it curious that the traditional position
regarding disclosure was reiterated in *Sieff v Fox* [2005] 1 WLR 3811, [37]—a decision playing an important part in this very development.

[79] See generally *Breakspear v Ackland* [2009] Ch 32.

[80] *Re Londonderry's Settlement* [1965] Ch 918, 937; *Breakspear v Ackland* [2009] Ch 32, [56].

appropriately characterizes (at any rate family) trusts.[81] One can see the sense in these insights. On the other hand, such problems will surely arise from the trustees' very decisions, eg the simple fact that the sister received more than the brother. To explain the thinking behind the decisions is unlikely to make matters worse, and might help. Moreover, one cannot satisfactorily note only the drawbacks of disclosure, and overlook the arguments in its favour, such as the spur it gives to trustees' compliance with their duties, and the boost it gives to the beneficiaries' 'ownership' of the trust.

All this is not the whole story, however. Information not otherwise available can sometimes be elicited in the event of litigation, either by a pre-trial order for the disclosure of relevant documents (once known as 'discovery'), or by the questioning of a witness. A beneficiary who sues the trustees, therefore, might force them to disclose their thinking in one of these ways.[82] While in theory this is possible only once the beneficiary has an arguable case for alleging breach of trust on the basis of other evidence, in practice that case might rest on inferences, the trustees being forced into the open in order to dispel these.

11.10 RULES AGAINST DISTRACTION

We have noted that trustees are fiduciaries, and must attend loyally to the trust objects' interests, taking no account of others, such as their own.[83] The third background factor promoting a satisfactory performance of their duties is a prophylactic rule, enjoining trustees and other fiduciaries from entering upon certain situations in which it is particularly predictable that they might do otherwise. This is the 'no conflict' rule,[84] whereby fiduciaries must not allow themselves to be so placed that their

---

[81] See section 2.4; D Hayton [2005] Conv 229.

[82] *Scott v National Trust for Places of Historic Interest or Natural Beauty* [1998] 2 All ER 705, 719; *Breakspear v Ackland* [2009] Ch 32, [13], [72].

[83] See sections 1.10, 7.5. As an off-shoot of this duty, they—and other fiduciaries—must confess to their principals any breach they may commit of their other duties: *Item Software (UK) Ltd v Fassihi* [2004] BCC 994. For the relationship between this and the anti-distraction duties discussed in the text, see R Lee [2009] Conv 236.

[84] Judicial statements and exemplifying decisions are legion; the most celebrated include *Aberdeen Railway Co v Blaikie Bros* (1854) 1 Macq 461, Scotland; *Bray v Ford* [1896] AC 44, 51; *Regal (Hastings) Ltd v Gulliver* [1967] 2 AC 134n; *Boardman v Phipps* [1967] 2 AC 46; *Hospital Products Ltd v US Surgical Corp* (1984) 156 CLR 41, Australia. Section 17.4 discusses the constructive trust that may arise when property is acquired in breach of this rule.

own interests (or their other duties, for example under another trust),[85] even *might* conflict with their duties under the trust.[86]

In turn, this rule is often portrayed in terms of a collection of more specific sub-rules and sub-sub-rules, described below. The differences between these sub-rules and sub-sub-rules reflect different ways in which trustees might be called upon to serve the objects' best interests, and in which they might be distracted from doing so. Their disaggregation of the no conflict rule is helpful in focusing its implications, but carries the danger of sight being lost of its essential point. The duty of loyalty, and the set of duties created by these further rules supporting it, are commonly, though not universally, referred to as 'fiduciary' duties.[87]

There are three principal sub-rules. One, the most general, prohibits trustees from entering into arrangements (most obviously, but not necessarily, taking bribes) calculated to influence their conduct of the trust.[88] The second is that a trustee must not purchase property from his trust.[89] The duty of a trustee selling trust property is to obtain as high a price as possible for it. A trustee purchasing it for himself would wish to pay as low a price as possible. To obviate the danger that the latter consideration might eclipse the former, trustees are barred from buying trust property.[90] The third sub-rule is that a trustee must not extract profit from his position as trustee. This in turn yields perhaps three sub-sub-rules. One prohibits a trustee from making an acquisition for himself that it was his duty to strive to make for the trust: a trustee contemplating the possibility of gaining for himself might neglect that duty.[91] The second requires trustees not to use the trust's shares to vote themselves into directorships of companies in which the trust is invested.[92] Their interest in the resulting

---

[85] For the issues that arise in this particular context, see M Conaglen *Fiduciary Loyalty* (2010) ch 6.

[86] For exploration of the idea that this rule is prophylactic, see particularly M Conaglen *Fiduciary Loyalty* (2010), especially ch 4.

[87] Compare eg M Conaglen *Fiduciary Loyalty* (2010) ch 3, applying the 'fiduciary' label only to the no conflict duty and its derivatives, not to the duty of loyalty itself; L Smith in J Getzler (ed) *Rationalizing Property, Equity and Trust: Essays in Honour of Edward Burn* (2003) ch 4, taking the opposite position. Other than as such a source of confusion, the question may be ultimately unimportant.

[88] *Vatcher v Paull* [1915] AC 372, 379; *Re Smith* [1896] 1 Ch 71.

[89] Commonly known as the 'self-dealing rule'. Another rule, the 'fair-dealing rule', states that trustees' purchases from their beneficiaries are the subject of suspicion. For the relationship between the two rules, see *Tito v Waddell (No 2)* [1977] Ch 106, 241; M Conaglen *Fiduciary Loyalty* (2010) 128–39.

[90] *Campbell v Walker* (1800) 5 Ves 678; *ex p Lacey* (1802) 6 Ves 625; *ex p James* (1803) 8 Ves 337. It is irrelevant whether the purchase is profitable for the trustee: that is why this rule does not merge with the next.   [91] *Keech v Sandford* (1726) Sel Cas t King 61.

[92] *Re Macadam* [1946] Ch 73; cf *Re Gee* [1948] Ch 284.

fees might distract them from their duty to cast the trust's votes for the most promising directors, so as best to promote its interests. The third prohibits trustees from paying themselves from the trust assets: if they could, their self-interest might lead them to maximize the extent of their work and so their charges, cutting across their duties to use their best judgement in deciding what work the trust needs, and normally to maximize the financial benefit to the objects.[93]

The rules can all be modified or excluded by the settlor,[94] by the consent of the beneficiaries,[95] or by the leave of the court.[96] The last of them, concerning the payment of trustees, has also attracted a collection of provisions negativing it, at first in narrow situations where there was inherently no danger of abuse[97] but latterly by way of a general regime whereby professional trustees and trust corporations can have 'reasonable remuneration' for their work.[98]

These anti-distraction rules are best understood as a response to the difficulties arising from the principal–agent problem associated with trustees and other fiduciaries, and explained in section 1.10. The agent's function is to act on his principal's behalf, but the agent's interests are not aligned with those of the principal, and, since the principal cannot well— even with a court's assistance—supervise the agent so as to see that his interests are indeed being loyally served, it is best to require the agent to ignore his own interests entirely.[99] Although thus intelligible, however, the rules are open to criticism.[100]

In practice, the rules are used not merely prospectively, to enjoin fiduciaries in general from embarking on a potentially disloyal course of action, but very often retrospectively, to render particular fiduciaries tangibly liable when they have done otherwise. When this occurs in the

---

[93] *Robinson v Pett* (1734) 3 P Wms 249.

[94] This seems to be the basis of *Edge v Pensions Ombudsman* [2000] Ch 602: the trust being structured so as to have beneficiaries as trustees, they were able to make a discretionary decision in their own favour. (Note also Pensions Act 1995 s 39.) While the duties under discussion are excludable, that which they are primarily calculated to promote, the duty to serve the beneficiaries' interests, is not: *Armitage v Nurse* [1998] Ch 241.

[95] In the case of contractually hired fiduciaries, such consent is commonly given by an express or implied term of the contract: *Kelly v Cooper* [1993] AC 205. But cf *Hilton v Barker Booth & Eastwood* [2005] 1 WLR 567.

[96] *Re Duke of Norfolk's Settlement Trusts* [1982] Ch 61 (trustees' remuneration); *Re Drexel Burnham Lambert UK Pension Plan* [1995] 1 WLR 32 (extracting a profit).

[97] *Cradock v Piper* (1850) 1 Mac & G 664.

[98] Trustee Act 2000 ss 29, 30. These provisions were preceded by narrower ones: Judicial Trustees Act 1896 s 1(5), Public Trustee Act 1906 ss 4(3) and 9, Trustee Act 1925 s 42.

[99] See J Getzler in A Burrows and A Rodger (eds) *Mapping the Law: Essays in Honour of Peter Birks* (2006) ch 31. [100] See especially J Langbein (2005) 114 Yale LJ 929.

absence of concrete ill-effects in the circumstances of the individual case, the result appears unjust. This comment can be made especially of two notorious cases in which a fiduciary made an acquisition for himself that he ought to have sought for his principal, though there was little or no chance of his actually obtaining it for the latter. In *Keech v Sandford*[101] a lease was held on trust. As the lease approached its end, the trustee tried to persuade the landlord to renew it in the trust's favour. When the landlord was unwilling, the trustee secured a renewal in his own favour. It was held that he should not have done so, and he was ordered to hold the new lease on trust too. Although commentators have found that the appearance may be deceptive or misleading,[102] the report of the case appears to suggest that there was *no* chance of a renewal in the trust's favour, in which event the decision is to be explained solely on the basis that the trustee, holding all the informational cards, should be given the disbenefit of any conceivable doubt;[103] or even as aiming to set a deterrent example to fiduciaries in general, by treating the individual facts as irrelevant.[104] Likewise in *Boardman v Phipps*[105] a trust's solicitor, treated as caught by the same rule,[106] discovered a business opportunity when working on the trust's behalf. He seized this opportunity to make a profit for himself, substantially benefiting the trust as well. Although there seems to have been no realistic prospect of the trust itself exploiting the opportunity in question, it was held that he should not have done so, and he was ordered to make his gains over to the trust. His duties required him to give uncontaminated consideration to the questions whether the trust could take the opportunity, and if so how this might be achieved.

---

[101] (1726) Sel Cas t King 61.

[102] See S Cretney (1969) 33 Conv 161; J Getzler in A Burrows and A Rodger (eds) *Mapping the Law: Essays in Honour of Peter Birks* (2006) ch 31; A Hicks [2010] CLJ 287.

[103] This proposition is certainly recognized and implemented in *ex p Lacey* (1802) 6 Ves Jr 625, 627; *ex p James* (1803) 8 Ves Jr 337, 345–6 (specifically connecting it with *Keech v Sandford* (1726) Sel Cas t King 61, though not by name); *ex p Bennett* (1805) 10 Ves Jr 381, 400. But J Langbein (2005) 114 Yale LJ 929, 944–51 argues that the proposition has now (note the antiquity of those decisions) been undermined by reforms in accounting procedures, making it easier to determine the actual facts.

[104] *Keech v Sandford* (1726) Sel Cas t King 61, 62; *Parker v McKenna* (1874) 10 Ch App 90, 124–5; *Korkontzilas v Soulos* [1997] 2 SCR 217, [33]–[34], [50], Canada.

[105] [1967] 2 AC 46. See too *Regal (Hastings) Ltd v Gulliver* [1967] 2 AC 134n.

[106] The solicitor was a fiduciary *vis-à-vis* the trustees, who employed him. Since they had a duty loyally to promote their beneficiaries' interests, they could not allow the solicitor to do otherwise. But *quaere* how he owed his duty directly to the beneficiaries, who were the claimants. The view that he did so is analogous to the position taken in *Colour Quest Ltd v Total Downstream UK Plc* [2010] 3 WLR 1192; see section 12.1.

It can also be argued that, while the anti-distraction rules are an intelligible response to the principal–agent problem, they are a sub-optimal one, even a counter-productive one. Suppression of all self-interest on the fiduciary's part may well entail not so much uncompromised pursuit of the principal's interest as, for the lack of any reason to do better, inertia. It is more helpful to align the two interests,[107] then allow the fiduciary to pursue his own after all.[108] This insight can be seen as the influence behind the use of 'stakeholder' trustees (see section 11.8) in general and, in particular, the erosion of the rule against trustees' remuneration, and the fact that other fiduciaries are generally remunerated, usually with the principal's consent.[109] A principal whose interests are aligned with his fiduciary's in any other way, too, should think himself fortunate rather than threatened. This was the position in *Boardman v Phipps*:[110] the solicitor's exploitation of the opportunity benefited, and was always intended to benefit, not only himself but also the trust. In fact, when the solicitor was ultimately ordered to make over his personal profit to the trust, he was compensated for his work in generating it. This outcome can be seen as consistent with the argument here, but it does not represent a full embodiment of it. The jurisdiction to compensate operates after the event and opaquely, so cannot incentivize trustees and other fiduciaries in the way that an upfront provision does. The courts have also said that the jurisdiction should not be used in such a way as to encourage fiduciaries to enter into situations of conflict:[111] a position that, if not precisely opposed to that under discussion, is certainly not sympathetic to it.

It is very possible, therefore, that the prophylactic anti-distraction rules are unjust to fiduciaries, and indeed harmful to principals. If so, they should be dropped, leaving only the original duty to serve the best interests of the trust.[112] Some judges have leant in this direction. They have said that a trustee or other fiduciary should be required to ignore his own interests only where there is a 'real sensible possibility of conflict';[113]

---

[107] For discussion of the design parameters, see eg D Sappington (1991) 5 *Journal of Economic Perspectives* 45.

[108] See further W Bishop and D Prentice (1983) 46 MLR 289.

[109] There is also the more basic point that without payment, people may be unwilling to serve in these roles at all, which is damaging in the way discussed in section 11.2.

[110] [1967] 2 AC 46. Similarly *O'Sullivan v Management Agency and Music Ltd* [1985] QB 428.   [111] *Guinness v Saunders* [1990] 2 AC 663, 701.

[112] See J Langbein (2005) 114 Yale LJ 929.

[113] Lord Upjohn in *Boardman v Phipps* [1967] 2 AC 46, 124. His Lordship dissented from the decision described above because he thought, given the unlikelihood of the trust pursuing the opportunity whether it had uncontaminated advice from the solicitor or not, that the solicitor's pursuit of it could not have distracted him from his responsibilities to the trust.

or only where attending to his own interests would verifiably cause loss to his principal.[114]

11.11 LEGAL ENFORCEMENT

A final factor conducing to satisfactory performance of trusts is the possibility of trustees who fail in their duties being legally liable.

This liability is primarily civil. The civil liability of trustees—its most protuberant component being known as their duty to 'account'—will be detailed in Chapter 13, but in essence it operates in the manner familiar from the laws of tort and contract, requiring them to rectify the consequences of the breach. This was not always the case, however. Until quite recently,[115] albeit decreasingly,[116] trustees were liable in at least some situations on a stricter basis. They were required not to rectify the consequences of their breach, but to ensure the proper state of the trust fund: that is, to maintain the fund (if necessary, augmenting it from their own pockets) in the state indicated by their authority regarding it. Say, for example, the trust property was stolen from the trustees. As the loss was not an authorized disbursement, they stood liable to correct it. In reality, the court would commonly excuse them in such a case,[117] but the onus was on them to prove the theft and persuade the court to do so; there were no promises; and the picture was patchy, as although loss by theft was generally excused, loss by fraud was not,[118] and nor indeed was loss by theft, if the stolen trust property had taken an unauthorized form (such as silver, when the trustees were permitted only to hold gold), notwithstanding that the theft was in no way a consequence of this.[119]

---

[114] *Murad v Al-Saraj* [2005] EWCA Civ 959, [82]-[83], [121], [158], suggesting also that while the anti-distraction rules may originally have been merited by the difficulties of supervision and proof characteristic of the principal–agent problem, improvements in the relevant procedures have reduced these difficulties to the point where they no longer require a special response.

[115] The old approach was (probably) finally abandoned in *Target Holdings Ltd v Redferns (a firm)* [1996] AC 421.

[116] *Speight v Gaunt* (1883) 22 Ch D 727, 9 App Cas 1 is iconic of a trend to reallocate some situations from the category in which they were treated thus to a category in which there was liability only if the trustees failed to exercise due care and skill, and only for such losses as were the reasonably foreseeable consequence of such failure (*Bristol & West Building Society v Mothew* [1998] Ch 1, 17). Loss of the trust property by theft or fraud, as in the example given in the ensuing text, would henceforth be dealt with in this way.

[117] See eg *Jones v Lewis* (1750) 2 Ves Sen 240.

[118] *Eaves v Hickson* (1861) 30 Beav 136.

[119] *Clough v Bond* (1838) 3 My & Cr 490.

The severity of these rules used to provide a powerful weapon against errant trustees, creating large incentives to manage their trusts perfectly. The unpredictability[120] of the rules' operation enhanced this effect, as preventing trustees from building a calculation around these incentives and concluding that, even given their magnitude, imperfection might nonetheless pay. As such, the rules operated not only reactively, to redress actual losses that one would ordinarily recognize (and today's law treats) as the trustees' responsibility, but also proactively, like the prophylactic rules discussed in section 11.10, to minimize the chances of such losses occurring in the first place. In terms of this chapter's theme of securing the performance of trusts, then, the old rules may appear an unqualifiedly good idea. If so, however, why the move away from them? Perhaps partly because they were perceived as downright unjust, but also because, again in terms of this chapter's theme, they came to be seen as counter-productive.[121] Remember what we saw in section 11.3: that the law promotes the performance of trusts better by keeping trustees' responsibilities within tolerable bounds, and thus securing a supply of them, than by greater harshness, which can simply deter people from acting as trustees in the first place. The old approach to liability, with its combination of severity and unpredictability, may have made functional sense in the past, as the then optimal response to the principal–agent problem that is, as explained in section 1.10, inherent in the relationship between trustees and trust objects (and fiduciaries and their principals generally). This point will be developed further in section 13.7, when we come to look at remedies against trustees in detail. But that problem may have diminished, or at any rate changed in its nature in such a way that the old liability rules no longer constitute an apt response to it; and/or, the countervailing imperative of not frightening people away from acting as trustees in the first place may have grown in relative importance, as a result of changes in, especially, the demography and (consequently) the functional vision of trusts.[122]

---

[120] For a remnant of the latter, see *Schmidt v Rosewood Trust Ltd* [2003] 2 AC 709, ruling that trustees must, as a facet of their duty to account, communicate to the beneficiaries only such information as the court may discretionally decide. See section 11.9.

[121] See *Speight v Gaunt* (1883) 22 Ch D 727, 740, 762.

[122] See J Anderson in W Cornish et al *The Oxford History of the Laws of England, Volume XII: 1820–1914 Private Law* (2010) Part One VI, especially 232–8, 268–9, 288–94, and further sources there cited (especially C Stebbings *The Private Trustee in Victorian England* (2001)). The essential points are that, during the nineteenth century, the population of express trusts grew greatly as a function of the increase and diffusion of wealth; and that, simultaneously and no doubt connectedly, such trusts came to be used as vehicles for mediating wealth taking forms other than land, involving more complex and strenuous activity—and more scope for things going wrong—than the traditional, essentially static, land trusts. Together, these

Some trustees are also subject to a further kind of civil intervention. The Charity Commission can make orders against trustees of charities, eg removing them or freezing the trust assets.[123] The Pensions Regulator may intervene in various ways against trustees of occupational pension fund trusts,[124] and the Pensions Ombudsman[125] can investigate maladministration and make such orders as are open to a court.[126] The Financial Ombudsman Service, which has jurisdiction over most corporate and unit trust trustees, can order them to pay such compensation as seems fair.[127] Though at times a little vaguely configured, and so apt to keep their objects on their toes, these jurisdictions operate in broadly the same way as the modern law on trustees' mainstream civil liability, just outlined.[128] They are thus calculated more to provide procedural advantages than to adjust trustees' substantive exposure. The main advantage is the more inquisitorial style of process, which is helpful in holding charity trustees to account when no individual may be interested enough in their activities to be relied upon to do so, and also in producing greater 'equality of arms' between those holding rights under pension fund trusts and unit trusts, or against corporate trustees, and their generally much better resourced opponents.

Sometimes, trustees' misbehaviour will also result in criminal liability. The principal crimes relevant to trustees are theft,[129] false accounting,[130] and fraud.[131] There is obviously the possibility of a deterrent effect here, but it is narrowly focused, not aimed at breaches of trustees' duties in general. For these offences have in common a requirement of dishonesty on the part of the accused, meaning that his behaviour must have been what reasonable people would regard as dishonest, and that he should have realized this.[132] This is in contrast with trustees' civil liability, which can arise for failure to reach the prescribed standard (say, 'such care and skill

changes increased both the demand for trustees, especially competent ones, and the difficulty of satisfying that demand.

[123] Charities Act 1993 s 18.

[124] Pensions Act 1995 ss 3–4, 6–12, 14–15, as amended and supplemented by the Pensions Act 2004, especially Part 1.

[125] Pension Schemes Act 1993 ss 146–51; Pensions Act 1995 s 157.

[126] *Hillsdown Holdings plc v Pensions Ombudsman* [1997] 1 All ER 862.

[127] Financial Services and Markets Act 2000 Part XVI and Sch 17.

[128] In particular, the Pension Ombudsman has jurisdiction to grant only such relief as a court could have granted: *Hillsdown Holdings plc v Pensions Ombudsman* [1997] 1 All ER 862.

[129] Theft Act 1968 s 1. Section 5(2), (3) removes difficulties which would otherwise affect the application of the offence to trustees.

[130] Theft Act 1968 s 17.

[131] Fraud Act 2006 s 1—especially in its variant 'fraud by abuse of position', s 4.

[132] *R v Ghosh* [1982] QB 1053.

as is reasonable in the circumstances')[133] through laziness or gullibility or even well-intentioned incompetence as much as through dishonesty. A trustee incurring criminal liability may be punished in the usual ways: fine, imprisonment, etc. The fact that the crime was committed by a trustee means that it attracts a more severe punishment than would otherwise have been given.[134]

---

[133] Trustee Act 2000 s 1: see section 7.2.
[134] *R v Barrick* (1985) 7 Cr App R (S) 143; *R v Clark* [1998] 2 Cr App R (S) 137.

Trustees' Duties and Beneficiaries' Rights

The 'definition' of the trust concept sketched in section 1.1 asserted in part that 'a trust is a situation in which property is vested in someone (a trustee), who is under legally recognized obligations, at least some of which are of a proprietary kind, to handle it in a certain way'.

In Chapters 7–9 and 11, we discussed the main types of obligations resting on trustees: their duties to respect the fact that the property is not beneficially their own and to keep it safe; to manage and invest it; to pay out to the trust's objects, with or without a preceding discretionary choice; and to avoid distraction. (Though we saw that the incidence and content of these duties varies to some extent from one trust, or class of trust, to another.) This chapter begins by thinking generally about the broad nature of these duties.

Where a trust has beneficiaries, the trustees' duties are mirrored by rights on the part of those beneficiaries. This chapter also considers the significance of this, and in particular examines an argument that it is the interest of a beneficiary in the trust property, rather than the trustees' duties, that lies at the heart of the trust concept.

12.1 THE NATURE OF TRUSTEES' DUTIES

Legal duties are commonly divided into two classes, 'proprietary' (or '*in rem*') and 'personal' (or '*in personam*'). In early times, trust obligations were probably personal. But over time, the law has come to the view that some of these obligations are necessarily proprietary.[1] This means, essentially, that they do not simply rest on the trustees personally, but are in effect charged on to, or attached to, the trust property.[2] Personal duties,

---

[1] *Tinsley v Milligan* [1994] 1 AC 340, 371; *Westdeutsche Landesbank Girozentrale v Islington LBC* [1996] AC 669, 705; *Foskett v McKeown* [2001] 1 AC 102, 108, 127. The European Court of Justice, however, treats English trustees' duties as personal: *Webb v Webb* (Case C–294/92) [1994] QB 696. Cf *Re Hayward* [1997] Ch 45.

[2] To say that such obligations are proprietary does not necessarily mean that they confer ownership of the trust property on the beneficiary. In principle an obligation can be attached

by contrast, apply to particular individuals, and follow from their actions or their particular characteristics.

Although the proprietary characterization of at least some trust duties seems now beyond doubt, the issue was once much debated.[3] The debate has potential for continued vitality as part of the question whether equitable notions are to be seen as indeterminate supplements on the law: the view that they are, is noted in section 1.12. Seeing obligations as configured on a case-by-case basis, that view must wish them to apply only personally. (Though the converse argument, that personal applicability necessarily predicates indeterminacy, would of course be incorrect.)

The attachment of trust obligations to the trust property manifests itself in various features of the law. Two are especially important.

The first concerns the impact of the trustee's insolvency. If I become bankrupt, my assets are taken and if necessary sold, to pay off my creditors. But assets in my hands are not mine to the extent that attached to them are obligations I owe to others—ie, to the extent that they are the subject of proprietary obligations upon me. If I borrow money from you, it is purely mine. My obligation to repay you does not attach to the money itself: it is only a personal obligation. But if I am your trustee, duties I owe you are attached to the trust property. Therefore, the property cannot be taken to pay my creditors as though unaffected by those obligations, in the way that borrowed money can.[4] The matter is sometimes expressed in the form that those to whom I owe trust obligations and other proprietary obligations have 'priority in bankruptcy', ie priority over my ordinary creditors, to whom I owe only personal obligations. The latter can demand only that my obligation to pay them be so far as possible met out of the proceeds of sale of the assets which have been taken from me. But the former can assert their claims in respect of the particular asset(s) in my hands to which the obligation in question is attached: in the case of trust obligations, the trust property.

---

to property, and thus proprietary, even though it confers less than ownership of that property: *Re Nisbet and Potts' Contract* [1905] 1 Ch 391, [1906] 1 Ch 386; *National Provincial Bank Ltd v Ainsworth* [1965] AC 1175, 1237–8. The extent to which beneficiaries do in fact enjoy ownership of trust property is considered in section 12.3.

[3] The victorious view was most famously stated by A Scott (1917) 17 Columbia LR 269; the defeated view by F Maitland *Equity* (ed J Brunyate) (1936) especially 106–16, and H Stone (1917) 17 Columbia LR 467. It may however be wrong to regard these works as simply antagonistic one to another, much as they may present themselves in that way. To an extent, they appear to talk across one another—to discuss slightly different issues.

[4] Where I am an individual, this rule is stated in the Insolvency Act 1986 s 283(3)(a). But it is accepted as obtaining equally where I am a corporation.

The second principal manifestation of the proprietary quality of trust obligations, ie attachment to the trust property, is that the obligations stay with that property when it is transferred from the trustees to other people, and so can affect those other people.[5] Say the trustee gives trust property to his sister. She is not free to enjoy it for herself, any more than the trustee was: just as he held it on trust, so now does she. The duties, being charged on to it, have accompanied it into her hands. A recipient of trust property is not always so bound, however. There are two situations in which he will not be.

One is where the trustee is authorized to make the transfer. Trustees are obviously authorized to pay money out in accordance with the terms of the trust, eg to pay a year's income from the trust assets to the beneficiary entitled to it. They are also generally authorized to treat their trust's assets as investments, selling them and buying others in their place.[6] When they transfer assets in accordance with this authority, the trust obligations are 'overreached', ie become detached from the assets, at the moment of sale: so the property that reaches the transferee is no longer trust property. (If the transaction is the realization of an investment, the obligations attach instead to the money that the trustee receives in return . . . and then to any new investment in which he subsequently places it, and so on.) But if a trustee acts outside his authority—say, he sells trust property as though it were his own, in return for a payment into his private account— there will be no overreaching, so a trust can arise against the transferee after all. In short, then, trust obligations will not affect recipients of the relevant property unless the transfer is *unauthorized*.[7]

The other situation in which a recipient of trust property is not bound is, in its classic form, where he is a 'bona fide purchaser of the property for value without notice'. Broadly, this formula exempts someone[8] who buys the piece of property, rather than being given it ('purchaser . . . for value'); and who, when he bought, neither knew nor ought reasonably to

---

[5] See further section 17.2.   [6] See section 7.4.

[7] 'Unauthorized', ie outside the trustees' authority, does not necessarily mean quite the same as 'wrongful', ie in breach of trust. Trustees' transfers of trust property can be in breach of trust in a number of ways, and it seems that only some of these count as outside their authority, so as to prevent overreaching; others count as within their authority, albeit wrongful, so that overreaching takes place but the trustees are liable for any loss that results. The issue has been discussed most extensively, though not necessarily to firm effect, in the context of trusts of land, where however it may be governed by different rules. See G Ferris and G Battersby (2002) 118 LQR 270 and (2003) 119 LQR 94; G Ferris in E Cooke (ed) *Modern Studies in Property Law, Volume 2* (2003) ch 6.

[8] And also anyone, even if not personally a bona fide purchaser without notice, acquiring from in turn such a purchaser: *Wilkes v Spooner* [1911] 2 KB 473.

have known that it was trust property ('bona fide... without notice').[9] In the modern law, the rule has been reshaped somewhat in certain contexts. In particular, where the trust property is land, a purchaser is generally speaking immune if the trust was not entered in the state register and the beneficiary was not himself in actual and apparent occupation of the land.[10]

It is sometimes argued that true proprietary obligations will affect *every* holder of the property to which they attach, and that the bona fide purchaser exception, and its derivatives, therefore mean that trust obligations cannot be proprietary and must be personal.[11] The argument is false, however. These obligations affect those whom they do affect not because of some action or characteristic personal to the latter, but because they are attached to the property so that they affect all save the excepted categories. They cannot properly be termed personal, therefore. If one insists on not terming them proprietary, some third label is thus required. In fact, in English law traditionally no obligation is binding on absolutely all holders of the property to which it relates, and obligations universally viewed as proprietary can bind distinctly fewer than all such holders.[12] A third label has not been sought, however: instead, the premise of the argument is generally rejected, and the term proprietary used after all.[13]

---

[9] The exact meaning of 'notice' varies between contexts. Possible meanings range from 'a situation in which a scrupulous purchaser would, by inquiry if necessary, have discovered the fact of the trust' to 'actual knowledge on the part of this individual purchaser'. The former meaning was characteristically used where the property in question was land, though in land cases the use of notice has largely been supplanted by the rules in the Land Registration Act 2002, noted below. The latter meaning is favoured in cases where the trust property is not land (*Polly Peck International plc v Nadir (No 2)* [1992] 4 All ER 769, 781–2), though it is evidence that this purchaser had the required knowledge that a reasonable person (though not an especially scrupulous one, nor after extensive inquiries) would have realized the fact at issue (*Eagle Trust plc v SBC Securities Ltd* [1993] 1 WLR 484, 493). See generally *Sinclair Investments (UK) Ltd v Versailles Trade Finance Ltd (in administrative receivership)* [2010] EWHC 1614 (Ch), [88]–[97].

[10] Land Registration Act 2002 s 29. Moreover, various rules combine to mean that trusts, especially over land, are in practice less likely than one might imagine to bind purchasers: see further S Gardner *An Introduction to Land Law* 2nd edn (2009) 306–14.

[11] This was the main ground on which the European Court of Justice held trust obligations personal in *Webb v Webb* (Case C-294/92) [1994] QB 696.

[12] This is the effect of eg *Miller v Race* (1758) 1 Burr 452; Sale of Goods Act 1979 ss 24, 25.

[13] B McFarlane *The Structure of Property Law* (2008) 21–39 (see too B McFarlane and R Stevens (2010) 4 J Eq 1), speaking in terms of rights rather than obligations, proposes a third label, 'persistent', and sees it as applying to rights under trusts; but it is aimed at a different issue. The issue under discussion in the text is whether, to count as 'proprietary', a right must bind *all* title-holders of the property in question. In McFarlane's terms, both 'proprietary' and 'persistent' rights can bind such holders and, as regards both classes, he seems content with the same answer as offered here, namely that there is no need for all holders to be bound; there can be exceptions (where there is what he calls a 'defence'). McFarlane is concerned rather

However, not all trust obligations are proprietary rather than personal. Proprietary quality appears to attach only to the basic duties of respecting the fact that the property is not beneficially a trustee's own, and of safeguarding it pending transfer, described in sections 7.1–7.2; duties beyond that being only personal.[14] The latter proposition certainly makes good sense, because such further duties cannot satisfactorily affect subsequent holders of the trust property. They are essentially positive duties, the performance of which is influenced by the identity of the trustee. Most notably, trustees are often required to form a judgement: to decide how to manage the trust, for example, or whom to pay in a discretionary trust. The trustees' individual perceptions and ways of thinking will naturally be influential in that process. Trustees appointed as such (either initially

to assert that, whereas some such rights—'persistent' rights—are effective *only* against title-holders of the asset in question, such as trustees and their successors, others—'proprietary' rights—are effective more widely. So, the *owner* of property, having a 'proprietary' right, can sue one who steals it or negligently damages it; but the *beneficiary of a trust* of the same property, having only a 'persistent' right, cannot: *MCC Proceeds Inc v Lehman Bros International (Europe)* [1998] 4 All ER 675; *Leigh and Sillavan Ltd v Aliakmon Shipping Co Ltd, The Aliakmon* [1986] AC 785, 812. McFarlane expresses his distinction in terms of the beneficiary having only a right to the trustee's right, rather than to the (relevant aspect of) the property itself. Notice, however, that if I have a right to *the entirety of* your right to some property, it is as accurate to say that I have a right to (the relevant aspect of) the property itself. There is a difference only if my right is to *less than* the entirety of your right; ie some elements of your right (eg the ability to sue for theft of the property) remain with you. This latter feature is necessarily present in the case of a trust, as otherwise the trustee would simply drop out of the picture and the beneficiary would own the relevant property outright (a position that did in fact obtain for a time, under the Statute of Uses 1536). Taking the idea of a 'trust' seriously, the trustee is present precisely so as, among other things, to hold the property on the beneficiary's behalf. The same need not, perhaps should not, be true of other kinds of equitable interest, which McFarlane sees as likewise 'persistent': in principle, there is no reason why they should not behave in the manner of the rights he calls proprietary, and indeed at least some avowedly do (see eg *Re Nisbet and Potts' Contract* [1905] 1 Ch 391, [1906] 1 Ch 386). Ultimately, therefore, McFarlane's point seems to be simply that trusts must be trusts. This is self-evident; though notice that the beneficiary rule and associated ideas, and the considerations behind these (see sections 12.2–12.4), make for a tendency towards full 'proprietary' effect even in their case. This is reflected in *Colour Quest Ltd v Total Downstream UK Plc* [2010] 3 WLR 1192, where a beneficiary (of an almost bare trust) was permitted to sue in negligence, so long as the trustee was made a formal party to the proceedings. Similarly, in *Boardman v Phipps* [1967] 2 AC 46 the court treated a solicitor's fiduciary duties to his employer, a set of trustees, as owed also to the trustees' beneficiaries.

[14]   See further R Nolan (2006) 122 LQR 232, and authorities there cited. Nolan sees the only proprietary duty as that to respect the fact that the property is not beneficially the trustees' own. The text adds the duty to safeguard the property in the meantime because that is the message of 'knowing receipt'. By the latter (see section 14.3), someone who receives improperly transferred trust property, but then loses it, is liable for the loss, thus implying that he comes under the duty to safeguard it.

by the settlor, or subsequently under the relevant mechanisms)[15] will thus generally be selected with an eye to their perceptions and ways of thinking. The courts have attached importance to this factor of selection as a reason for interfering little with the judgements that trustees make.[16] A transferee of the trust property would not be so selected, and to impose on him the transferring trustee's duties to form judgements would thus be inappropriate.

So the personal status of most trust duties is intelligible enough. It is in fact more difficult to say why the remaining duties should be proprietary. To be sure, it makes sense that if any trust duties are to be proprietary, these should be—as is the case—the duties to respect the fact that the property is not beneficially the trustee's own, and to safeguard it. Together, these duties help ensure the property's rendition (if not to the objects themselves, then) into the hands of the original or a replacement trustee, who will be under the personal duties too, so reinstating the full trust. But it remains to be established that these two duties positively should be proprietary. For the law's default position is that obligations should be personal: proprietary status requires active justification, in the form that the obligation in question has an important social role that it can perform only if it has that status.[17] And it is not clear why trusts should be seen as having such a role, rather than as being personal to their trustee. If trusts consisted only of personal obligations, trust property would not be immune from the trustee's insolvency, and, if wrongfully alienated, could not be recovered from the alienee; but the trustee would be liable to make good the loss. This would certainly leave the objects in a less advantageous position than they enjoy under the law as it stands, but not in a plainly inadequate one (in one no worse than a party to a contract, for example), which is what we should expect to see demonstrated when encountering proprietary status. The question is taken further in section 12.3.

---

[15] Section 11.1.   [16] *Edge v Pensions Ombudsman* [2000] Ch 602, 630.

[17] This is the '*numerus clausus*' principle: see further S Gardner *An Introduction to Land Law* 2nd edn (2009) 9–12. According to B McFarlane *The Structure of Property Law* (2008) 218, and B McFarlane and R Stevens (2010) 4 J Eq 1, 2, 'persistent' rights—such as those under trusts—are not subject to the *numerus clausus* principle, so no justification need be offered for their status as such: they can be made whenever their creator so desires. The supportability of this claim depends on the reasons behind the *numerus clausus* principle. If these include the protection of transferees—whether for their own sake, or for the good of the market—it cannot be supported, for transferees are affected by 'persistent' rights as much as by (other) proprietary rights. It seems likely that that is the case. See Gardner *ibid*, and further materials cited there.

12.2 BENEFICIARIES' RIGHTS;
THE BENEFICIARY RULE AND
THE INTEREST THESIS

Where a trust has beneficiaries, the beneficiaries have rights mirroring its trustees' duties. Whatever the trustees are required to do is for the benefit of the beneficiaries, and the beneficiaries are entitled to have it done. In an express trust in favour of beneficiaries, for example, the trustees must pay the beneficiaries as the settlor has stipulated: and the beneficiaries are entitled to have them do so. The beneficiaries' rights are said to be 'correlative' to the trustees' duties. Because beneficiaries' rights relate to trustees' duties in this way, information about the duties can be read across to the rights. So rights correlative to trustees' proprietary duties are themselves proprietary, ie attached to the trust property.

According to one thesis,[18] however, the last paragraph distorts the true picture. It is wrong, this thesis maintains, to see trustees' duties as central to the trust concept, and the rights of any beneficiaries as merely the obverse of whatever those duties might be. On the contrary, the thesis continues, the very mission of the trust concept is to permit beneficiaries to have interests in the trust property: and trustees' duties ensue to effectuate these interests. Trusts must therefore have beneficiaries. This latter element in the thesis, insisted on in a number of decisions,[19] is known as the 'beneficiary rule'. It may be better known than the full form of the thesis. The latter, however, places the rule in a justifying context. Beneficiaries are required as the repositories of the interests in the trust property that are the true heart of the trust concept. Call this thesis, therefore, the 'interest thesis'.

Accounts of the interest thesis[20] are often imprecise on the question of the exact nature of the 'interest in the trust property' that they demand. The requirement might simply be for rights attached to the

---

[18] Described especially in *Re Astor's Settlement Trusts* [1952] Ch 534, 541–2; P Millett (1985) 101 LQR 269; P Matthews in A Oakley *Trends in Contemporary Trust Law* (1996) ch 1; J Penner *The Law of Trusts* 7th edn (2010) 244. *Commissioner of Stamp Duties (Queensland) v Livingston* [1965] AC 694, 708 contrasts this view of trusts with the duty-centred account, which it applies to the relationship between the executor of a deceased person's estate and someone entitled to the as yet unestablished residue of that estate, who by the nature of things cannot yet have an interest in particular property. For discussion, see R Cotterrell in S Goldstein (ed) *Equity and Contemporary Legal Developments* (1992) 302; (1993) CLP 75.

[19] *Bowman v Secular Society Ltd* [1917] AC 406, 441; *Re Wood* [1949] Ch 498, 501–2; *Re Shaw* [1957] 1 WLR 729, 744–6; *Leahy v A-G for New South Wales* [1959] AC 457, 478–9, 484; *Re Endacott* [1960] Ch 232, 246, 250–1.   [20] Note 18 above.

trust property.[21] As we saw in the last section, however, all trustees have duties attached to the trust property (whether or not all their duties are so attached); so the beneficiaries' rights correlative to these duties are necessarily likewise attached. This conception of the required interest would therefore accommodate the thesis to all arrangements, otherwise recognizable as trusts, in which trustees owe proprietary duties to beneficiaries. That is, the substantive impact of the thesis would consist only in the beneficiary rule, ie a demand that trusts have beneficiaries. Unsurprisingly, then, these imprecise accounts of the thesis appear in fact to be unauthentic. The authentic version of the thesis reads the required 'interest in the trust property' more tightly, demanding that the beneficiaries' rights amount to *a claim to the property itself*, rather than merely a claim, attached to the property, to the trustees' proper performance of their duties.[22] Understood in this way, the interest thesis has a substantive message over and above the beneficiary rule: that the trust concept is confined to arrangements in which the beneficiaries have such a claim—that is, enjoy equitable ownership of the very trust property.

12.3 RIGHTS AND DUTIES IN THE CURRENT LAW

The matter has a history. There seems to be no evidence that the earliest ancestors of today's trusts did not always feature beneficiaries, but this could be merely because no one tried any variation; and even if that in turn was the result of the contemporary vision of what was possible, it could hardly be eternally determinative. Originally the beneficiaries were regarded as having merely a right to the performance of the trustee's obligation, which they could neither enforce against a third party (ie the obligation and right were personal) nor assign themselves. The latter point was especially insisted upon by Sir Edward Coke at the end of the

---

[21] This view seems to be taken by P Matthews (1998) 12 TLI 98, 99.

[22] See eg J Harris (1971) 87 LQR 31; J Davies [1970] ASCL 189; J Penner *The Law of Trusts* 7th edn (2010) 244: 'The very existence of a trust turns on there being a trust obligation to someone who, in consequence, has equitable ownership of the trust property ... The essence of the [beneficiary] principle is that for a trust to exist, there must be someone other than the trustee who has the real beneficial ownership of the trust property. If there is no such person, then not only is there no person *to enforce* obligations against the trustee, but more fundamentally, there are *no trust obligations to* enforce, for the legal owner owns it for his own benefit absolutely.'

sixteenth century.[23] Coke's view however was reversed in the seventeenth century, particularly by Lord Nottingham, who promoted the vision of beneficiaries' rights as analogous to legal estates, ie slices of the ownership of the assets.[24] The interest thesis, in its authentic version, thus certainly reflects Lord Nottingham's view. The question for us is whether matters rested there, or whether that view has in turn been replaced by a further new conception, in particular one focusing on the trustees' duties and holding beneficiaries and their rights inessential to the idea of a trust.

It evidently has. Neither the demand for a claim to the trust property, nor that for beneficiaries with or without such a claim, is reconcilable with the trust phenomenon as it has been developed to date. The law has accepted various kinds of trusts where the trustees' duties do not mirror claims to the trust property, or, in many cases, rights of any kind, on the part of beneficiaries.[25]

Vast numbers of trusts do involve beneficiaries, of course; and such beneficiaries have rights to the performance of the trustees' duties, which are in at least some cases attached to the trust property, as we saw in section 12.1. Furthermore, there certainly exist cases in which a beneficiary can be said to have a claim to the trust property. This is least controversially so[26] where the trust is a 'bare' one, ie one in which the trustees hold

---

[23] Curiously, however, at the same period, a trustee's liability to account was being explained and justified on the basis that the beneficiary had something like a 'proprietary' right to the trust assets. See S Stoljar (1964) 80 LQR 203, 210–12.

[24] On all this, see D Yale *Lord Nottingham's Chancery Cases* vol II (1961) introduction 88–101. Lord Hardwicke LC therefore said in *Hopkins v Hopkins* (1739) West temp Hard 606, 619: 'It is the maxim of this court that trust estates, which are the creatures of equity, shall be governed by the same rules as legal estates, in order to preserve the uniform rule of property: and that the owner of the trust shall have the same power over the trust as he should have had if he had had the legal estate for the like interest or extent.' And Lord Mansfield CJ said in *Burgess v Wheate* (1759) 1 Eden 177, 223: 'The *forum* where they are adjudged is the only difference between trusts and legal estates. Trusts are [in Chancery] considered as between *cestuy que trust* and trustee (and all claiming by, through, or under them, or in consequence of their estates), as the ownership or legal estate, except when it can be pleaded in bar of the exercise of this right of jurisdiction. Whatever would be the rule of law, if it was a legal estate, is applied in equity to a trust estate.' This section of Lord Mansfield's judgment—at 215–27—offers an account of the development of trusts to this point. For the continuation of the same ideas into a more recent period, but also signs of discomfiture with them, see too J Anderson in W Cornish et al *The Oxford History of the Laws of England, Volume XII: 1820–1914 Private Law* (2010) Part One VI, 246–52.

[25] Though Lord Millett in *Twinsectra Ltd v Yardley* [2002] 2 AC 164, [90]–[91], equates the absence of a beneficial interest with a failure to make a complete trust, generating a resulting trust. The correctness of that equation is the issue under discussion; Lord Millett fails to deal with the evidence against it.

[26] But cf *Nelson v Greening & Sykes (Builders) Ltd* [2007] EWCA 1358, [49]–[58], holding that where I hold property on trust for you, and you hold it on a bare sub-trust for John, you do not simply drop out of the picture, leaving me holding directly on trust for

the property for a sole adult beneficiary of unimpaired capacity, upon whose entitlement there are no conditions, and must transfer it to him on demand, under the rule in *Saunders v Vautier*.[27]

A beneficiary entitled to 'the trust income' for his life has been treated, in *Baker v Archer-Shee*,[28] as likewise having a claim to the very trust assets. This view was taken despite two difficulties. First, the arrangement contained features attenuating the beneficiary's entitlement to the trust property, such as the trustees' right to deduct expenses from periodic transfers of income to him. These features were however depicted as mandated by the beneficiary, and so not antithetical to his having a claim to the property. Secondly, such a beneficiary cannot single-handedly demand transfer of the trust property: he can invoke the rule in *Saunders v Vautier*[29] only in collaboration with his fellow-beneficiaries, entitled after his death. It must have been reckoned, therefore, that his claim to the property was only for the period of his own entitlement, but that this sufficed for the purposes of the (tax) context in question. These answers to the difficulties may be accepted, but it is unsurprising that some judges dissented, denying that the beneficiary had a claim to the very trust property, implicitly regarding him as having only a right to the proper performance of the trustees' duties after all. This dissenting view was found by a further decision[30] correctly to state New York law, which in principle had no reason to be different.

This seems to be as far as the idea of a 'claim to the very trust assets' can be taken, however. Some kinds of beneficiaries' rights cannot possibly be regarded as amounting to such claims. Take trusts involving dispositive discretions: discretionary trusts, or trusts with powers to appoint, advance, maintain, or accumulate.[31] A beneficiary of such a trust certainly has a right that the trustees shall take their discretionary decisions in a proper way. But he has no claim to the assets, which the trustees may, but need not, pay over to him. The point is most obvious in the case of a discretionary trust for a large number of potential payees, but analytically

---

John. However, the crucial issue in that decision was whether you remain a trustee. The proposition that you do is compatible with the proposition that John has a claim to the very trust property, which is our current focus. Nothing in the present discussion involves denying the existence of a trust; nor could it, though, as section 12.4 explains, that is the interest thesis's tendency.

[27] (1841) 4 Beav 115, Cr & Ph 240; see section 10.4.   [28] [1927] AC 844.
[29] (1841) 4 Beav 115, Cr & Ph 240.   [30] *Archer-Shee v Garland* [1931] AC 212.
[31] See section 11.2. Beneficiaries' rights in trusts of land (governed by the Trusts of Land and Appointment of Trustees Act 1996) are in some respects, especially that of occupation (s 12), also too dependent on discretion to amount to firm claims.

it is equally applicable to narrower situations, and it has been judicially accepted in the latter type of case.[32]

Moreover, some trusts have no beneficiaries, so for that reason cannot involve claims to the very trust assets. Such trusts are termed 'purpose trusts'. The most notable of them are trusts for charitable purposes, discussed in Chapter 6.[33] To count as charitable, a trust must make provision in some way for the public rather than for particular individuals. Charities for the relief of poverty can stipulate for payments to individuals, but must be differentiated from trusts for individuals (beneficiaries) required to be poor;[34] the distinction can be a narrow one on the facts, but the difference of principle is that the latter have the right to enforce the trust, while the former do not. Charitable trusts are enforced by the Charity Commission or Attorney General,[35] who are not however beneficiaries, because they are not themselves benefited. Statements of the beneficiary rule and interest thesis note, but do not cavil at, the non-conformity of charities: they portray it as exceptional.

The courts have also held valid certain non-charitable purpose trusts. The cases fall into two classes. One class is usually indicated by reference to *Re Denley's Trust Deed*.[36] The trust there provided a sports field for a company's employees. Some view the trust as being for the employees as beneficiaries in the ordinary sense.[37] If this were correct, the employees could have claimed the sports field's monetary value, rather than merely the use of the sports field itself.[38] The judge, however, took the trust as being for the purpose of providing the employees with a sports field, and

---

[32] *Gartside v IRC* [1968] AC 553; *Sainsbury v IRC* [1970] Ch 712. It is true that the beneficiaries of a discretionary trust may, if adult and of unimpaired capacity, unite to invoke *Saunders v Vautier* (1841) 4 Beav 115, Cr & Ph 240: *Re Smith* [1928] Ch 915. This does not however entail that the rights enjoyed by *each* beneficiary amount to a sufficient 'interest'.

[33] See section 6.1; *A-G v Cocke* [1988] Ch 414, 419–20; *Catholic Care (Diocese of Leeds) v Charity Commission for England and Wales* [2010] 4 All ER 1041, [62]–[63].

[34] *Re Scarisbrick* [1951] Ch 622; *Re Cohen* [1973] 1 WLR 415; *Re Segelman* [1996] Ch 171.

[35] Persons 'interested in the charity' can enforce, but only with the leave of the Charity Commission, which may not normally be given if the Commission could proceed itself: Charities Act 1993 s 33. Evidently, the section uses the word 'interested' in a different sense from the interest thesis.

[36] [1969] 1 Ch 373; for the relationship with the interest thesis see J Davies [1968] ASCL 438. For further instances of the same idea, see *Re Trusts of the Abbott Fund* [1900] 2 Ch 326; *Re Aberconway's Settlement Trusts* [1953] Ch 647; *Re West Sussex Constabulary's Widows, Children and Benevolent (1930) Fund Trusts* [1971] Ch 1.

[37] See especially *Re Grant's Will Trusts* [1980] 1 WLR 360, 370–1; seemingly also *Re Lipinski's Will Trusts* [1976] Ch 235. These rely on *Re Bowes* [1896] 1 Ch 507, reading an apparent purpose trust as one for beneficiaries by treating the purpose as merely the motive with which an unrestricted entitlement is conferred (see section 3.5).

[38] *Saunders v Vautier* (1841) 4 Beav 115, Cr & Ph 240: see section 10.4.

upheld it on the footing that a trust without beneficiaries in the ordinary sense is nonetheless valid if there are persons—such as the employees—who are directly and tangibly benefited by its performance, they being able to enforce it if the trustees fail to perform. Apparently cognate with *Re Denley's Trust Deed*,[39] too, is *Barclay's Bank Ltd v Quistclose Investments Ltd*,[40] the most famous of a group of cases in which money is transferred on the understanding that the payee will spend it in a particular way, it being held that the transferee therefore holds the money on trust to spend the money in that way (failing which, to return it to the transferor).[41] In that case, for example, a finance house lent money to a company to allow the latter to pay a dividend to its shareholders. In at least some of these cases, spending the money in the designated way will benefit one or more persons, such as the shareholders there, but the trust is once again not for them as beneficiaries, so as to entitle them to the money without strings;[42] it can be spent only in the designated way. Here too, those who are benefited have the right to enforce the trust.[43] In one of these cases, the payer–settlor was itself benefited by the performance of the purpose, and was therefore recognized as entitled to enforce in this way.[44]

The other class comprises decisions declaring valid trusts for constructing and/or maintaining particular graves and monuments;[45]

---

[39] [1969] 1 Ch 373.   [40] [1970] AC 567.

[41] There is another interesting feature of these decisions. The transfer is frequently a loan. In the ordinary way, the borrower would then owe the lender the relevant sum as a debt. If the borrower spends the money in the designated way, that is indeed the result. But if not, the borrower instead holds the money in question on trust for the lender, with the advantages (especially in the borrower's insolvency) that that entails. It can be argued that the law should not allow this: see section 2.5.

[42] This was explicitly recognized in *Carreras Rothmans Ltd v Freeman Mathews Treasure Ltd* [1985] Ch 207, 223.

[43] This understanding was however rejected, on the basis that trusts cannot exist without exhaustive beneficial interests—the proposition we are seeking to test—in *Twinsectra Ltd v Yardley* [2002] 2 AC 164, [90], Lord Millett (though curiously, in *Armitage v Nurse* [1998] Ch 241 the same judge implicitly rejected the interest thesis: see J Penner in P Birks and A Pretto (eds) *Breach of Trust* (2002) ch 8). For efforts to reinterpret these '*Quistclose*' trusts see especially P Millett (1985) 101 LQR 269; R Chambers *Resulting Trusts* (1997) ch 3; *Twinsectra Ltd v Yardley ibid*, [96]–[100]. And see further J Payne in P Birks and F Rose (eds) *Restitution and Equity: Resulting Trusts and Equitable Compensation* (2000) ch 5; W Swadling (ed) *The Quistclose Trust—Critical Essays* (2004); cf P Parkinson [2002] CLJ 657.

[44] *Carreras Rothmans Ltd v Freeman Mathews Treasure Ltd* [1985] Ch 207, where a tobacco company placed money on trust with its advertising agency to pay the advertising bills that the agency had run up on its behalf with some newspapers; failing the payment of which, the newspapers would have blacklisted it. See too *Barclay's Bank Ltd v Quistclose Investments Ltd* [1970] AC 567, 581.

[45] eg *Trimmer v Danby* (1856) 25 LJ Ch 424; *Re Hooper* [1932] 1 Ch 38. Trusts to enhance or maintain churches or graveyards as such are charitable: *Re Vaughan* (1886) 33 Ch D 187.

privately saying masses;[46] maintaining particular animals;[47] and 'miscellaneous' other purposes, a category apparently consisting solely of the promotion of fox-hunting.[48] Extension of the list, even by analogy, has been discountenanced,[49] for these trusts have been characterized as 'anomalous'. They fail to conform not only with the beneficiary rule and interest thesis, but also with the thinking in *Re Denley's Trust Deed*:[50] they do not feature people particularly benefited by the achievement of the purpose. To these classes of English decisions may be added the statutory regimes introduced in a number of other jurisdictions under which non-charitable purpose trusts are in principle valid, commonly so long as there is someone to enforce them:[51] perhaps the most famous among such regimes being that of the Cayman Islands, known as STAR.[52]

So the interest thesis and beneficiary rule do not satisfactorily describe the shape that, given this material, the trust concept has in the existing law. It is in reflection of this that the 'definition' given in section 1.1 does not track the thesis and rule, but focuses instead on the trustees' obligations, which are essential to all the kinds of arrangement that are in fact denominated trusts.[53]

On the other hand, we cannot regard the law as uncomplicatedly settled along the latter lines. Certain aspects of it are easier to understand if the interest thesis, requiring beneficiaries having a claim to the very trust property, is accepted after all.

---

[46] *Bourne v Keane* [1919] AC 815. Trusts for public masses are charitable: *Re Hetherington* [1990] Ch 1.

[47] eg *Pettingall v Pettingall* (1842) 11 LJ Ch 176; *Re Dean* (1889) 41 Ch D 552. The latter overlooks the requirement (see section 2.5) that such trusts have a maximum duration of 21 years. Trusts for animals generally may be charitable: see section 6.4.

[48] *Re Thompson* [1934] Ch 342. Trusts for this purpose will no longer be valid, unless they extend to a form of fox-hunting not prohibited by the Hunting Act 2004.

[49] *Re Endacott* [1960] Ch 232. It used to be thought that trusts for unincorporated associations had a place on the list, but they are nowadays handled by other analyses: see section 3.11.   [50] [1969] 1 Ch 373.

[51] See P Matthews in A Oakley (ed) *Trends in Contemporary Trust Law* (1996) ch 1. D Hayton (2001) 117 LQR 96 argues that English law too should accept the presence of an enforcer, appointed by the settlor, as validating an otherwise invalid purpose trust, and suggests that the first step towards this position may be the recognition of such trusts established in off-shore jurisdictions.

[52] Introduced by the Cayman Special Trusts (Alternative Regime) Law 1997; see P Matthews (1997) 11 TLI 67; A Duckworth (1998) 12 TLI 16; P Matthews (1998) 12 TLI 98.

[53] Likewise the definitions given in the Hague Convention on the Law Applicable to Trusts and on their Recognition; in D Hayton et al *Principles of European Trust Law* (1999); and in C von Bar et al (eds) *Principles, Definition and Model Rules of European Private Law: Draft Common Frame of Reference: Outline Edition* (2009) section X.—1:201. (On the latter document, see N Jansen and R Zimmermann [2010] CLJ 98.)

In particular, in section 10.4 we encountered the rule in *Saunders v Vautier*,[54] whereby someone who is entitled to the entire beneficial interest under a trust can, if he is an adult and of unimpaired capacity, demand that the trust be dismantled, and its capital transferred to him. In the present section, indeed, we have seen how invoking this rule makes it easier to see beneficiaries' interests as amounting to ownership. To be sure, the rule cannot in reality operate (not only in purpose trusts, but also) in trusts, which will usually be discretionary trusts,[55] having large numbers of beneficiaries, who will never in practice band together so as to take advantage of it. For present purposes, however, the important point is this: for the rule to make sense in the cases where it does operate, the law must assume that a beneficiary's interest consists in an entitlement not merely to the trustees' performance of their duties under the trust—that would entail the trust *not* being dismantled, but remaining on foot—but to the trust property itself, as proposed by the interest thesis.

Then, in section 12.1 we saw that at least some of the obligations upon trustees are proprietary, rather than personal. We noted that this fact requires an explanation—for the law's default position is that obligations should be personal, proprietary status requiring positive justification—but struggled to find one. If we accept the interest thesis, however, the problem is solved. According to the thesis, the trustees' obligations must reflect rights on the beneficiaries' part amounting to the ownership, or (as with an entitlement for life)[56] slices of the ownership, of the trust assets. Ownership is the quintessential proprietary interest; the very statement that you are the owner of some asset necessarily tells us, among other things, that your right regarding the asset has the capacity to bind others into whose hands the asset comes, and survives the insolvency of any other person in whose possession the asset may be.

Again, if we accept the interest thesis, the idea that a trustee cannot benefit from the trust[57]—and its corollary, that he is a fiduciary, and all that flows in turn from this[58]—follows inevitably. Approached thus, there can be no trust unless the beneficiary has ownership of the property lying in the trustee's hands. And if that is the position, there is obviously no room for the trustee to have any stake in the property; he cannot be other

---

[54] (1841) 4 Beav 115, Cr & Ph 240. For the relationship between this and the interest thesis, see further P Matthews (2006) 122 LQR 266.

[55] Though it applies to such trusts in theory: *Re Smith* [1928] Ch 915.

[56] *Baker v Archer-Shee* [1927] AC 844; see n 28.   [57] See section 1.10.

[58] See sections 7.5, 11.10, and 13.2–15.8.

than a fiduciary for the beneficiary. To be sure, the reverse is not true. If someone holds property for a purpose, or for a beneficiary or set of beneficiaries not enjoying ownership, it does not follow that he *must* have a stake in the property, or *cannot* be a fiduciary, and so cannot hold on what we regard as a trust. That is, in this scenario, we can choose to say that the property-holder holds on trust, ie does not have a stake and so is a fiduciary. The law does in fact so choose, by recognizing trusts in this scenario in the manner we have reviewed in this section. But in order to do this, we, and the law, have positively to stipulate for the presence of a trust. We do so on the basis that it is valuable to allow fiduciary status to be positively attached in this way to those who hold property for such purposes or persons.[59] The trust does not arise inevitably, as it would if the situation had to comply with the interest thesis.[60]

The rule that, once made by its settlor, a trust is irrevocable[61] is another necessary consequence of the interest thesis. If, by definition, the trust passes ownership to the beneficiary, the rule could not be otherwise; the very idea of passing ownership denotes, among other things, that the property's previous owner cannot simply demand it back again. Again, it is obviously possible to have the same rule in the absence of passing ownership, and indeed the current law does so; but, also again, this needs to be posited.

In the end, then, we have seen that the law contains material that cannot co-exist with the interest thesis whereby an express trust cannot arise unless it is for a beneficiary or beneficiaries having a claim to (ie ownership, or a slice of ownership, of) the very trust property, implying instead that trusts need only trustees' obligations;[62] but also other material suggestive of that thesis. In offering any sort of definition of a trust, as in section 1.1, one has to choose to emphasize one of these sets of material over the other—the choice made in this book being to emphasize the former.

---

[59] Which is not, of course, to say that it is the better choice in all cases. Commonly—and entirely understandably—a property-holder, while owing duties, nevertheless does have a personal stake, and so is not a fiduciary or a trustee. This is the situation, for example, where I own land but you have a right of way or similar over it. Say I sell the land: I, not you, take the proceeds.

[60] Notice that this discussion has treated the idea of a 'fiduciary', who cannot have any personal interest, as sharply distinct from that of a 'non-fiduciary', who can and generally does. This distinction represents the conventional vision of the matter, but it can be challenged. In particular, W Bishop and D Prentice (1983) 46 MLR 289 argue that principals may be better served by agents (trustees etc) who do have a personal stake. See further section 11.10.

[61] *Ellison v Ellison* (1802) 6 Ves Jr 656.

[62] See further D Hayton (2001) 117 LQR 96; P Parkinson [2002] CLJ 657.

If the choice is not to be arbitrary, however, it should be made on the basis of arguments as to which position the law *should* adopt. To these we now turn.

12.4 RIGHTS AND DUTIES: ARGUMENTS OF PRINCIPLE

So is it better in principle to conceive trusts in terms of trustees' duties, regarding correlative beneficial rights as inessential; or do the interest thesis and beneficiary rule reflect persuasive considerations?

The debate is commonly conducted on the wrong wavelength. Assertions are made to the effect that one or the other answer is doctrinally, conceptually, inevitable. Given that—as we saw in section 12.3—there exist perfectly understandable and operable rules pointing to both answers, such assertions are clearly wide of the mark. The point can be readily appreciated if we consider statements that trusts must, as a matter of definition, have beneficiaries, but simultaneously accepting the existence of charities as 'exceptions' to that position. If charities can exist within the trust universe at all, it must be because beneficiaries are not conceptually necessary: there can be no exceptions to an inevitability. To permit of exceptions, the requirement for beneficiaries must instead be a predicate of policy.

Indeed, the very terms in which the discussion is carried on—the distinction between 'trusts for beneficiaries' and 'purpose trusts'—are not pre-ordained. All express trusts are purpose trusts, in the sense that the settlor vests the property in the trustees to be used by them in such-and-such a way. So 'trusts for beneficiaries' are purpose trusts too, but are singled out from the remainder (which are then labelled 'purpose trusts') by reference to the particular type of purpose they involve, this being the transfer of capital, or income in cash, to one or more persons, these being called 'beneficiaries'. It is not self-evident that a distinction should be made on this basis. It would be just as possible to distinguish among trusts on some other basis, such as whether they provide say a supply of food or water, or indeed to make no distinction between them at all. The decision to distinguish at all, and to do so in terms of whether the trust is for a 'beneficiary', is a choice. It can only have been made, once again, for reasons of policy.

So our inquiry should proceed in terms of policy; of the work we think the law wants, or should want, trusts to do.

In seeking a basis for a conception of trusts in terms of trustees' duties, we need look no further than the logic of the facilitative project.[63] The law maintains express trusts so as to give settlors the means to do as they will with their property. Some wish to put their property to purposes other than outright payments to beneficiaries. Facilitative logic requires the trust notion to accommodate that wish.

As explained in Chapter 2, however, facilitative logic should yield, and does, where the settlor's goal is sufficiently inimical to some other policy consideration. A trust to promote genocide, whilst as valuable as any other in facilitative terms, should and would be rejected as heavily objectionable to rights concerns. An argument of this kind can be made for restricting the trust device in the way proposed by the interest thesis, to arrangements giving the beneficiaries a claim to the very trust property.

The concerns relevant to this argument are those regarding rights and economic utility, as explored in sections 2.5–2.6. The former asks that people be able to enjoy their property (as other aspects of their identity) in a full way; the latter that property be exposed to market influences, which means its being owned by someone with complete liberty over its disposal. A facility for settlors to make trusts howsoever they please is likely to result in infringement of both these precepts, as some settlors seek to confer heavily qualified entitlements on beneficiaries or to have money spent in particular ways rather than being paid to beneficiaries as cash. A beneficiary of a discretionary trust, for example, while able freely to spend what the trustees decide to pay him, lacks untrammelled entitlement to particular property. A trust to promote a purpose advantageous to certain people, say by providing a sports field for a company's employees, prevents those advantaged from spending the money as they wish. Trusts for purposes not advantageous to particular people, say those to erect monuments, in a sense escape this criticism: but only because the settlors of such trusts commit what, for at any rate the economic utility argument, is the still greater sin of directing the money altogether away from enjoyment by people. The money provided by every purpose trust, moreover, has to be spent on particular commodities needed to achieve the purpose: in the case of a sports field, land, turf, drainage pipes, etc. Except within the limits of those commodities, therefore, the use of the money is immune to market influences.

---

[63] See section 2.2.

The kinds of trust arrangement compatible with the interest thesis do not raise these concerns. A beneficiary with a full claim to the trust assets, especially one able to invoke *Saunders v Vautier*[64] so as to free them from the trust, can enjoy those assets as he himself wishes rather than as prescribed by the settlor; and in that enjoyment he will be open to market influences. A beneficiary having a claim on only the income from the trust assets, as Adam in the arrangement 'for Adam for life, thereafter to his children', is in a weaker but essentially similar position.[65] Whilst unable alone to take the capital assets using *Saunders v Vautier*,[66] he can likewise enjoy the income in his own way, and in that enjoyment will again be exposed to market influences. (Note that this holds good whether or not one considers the beneficiary's claim to be to the gross income, rather than only to the sum properly payable, after deductions, by the trustees.[67] There seems to be no advantage from the viewpoint of the present arguments in requiring interests to be of the former kind.)

The interest thesis can thus be understood as reflecting limits that rights and economic utility arguments would put on the facilitative project. But those arguments do not have a monopoly on this area of discourse. Some putative trusts inimical to them can nevertheless be supported by, especially, communitarian and broader utilitarian arguments, as explored in sections 2.4–2.5, where the trust in question is calculated to do good in a way intelligible to these arguments. At least some types of trusts accepted by the law, but not reconcilable with the thesis, can be accounted for in this way. This is especially so as regards charitable trusts, which must by definition benefit the public. Large discretionary trusts, say for a company's workforce, can be seen similarly, as can trusts for purposes advantageous to particular individuals. Likewise trusts for the kinds of purposes tolerated in the 'anomalous' cases: significantly, these (care of a testator's pets, provision of tangible and spiritual memorials) are located in the culture of the family.

---

[64] (1841) 4 Beav 115, Cr & Ph 240; see section 10.4.

[65] But note the likely reading of the arrangement 'for my widow, in the knowledge that she will look after our children' not as a trust for the widow for life, then for the children, but as conferring a capital entitlement on the widow, with only a moral duty on her to provide for the children: see section 3.4.

[66] (1841) 4 Beav 115, Cr & Ph 240. If and when Adam and his children are all adult and of unimpaired capacity, they can however agree together to use this facility. For the political significance of *Saunders v Vautier*, see further J Getzler (2009) 10 *Theoretical Inquiries in Law* 355.   [67] Cf *Baker v Archer-Shee* [1927] AC 844, n 28 above.

In short, then, we have seen that, among all the purposes at which set-tlors might want to aim their trusts, certain kinds have been privileged, trusts for them being accorded validity while those aimed at other kinds are denied it. Those which comply with the beneficiary rule and the inter-est thesis are privileged because they are particularly aligned with consid-erations of rights and economic utility. Charitable purposes, those for the benefit of particular individuals, and those accepted in the 'anomalous' cases are privileged because, in their different ways, they are particu-larly aligned with respectable communitarian and/or broader utilitarian considerations.

Seeing matters in this way, we realize that we do not have to privilege one such kind of purpose *rather than* the other, so long as we are pre-pared to regard the various explanatory considerations not as inevitably antagonistic, but as different ways of achieving some deeper good, such as 'optimal human fulfilment'.

This perspective allows us to react more sympathetically to the favour with which some regard the interest thesis, demanding a beneficiary enjoying an interest in the nature of ownership. This favour is otherwise puzzling, for it is obvious to all that this position is far from reflective of the actual state of the law, failing—as we have seen—to account not only for charities and other forms of 'purpose trust', but also for discretionary trusts, and indeed struggling even with fixed trusts involving anything more complicated than a single absolute interest. We can now see the favouring of this position as denoting an attraction to the policies underly-ing it. Such an attraction is clearly intelligible. It might be combined with a revulsion from other policies, those explaining the kinds of trust that the position would not support. But it does not have to be so combined, and many would find such single-mindedness rather troubling. One can easily prefer an intelligently nuanced blend of routes to optimal human fulfil-ment. Given the manner in which English law is made, it is unsurprising that such a preference should represent the best explanation for the law's own current make-up. It is also persuasive enough, on account principally of its richer, more sympathetic appreciation of the human condition, to be adopted in this book as the way the law should orientate itself, at the level of principle. That is why the 'definition' of a trust given in section 1.1 is not limited in the manner indicated by the beneficiary rule or interest thesis, but accommodates the various kinds of purpose trust that the law has accepted.

Notice, however, the extent to which both these two stances—a pure commitment to considerations of rights and economic utility on the one hand, and an attraction both to those considerations and to communitarian and/or broader utilitarian concerns on the other—entrench upon the facilitative ideal. To be sure, settlors can create the trusts they wish, but only so long as these fit the law's policy template: not merely in the trite sense that an outrageous project, such as a trust to promote genocide, will be disallowed, but in the much stronger sense that trusts will be allowed only where they quite firmly benefit people, or even (following the beneficiary rule and interest thesis) where they do so specifically by putting capital or cash income in people's hands.

Notice also, finally, that the two stances are not the only conceivable ones. That is, one might wish the law to support, either as well as or instead of those purposes that it currently supports, purposes of kinds that it does not. In particular, observing that the familiar rules and their underlying principles are aimed at optimal *human* fulfilment, and arguing that this should not represent the (only) ultimate goal, one might urge the acceptance of purposes reflecting less anthropocentric concerns; for example saving the whales.[68] But the law of trusts is not, perhaps, the area where those of this persuasion would reckon to fight their principal battles.

12.5 THE ENFORCEMENT OF TRUSTEES' DUTIES

Where trustees' duties do correlate to beneficiaries' rights (whether claims to the trust property or otherwise), these duties can be enforced by the beneficiaries: and by the beneficiaries alone, so by no one else if the beneficiaries choose not to.[69]

Charities are enforceable by the Charity Commission or the Attorney General, and by no one else except interested individuals with the Commission's permission.[70] Trusts for purposes beneficial to particular individuals are enforceable by those individuals. In *Re Denley's Trust Deed*,[71] for example, the employees could have enforced if the trustees erred from their duty to provide the sports field. But again, if the benefited individuals choose not to enforce, no one else can. So if a trust provides for a company's employees to have a sports field, but the employees do not want the sports field and the trustees propose to

---

[68] That is, *for the whales' own sake*. A trust to save whales *for the public (ie human) benefit* is valid under the existing law, as being charitable: Charities Act 2006 ss 2(1)(b), 2(2)(i) or (k); section 6.5.

[69] *Shaw v Lawless* (1838) 5 Cl & Fin 129; *Gandy v Gandy* (1885) LR 30 Ch D 57.

[70] Charities Act 1993 s 33.   [71] [1969] 1 Ch 373.

sell it for development, neighbouring landowners opposed to this cannot enforce the trust instead.[72]

So far as 'anomalous' purpose trusts are concerned, the remainder-men, ie the people entitled to the sum remaining after the achievement of the purpose, have the right to enforce;[73] no suggestion of any alternative enforcers has been made, other than those appointed as such under regimes such as the Cayman Islands' STAR, considered in section 12.3. The remaindermen will want to sue if the trustees wrongfully reduce that sum, say by overspending on the monuments or animals. But they have no incentive to sue, indeed they have an incentive not to sue, where the trustees underspend on the purpose, so maximizing the amount remaining.

Two features of the picture regarding enforcement should be noticed. First, the regime is by and large not one calculated to secure the trustees' performance of their duties *as established by the settlor*. Where the person having the right of enforcement chooses not to enforce, that choice prevails, even if the settlor is or would have been chagrined thereby.[74] It is easy to discern this in the case of trusts for beneficiaries: the beneficiaries' preferences might easily differ from the settlor's stipulations, and the law attaches positive importance to the precedence of the former, as announced in the consent principle[75] and *Saunders v Vautier*.[76] (This may well be another reflection, or product, of the interest thesis: if the effect of a trust is to transfer ownership of its assets from settlor to beneficiary, its enforcement or otherwise, being a facet of that ownership, must obviously be the beneficiary's prerogative.) But, albeit without such an overt announcement of primacy, precedence is also given to the enforcer's wishes in other cases. This is true even as regards charities, where in reality the Charity Commission or Attorney General can be expected not necessarily to enforce the settlor's stipulations without compromise. In jurisdictions that have introduced the appropriate regime, however, a

---

[72] *Re Denley's Trust Deed* [1969] 1 Ch 373, 383, referring to situations where the performance of the trust 'would benefit an individual or individuals, where [the] benefit is so indirect or intangible or . . . is otherwise so framed as not to give those persons any *locus standi* to apply to the court to enforce the trust'.

[73] *Pettingall v Pettingall* (1842) 11 LJ Ch 176; *Re Thompson* [1934] Ch 342.

[74] Sometimes, the settlor may be able to enforce, but only because he simultaneously occupies another position, in the capacity of which he is entitled to do so. Thus, a settlor may also be a beneficiary; or he may be a 'benefited individual' within the principle in *Re Denley's Trust Deed* [1969] 1 Ch 373, as in *Carreras Rothmans Ltd v Freeman Mathews Treasure Ltd* [1985] Ch 207. There, the settlor, a tobacco company, placed money in trust so as to ensure that newspapers were paid for carrying its advertisements. The settlor company wanted this trust performed so that the newspapers would continue to accept its advertising. It was able to enforce.   [75] See section 10.3.

[76] (1841) 4 Beav 115, Cr & Ph 240; see section 10.4.

settlor can appoint an enforcer[77] or 'protector'[78] with the right to enforce against the trustees. Unless the appointment has been made with some other aim (a particular beneficiary could for example be appointed protector, with the aim of privileging his position *vis-à-vis* that of his fellow beneficiaries), the enforcer or protector can be expected generally to seek performance of the settlor's stipulations: though again, not in the last resort necessarily without compromise.

Secondly, there will not be enforcement in every case where the person(s) entitled to enforce would in principle wish to do so. Theoretical rights to enforce are in practice diminished by lack of information, energy, strength, or resources, deficiencies in all these respects being routine features of life, even for the Charity Commission and Attorney General.

12.6 MUST TRUSTEES' DUTIES BE ENFORCEABLE?

Prominent judicial statements can be found of an 'enforceability principle': ie that a trust cannot be validly created unless its trustees' duties will be enforceable against them. The most celebrated such statements are by Sir William Grant MR and Lord Eldon LC in *Morice v Bishop of Durham*.[79] That decision focused on the need[80] for certainty in the detailing of the trustees' duties, as explained in Chapters 8 and 9: for instance, the requirement, in the case of a trust requiring equal division of property between the beneficiaries, that the number of beneficiaries be known. Certainty was required so that the trustees' duties could be defined, this in turn being necessary so that the court could enforce them.

These statements have led to assertions[81] that a trust must have a beneficiary or other person to enforce it, thus denying validity to trusts for

---

[77] Where the law permits it, enforcers can be used to validate otherwise invalid purpose trusts; but the device can also be extended to a trust with beneficiaries, to the exclusion of the beneficiaries' rights of enforcement (and non-enforcement) or otherwise. That is the position in, especially, the Cayman Islands. For a discussion of the latter, see P Matthews (1997) 11 TLI 67; A Duckworth (1998) 12 TLI 16; P Matthews (1998) TLI 98.

[78] D Waters in A Oakley (ed) *Trends in Contemporary Trust Law* (1996) ch 4.

[79] (1804) 9 Ves 399, 404–5, (1805) 10 Ves 522, 539. See also *Re Astor's Settlement Trusts* [1952] Ch 534, 541–2; *Re Shaw* [1957] 1 WLR 729, 744–5; *Leahy v A-G for New South Wales* [1959] AC 457, 479, 484.

[80] Except in charitable trusts: an insufficiently defined charitable purpose will be given shape by a 'scheme' devised by the Charity Commission (Charities Act 1993 s 16) or court.

[81] See eg *Leahy v A-G for New South Wales* [1959] AC 457, 478, which however refers only to trusts for beneficiaries or charitable purposes. For further discussion, see D Hayton (2001) 117 LQR 96; P Parkinson [2002] CLJ 657.

purposes that are neither charitable nor, as *Re Denley's Trust Deed*[82] points out, to the advantage of identifiable people (or, under a regime such as STAR, having an appointed enforcer). Although enforceable by their remaindermen, the 'anomalous' trusts for other purposes are not enforceable as this principle requires,[83] for, as we saw in section 12.5, the remaindermen have no reason to intervene against underspending, as opposed to overspending, on the purpose.

But is it correct to see the enforceability of the trustees' duties as essential to the trust concept in this way?

It might be said that it is correct, on the basis of facilitative logic. The argument would be this. If the law offers the trust as a vehicle whereby a settlor can effectuate his intentions, but it cannot guarantee the trustees' performance of their duties embodying those intentions, the settlor is potentially led up the garden path: he may put assets into the trust only for his intentions to be subverted, say by the trustees keeping the money for themselves.[84] There are two difficulties about a justification for the enforceability principle in these terms, however.

The first is that a requirement of enforceability would not necessarily serve facilitative policy well. By holding the trustees to their duties, such a requirement facilitates projects that can be enforced. These cases are easy. But there is a dilemma for the policy regarding projects that cannot be enforced, notably purpose trusts (other than those caught by *Re Denley's Trust Deed*[85] and charities). Demanding enforceability prevents frustration of settlors by the subversion of their intentions, but simultaneously itself frustrates them by denying such projects validity as trusts at all. Not demanding enforceability allows such trusts to exist, but at the cost of a risk of subversion. Either response promises only a partial vindication of settlors' wishes, therefore. It is not inevitable that the preference should be for enforceability and so invalidity. There is a parallel here with the treatment of certainty. Take, for example, the trustees' apparently simple duty to pay the settlor's designated objects and no one else. As we saw in section 8.6, a duty in this form might well be what settlors want; but it would require so much certainty that trusts would routinely fail for uncertainty. Reducing the duty to something more practicable would allow people to make valid trusts, but it would mean sacrificing strict fidelity to their wishes. The facilitative policy finds itself in a dilemma between these two

---

[82] [1969] 1 Ch 373.   [83] *Re Shaw* [1957] 1 WLR 729, 745.

[84] *Leahy v A-G for New South Wales* [1959] AC 457, 484 explicitly puts the enforceability principle in terms of enforcement *of the settlor's wishes*.

[85] [1969] 1 Ch 373.

positions. The latter approach has in fact prevailed: the duties are relaxed, and trusts upheld. Half a loaf is treated as better than none. Consistency argues that purpose trusts should be upheld too. Their being valid but unenforceable can be seen as the half a loaf that is better than the no bread of invalidity.

The second difficulty about ascribing the enforceability principle to facilitative thought is that, as we saw in section 12.5, the law's prevailing enforcement regime is not in fact generally calculated to secure the trustees' performance of their duties *as established by the settlor*. In an ordinary trust for beneficiaries, especially, the settlor's stipulations will be enforced only to the extent that this suits the beneficiaries; the settlor himself having no legal right to intervene. Facilitative logic is overlain with considerations about maximizing the rights of the recipients.

The loss of a foundation in facilitative logic is not necessarily fatal to the enforceability principle, however. The principle might be justified instead on another basis. The obvious candidate is an argument that the availability of legal enforcement is intrinsic to the concept of a legal duty (and, where applicable, a legal right). Owners without duties to the contrary can enjoy their property as they wish. Trustees are in principle owners of the trust property: the trust consists in the fact that their duties oblige them not to enjoy the property themselves but to deploy it in the required way. Unless these duties can be enforced, it might be said, they amount to nothing, leaving the trustees with full ownership. Such thinking is perceptible in at least some statements of the enforceability principle.[86] It is certainly intelligible. But on examination, at any rate as applied to express trusts, it fails to capture the whole truth.

The argument certainly cannot be that legal enforcement is all that prevents trustees from breaching their duties. In the vast majority of cases, trustees will perform their duties regardless of the prospect of legal enforcement, for the kinds of reasons described in Chapter 11. (Express trust duties may differ in this respect from some others: perhaps legal enforcement is required to give practical substance to family provision law, for example.) Rather, the argument needs to be that trusts cannot intelligibly exist *as legal institutions* unless trustees' duties are legally enforceable: that we cannot intelligibly speak of legal duties, such as would have to exist in an unenforceable trust, if these duties could not be legally enforced. That seems implausible, however. As we saw in section 12.5, even those duties that someone has the right and motivation to enforce are only

---

[86] *Morice v Bishop of Durham* (1804) 9 Ves 399, 404–5; *Re Astor's Settlement Trusts* [1952] Ch 534, 541–2; *Armitage v Nurse* [1998] Ch 241, 253.

adventitiously enforceable in practice (and the point is hardly confined to trusts); yet this does not prevent us thinking of them as legal duties. Their legal quality makes a difference in the eyes of the trustee who wishes to perform them despite the lack of legal sanction if he does not. For the same reason, one can intelligibly identify as involving distinctively legal duties a trust, such as an 'anomalous' purpose trust, which no one has the right and motivation to enforce.

In the hands of compliant trustees of this kind, indeed, an unenforceable trust is not only an intelligible concept; but also one distinct from other concepts such as a power, a moral obligation, and absolute ownership. Telling such trustees that they had any of these would create different effects in their minds, and thus in their behaviour, from telling them that they had a trust. A power would signify that it was for them to choose whether to carry out the object in question or not.[87] A moral obligation would point definitely towards the promotion of the object, but its merely moral character means that even a trustee seeking to perform his legal duties would be right to weigh it against, and where appropriate postpone it to, contradictory moral obligations: for example, someone given money with a merely moral obligation to care for a horse could validly conclude that it should be spent instead on his starving children. And a person prepared to be a compliant trustee but in fact given absolute ownership would see himself, correctly, as under no relevant duties. Uncompliant trustees with unenforceable duties might treat these as of no moment; but compliant trustees regard their legal duties as such and try to perform them properly, irrespective of their enforceability. As most trustees seem to be compliant, this observation can properly persuade us to regard trusts without legally enforceable duties as nonetheless legal institutions. Consider also the position where the compliant trustee becomes insolvent. Any property that he owns himself, even with a moral obligation attached, will pass to his creditors; but if, despite not having to, he points out that he holds a certain item of property on trust, it will not so pass.

Indeed, not only is it intelligible to see trusts as legal institutions notwithstanding that the duties in them may not be legally enforceable. Arguably, at least some express trusts *ought not to be* the subject of legal

---

[87] It is sometimes suggested that unenforceable purpose trusts should be salvaged from failure, if that would otherwise be their fate, by regarding them as purpose powers. (That is the effect of the Ontario Perpetuities Act 1966 s 16 and similar statutory provisions, but English decisions have ruled it out: *Re Shaw* [1957] 1 WLR 729, 746; *Re Endacott* [1960] Ch 232, 246.) The point in the text weighs against such an easy equation of unenforceable trust with power. It is also not clear that objections to purpose trusts are inapplicable to powers: see section 9.2.

enforcement. The proposition here is that such trusts are to that extent best seen as self-contained, autonomous, institutions, zones of self-regulation into which judges positively should not intrude. The origins of many express trusts in an act of generosity, and their place in contexts such as the family, make this proposition plausible: they lend themselves to an argument that legalism, and so judicial enforcement, is inappropriate to them on communitarian grounds.[88] This observation has less relevance to other kinds of express trusts, such as pension fund trusts. But one could defensibly argue against judicial intervention more widely, for a further reason. The operation of most express trusts is not a purely mechanical exercise, but requires finesse and judgement. Trustees being chosen for their personal qualities in these respects,[89] their oversight by an outsider such as a judge might easily be inappropriate. This point seems to be taken in several features of the law itself, revealing a judicial reluctance to intervene in trusts. If trustees run into difficulty, the normal course is for the court to deal only with the specific problem, rather than to take on the whole administration of the trust. Trustees will not normally have to disclose the thinking behind their discretionary decisions.[90] If a discretionary decision is questioned in court, the judge considers merely whether the discretion has been exercised properly, not whether he or she agrees with the conclusion reached.[91] And if trustees are found to have gone wrong in the exercise of their discretion, the remedy is as conservative as possible: they may be told to try again,[92] or an order may be made to carry out a course of action favoured by some of them but blocked by others,[93] or else to give effect to the beneficiaries' own wishes; the judge may exercise the discretion personally,[94] but generally[95] only as a last resort.

---

[88] See section 2.4. Compare the way that agreements between members of families are not normally enforceable as contracts, as 'lacking intention to create contractual relations'.

[89] See section 11.8.

[90] See section 11.9, reflecting *Re Londonderry's Settlement* [1965] Ch 918; *Schmidt v Rosewood Trust Ltd* [2003] 2 AC 709; *Breakspear v Ackland* [2009] Ch 32. The latter, at [56], explicitly connects this position with a desire to keep the conduct of trusts away from the courts.

[91] *Gisborne v Gisborne* (1877) 2 App Cas 300; *Tabor v Brooks* (1878) 10 Ch D 273; *Tempest v Lord Camoys* (1882) 21 Ch D 571; *Edge v Pensions Ombudsman* [2000] Ch 602, 630 (expressly referring this attitude to the importance of the trustees' identity). Review of protectors' decisions may be especially attenuated: D Waters in A Oakley (ed) *Trends in Contemporary Trust Law* (1996) ch 4.

[92] *Re Locker's Settlement Trusts* [1977] 1 WLR 1323; *Turner v Turner* [1984] Ch 100.

[93] *Klug v Klug* [1918] 2 Ch 67.

[94] *McPhail v Doulton* [1971] AC 424, 457; *Mettoy Pension Trustees Ltd v Evans* [1990] 1 WLR 1587, 1617, 1632; *Thrells Ltd v Lomas* [1993] 1 WLR 456.

[95] Aberrantly, judicial exercise is the norm in the case of the discretions given to trustees of land: Trusts of Land and Appointment of Trustees Act 1996 s 14.

In the end, then, the view that trustees' duties (and, where they arise, beneficiaries' rights) need *not* be legally enforceable seems more support- able than the contrary view.

12.7 WHAT PRICE FACILITATION?

In this chapter, we have seen that the facilitative project—the idea that the law operates express trusts so as to effectuate a settlor's intentions—does not account for some key rules regarding the validity of trusts: instead, as section 12.4 explained, these rules track rights, utilitarian (including eco- nomic utilitarian), and communitarian considerations. We have also seen, in section 12.5, that facilitative ideas do not shape the position regarding the enforcement of trusts: this is the prerogative of another member of the trust's cast (unless, coincidentally, the settlor has another role car- rying that prerogative), inevitably influenced to at least some extent by that member's own constraints and agendas. And in section 12.6, we saw that facilitation cannot form the basis of the demands often found for trusts to be enforceable; indeed, it probably suggests the opposite of those demands.

Given all this divergence between important aspects of the prevailing vision of trusts on the one hand and the facilitative project on the other, what is the standing of the latter? In Chapters 1 and 2, we depicted express trusts as arising in furtherance of that project, ie so as to effectuate a set- tlor's wishes.[96] In the light of what we have seen in the present chapter, do we need to abandon this vision, instead seeing the settlor's role as being to provide the trust assets but then disappear?

The way to understand the matter is as follows. It tracks the analysis advanced in Chapter 2. At bottom, express trusts assuredly are facilita- tive. Sometimes, the law does reallocate property away from its hitherto owner without regard to the latter's wishes, as when it levies taxes, or indeed imposes a constructive trust. But this is not how express trusts work. Unless the settlor wants them to arise, they do not. Among facili- tative devices (others being covenants, gifts, and testamentary transfers; perhaps contracts too, but more probably not), the work of express trusts is to permit dispositions of property more sophisticated than a simple absolute transfer. But it does not follow that they must permit any dispo- sition that a settlor might want. Influenced by other considerations, the law might quite understandably limit the facility they afford. As indeed

---

[96] See sections 1.3–1.4, 2.1–2.2.

it does, on the bases (paternalist, communitarian, utilitarian, and rights-focused) reviewed in sections 2.3–2.6. The limits, however, may be more constraining, or less. A ban only on trusts for the promotion of genocide and the like would constrain little, leaving plenty of scope for settlors still to devise their own forms of disposition. At the other extreme—very constraining indeed—is the vision of the express trust embedded in the interest thesis, which we have now come to appreciate. According to this vision, a settlor can use the trust device only to transfer ownership (as a whole or in slices); that is, to make what, in comparison with the possibilities that are excluded, is little more than a gift.[97] The trust remains facilitative, but the facility is not a spacious one. On this view, the law's message to settlors is akin to Henry Ford's remark about his Model T automobile in 1909: 'any customer can have a car painted any color that he wants so long as it is black'.[98] An express trust device limited in this way can be explained, in the manner noted in section 12.4. But, as also noted there, it is hard to regard the preferences involved in its adoption as optimal ones.

---

[97] Though also, by way of tolerated exception, to provide for a charitable purpose; and perhaps too, by way of barely tolerated exception, to provide for an 'anomalous' non-charitable purpose.   [98] H Ford *My Life and Work* (1924) ch 4.

13

Breach of Trust and Remedies

Chapter 11 concerned the factors helping to ensure that trustees perform their duties properly. Sometimes, however, trustees fail to live up to what is expected of them. In that event they may be sued, ie a legal remedy sought against them.[1] This chapter examines when they can be successfully sued, and the remedies that may be available against them.[2]

13.1 ORDERING PERFORMANCE

The basic remedy available against trustees is an order requiring them to perform their obligations under the trust, or to refrain from breaching those obligations. (There is a resemblance to specific performance and injunctions in the law of contract.) So say trustees have placed trust money in a prohibited investment: they can be ordered to sell this investment and to reinvest the proceeds properly. Likewise, trustees who fail to pay some money to the beneficiary entitled to it, and who still have it available, can be told to repair the omission. Trustees who fail to think properly about a discretion can be told to do so.[3] One who holds property on constructive trust can often be told to hand it over to the beneficiary.[4]

Sometimes, the goal remains that of securing the future performance of the trust, but a different approach needs to be taken to achieving this, as for one reason or another the existing trustees cannot, or should not, simply be ordered to perform. In particular, there may well (otherwise why sue them

---

[1] Section 12.6 suggests, however, that the possibility of suing the trustees should not be seen as essential to the trust concept.

[2] See further R Chambers in P Birks and A Pretto (eds) *Breach of Trust* (2002) ch 1.

[3] As in *Re Locker's Settlement Trusts* [1977] 1 WLR 1323 and *Turner v Turner* [1984] Ch 100. It is said that where a power of appointment must be exercised, if at all, by a date which has now passed, the trustees cannot be ordered to consider exercising it: *Re Allen-Meyrick's Will Trusts* [1966] 1 WLR 499, 505; *Breadner v Granville-Grossman* [2001] Ch 523, [52]. But this rule overlooks the *duty* that the trustees have, even in a power (so long as it is a fiduciary power: see sections 9.2, 9.5) to consider exercise; performance of a duty was ordered out of time in *Re Locker's Settlement Trusts*.   [4] See section 18.5.

at all?) be misgivings about the existing trustees' continued handling of the trust. In this event, the court may secure the trust's future performance by replacing the existing trustees,[5] leaving the new trustees to perform in their stead.[6] Alternatively, the judge may act in the trustees' stead. This response is unproblematic if the duty in question requires a specific action, such as the transfer of some property. There is greater difficulty in the case of a duty properly to reach a decision, for example a duty to choose an investment or a beneficiary for payment in a discretionary trust.[7] The law is committed to the view that there is no single right way of performing such a duty;[8] that the choice between possible ways must be that of the trust's own trustee. A judge, therefore, appears to have no business to make it.[9]

Plainly, an order requiring trustees to perform their obligations in respect of particular trust property can be made only if they do indeed hold that property. At the extreme, an order requiring the performance of trust obligations cannot be made against one who does not hold trust property at all. And an order requiring the trust property to be transferred to new trustees, for them to perform the obligations, or allowing a judge to perform the obligations, can be made only if the trust property is available for such treatment. So such orders are possible when a trustee has, for example, improperly put trust property into his own pocket but still has it, for it nonetheless continues to exist, and to be claimable as trust property. On the other hand, if he has handled it in such a way that it can no longer be identified in his hands, as for example by spending it on taking a holiday, it is no longer practicable to think simply in terms of having him,

---

[5] See section 11.1.

[6] This used to be thought the only response when trustees with a power of appointment neglect their duties of consideration (*Re Gestetner Settlement* [1953] Ch 672, 688; *Re Manisty's Settlement* [1974] Ch 17, 25–6); but that restrictive view no longer obtains: *Mettoy Pension Trustees Ltd v Evans* [1990] 1 WLR 1587, 1617–18.

[7] The possibility of judicial performance of such a duty was accepted in *McPhail v Doulton* [1971] AC 424, 457; *Mettoy Pension Trustees Ltd v Evans* [1990] 1 WLR 1587, 1617, 1632; *Thrells Ltd v Lomas* [1993] 1 WLR 456.

[8] *Gisborne v Gisborne* (1877) 2 App Cas 300; *Tabor v Brooks* (1878) 10 Ch D 273; *Tempest v Lord Camoys* (1882) 21 Ch D 571; *Edge v Pensions Ombudsman* [2000] Ch 602.

[9] The opposite position—that judges can exercise discretions on the trustees' behalf—was assumed in the previous law, when indeed judges, instead of simply carrying out a particular duty in the trustees' place, regularly took over the entire administration of the trust, in effect appointing themselves trustees. The final expressions of the old position were perhaps *Re Hodges* (1878) 7 Ch D 754 and *Re Roper's Trusts* (1879) 11 Ch D 272, and the practice of taking over the whole trust largely died out around the same time. (It may be significant that the beneficiaries in even these cases were wards of court, in the protection of whose interests judges are abnormally interventionist.) The old approach has, however, been revived where the trust is of land (Trusts of Land and Appointment of Trustees Act 1996 s 14); probably inadvisedly, for the reason given in the text.

or anyone else, perform his duties regarding it. Having been turned into the holiday, and the holiday taken, the trust property has evidently disappeared from the trustee's ownership, just as if he had burned the very banknotes in question. The position in these two examples is straightforward and obvious. More thought is however needed in other cases, in which the trustee likewise no longer has the trust property in its original form, but nor has it simply disappeared from his hands in this way: as where he spends trust money on a painting, or where he mixes it in a bank account with his own money. In such cases, it cannot be said that he either does or does not still have the trust property, by the light of nature: all depends on how the law itself treats the matter. In fact, the law sees him as still having the trust property in many such cases, despite the complications. It does so via the 'tracing' rules, described in section 17.5.

13.2 ACCOUNT

As just noted, it is impossible to make an order requiring a trustee to perform the trust obligations (or to transfer it to a new trustee, or to give over the function to a judge) if the trust property no longer exists in his hands. Where this is the case, however, the law addresses the difficulty by inserting a preliminary step, requiring the trustee *first* to repair the loss to the trust fund and *then* to perform his duties regarding it (or transfer it, etc). So if a trustee has squandered trust money on a holiday for himself, he can be ordered to pay the sum in question back into the trust, before once again using the reinstated fund in accordance with the terms of the trust. Or if he has placed the trust's assets in a prohibited investment, and there they have lost value, he can be ordered not only to retrieve them, but also to make up the loss, before re-investing the combined sum properly. The trustee's liability to make up the trust fund in this way is an aspect of his duty to 'account', ie to report periodically on the state of the trust fund—what assets he holds for the trust, and what movements have taken place into and out of those assets[10]—and to ensure that it in fact contains the assets that it should.

Sometimes, indeed, the making good of the fund is the only aspect of the case that requires attention. There may be no difficulty about leaving the trustees to continue performing the trust once the fund has been reinstated, as where they have unfortunately but innocently paid out some

---

[10] Hence the ascription to their duty to account of the trustees' obligation to disclose information about their conduct of the trust: *Schmidt v Rosewood Trust Ltd* [2003] 2 AC 709, section 11.9.

trust money in an unauthorized way. Or performing the trust may involve simply transferring the trust assets to the objects, as where the trust's beneficiaries simultaneously wind it up,[11] or where there is a single beneficiary, immediately entitled, as is commonly the case with a constructive trust. In that event, the order will not require the trustee to reinstate the trust fund and then, separately, transfer the latter; it will order him straightforwardly to pay the money in question directly to those ultimately entitled to it, such an order sometimes being called one for 'equitable compensation' (though this expression is also used more widely, as meaning an order 'to make good the trust fund' generally).

The liability to account, then, involves a liability on the part of trustees, where the value of the assets that they hold on trust is lower than it should be, to make up the difference. There appears to be a resemblance to an award of damages for, say, breach of contract. It is often asserted, however, that this appearance is partly—though only partly—misleading.[12] The most famous statement of this position is by Millett LJ in *Bristol and West Building Society v Mothew*.[13] In fact, this statement goes into detail only about certain aspects of the matter, leaving the remainder to be gathered from other sources. But we shall refer to the whole assemblage as 'the *Mothew* position'. It exercises a powerful influence over contemporary thinking about this area, though, as we shall see, it states neither the present nor the previous law fully accurately, let alone unproblematically.

13.3 ACCOUNT: TWO KINDS OF DUTY?

The *Mothew* position draws a distinction between, on the one hand, duties requiring the exercise of care and skill, such as the duty to use care and skill in choosing the trust's investments; and, on the other hand, fiduciary and other absolute duties, such as the duty not to use unauthorized types of investments.[14] It accepts that the liability to account in respect of the

---

[11] Under the rule in *Saunders v Vautier* (1841) 4 Beav 115, Cr & Ph 240: see section 10.4.

[12] See eg S Elliott (2002) 65 MLR 588, 590. Cf R Chambers in P Birks and A Pretto (eds) *Breach of Trust* (2002) ch 1, 8–10.

[13] [1998] Ch 1, 17–18. This statement had precursors: *Girardet v Crease & Co* (1987) 11 BCLR (2d) 361, 362 (Canada); *Permanent Building Society (in liquidation) v Wheeler* (1994) 11 WAR 187, 237–9, Australia.

[14] Strictly, *Bristol and West Building Society v Mothew* [1998] Ch 1, 17–18 itself deals only with duties of care and skill on the one hand, and *fiduciary* duties on the other. But it is generally accepted, following eg *Clough v Bond* (1838) 3 My & Cr 490, that other absolute duties are to be grouped with the latter. Thus *Youyang Pty Ltd v Minter Ellison Morris Fletcher* (2003) 212 CLR 484, Australia, regarding the duty to invest, and otherwise to disburse, the trust assets only as authorized.

former is analogous to the 'secondary' liability to pay damages for breach of contract, in arising only where the trustee has breached his 'primary' duty—that is, has failed to deploy the necessary care and skill—and aiming to redress the consequences of that breach.[15] But in respect of absolute duties, the *Mothew* position denies this approach. So if the trustee makes, for example, an unauthorized investment, and the fund loses value as a result, it sees his liability to correct this loss *not* in terms of his breaching a primary duty to use only authorized investments and a secondary duty to make good the consequences of that breach. Rather, it depicts him as owing *only* a primary duty, this being to 'ensure the proper state of the trust fund'. It regards his liability to correct the loss flowing from his unauthorized investment as simply an instantiation of this duty, and an order requiring him to do so as an order to perform the latter. If we wish to find an analogy in the law of contract, it is with the very—primary— duty to perform the contract itself, enforced by specific performance or injunction.

Although this division between the two kinds of duty seems to represent the modern orthodoxy, it is in fact dubious. There is much support, overlooked in *Bristol and West Building Society v Mothew*,[16] for assimilating the two contexts. On the one hand, some previous decisions treated duties of care and skill in the same way as the *Mothew* position does absolute duties, ie as involving only primary liabilities.[17] On the other, as section 13.5 will explain, a more recent previous decision[18] had gone some distance in the other direction, treating the absolute duty context rather as the *Mothew* position treats duties of care and skill. Moreover, the idea of differentiating between the two kinds of duty is unsatisfactory in principle. Duties of care and skill are surely aimed at putting flesh on the trustee's basic duty to respect the fact that the trust property is not his own.[19]

---

[15] For the division of contractual obligations into 'primary' and 'secondary' classes, see *Photo Production Ltd v Securicor Transport Ltd* [1980] AC 827, 849.

[16] [1998] Ch 1.

[17] *Caffrey v Darby* (1801) 6 Ves Jr 488, 496; *Nocton v Lord Ashburton* [1914] AC 932, 958, 965; *Bartlett v Barclays Bank Trust Co Ltd (Nos 1 and 2)* [1980] Ch 515, 543–5. See too *Youyang Pty Ltd v Minter Ellison Morris Fletcher* (2003) 212 CLR 484, [39], Australia; *KM v HM* [1992] 3 SCR 6, Canada.

[18] *Target Holdings Ltd v Redferns (a firm)* [1996] AC 421.

[19] This appears to be the very point of *Nocton v Lord Ashburton* [1914] AC 932; and the classic formulation of the duty of care and skill—that a trustee should emulate an ordinary prudent businessman looking after the interests of others (*Re Whiteley* (1886) 33 Ch D 347, *Learoyd v Whiteley* (1887) 12 App Cas 727; see section 7.2)—was expressly informed by the reflection that a trustee is a fiduciary (see (1886) 33 Ch D 347, 355). See further J Getzler in P Birks and A Pretto (eds) *Breach of Trust* (2002) ch 2; J Heydon in S Degeling and J Edelman (eds) *Equity in Commercial Law* (2005) ch 9; J Getzler *ibid* ch 10; but cf D Hayton *ibid* ch 11.

13.4 ACCOUNT: BREACH

Remember the *Mothew* position's treatment of absolute duty cases. Seeing the trustee's liability to make up the trust fund in such cases as primary—a duty of 'ensuring the proper state of the trust fund'—means that it can, and indeed should, be elaborated and applied without reference to the idea of his being in *breach* of his obligations.[20]

Historically, this vision had substance. If he was not to have to make up a loss to the trust assets, the trustee—the onus being on him—either had to show that the loss was proper (as in the case of an authorized investment, or a legitimate payment to an object), or had to be excused in respect of it, if not by the objects themselves, then by the court (as where, despite his taking proper care of the assets, they had been stolen).[21] The question whether he should be excused, or 'relieved', was not discussed in the language of whether he had a duty to avoid or prevent the loss in question, and had breached this duty.[22]

But of course such language could have been used, and indeed would better have been, if the relevant decisions were not to be made randomly, but were to follow a consistent and substantively appropriate pattern. The only sensible way to think about whether a trustee ought to be excused is to ask whether he should, for whatever good reason, be expected to have behaved differently; *alias* whether the fund is smaller than the law says, positively, it should be; *alias* whether the trustee went wrong—there is no reason to avoid saying, breached his duties—in causing or allowing it to be at a lower level. This latter mode of expression is the more transparent, and so appealing to Rule of Law values; and substantively, it gives a guarantee of reasonable treatment, where the traditional approach, involving

---

[20] See eg C Mitchell and S Watterson in C Mitchell (ed) *Constructive and Resulting Trusts* (2010) ch 4, 126.

[21] *Jones v Lewis* (1750) 2 Ves Sen 240. In practice, losses were not excused if the trustees could have come to court for guidance before doing the act that resulted in them, meaning that the possibility of excuse arose only in respect of unforeseeable events (such as theft). For this praxis, and the view that it was too ponderous to represent a satisfactory way of profiling trustees' liability, see House of Commons Select Committee on the Administration of Trusts, *Report* (1895 HC 248), *Minutes of Evidence* q 462; see too qq 422–5.

[22] In fact, this vision chimed better with the way in which liability to account was formerly assessed at common law (largely by auditors, rather than judicially), than with the approach taken in equity (more judicially, since the judicial procedure was itself more inquisitorial). (See S Stoljar (1964) 80 LQR 203, 214–15, 220.) The vision's adoption in equity thus appears a calculated position, not easily explicable, since the information deficits justifying the common law's approach (see section 13.7) were lessening as—and partly because—the equitable one became prominent. At all events, it was ultimately disavowed as counter-productive, in the way about to be described in the text.

relief, offered only a hope. Informed at least partly by a desire to ensure
that people were not frightened away from becoming trustees by the
severity of the demands upon them,[23] an important decision on liability
towards the end of the nineteenth century, *Speight v Gaunt*,[24] conspicu-
ously proceeded in terms of duty and breach, emphatically addressing the
trustee's liability for the loss of trust property via the question whether he
had failed to exercise due care and skill.[25,26] This vision of trustees' liability is also more firmly, indeed institutionally, represented in today's law
than proponents of the contrary position tend to notice.[27]

We should therefore reject the view that, except where the loss is said
to arise from a failure to exercise appropriate care and skill, the trustee is
required (where necessary) to make up the trust fund because of a primary
obligation to ensure the proper state of the trust fund. The better course is
to see a trustee's liability to make up shortfalls in the trust fund—both in
cases where he breaches a duty of care and skill, and in every other case as
well—as an obligation to repair the harmful consequences of a breach of
his duty to perform his genuine primary obligations under the trust.

We must, therefore, consider when a breach is to be found. In outline
terms, a breach of trust is a failure by a trustee to perform a duty binding
him: as modified, if relevant, either by the terms of the individual trust or

---

[23] See section 11.2.

[24] (1883) 22 Ch D 727, 9 App Cas 1; see especially (1883) 22 Ch D 727, 740, 762 (see further
section 7.2). Though iconic, however, the decision was not the first occasion on which matters
were analysed in this way. The same approach is visible, for example, in the (unsuccessful)
arguments of counsel in the older decision, *Eaves v Hickson* (1861) 30 Beav 136.

[25] The decision might be depicted as a mere technical adjustment of the boundary between
absolute duty cases and care and skill cases, posing no challenge to the rules applicable to those
cases themselves. But its real point was surely, to the extent permitted by the case's ambit, a
rejection of the old excuse-based approach, and the installation of a duty-based approach in
its place.

[26] The decision was intended to be complemented by the Judicial Trustees Act 1896 s 3,
re-enacted as the Trustee Act 1925 s 61, allowing a court, after a trustee has been found in
breach, to relieve him from liability if he acted 'honestly and reasonably'. (See House of
Commons Select Committee on the Administration of Trusts, *Report* (1895 HC 248) iv, and
Minutes of Evidence qq 422, 462, 552–4.) This provision will rarely if ever be applied to a
breach of a duty of care and skill (a trustee acting honestly and reasonably will not commit
such a breach), but goes some way towards turning all other obligations into ones of care and
skill (a generalized position on these lines being acknowledged as the goal: *ibid* q 482). How far,
however, depends on the extent to which a trustee can rely on it. This is a contentious issue, but
the dominant view is that he cannot: see section 10.2. If so, however, the provision represents
no advance upon the old excuse-based approach.

[27] For example, the phrase 'breach of trust' is used in the Trustee Act 1925 s 61 and the
Limitation Act 1980 s 21(3), and no one seems to regard this as preventing their application to
absolute duties, or even as infelicitous. Even *Bristol and West Building Society v Mothew* [1998]
Ch 1, 18 itself uses the word 'breach' in the context of fiduciary duties.

by a general rule.[28] The essential principle is the same whether the trust is express, resulting, or constructive. The trustee's duties probably vary between the categories,[29] however, and certainly vary from one trust to another within them. Chapters 7–9 contained a survey of some of the main kinds of duty.

Many trust duties demand a reasonable performance rather than an impeccable one: for example, in management operations, trustees are commonly required to show 'such care and skill as is reasonable in the circumstances'.[30] Breach of such a duty consists in failing to display this level of care and skill, rather than in mismanagement in an absolute sense. Some duties, however, are absolute, demanding the performance of a particular task, positive or negative: eg avoidance of certain investments.[31] Here, non-performance will be a breach even if reasonable, as where trustees pardonably misunderstand their investment instructions.[32]

In regard to discretions, the question is not whether the judge would have come to a different determination in the trustees' place.[33] The trustees' duty is to consider the question properly: that is, to give it active thought, taking relevant matters into account and leaving irrelevant ones aside, as explained in sections 7.3–7.4 and 9.5–9.6. As seen there, this rule has different aspects. As regards the particular duty to think at all, and that not to entertain improper motives, breach—called 'fraud on a power', though there is no requirement of dishonesty—consists simply in a failure to do so. Regarding the rule in *Re Hastings-Bass*[34] (the duty to be appropriately informed),[35] however, the cases have taken a more complicated position. It has been said the rule is transgressed only if the trustees

---

[28] See Ch 10.   [29] See sections 7.1, 18.5.

[30] Trustee Act 2000 s 1, Sch 1 para 1.

[31] The Trustee Act 2000 s 6 allows settlors to restrict the range of investments open to the trustees: eg so as to confine them to ethical investments.

[32] Though such a breach may well be excused, ie the trustees exonerated from liability, under the Trustee Act 1925 s 61: see section 10.2.

[33] *Gisborne v Gisborne* (1877) 2 App Cas 300; *Tabor v Brooks* (1878) 10 Ch D 273; *Tempest v Lord Camoys* (1882) 21 Ch D 571; *Edge v Pensions Ombudsman* [2000] Ch 602. (The older contrary approach—see eg *Re Hodges* (1878) 7 Ch D 754; *Re Roper's Trusts* (1879) 11 Ch D 272—has been resurrected for trusts of land by the Trusts of Land and Appointment of Trustees Act 1996 s 14, but probably not as a test for beach: only to the extent of allowing a judge to exercise a discretion in the trustees' place.)

[34] [1975] Ch 25, 36, 41; *Mettoy Pension Trustees Ltd v Evans* [1990] 1 WLR 1587, 1621–6; *Sieff v Fox* [2005] 1 WLR 3811; R Walker (2002) 13 King's College LJ 173; C Mitchell (2006) 122 LQR 35; M Ashdown (2010) 16 T & T 826.

[35] The matters of which they should be informed include not only the legal but also the practical effects of the course of action in question, including the tax consequences: *Smithson v Hamilton* [2008] 1 WLR 1453, [53]; *Pitt v Holt* [2010] 1 WLR 1199, [31], [40]–[43] (where the point was challenged by the Revenue authorities for the first time); *Futter v Futter* [2010]

would (or sometimes, might)[36] have come to a different determination if they had been appropriately informed.[37] It has also been said that the rule can be transgressed even without a breach of trust,[38] but this may be doubted. Certainly, the rule may be transgressed even though the oversight of the crucial information involves no *independent* breach, such as a failure to exhibit due care and skill.[39] But it is hard to see, in principle, why a transgression is not, like a fraud on a power, a breach in its own right.[40] There will also be a breach, even if it is impossible to identify a particular failure in their thinking, if trustees reach a conclusion that is unreasonable, in the sense[41] that no reasonable trustees, thinking about the question

EWHC 449, [23]–[24]. At the time of writing, the latter two decisions were being appealed, creating an opportunity for the Court of Appeal to review the doctrine generally.

[36] *Sieff v Fox* [2005] 1 WLR 3811, [77]. 'Would' is presumably to be understood as meaning 'would, on at least a balance of probabilities', ie the chance of a different determination is greater than 50 per cent; while 'might' refers to a chance of less than 50 per cent—so the difference is one of degree. 'Might' applies if the trustees had to act in some way, the question for their determination being just how: as in the case of a discretionary trust, where they must distribute the available funds, but can choose (within limits) in what way. 'Would' applies elsewhere, ie where the trustees did not have to act at all, but decided both to do so and how, as in the case of a power of appointment. The distinction is intelligible, but not inevitable: the less generous 'would' variant probably betrays an underlying desire to limit the frequency with which the doctrine destabilizes trustees' determinations (cf *Scott v National Trust for Places of Historic Interest or Natural Beauty* [1998] 2 All ER 705, 718; *Breadner v Granville-Grossman* [2001] Ch 523, [58]–[61]). For another suggestion, proposing that 'would' should apply in pension fund trusts and 'might' elsewhere, see D Hayton [2005] Conv 229, 238–9.

[37] There is doubt whether a transgression renders the flawed determination *ipso facto* void, ie of no legal effect whatsoever; or voidable, ie effective unless set aside by the court's judgment, perhaps only under certain circumstances or upon certain conditions (eg not after a long lapse of time); or something between the two: cf *Sieff v Fox* [2005] 1 WLR 3811, [78]–[83], *Futter v Futter* [2010] EWHC 449 (Ch), [33]–[34]. Although the issue is often addressed in terms of doctrinal logic (see eg R Nolan [2009] CLJ 293, 316–21), the message of the latter is unclear, and it is more realistically seen in terms of a concern, identified in n 36, over the extent of the doctrine's impact. See further D Hayton [2005] Conv 229, 239–40, suggesting a wholly 'remedial', ie discretionary, approach.

[38] *Sieff v Fox* [2005] 1 WLR 3811, [80], [119].

[39] The contrary was asserted in *Abacus Trust Co (Isle of Man) Ltd v Barr* [2003] Ch 409, [22]–[25], which was rightly therefore doubted in *Sieff v Fox* [2005] 1 WLR 3811, [80], [119].

[40] Indeed, the rule is usually formulated in terms of the trustees' failure to take into account matters which they 'should' have taken into account, or had a 'duty' to take into account: see eg *Mettoy Pension Trustees Ltd v Evans* [1990] 1 WLR 1587, 1621, 1624; *Sieff v Fox* [2005] 1 WLR 3811, [49], [76], [90], [114], [119]; *Smithson v Hamilton* [2008] 1 WLR 1453, [97]; *Futter v Futter* [2010] EWHC 449 (Ch), [26]–[27]. It is true that the transgression sometimes consists in a mistake that the trustees could hardly have avoided (see eg *Re Abrahams' Will Trusts* [1969] 1 Ch 463); but to disburse trust money without a proper basis, however understandably, remains a breach: see eg *Chichester Diocesan Fund and Board of Finance Inc v Simpson* [1944] AC 341.

[41] Sometimes called '*Wednesbury* unreasonableness', after the reference to it in the public law decision *Associated Provincial Picture Houses Ltd v Wednesbury Corp* [1948] 1 KB 223, 230.

properly, could have arrived at it.[42] The latter rule has been little relied on, but is potentially useful against trustees who decline to disclose their thinking, as they are generally permitted to do.[43]

13.5 ACCOUNT: 'DEFICIENCY'

The trustee's liability to account thus allows the trust objects to demand that he make up a shortfall in the trust assets, where that shortfall stems from a breach on his part. More needs to be said, however, about the concept of a shortfall, or, as it is more usually called, a 'deficiency'.

First of all, a deficiency can take more than one form. Most straightforwardly, it can be an actual loss, as where the trustee makes an unauthorized investment that then loses value, or pays out trust money in a way he should not have, or allows the trust's interests to suffer in a situation where those interests conflict with his own. When the trustee presents his accounts, the entry showing such a fall in value—being the result of a breach on his part—will be 'falsified', ie disallowed; so the overall account will to that extent show a deficit, which the trustee will have to rectify (whether using cash from his own pocket, or, if he can, by replacing the very property that has been lost, eg the requisite number of shares in a particular company).[44] Alternatively, the point may be that the trust fund has not grown as it would have done if the trustee had properly performed his duties, as again where he makes an unauthorized investment that then, even if it does not actually lose value, underperforms authorized investments.[45] In this event, the trustee's accounts will be 'surcharged' by the

---

[42] *Edge v Pensions Ombudsman* [2000] Ch 602, 627–30, 636.

[43] See section 11.9, referring to *Re Londonderry's Settlement* [1965] Ch 918; *Breakspear v Ackland* [2009] Ch 32. In *Re Beloved Wilkes' Charity* (1851) 3 Mac & G 440, 448 it is said that trustees who disclose their reasoning will be in breach if it does not support their conclusion, but that was rejected (disclosure of reasoning makes it easier to apply the usual rule, but nothing more) in *Dundee General Hospitals Board of Management v Walker* [1952] 1 All ER 896, 900; *Scott v National Trust for Places of Historic Interest or Natural Beauty* [1998] 2 All ER 705, 718–19. The review of the position in *Breakspear v Ackland* does not clarify the law.

[44] Contrast situations where an entry showing a fall in value is not falsified, so there is no liability: for example, where the trust's assets have been correctly distributed to its object(s), or been placed in an authorized and satisfactory investment that has unfortunately lost value, or lost (eg stolen by a third party) in circumstances not involving unauthorized action, nor a want of care and skill, on the trustee's part.

[45] Or where he makes an authorized investment but chooses it unsatisfactorily, and it underperforms the kind of authorized investments that he might satisfactorily have chosen. But it is not easy to quantify, or even prove, the shortfall in such a case: cf *Nestle v National Westminster Bank plc* [1993] 1 WLR 1260.

sum in question, and will therefore again show a deficit, which the trustee will once more have to rectify.

Then it is necessary to say how a deficiency is to be assessed. The *Mothew* position requires us once again to distinguish between cases where the trustee's breach is of a duty requiring the exercise of care and skill, such as the duty to choose appropriate investments; and other cases, ie those involving breach of an absolute duty, such as the duty not to use unauthorized types of investments. It claims that deficiencies arising from the two kinds of breach are handled in different ways.

Deficiencies arising from breach of a duty of care and skill are, it asserts, to be assessed in the same way as those arising from comparable breaches in other areas of the law.[46] In fact, this is not a fully helpful position, as duties of care and skill are found in at least two other areas, namely tort—in the shape of negligence—and contract, and the quantum rules for these differ as between themselves;[47] but the assumption seems to be that the analogy is with the tortious negligence rule. Knowing this, indeed, does not answer all our questions, as 'the tort rule' is itself neither wholly clear nor uncontroversial. But to put it in broad terms, losses must first be caused by the wrongdoer, in the basic sense that his act is a *sine qua non* of their occurrence. Even though established in this sense, however, the wrongdoer's causation of the loss can sometimes be negatived on account of the intrusion of another cause, commonly referred to as a *novus actus interveniens*;[48] and, even if the wrongdoer is held to have caused the loss, he will be liable for it only if loss of its type was a reasonably foreseeable consequence of his tort.[49] Applying this to the trusts context, then, say the trustee is authorized to invest the trust assets in paintings. He buys

---

[46] *Bristol and West Building Society v Mothew* [1998] Ch 1, 17. This ruling is however contrary to, and *per incuriam* of, previous authority: see eg *Caffrey v Darby* (1801) 6 Ves Jr 488, 496; *Nocton v Lord Ashburton* [1914] AC 932, 958, 965; *Bartlett v Barclays Bank Trust Co Ltd (Nos 1 and 2)* [1980] Ch 515, 543–5. According to these latter decisions, deficiencies arising from breach of a duty of care and skill are to be assessed in the same way as deficiencies arising from breach of an absolute duty (though we shall see below that the latter are nowadays assessed differently from how they were at the time of these decisions). See further J Getzler in P Birks and A Pretto (eds) *Breach of Trust* (2002) ch 2; J Heydon in S Degeling and J Edelman (eds) *Equity in Commercial Law* (2005) ch 9; J Getzler *ibid* ch 10 (and n 17 above).

[47] The tort rule is described in the text below. The contract rule is more favourable to the wrongdoer, demanding that, to be recoverable, a loss should have been foreseeable as a serious possibility, or something of that kind: *Koufos v C Carnikow Ltd, The Heron II* [1969] 1 AC 350.

[48] See eg *Jobling v Associated Dairies Ltd* [1982] AC 794; *McKew v Holland Hannen & Cubitts (Scotland) Ltd* [1969] 3 All ER 1621.

[49] *Overseas Tankship (UK) Ltd v Morts Dock and Engineering Co Ltd, The Wagon Mound* [1961] AC 388; *Hughes v Lord Advocate* [1963] AC 837.

a painting, but his choice is careless. The painting is then stolen and never recovered.[50] It might be argued that he should be liable for the loss because this particular painting was only among the trust's assets at all as a result of his breach. The argument would not prevail, however. By analogy with the tort rule, the thief's intervention should be seen as a *novus actus interveniens*, eclipsing the trustee's part in the occurrence of the loss, and so preventing the ascription of the loss to the trustee.[51]

But according to the *Mothew* position, while this is the correct approach in the context of the trustee's duties of care and skill,[52] it does not apply in the context of his absolute duties. As regards the latter, it depicts his liability not as one *to remedy the consequences of the breach*—the task being then to settle the proper content of the word 'consequences', as undertaken above—but as one *to restore the trust fund to the position it was in before his breach*. This follows from its perception of his duty, noted in sections 13.2–13.3, as one of ensuring the proper state of the trust fund. So say that the trustee invests trust assets in a painting when the terms of the trust forbid his doing so; that the investment should nonetheless have been substantively satisfactory; but that the painting is then stolen by thieves. According to the *Mothew* position, he has to make good the resulting deficiency, because this is the step needed to restore the trust fund to the position it was in before his breach, the unexpectedness and complex aetiology of the loss being irrelevant. Likewise, say he sells some shares from among the trust assets in order to spend the proceeds in some unauthorized way. He is not liable merely for their value at the time he sold them: he has actually to replace them, or pay in the cost of doing so, even at such higher price as they might fetch when the objects complain. Or say he wrongfully alienates assets that, if kept in the trust, would have attracted a tax liability. He has simply to replace the assets, or pay for their replacement, and cannot deduct the tax that would have been payable.

In dealing with breaches of absolute duties in this way, the *Mothew* position certainly captures the traditional law regarding this area,[53] though (as

---

[50] Its loss would normally be covered by the insurance he ought to have taken out. Any failure to do so would however be a separate breach and dealt with in its own right.

[51] The trustee would be liable, however, if his breach was of his duty to look after the painting carefully, and this allowed its theft. A loss occurring thus—in the very manner that the duty is aimed at preventing—is not regarded as too remote, or the product of a *novus actus interveniens*: *Stansbie v Troman* [1948] 2 KB 48.

[52] For further exploration, see S Elliott (2002) 65 MLR 588.

[53] For authority supporting the *Mothew* position's treatment of the examples just given, see *Clough v Bond* (1838) 3 My & Cr 490; *Re Massingberd's Settlement* (1890) 63 LT 296; *Re Bell's Indenture* [1980] 1 WLR 1217, 1235–7 (cf the opposite position in tort: *British Transport Commission v Gourley* [1965] AC 185).

already said) it errs in differentiating breaches of duties of care and skill, which were traditionally treated likewise.[54] This traditional approach was always vulnerable, however. As soon as one introduces a reference to the trustee's breach—as section 13.4 showed one should—one encounters difficulty in explaining why he should have to restore the trust fund to its previous condition, *regardless of whether the deficiency in question can satisfactorily be ascribed to the breach*, rather than having only to put right the consequences of that breach. Unsurprisingly, therefore, the traditional rule has been abandoned. On facts analogous especially to those of the final example in the previous paragraph, in *Target Holdings Ltd v Redferns (a firm)*[55] the House of Lords held that a consideration such as the tax liability in that example should be taken into account, in reduction of the amount that the trustee has to make up. The message is that the trustee is required *not* to restore the trust fund to the position it was in before his breach, but instead to remedy the consequences of his breach.[56] The content of the idea of 'consequences' in this context is however different from its counterpart in the tort of negligence, discussed above. The requirement of reasonable foreseeability, which impacts on the latter, is irrelevant here, its place being taken by 'common sense';[57] apparently a stricter test, taken to require only that the loss should have flowed directly from the breach, whether foreseeably or not.[58]

---

[54] See eg *Caffrey v Darby* (1801) 6 Ves Jr 488, 496; *Nocton v Lord Ashburton* [1914] AC 932, 958, 965; *Bartlett v Barclays Bank Trust Co Ltd (Nos 1 and 2)* [1980] Ch 515, 543–5.

[55] [1996] AC 421. On the facts assumed for the proceedings, a finance company planned to loan about £1.5m to a property developer, to allow the latter to acquire some land. The finance company placed the money on trust with a solicitor, stipulating that he should pay it to the developer only when the latter granted the finance company a mortgage over the land in question. The solicitor, however, paid out the money before the grant of the mortgage, thereby breaching his trust. Later, the developer defaulted on the loan, and the finance company, invoking its mortgage, repossessed and sold the land. The sale realized only £0.5m, so the finance company lost £1m. The finance company sued the solicitor, asking that he be ordered to restore the fund to its £1.5m value before his breach, ie pay over the outstanding £1m. The claim failed, on the ground that, even if the solicitor had obtained the mortgage before forwarding the money, the finance company would still have made a loan of £1.5m on the basis of a security worth only £0.5m, and would therefore have sustained the same loss of £1m. That is, the solicitor was liable only for the actual consequence of his breach, namely zero. To revert to the text's example: if it had not been for the breach, the trust would have incurred the tax liability; so by this decision, the deficiency—the trustee's liability—should be reduced by the amount of that liability.

[56] [1996] AC 421, 432–3, 435, 438–9.   [57] [1996] AC 421, 438–9.

[58] *Collins v Brebner* [2000] Lloyd's Rep PN 587, [60]–[63]. The model is liability for the tort of fraud, on which see *Smith New Court Securities Ltd v Citibank NA* [1997] AC 254. The test of whether the loss 'flowed directly' from the breach can be harder to apply than it may sound, especially where the question arises whether, or how, to consider the ways in which the

The reasoning in *Target Holdings Ltd v Redferns (a firm)*[59] is not as clear as it might have been.[60] It has also been criticized for its departure from the old understanding, and in some quarters the latter continues to be espoused notwithstanding it.[61] Most recent authority, however, treats it as having indeed changed the law in the way described.[62] But if the *Mothew* position holds sway otherwise, the rule is now that a trustee is required to rectify the consequences of breach of both types of duty... but that the idea of 'consequences' varies between them. In the case of an absolute duty (the duty in question in *Target Holdings* being such a duty), it takes the form just described. But in the case of a duty of care and skill, the *Mothew* position applies, and dictates that it takes the slightly different form found in the tort of negligence. This divergence seems a needless and unprincipled complication.[63]

claimant and others might have behaved if the breach had not occurred. For the position in tort, see P Mitchell (2009) 125 LQR 12; M Stiggelbout (2010) 30 LS 558. For the position in the liability to account, see *Swindle v Harrison* [1997] 4 All ER 705.

[59] [1996] AC 421.

[60] It is not always clearly articulated in general; and it is unclear on the particular question whether the new rule applies in every case where the trustee breaches a fiduciary or other absolute duty. Arguably (see at 434–5), the new rule is confined to cases involving a non-'traditional' trust, presumably leaving other cases to continue to be governed by the previous rule. 'Traditional' trusts apparently comprise family settlements and the like, but no sharper definition is offered, nor is it explained why the rules for the two classes should, or indeed satisfactorily could, be different. So the text assumes that the new rule applies to all cases.

[61] Perhaps in *Bristol and West Building Society v Mothew* [1998] Ch 1, 17; and explicitly in eg C Mitchell and S Watterson in C Mitchell (ed) *Constructive and Resulting Trusts* (2010) ch 4, 124; P Millett (1998) 114 LQR 214. At 227, Millett observes that the decision's result was nonetheless correct in terms of the traditional understanding, since the later mortgage itself rectified the breach, or its effects: after this, the line in the account showing the loss of £1m could no longer be falsified. It would have been different, however, if the mortgage had never been granted, leaving the breach unrectified: the line could then be falsified, and the £1m recovered (as in *Youyang Pty Ltd v Minter Ellison Morris Fletcher* (2003) 212 CLR 484, Australia, where the facts were such, this approach was taken, and this conclusion reached: see S Elliott and J Edelman (2003) 119 LQR 545). But on the House of Lords' reasoning, the £1m would remain unrecoverable, since its loss was still *not a consequence of the breach*: even if the solicitor had taken the mortgage, the security would still have been worth £1m less than the loan, so the finance company would have lost that amount anyway.

[62] See especially *Swindle v Harrison* [1997] 4 All ER 705, 718,728,733, 735 (though the reasoning here is somewhat disorderly); *Collins v Brebner* [2000] Lloyd's Rep PN 587, [57]–[64]; *Gwembe Valley Development Co Ltd v Koshy* [2003] EWCA Civ 1048, [147].

[63] Cf S Elliott (2002) 65 MLR 588 for a suggestion that, going forward, the test would best be shaped not by the kind of duty involved, but by the nature (fraudulent or negligent, etc) of the actual breach.

13.6 ACCOUNT: A SUMMARY

As we have seen, the law is in some disarray in terms of authority. But let us assume that *Target Holdings Ltd v Redferns (a firm)*[64] applies to absolute duties, and the *Mothew* position applies otherwise. To sum up where this leaves the law, let us revert to the case in which a trustee invests trust assets in a painting, which is then stolen, though not through want of reasonable care on the part of the trustee.[65]

First, if the trustee was authorized to buy the painting and exercised appropriate care and skill in doing so, he is of course not liable for the loss. At one time, this outcome was reached by saying that a trustee who suffered a theft of the trust assets was to that extent 'relieved' from his duty to ensure the proper state of the trust fund.[66] For a long time now, however, it has been seen as the result of his having committed no breach.[67]

Second, if the purchase of the painting involved a breach of a duty of care and skill—say, the trustee chose the particular painting carelessly—then, again, he is not liable for the loss. He is liable for deficiencies consequent upon his breach. But the test for this, as regards breaches of this type, is whether the kind of loss in question is a reasonably foreseeable result of the breach.[68] And the theft of the painting is not. Rather, it is the result of a *novus actus interveniens* on the part of the thief.

Third, if the trustee was not authorized to invest the trust's assets in paintings at all, then he is in breach on that basis. Under the law as it stands today,[69] however, he is not liable for the loss. He is liable for the direct (even if not reasonably foreseeable) consequences of his breach, but again, the loss of the painting is instead the result of a *novus actus interveniens* by the thief.

---

[64] [1996] AC 421.

[65] If the theft *were* the result of such want of care, the trustee would certainly be liable for the loss: *Speight v Gaunt* (1883) 22 Ch D 727, 9 App Cas 1.

[66] *Jones v Lewis* (1750) 2 Ves Sen 240. Bizarrely, the opposite result followed in a case where the trustee was instead *defrauded* of the painting: *Eaves v Hickson* (1861) 30 Beav 136. Perhaps the reason lies in the practice (see n 21 above) of relieving trustees only in respect of losses that could not have been prevented by the trustees coming to court for guidance, ie those arising only from unforeseeable events happening to the trustees, such as theft, rather than those involving voluntary action on their part—which would include loss by fraud.

[67] *Speight v Gaunt* (1883) 22 Ch D 727, 9 App Cas 1—under which, reassuringly, the result is the *same* where the trustee is instead defrauded of the painting. In the case itself, a trustee was defrauded of trust money by a stockbroker to whom he entrusted it. He was held not liable for the loss, on the basis that he had committed no breach—he was required to take as much care as an ordinary prudent man of business, and had done so.

[68] *Bristol and West Building Society v Mothew* [1998] Ch 1, 17.

[69] *Target Holdings Ltd v Redferns (a firm)* [1996] AC 421.

Contrast, however, the handling of the second and third situations by the law as it stood in the past. The rule was that the trustee had to make good the fund as it stood before his breach. This meant that he had to restore the painting's value, with no question of pointing instead to a *novus actus interveniens* on the part of the thief.[70] Although one can follow the internal logic involved, this result appears substantively harsh: in truth, the loss of the painting is no more ascribable to a wrong by the trustee here than in the first situation. Its rejection by the present law seems unsurprising. Section 13.7, however, considers why it should formerly have prevailed.

13.7 ACCOUNT: A RESPONSE TO THE PRINCIPAL–AGENT PROBLEM

The most promising explanation of the liability, especially in its traditional—harsh—form, to account views it as a legal tool specifically adapted to address the principal–agent problem.[71] As explained in section 1.10, this problem besets trusteeship, as a consequence of the idea, essential to the very concept of a trust, that trustees hold the trust property solely for the objects, having no stake of their own, and so must be fiduciaries.

Consider the relationship between a medieval lord and his bailiff. During the lord's frequent and extended absences from his estates, and given the difficulty of communications at such times, he had little choice but to leave his affairs in the hands of a bailiff. By the same token, however, the situation gave the bailiff plentiful opportunities to fail his lord, and simultaneously made it hard for the lord even to know when this occurred, let alone protect himself and if necessary achieve redress.[72] It thus called for a reaction, lest lords should in effect be confined to their own estates and unable to do useful other work, such as fighting the king's wars. Or consider, as England developed its long-distance trade, the relationship between the trader, remaining at home, and his agent ('factor'), operating on his behalf at large. Once more, until very recently there were no useful

---

[70] *Caffrey v Darby* (1801) 6 Ves Jr 488, 496; *Clough v Bond* (1838) 3 My & Cr 490.

[71] For the connection between account and the principal–agent problem, see also J Getzler in A Burrows and A Rodger (eds) *Mapping the Law: Essays in Honour of Peter Birks* (2006) ch 31, 590–7. And see further P Brand, *Kings, Barons and Justices* (2003) 65–6, describing the harshness of the law's response from the (thirteenth century) earliest days of account as a means of controlling agents.

[72] The problem was exacerbated by the late (seventeenth century) arrival, in England, of modern book-keeping.

means of communication between the two, so the same sorts of problems arose. To avoid trade being cramped for this reason, to the nation's detriment, a response was again needed.

The traditional rule requiring a trustee—and a fiduciary of other kinds, and thus a bailiff or factor—to maintain the fund in accordance with his authority, with all that we have seen this to entail, can be viewed as aimed at providing this response.[73] Avoiding reference to the 'consequences' of the fiduciary breach, and even (as we saw in sections 13.3–13.4) to the idea of a 'breach' at all, it precisely addressed the weakness of the principal's position, namely that he would, by definition, have been in a poor position to adduce the facts needed to establish such things.[74] It simply required the fiduciary to deliver the state of affairs that was to be expected if all had gone smoothly, unless he himself could point to some good reason why he should not.[75] And relying on the court's discretion to recognize such a 'good reason' when it saw one, rather than covering the point with a rule, it kept the fiduciary guessing about what, if anything, he could get away with. It thus prevented the fiduciary from calculating that he could profit from malfeasance in the way that a predictable liability, however stern, could not, and so gave him an incentive to exert himself to his utmost on his principal's behalf—which in turn afforded a surrogate for the supervision that the distant principal himself could not provide.

Which is not, of course, to say that the same approach is warranted nowadays. Clearly, there has in fact been a movement towards a less strict approach. We have noticed some mileposts of this movement in our discussion so far. They include the affirmation that the trustees' duties regarding the safeguarding, investment, and management of the trust assets are duties of care and skill rather than absolute, and that the level of care and skill in question is that of the ordinary prudent man of business;[76] the (*Mothew* position's) assertion that, where such duties are concerned, deficiencies in the trust assets are determined using the relatively lenient tortious negligence rule;[77] and the adoption of the position

---

[73] Likewise M Conaglen *Fiduciary Loyalty* (2010) 263–4, ascribing the law's other main response to the principal–agent problem, ie the anti-distraction rules (section 11.10), to a desire to protect fiduciary relationships as 'institutions [of] societal importance'.

[74] For the significance of such information deficits on another aspect of the law's treatment of trustees and other fiduciaries, see eg *ex p Lacey* (1802) 6 Ves Jr 625, 627; *ex p James* (1803) 8 Ves Jr 337, 345–6; *ex p Bennett* (1805) 10 Ves Jr 381, 400; see section 11.10.

[75] For the development of account from such origins, see S Stoljar (1964) 80 LQR 203.

[76] *Speight v Gaunt* (1883) 22 Ch D 727, 9 App Cas 1; *Re Whiteley* (1886) 33 Ch D 347, *Learoyd v Whiteley* (1887) 12 App Cas 727.

[77] *Bristol and West Building Society v Mothew* [1998] Ch 1, 17. It is curious that the judge responsible for this assertion, Millett LJ, has also (P Millett (1998) 114 LQR 214) expressed

that deficiencies in respect of other duties are likewise to be assessed as consequences of breach, even though here the idea of 'consequences' is somewhat harsher.[78] The question is whether this movement is justified and, if so, whether it has arrived at the optimal position for contemporary purposes.

Certainly, the relationship between today's trust objects and their trustees is shaped differently from that between medieval lords and their bailiffs, or between traders and their factors in times of poor telecommunications. And along the way, also relevantly to the movement under discussion, it has been found important not to damage the supply of essentially decent trustees by requiring too much of them.[79] So on the face of things, it is not surprising to find a trend to reduce the stringency of the liability to account. However, there is still a principal–agent problem in play, especially in the fact that, in many cases, the trustee (or other fiduciary) will have a much better grasp than the objects (or other principals) on the issues relevant to the running of the trust, and the investment opportunities available to it. The trustee is required to provide the objects with appropriate information,[80] which goes some way towards redressing matters, but information is not the same as understanding; nor is the need always to know what the trustees know, for sometimes it is to know what they might have known but did not.[81] So although the traditional notions of the liability to account should certainly not be preferred out of mere antiquarianism, there may remain a considerable functional case for adhering to them, or at any rate against retreating any further from them.[82] While these more modern facets of the principal–agent problem may merit the law's solicitude, however, it needs to be carefully considered whether that solicitude should continue to take the shape evoked by their predecessors, or whether a rather different shape would address them better.

---

himself *against* the development mentioned next in the text, for on the face of it they are both steps along the same journey.

[78] *Target Holdings Ltd v Redferns (a firm)* [1996] AC 421.

[79] See section 11.2. The connection is made in *Speight v Gaunt* (1883) 22 Ch D 727, 740, 762.

[80] *Schmidt v Rosewood Trust Ltd* [2003] 2 AC 709; see section 11.9.

[81] See eg *Nestle v National Westminster Bank Plc* [1993] 1 WLR 1260, where the claimant failed to prove how much she had lost as a result of her trustee's underperforming investment policy. However, the claim was for a surcharge under the traditional view of account, so the law in play was already at its most favourable to her.

[82] See further J Getzler in S Degeling and J Edelman (eds) *Equity in Commercial Law* (2005) ch 10.

13.8 ACCOUNT: A CHOICE OF REACTIONS

One final section on the trustee's liability to account. As we have seen, where he is in breach of his trust, the objects can require him to account for any resulting deficiency in the trust assets. Obviously, they do not have to: for all sorts of reasons, they can decide not to sue in this way, or be prevented from doing so. Most interestingly, however, they sometimes have a choice between doing so and another course of action *that may be more advantageous to them*. This section explores this choice.

The essential point is this: while the objects are, as we have seen, able to reject impeachable features of the trustee's account that they do not like, they can also accept features that, although equally impeachable, they do like. That is, the trustee's breach allows the objects to require him to make good such deficiency in the trust assets as it gives rise to. By complaining about the breach, they can shift the impact of the deficiency from themselves to him. But the reverse effect can also be had. If the breach brings assets in, then by *not* complaining about the breach but instead treating the act in question as one done on behalf of the trust, the objects can take those assets for the trust.

Say a trustee makes an unauthorized investment. If it loses value, the objects will wish to falsify the trustee's accounts in respect of the breach, and so require him to make the loss good. But if the unauthorized investment does well, the objects, choosing to regard the breach as not a breach after all but an act done on behalf of the trust, can treat the investment as having been properly acquired for the trust, so that it forms part of the trust assets, and must be included in the trustee's account of those assets. So long as he still has it, he can thus be ordered to deal with it in accordance with the trust, in the manner discussed in section 13.1. But if he has wrongfully lost it, he will have committed a further breach, about which the objects will doubtless complain, falsifying his account in this respect and requiring him to make up the deficiency.

Frequently, though not always, a breach that brings a gain to the trustee will also entail a loss to the trust. As explained, the objects can focus on the trustee's gain: that is, they can overlook his breach, regarding the act in question as done on behalf of the trust; treat the property in his hands as therefore held by him on the trust; and take an order requiring him to perform his duties regarding it. Remember, however, that this is not a course that the law forces upon them, but a choice that it allows them to make. So they can decide instead to draw attention to the breach, treat the property in question as now the trustee's own, and require him to make up the deficiency in the account that this decision entails. For example, where the trustee transfers a sum of trust money into his personal bank account and so breaches his duty to keep it safe, the objects can either, treating his act as nonetheless done on the trust's behalf, assert that the money remains trust property and claim an order that he perform his duties regarding it; or, instead, treat it as having thereby become the trustee's own, falsify his account in respect of its loss, and demand that he make the resulting deficiency good.[83]

Sometimes the objects will prefer the latter course. Identifying an asset in the trustee's hands as trust property despite his breach will often involve resort to the tracing rules, as where the breach consists in the trustee's exchange of the original trust property for something else, or his mixing it with other property. As will be seen in section 17.5, these rules are complex and sometimes uncertain, and applying them to the circumstances of a particular case can also demand daunting factual inquiries. Faced with such difficulties, the trust's objects might well prefer to let the property in question go to the trustee, instead (thus) point to his breach as having left a deficiency in the account, and require him to make the latter good.

On the other hand, the objects will often find advantage in taking the other course, ie treating the trustee's act as done on the trust's behalf and pointing to the asset he has acquired as therefore the trust's. This will be preferable, for example, if the trustee has become insolvent. Sections 1.9 and 12.1 explain that at any rate the basic trust obligations are *proprietary*, and that this means (among other things) their being unaffected by the trustee's insolvency. By contrast, a breaching trustee's liability to make good a deficiency in his account is a *personal* one, meaning that it ranks equally with his liabilities to all his other ordinary creditors, which of course will outstrip his worth. So in the event of his insolvency, pointing to and suing for a breach via their personal claim will mean the objects recovering only a (usually rather small) proportion of the sum at stake; whereas treating the asset in question as trust property, and so exercising their proprietary claim to it, will mean their taking it in full. Treating the asset as trust property will also entitle the objects to claim any profit accruing. Say a trustee uses £2,000 trust money to buy himself a painting, which turns

---

[83] In fact, the choice is less stark. If the trustee has gone on to trade with the money, or perhaps more generally gained from having the use of it, he can be made to make good the value of the money *plus compound interest on this*. His liability to interest can be seen as a proxy for his liability to disgorge the actual profits in question: if the objects were able to prove such profits, they could treat them as made on behalf of the trust in the first place, and choose to claim them that way. See *Westdeutsche Landesbank Girozentrale v Islington LBC* [1996] AC 669, 701–2.

out to be worth £3,000. By treating the trustee's (wrongful) act as done on the trust's behalf, the objects can claim the painting; whereas pointing to the breach, falsifying his expenditure of the £2,000, and thus treating the painting as the trustee's own, will allow them to demand only that he make good the £2,000. (Conversely, of course, if the painting turns out to be worth only £1,000, the objects will do better to take the opposite route.) Further, the two approaches may attract different limitation rules, these being the rules preventing a claim being mounted once a certain period has elapsed from the moment it first arose. Claims in respect of trusts are governed by the Limitation Act 1980. There is no period of limitation—ie claims can in principle be brought indefinitely—in respect of claims to recover property from a trustee, which must be based on an assertion that he holds it as part of the trust fund, and has a duty now to transfer it.[84] Other claims, including therefore all claims to reinstatement of the trust fund, have a limitation period of six years,[85] unless they involve a factor making it right to be abnormally ungenerous to the defendant, namely that the breach was fraudulent,[86] or the loss consisted in the trustee's taking the assets for himself.[87]

Why should the law allow objects to choose how to react to a trustee's breach in the manner discussed in this section? One might reply, because the option follows logically from the trustee's liability to account: he must report to them on his activities as trustee, whereupon they can impeach any impeachable deficiencies if they want to, but, obviously, can choose not to. But that is not a good enough answer. It proves only that the objects need not complain about a breach, not that they can require the law to treat it as a non-breach, and so claim the benefits of it. The option—or, if you like, the relevant dimension of the liability to account—thus needs to be explained in its own right.

The explanation seems once again to be that the law is seeking to foster the use of trusts by addressing the principal–agent problem inherent in the relationship between a trustee and his trust objects, and indeed any other fiduciary and his principal: see section 1.10. Section 13.7 suggested that other aspects of the liability to account reflect a concern to offset the information deficit that exists between the parties to such a relationship, or more especially, typically did exist at the period when the ideas comprising account took shape. The present rule addresses a different facet of the problem, namely the fact that the agent (trustee) has effective control

---

[84] Section 21(1)(b).   [85] Section 21(3).   [86] Section 21(1)(a).

[87] Section 21(1)(b), 'to recover from the trustee trust property or the proceeds of trust property... previously received by the trustee and converted to his use'.

over assets that are essentially not his but his principal's.[88] This leaves the principal especially vulnerable to injury at the hands of an errant agent. The rule is calculated to support the principal by, so far as possible, negativing the agent's incentive to err. It does so by allowing the objects not only to claim any losses arising from their trustee's misbehaviour, but any gains he may make from it. He cannot, therefore, rely on being—so long as he pays off any actual losses to the trust—able to keep any trust property he may divert to himself, or any profits he makes from 'borrowing' and speculating with the trust assets.[89] Moreover, he is not only liable to disgorge such gains. As we saw above, he holds them on trust from the moment he acquires them. This, meaning that the gains never beneficially accrue to him at all, represents the most thorough-going possible way of removing his incentive to err. It is no surprise, however, that the objects can choose instead to focus on the losses arising from their trustee's breach, as in the particular situation we considered midway through this section, if they find it more advantageous to do that. The law's whole mission here is to reduce the principal's vulnerability by giving the agent no place to hide.

[88] But remember the rule (n 83) whereby objects can require a trustee who takes trust property and uses it for his own gain not only to reimburse its value, but also to pay compound interest on the latter. This rule allows objects who cannot prove what profit the trustee has actually made and so claim this as such, nonetheless to take claim his profits on a notional basis. It can therefore be seen as reacting to an information deficit.

[89] Compare *A-G v Blake* [2001] 1 AC 268, introducing a profit-stripping rule to the law of contract, likewise so as to attack undesirable cynical breaches.

14

Liabilities of Strangers

Chapter 13 focused on the liabilities of trustees. We turn now to instances in which people who are not themselves trustees ('third parties', 'strangers') can find themselves liable for wrongs to trusts.

There are commonly said to be three classes of this additional form of liability,[1] known as 'dishonest assistance', 'trusteeship *de son tort*', and 'knowing receipt'—but in section 14.3 we shall in fact see that the latter does not in truth belong in this group, being a liability for breach of trust on the part of someone who is actually a trustee, having taken an unauthorized transfer of trust property from its previous trustee. We shall consider the three classes in turn.

14.1 DISHONEST ASSISTANCE

A person who dishonestly helps trustees to commit a breach of trust is liable to make good to the trust the sum involved, alongside the breaching trustees. This form of liability is termed 'dishonest assistance'.[2]

Losses caused by breach of trust are ones that the law regards as meriting redress, and this rule treats such redress as exigible from not only the breaching trustees themselves but also others sufficiently culpably involved in the occurrence of the breach and loss: it imposes on them a duty not to so involve themselves. Given the proprietary quality of trusts, it is unsurprising that the law requires others to respect it in this way (as well as imposing duties on those who acquire trust property). Similar duties not to contribute to legally recognized wrongs are found more widely, however. They exist in respect of crimes,[3] torts, and breaches of

---

[1] *Metall und Rohstoff AG v Donaldson Lufkin & Jenrette Inc* [1990] 1 QB 391, 481 denies that there is a further class in the shape of a tort of 'procuring a breach of trust' analogous to the tort of interference with contractual relations.

[2] See further C Mitchell in P Birks and A Pretto (eds) *Breach of Trust* (2002) ch 6; S Elliott and C Mitchell (2004) 67 MLR 16; P Ridge (2008) 124 LQR 445; C Mitchell and S Watterson in C Mitchell (ed) *Constructive and Resulting Trusts* (2010) ch 4, 150–4.

[3] 'Complicity'.

contract.[4] At any rate contractual obligations are not proprietary, as trust obligations at least sometimes are. This suggests that acting as accessory to a legally recognized wrong is objectionable in its own right. That is intelligible: by definition, accessories increase the chances of the wrong occurring or of harm resulting, and those are the evils against which the law aims the wrong in the first place.

So, say I am trustee of a pension fund, while you are not a trustee but the fund's auditor. I embezzle £1 million from the fund. You know what I am doing, but cover it up, perhaps hoping that this will make me want to continue employing you. Assuming that a judge would regard you as dishonest in this, as seems likely, you are liable (in dishonest assistance) alongside me (in breach of trust) to restore the £1 million. The portrayal of the helper in this example as an auditor reflects the fact that a trust's professional agents—auditors, solicitors, bankers—will routinely, given the nature of their work, be caught up in a breaching trustee's activities. Whether, as a result, they find themselves liable for the trustees' breaches depends on the exact profile of the liability.

At one time, there could be no liability of this kind unless the trustee's breach was itself dishonest,[5] but that limitation has now been removed,[6] so someone who dishonestly helps in even a careless or unwitting breach will be liable. (Then, the dishonest 'helper' may well be the prime mover of the breach, the trustee committing his breach as the helper's tool.) The help must be of some substance: cooking a good breakfast for a trustee about to embezzle from his trust does not entail liability for the cook.[7]

However, the helper incurs liability only if he himself acts dishonestly.[8] In this context, he acts 'dishonestly' only if his deeds, given his

---

[4] 'Interference with contractual relations'.

[5] *Barnes v Addy* (1874) 9 Ch App 244. At the time of this decision, trustees could be required to account for any unauthorized depletion of the trust assets, however carefully they had acted, unless relieved by the court. As explained in section 13.4, *Speight v Gaunt* (1883) 22 Ch D 727, 9 App Cas 1 affirmed that this approach should be left behind, and that trustees should be liable for losses arising from their stewardship of the trust assets only if they acted carelessly. *Barnes v Addy* can be seen as anticipating this move, so far as the issue affected trustees' helpers. It ensured that, even if the trustees' own liability remained (for the moment) potentially excessive, their helpers would not suffer by this. The judges were also moved by a desire to minimize the exposure of trustees' helpers (solicitors, banks, etc) for its own sake, reflecting that if exigent liability drove them away, trusts would actually be worse off: see 251–2, 254, 256.

[6] *Royal Brunei Airlines Sdn Bhd v Tan* [1995] 2 AC 378; *Twinsectra Ltd v Yardley* [2002] 2 AC 164.   [7] Cf *Brinks Ltd v Abu-Saleh (No 3)* [1996] CLC 133.

[8] *Royal Brunei Airlines Sdn Bhd v Tan* [1995] 2 AC 378; *Twinsectra Ltd v Yardley* [2002] 2 AC 164; *Barlow Clowes International Ltd v Eurotrust International Ltd* [2006] 1 WLR 1476. It is sometimes suggested that the *Eurotrust* decision gave precedence to Lord Millett's dissenting view in the *Twinsectra* case, and that that view requires only that the helper should know of

knowledge, belief, or suspicion[9] as to what is afoot,[10] and seen in the context of the circumstances and his motives and attitudes,[11] are dishonest by the ordinary standards of reasonable and honest people.[12] A helpful proxy, formulated appropriately to a commercial context but applicable *mutatis mutandis* more generally, is the question whether the assister is 'guilty of commercially unacceptable conduct in the particular context involved'.[13] But ordinary standards of honesty, and the idea of unacceptable conduct, are concepts not free of doubt or unchanging. The judges must therefore construct them, necessarily via value judgements of their own. Take someone who knows about a breach of trust, could stop it by reporting it, but fails to do so because he regards it as 'none of his business'. Deciding whether he is dishonest by the ordinary standards of reasonable and honest people, or guilty of unacceptable conduct, requires the judge in effect to legislate whether, in the context concerned, there is a duty not to turn a blind eye to wrongdoing in this way.

What should be the courts' vision of unacceptable conduct in respect of the kind of situation at issue here? There are many variables, so a comprehensive discussion is impossible. But one central question is whether a person, especially a professional agent, should guard against the possibility that those with whom he deals are trustees in breach of their trust, or may content himself with the appearance that they are not. The answer is not self-evident and, before the establishment of the dishonesty rule,

---

the breach of trust in question, not that he should have acted 'dishonestly'. But although Lord Millett seems to have thought the helper would usually be liable if he knew of the breach, he did not reject the requirement of 'dishonesty', with the greater space for evaluative reflection that it affords. So, it is possible (if rare) to know of the breach and not necessarily be dishonest; and also *not* to know of the breach, and still be dishonest—as where the helper turns a blind eye when he should be more inquisitive.

[9] Suspicion is certainly enough: *Abou-Rahmah v Abacha* [2006] EWCA Civ 1492, [23].

[10] He need not appreciate that it is a breach of trust. It is enough if he believes or suspects that he is helping in a 'misappropriation', or in the evasion of exchange controls or tax liabilities, or in money laundering—potentially, therefore, of any kind of wrongful act. See *Abou-Rahmah v Abacha* [2006] EWCA Civ 1492, [23], [37]–[39].

[11] *Royal Brunei Airlines Sdn Bhd v Tan* [1995] 2 AC 378, 390–1.

[12] *Barlow Clowes International Ltd v Eurotrust International Ltd* [2006] 1 WLR 1476. This, however, is a decision of the Privy Council, departing from, or turning a blind eye to, a previous ruling of the House of Lords (*Twinsectra Ltd v Yardley* [2002] 2 AC 164), which additionally required the helper *to be aware* that his deeds were dishonest by ordinary standards (following the formulation of 'dishonesty' in the criminal law case *R v Ghosh* [1982] QB 1053). It has not yet been authoritatively decided that *Barlow Clowes* takes precedence (see *Abou-Rahmah v Abacha* [2006] EWCA Civ 1492, [23], [90]–[94], cf [64]–[69]), but it appears likely.

[13] *Cowan de Groot Properties Ltd v Eagle Trust plc* [1992] 4 All ER 700, 761; adopted in *Royal Brunei Airlines Sdn Bhd v Tan* [1995] 2 AC 378, 390.

different judges came out for[14] and against[15] a rule requiring people so to guard. The principal considerations can however be explained.[16]

A vision of dishonesty demanding actual knowledge of the breach generates liability less frequently, and generates incentives to less work, than one requiring alertness as to the possibility. The former vision thus tracks a public interest in minimizing the financial exposure and the amount of 'red tape' to which commercial undertakings, such as trustees' professional agents, are subject: their competitiveness is thus enhanced, and more wealth is created. It also tracks a further interest in not undermining such agents' willingness to work for trusts, in that their work conduces importantly to the satisfactory performance of trusts; though there was more anxiety over this in the past than there is today. Conversely, a vision requiring alertness as to the possibility of breach generates liability more frequently, and creates incentives to more work. As professional agents will carry insurance against this liability, the cost of the premiums being reflected in their charges to the trust and so deducted from the payments out to the objects, such a vision thus comes closer to requiring objects to insure themselves against the possibility of depredation by their trustees: which may be felt desirable, particularly in contexts such as family and especially pension trusts, where the objects' prosperity is substantially at stake but they might well not take insurance on their own initiative. And incentivizing such agents to police their trustee clients' activities may also be thought desirable: experience suggests the job to be worthwhile, these agents are particularly well placed to perform it, and it chimes with what is already required of them by their own professional standards and by anti-money laundering legislation.[17] In recent times the dominant judicial proclivity has been to minimize professional agents' liabilities. The period has, however, been punctuated by notorious episodes revealing complacency on auditors' part to the possibility of fraud, to which there has been a strong reaction demanding higher standards. It would be unsurprising, therefore, to find at least some signs of a willingness to treat slackness on professional agents' part as 'unacceptable conduct', falling short of ordinary standards of honesty.

---

[14] Thus eg *Selangor United Rubber Estates Ltd v Cradock (No 3)* [1968] 1 WLR 1555, 1590.

[15] Thus eg *Agip (Africa) Ltd v Jackson* [1990] Ch 265, 292–3. (The decision was affirmed, but more equivocal statements made as to the present issue, on appeal: [1991] Ch 547, 567, 569–70.)

[16] For expansion of what follows, see S Gardner (1996) 112 LQR 56, 71–85.

[17] In especially the Proceeds of Crime Act 2002 Part 7; Serious Organised Crime and Police Act 2005 ss 102–9; Money Laundering Regulations 2007 SI No 2157.

One factor distorts the natural calculus, pushing the law to narrow the liability. Someone liable in dishonest assistance is liable, alongside the breaching trustees, to make good the whole loss following from the breach of trust. Say I, a trustee, embezzle £1,000, and you dishonestly help me. We shall both be liable for £1,000. That is, the claimant can sue either or both of us for all or any part of that sum, so long as he does not recover more than £1,000 overall. Liability of multiple defendants organized in this way is called 'joint and several', and is a characteristic, but controversial,[18] feature of English law. A defendant made to pay for all of a loss under this doctrine can recoup himself against others who might have been sued using the process known as 'contribution', whereby a loss is apportioned amongst those responsible for it;[19] but any difficulty in doing so, eg the disappearance or bankruptcy of another defendant, is his problem rather than the claimant's. This rule has an especially significant impact in the context of dishonest assistance. A claimant will commonly have little chance of recovering the loss from the breaching trustee, but a much better chance of recovering it from the trustee's professional agent helpers, if they are liable at all. The agents' correct share will normally be less than half, as the main instigator will have been the breaching trustee. But the agents will have equally little chance of obtaining contribution from the trustee. So they will in practice be left bearing the entire loss, rather than their correct share. This is an unsatisfactory outcome. A narrow construction of dishonesty helps to avoid it, by making it likely that the helper will not be liable at all. Having the helper emerge not liable at all is also an unsatisfactory outcome, but no liability is closer to the correct outcome, a less-than-half share, than is full liability.

14.2 TRUSTEESHIP *DE SON TORT*

A person who is not a trustee, but who acts as though he were, is known as a 'trustee *de son tort*' (or a 'de facto trustee').[20] As such, he becomes subject to all the duties incumbent on the genuine trustees of the trust in question (these of course vary from one trust to another). He is accordingly liable to the same remedies as are available against trustees, though it would

---

[18] In 1995 the Law Commission concluded that it would nevertheless not be justified in exploring reform. This surprised many and caused the government to consult more widely: Department of Trade and Industry *Feasibility Investigation of Joint and Several Liability* (1996). No reform has ensued, however, other than a rule allowing a company to relieve its auditors from liabilities that they would otherwise incur to, or alongside, the company: Companies Act 2006 ss 532–8.   [19] Civil Liability (Contribution) Act 1978 s 1.

[20] *Dubai Aluminium Co Ltd v Salaam* [2003] 2 AC 366, [138].

be curious to make a demand for the performance of the trust's primary obligations against someone who is not in fact a trustee: the claim will generally be rather for the making good of a deficiency in the trust fund after a breach. The special feature of this liability thus lies not in the duties and liabilities it involves, but in its application to non-trustees of rules normally applicable to trustees. This is justifiable where the non-trustee makes himself responsible for the trust: and that is, by definition, what someone acting as though he were a trustee does.

Say I am personal assistant to the single trustee of a trust, and when he dies I carry the trust on. Or say I am clerk to a group of elderly trustees and take all their decisions for them. If for example I invest the trust's assets in an unauthorized way, or carelessly, and at a loss, I have come under and breached the duties against such behaviour, and can therefore be required to make good the loss.[21]

There is no requirement of culpability before someone is held a trustee *de son tort* (though presumably some kind of awareness that one is encroaching on the role of trustee is required). The only culpability required for this kind of liability is that, if any, required for breach of the duty in question by a genuine trustee. So someone who helps trustees as they put themselves in breach of trust, and who is honest and so not liable in dishonest assistance, is nonetheless liable for the breach if he is a trustee *de son tort*. The concept of 'acting as though one were a trustee', limiting the scope of the latter possibility, thus decides where the requirements for dishonest assistance can in effect be undermined. The courts have been mindful of this point,[22] and once again concerned to protect, in particular, professional agents from liability,[23] a position intelligible (though not inevitable) for the kinds of reasons considered in section 14.1. They have accordingly circumscribed the concept of 'acting as though one were a trustee' by contrasting it emphatically with the phenomenon of associating oneself with the carrying on of the trust while acknowledging one's non-trusteeship.[24]

Some judicial treatments assert that a person becomes a trustee *de son tort* only where he takes control of the trust assets.[25] Others, while not expressly denying such a requirement, do not assert it.[26] The demand is presumably not for the acquisition of title to the trust assets alongside or

[21] *Blyth v Fladgate* [1891] 1 Ch 337.

[22] *Barnes v Addy* (1874) LR 9 Ch App 244, 251; *Williams-Ashman v Price & Williams* [1942] Ch 219, 228. [23] *Barnes v Addy* (1874) LR 9 Ch App 244, 251–2, 255.

[24] *Mara v Browne* [1896] 1 Ch 199; *Williams-Ashman v Price & Williams* [1942] Ch 219.

[25] *Morgan v Stephens* (1861) 3 Giff 226, 236; *Re Barney* [1892] 2 Ch 265; *Williams-Ashman v Price & Williams* [1942] Ch 219, 228. [26] *Mara v Browne* [1896] 1 Ch 199.

in place of the proper trustees: someone who, without proper authorization, acquires title to the trust assets incurs a constructive trust,[27] and is thus liable *as* a trustee, rather than *as though he were* a trustee. The demand should therefore be understood as one for de facto control. It is calculated to narrow further the ambit of this liability. It seems essentially unprincipled, however. As noted above, trusteeship *de son tort* is justifiable as imposing trust duties on someone who makes himself responsible for the performance of those duties. And it seems possible for a person to fit the latter description even if he does not take control of the trust assets: as where the trustees defer to him, and he colludes in their doing so, specifically in the operation of a trust's dispositive discretions.

14.3 KNOWING RECEIPT

In section 12.1, we saw that the basic duties of trustees—those of respecting the fact that the property is not beneficially their own, and of safeguarding it pending transfer—are proprietary, ie capable of binding those to whom the trust property is transferred. As a result, if a trustee, acting outside his authority to do so, transfers trust property to someone else, then, unless the transferee is a bona fide purchaser of the property for value without notice of its provenance, he will hold the property on a constructive trust:[28] this being another way of saying that he incurs the duty to respect the fact that it is not beneficially his own.

So long as the transferee still has this property, or further property identified by the tracing rules,[29] he can thus be obliged to transfer the property to the original or new trustees, or, if they are immediately entitled to the capital assets, to the trust objects themselves. If, however, the trust property is lost from the transferee's hands in turn, the transferor will be liable to repair the loss in the ordinary way—but so too may the transferee, via a form of liability known as 'knowing receipt'. As with dishonest assistance and trusteeship *de son tort*, therefore, trust objects are thus valuably enabled to increase the number of those against whom they can proceed in respect of a given loss.

Say I give you some money as a present. The money is in fact money that I hold on trust for Adam, and I act outside my authority in giving it to you. So long as you retain it, in either its original or a traceable form, you hold it on constructive trust and must give it back to me, or more likely to a new trustee appointed to replace me, or perhaps to Adam himself. But

[27] See section 17.2.   [28] This constructive trust is discussed further in section 17.2.
[29] See section 17.5.

say you spend it so that there are no traceable proceeds, eg on a holiday. If at that point you know or ought to know that it came to you in breach of trust, you are liable, in knowing receipt, to reimburse Adam's trust.

According to this statement, then, to incur liability in knowing receipt, it must be the case that the transferee, before misappropriating or losing the property he has acquired, 'knows or ought to know' that it is trust property (ie was transferred to him by a trustee acting outside his authority). The formulation used by the prevalent authority, however, is that 'the recipient's state of knowledge must be such as to make it unconscionable' for him, having had the trust's property, not now to repay the trust.[30] Once the latter is deciphered, the two statements come to the same thing.

A formulation in terms of 'unconscionability' is opaque, and was rejected on this ground in the context of dishonest assistance.[31] But the court seems to have chosen it for knowing receipt as offering the flexibility to have the best of both worlds between two other positions, acknowledging each as to an extent attractive. According to one, there should be liability only if the recipient actually knows of the property's provenance. This view is especially calculated to eliminate the delays and costs, and so damage to commerce, which would ensue if recipients of property could not accept it at face value but had to check its provenance;[32] and to recognize that those presented with property as a gift will find it hard not simply to accept it at face value.[33] According to the other position, there should be liability also if, with a certain amount of diligence, the recipient could have discovered the property's provenance, whether he did so or not:[34] a view conducing more to commercial responsibility.[35] The reference to unconscionability instructs the judge to decide how far it is right to go in the direction of the second of these positions, not as a general proposition but for the purposes of the individual case. A transferee's failure to discover the property's provenance will be unconscionable if, but only if, he not only *could* have discovered it but also *should* have exercised the diligence necessary to discover it. And that judgement depends on the context (traditionally, for example, great diligence has been expected where the

---

[30] *Bank of Credit and Commerce International Ltd v Akindele* [2001] Ch 437, 455.

[31] *Royal Brunei Airlines Sdn Bhd v Tan* [1995] 2 AC 378, 392.

[32] *Manchester Trust v Furness* [1895] 2 QB 539, 545.

[33] *Re Montagu's Settlement Trusts* [1987] Ch 264.

[34] A state of affairs commonly described as 'notice', but that term has been used with a number of meanings, including sometimes merely knowledge: eg *Eagle Trust plc v SBC Securities Ltd* [1993] 1 WLR 484, 494–5, 504–6.

[35] *Agip (Africa) Ltd v Jackson* [1990] Ch 265, 291; *Houghton v Fayers* [2000] 1 BCLC 511, 516.

property is land), and will also vary over time (some periods being more *laissez-faire* than others). One could thus paraphrase the inquiry as one whether the transferee, in failing to discover the property's provenance, is guilty of unacceptable conduct in the particular context involved. In effect, then, 'unconscionability' seems to be identical to the idea of 'dishonesty' as used in dishonest assistance, discussed in section 13.1.[36] Judges applying it will be influenced by the same kinds of considerations as were explored in that discussion.

This chapter began by noting that knowing receipt is commonly presented as a liability arising, like dishonest assistance and the liability of a trustee *de son tort*, against persons who are not themselves trustees. This view of it is incorrect, however. The best way to see knowing receipt is as simply the application to the particular context under discussion of the principles governing the ordinary liability of trustees. Remember that the transferee is in fact trustee of the acquired assets, as explained at the start of this section. As such, he incurs duties to recognize that the assets are not his own, and to safeguard them. It seems likely that these duties arise only from the time when he knows, or ought to know, that he does indeed hold the assets on trust.[37] If he then misappropriates the assets or carelessly loses them, he breaches his duty and can be required to make good the loss accordingly, in the manner described in Chapter 13.[38] There is no reason to doubt that he incurs this liability; or that it exactly corresponds with knowing receipt.[39]

---

[36] The court in *Bank of Credit and Commerce International Ltd v Akindele* [2001] Ch 437, 448–50 rejected a 'dishonesty' test, but did so out of unhappiness with the additional element which 'dishonesty' at that time possessed in dishonest assistance, namely a requirement that the defendant be *aware* that his conduct is unacceptable by ordinary standards (*Twinsectra Ltd v Yardley* [2002] 2 AC 164). This additional element was subsequently extirpated from dishonest assistance too (*Barlow Clowes International Ltd v Eurotrust International Ltd* [2006] 1 WLR 1476), meaning that there is no longer any reason to distinguish between 'dishonesty' and 'unconscionability'.

[37] Lord Browne-Wilkinson in *Westdeutsche Landesbank Girozentrale v Islington LBC* [1996] AC 669, 705 proposes instead that the transferee *does not hold the property on trust at all* until he knows or should know it to be trust property. Section 1.13 discusses this view, suggesting that it is a (flawed) proxy for the position taken in the text. At all events, his Lordship continues (707) that on acquiring the necessary knowledge, the transferee may 'become a constructive trustee... on the basis of knowing receipt'—thus also arriving at the suggestion in the text.

[38] Likewise, *Sinclair Investments (UK) Ltd v Versailles Trade Finance Ltd (in administrative receivership)* [2010] EWHC 1614 (Ch), [82]–[98] carefully separates the questions whether the recipient (being a purchaser for value) has notice, so as to incur the trust in the first place, and whether he then becomes liable for knowing receipt if he later loses the property in circumstances making it unconscionable for him not to be liable for this.

[39] Knowing receipt seems to be depicted thus in *Re Montagu's Settlement Trusts* [1987] Ch 264, 272–3; *Westdeutsche Landesbank Girozentrale v Islington LBC* [1996] AC 669, 707. This analysis is also supported by C Mitchell and S Watterson in C Mitchell (ed) *Constructive*

Many, however, regard knowing receipt in a different light. In particular, it has been repeatedly portrayed as essentially a standard restitutionary liability, aimed at reversing the unjust enrichment at the trust objects' expense that the acquisition of trust property, transferred without authority, is said to bring the transferee.[40] Applying the classic account of restitution to this view, the law should not ask whether the transferee knew or should have known of the property's provenance before imposing liability, but should make him repay on a strict liability basis, ie on the basis of having had the enrichment pure and simple.[41] A liability seemingly of this kind does exist not far from, though not quite in, the context of misapplied trust property: if someone receives property to which he is not entitled in the distribution of a deceased person's estate (rather than from a trustee, but there are similarities), he is liable to repay the estate even if he had no reason to doubt his entitlement.[42] But when invited to take the step of moulding knowing receipt on similar lines, the English courts have so far declined to do so.[43] Their reluctance is understandable and indeed commendable, for the restitutionary vision of knowing receipt has fundamental internal difficulties.[44] According to the standard analysis of restitutionary liability, it requires that the defendant (here, the transferee) be 'enriched', 'at the expense of' the claimant (here, the trust objects), in an 'unjust' manner: which, if one takes the widest view, means by way of a transfer to him from the claimant that lacks any juridical basis.[45] These requirements are simply not made out. As noted earlier, a recipient of trust property transferred without authority takes the property not as

---

and Resulting Trusts (2010) ch 4—though acceptance of the analysis need not entail acceptance of all that is said there about what follows. In particular, they prefer to speak of liability in knowing receipt in terms of the recipient having to account for the trust property and, in the circumstances, not being relieved. This approach is criticized in section 13.4.

[40] P Millett (1991) 107 LQR 71; P Birks in P Birks (ed) *The Frontiers of Liability Volume 1* (1994) ch 3; Lord Nicholls in W Cornish et al (eds) *Restitution: Past Present and Future* (1998) ch 15; P Birks in P Birks and A Pretto (eds) *Breach of Trust* (2002) ch 7; *El Ajou v Dollar Land Holdings Plc* [1993] 3 All ER 717, 736–9; *Royal Brunei Airlines Sdn Bhd v Tan* [1995] 2 AC 378, 386; *Twinsectra Ltd v Yardley* [2002] 2 AC 164, [105].

[41] In the law of restitution, however, an ignorant recipient is not liable to the extent that he incurs additional expenditure in the belief that the enrichment is his to keep, under the defence of 'change of position': *Lipkin Gorman v Karpnale Ltd* [1991] 2 AC 548.

[42] *Ministry of Health v Simpson* [1951] AC 251.

[43] *Bank of Credit and Commerce International Ltd v Akindele* [2001] Ch 437, 455–6. The Canadian courts have made the move (*Gold v Rosenberg* [1997] 3 SCR 767; *Citadel General Assurance Co v Lloyds Bank Canada* [1997] SCR 805); but it has been disavowed in Australia (*Farah Constructions Pty Ltd v Say-Dee Pty Ltd* [2007] HCA 22, [130]–[158]).

[44] See further L Smith (2000) 116 LQR 412. There are also more practical arguments pointing the same way: *ibid*, and also G Watt in E Cooke (ed) *Modern Studies in Property Law, Volume 3* (2005) ch 5.   [45] P Birks *Unjust Enrichment* 2nd edn (2005) ch 5.

his own, but on constructive trust for the claimant trust objects. So he is not enriched at their expense in the way that, outside the trust context, a recipient of a simple mistaken payment is enriched at the claimant's expense when the claimant loses, and the recipient acquires, ownership of the money in question.[46] Nor, in our context, is it apparent why any enrichment on the recipient's part is 'unjust': one cannot point to a transfer lacking in juridical basis from the claimant objects to the defendant recipient, because there is no transfer between them at all. It all boils down to the same quite basic point: no value passes from the objects to the recipient, so nothing in respect of which there could be a restitutionary claim between them.

There is an important exception from knowing receipt. There is no liability for someone who, in receiving and then depriving the trust of the property, acts as agent for someone else. Imagine a situation in which I would be liable. Now imagine a situation which is otherwise the same but in which I acquire the trust property, transferred without authority, not in my own right but as agent for you, and am adhering to your instructions when I deprive the trust of it. In the latter case, I myself am not liable, though you should be.

This exemption is available not only to agents properly so called, but also to banks: in the example above, I am not liable if I am your bank and receive the trust assets as a payment into your account with me.[47] Technically, this extension of the rule to banks is surprising. When money is 'paid into' a customer's account, the bank acquires it not as the account-holder's agent but in its own right: the credit to the customer's account is a debt that the bank undertakes to the customer in return. That the law nonetheless treats the bank as the customer's agent, so immunizing it against liability in knowing receipt, suggests that, like certain aspects of the law on dishonest assistance and trusteeship *de son tort*, the immunity reflects a project of protecting 'professional agents'. Within such a project, it is understandable that banks should be bracketed with agents proper.

One would wish the immunity to be explicable in a principled way, however. The best view might be the following. Remember the thesis, explicating the test of unconscionability, that the liability should be imposed only where the recipient knows of the property's provenance, or, in not

---

[46] *Lipkin Gorman v Karpnale Ltd* [1991] 2 AC 548 seems to show that a defendant can be liable as though for unjust enrichment even though he never acquires the asset, which remains the claimant's throughout: but the thinking behind this is difficult, and its message for knowing receipt conjectural.   [47] *Agip (Africa) Ltd v Jackson* [1990] Ch 265, 292.

knowing, is guilty of unacceptable conduct. Arguably, it should be seen as acceptable for agents and banks not to probe their customers' dealings, so that they should incur no liability if they take matters at face value (though it ought to follow that they should be liable if they actually know of the impropriety). But one could controvert that argument, and, regarding it (as the money laundering legislation does) as both feasible and desirable for professional agents to undertake such probing, aver that they should incur liability for knowing receipt accordingly.

15

Constructive Trusts 1

So far, we have concentrated on express trusts. In the remaining chapters, we turn to the two types of trust with which express trusts are customarily contrasted, namely resulting and constructive trusts. We begin by trying to understand constructive trusts in general, since in some ways they are less problematic than resulting trusts; then, in Chapter 16, move on to resulting trusts, and the question of their relationship with constructive trusts; and finally, in Chapters 17 and 18, review a number of particular kinds of such trusts, and also (in section 18.5) consider the duties that arise in constructive and resulting trusts.

15.1 THE NATURE OF CONSTRUCTIVE TRUSTS

The essential difference between express and constructive trusts is easily stated. Remember the 'definition' of a trust that was offered in Chapter 1:

> A trust is a situation in which property is vested in someone (a trustee), who is under legally recognized obligations, at least some of which are of a proprietary kind, to handle it in a certain way, and to the exclusion of any personal interest. These obligations may arise either by conscious creation by the previous owner of the property (the settlor), or because some other legally significant circumstances are present.

In these terms, express trusts arise by the settlor's conscious creation, whilst constructive trusts arise because some other legally significant circumstances are present.

Contrast this way of expressing the distinction with two other, apparently similar, but in fact problematic formulations of it. According to one, express trusts are intended by a settlor, whereas constructive trusts are not. This is incorrect because some constructive trusts are intended: for example, those that effectuate secret trusts.[1] According to the other,

---

[1] See section 5.6. As noted there, the fact that settlors can so easily engineer these constructive trusts generates the worry that they can in effect opt out of the Wills Act.

express trusts arise because of the settlor's intention, whereas constructive trusts arise by operation of law. This deals with the point just made, but errs in contrasting the settlor's intention with the operation of law. All trusts arise by operation of law, in the sense that trusts involve legal obligations, and only the law can place legal obligations upon people. The question is rather why the law does so. In express trusts, its reason is to give effect to the settlor's wish;[2] while in constructive trusts it is something else. Hence the wording of the 'definition' referred to above.

This distinction between express and constructive trusts is important not only for a proper understanding of their bases. The law draws upon the distinction when it rules that the two kinds of trust shall be treated differently.[3] In particular, by virtue of s 53(2) of the Law of Property Act 1925, constructive trusts[4] are exempted from the formality requirements of s 53(1), described in Chapter 5. A requirement of formality in making a trust can, in the nature of things, be complied with only by someone who knows that he is making a trust. That is the case with express trusts, since these are necessarily associated with a settlor's intention. But it is not the case with constructive trusts, which by definition may not be associated with such an intention and moreover, as we shall see, may arise in circumstances such that no one may realize a trust is at issue. If they applied to these trusts, therefore, the formality requirements would be very frequently not complied with, leading to the trusts' invalidity, so negating the law's concern that in the relevant circumstances such a trust should arise.

It ought to be unnecessary to stress that a situation cannot be a constructive trust unless it qualifies as a *trust*: ie, following our 'definition', property must be vested in the trustee, who must be under legally recognized obligations, at least some of which must be of a proprietary kind, to handle it in a certain way, to the exclusion of any personal interest. The expression 'constructive trust' has however been used to describe two kinds of situation that do not conform to this pattern, and that are not therefore properly trusts at all. In one of these, I am required to compensate the trust's objects when I cause them damage.[5] My obligations

---

[2] Ostensibly, at any rate. In fact, in some cases, a settlor's intention—and so an express trust—is 'found' less because it really exists than because the judge wishes there to be a trust for some other reason, which is tantamount to imposing a constructive trust: eg *Paul v Constance* [1977] 1 WLR 527: see section 3.3.

[3] See further P Matthews in C Mitchell (ed) *Constructive and Resulting Trusts* (2010) ch 1.

[4] Together with resulting and 'implied' trusts. 'Implied' here is normally read not as 'express but not clearly stated' (exempting such trusts would undermine the requirements in s 53(1) for express trusts) but as 'arising for reasons other than the settlor's conscious creation'. Implied trusts thus comprise nothing that would not be a constructive trust anyway.

[5] Thus especially 'dishonest assistance': see section 14.1.

do not require me to handle particular property in a particular way. They require me rather to pay the claimants the amount in question out of my general assets, ie they are personal rather than proprietary.[6] In the other, I am required to honour a promise I made regarding my use of a particular piece of property, but my obligation is neither of a proprietary kind nor to the exclusion of any interest in the property on my own part.[7] Since these situations are not properly trusts at all, they should not be referred to as constructive trusts.

Where the holder of some property has proprietary obligations arising in the appropriate way to use it in a particular manner for another's benefit, the term 'constructive trust' is correctly used. This does not mean, however, that a constructive trust will arise whenever I owe you an obligation and hold some property to which it might arguably be attached. Sometimes the circumstances will call for a legal response, and a constructive trust will be a candidate because a particular piece of property is at issue, but the law will instead impose a personal liability. Take the example of your accepting a bribe to neglect your duty to me. The authorities are divided over whether you hold the bribe on constructive trust for me, or merely owe me the amount in question by way of a personal liability.[8] Or take the situation where you are my agent and sell my goods. In some such cases, identified by reference to the precise arrangement between us, you will hold the proceeds of the sale on trust for me; otherwise you will be able to take them into your own funds and then have a personal liability to pay me the sum in question from those funds.[9] The type of liability chosen, when either is possible, matters above all because proprietary obligations give me priority in your bankruptcy; personal obligations do not.[10] The law must ensure that the circumstances in which constructive trusts arise (the 'other legally significant circumstances' of our 'definition') justify not only some response, but also a response of a proprietary nature.

---

[6] For this distinction, see sections 1.9, 12.1.

[7] *Binions v Evans* [1972] Ch 359, 368–9; *Swiss Bank Corporation v Lloyds Bank Ltd* [1979] Ch 548, 571; *Lyus v Prowsa Developments Ltd* [1982] 1 WLR 1044; *Ashburn Anstalt v Arnold* [1989] Ch 1, 22–6: see section 18.1.

[8] See *Lister & Co v Stubbs* (1890) 45 Ch D 1; *A-G for Hong Kong v Reid* [1994] 1 AC 324; *Sinclair Investments (UK) Ltd v Versailles Trade Finance Ltd (in administrative receivership)* [2010] EWHC 1614 (Ch), [23]–[80]. The issue is discussed in section 17.4.

[9] See section 17.3.   [10] See sections 1.9, 12.1.

15.2 WHY DO CONSTRUCTIVE
TRUSTS ARISE?

It is accurate to say that constructive trusts are generated by considerations other than a project of effectuating settlors' wishes, but so far we have learnt nothing about what those considerations might be. In fact, constructive trusts arise as a reaction to (on the face of it) a number of sets of circumstances. Some of these are detailed individually in Chapters 17 and 18. But the catalogue given there is certainly not exhaustive. Indeed, it is probably impossible to produce an exhaustive catalogue. There is nothing, either in practice or (more importantly) in theory, to prevent a new set of circumstances being identified that, on reflection, seems to require the imposition of a constructive trust.

It would be otherwise if the sets of circumstances in which constructive trusts arise all had a common factor, it being this that generates the constructive trust. No set of circumstances lacking that factor could then properly elicit such a trust. Attempts have been made to identify such a common factor, but none has yet given a satisfactory account of the circumstances in which constructive trusts do in fact arise in English law. The most famous of these attempts asserts that constructive trusts exist solely to deprive the trustee of an unjust enrichment that he has received at the beneficiary's expense.[11] This view seems to be generally held as regards the law of the United States,[12] but in other jurisdictions, whilst it is probably correct to say that one of their bases may be the reversal of unjust enrichment, it is clear that constructive trusts arise also in other circumstances.[13] Other attempts at a general theory of constructive trusts seek exhaustively to describe these other circumstances. According to one view, for example, constructive trusts also exist to deprive a person of property obtained in breach of a fiduciary duty;[14] another view adds an aim of perfecting incomplete dispositions.[15] Whatever their accuracy in

---

[11] D Waters *The Constructive Trust* (1964).

[12] See eg American Law Institute *Restatement (First) of Restitution* (1937) §160 and Commentary.

[13] In Canada, the United States view, previously held (see eg *Rawluk v Rawluk* [1990] 1 SCR 70, 101–3), was rejected in *Soulos v Korkontzilas* [1997] 2 SCR 217. As regards Australia, see *Muschinski v Dodds* (1985) 160 CLR 583, 616–17.

[14] *Soulos v Korkontzilas* [1997] 2 SCR 217, Canada.

[15] G Elias *Explaining Constructive Trusts* (1990). Elias also adds the project of securing reparation for loss wrongfully caused. But at least some of this work is carried on not by constructive trusts but by personal responses, such as 'dishonest assistance' (see section 14.1), albeit that these have sometimes been wrongly called 'constructive trusts': see section 15.1.

accounting for some instances of constructive trusts, however, these theses fail in their aim of exhausting the circumstances in which constructive trusts in fact occur. A major instance covered by none of them is the constructive trust that especially English law erects in certain cases regarding family homes, which we shall look at in section 18.3.

The discussion of constructive trusts in Chapters 17 and 18 in fact suggests that most of the trusts addressed there rest on four kinds of basis.[16] But there is nothing about these to lead one to think that such trusts cannot, in principle, arise on any other basis. So far as producing a general theory goes, therefore, we can say only that constructive trusts arise in circumstances where, for whatever reason, it is right that the owner of some property should not enjoy it personally, but should hold it on trust for another. In some quarters, this is regarded as a reason for opprobrium.[17] It is unclear why. It simply reflects the idea—surely not a threatening one—that a number of situations may merit the same response for differing reasons (just as various different scenarios, for different reasons, can lead to awards of damages). The important question is whether the reasons, albeit differing, are good ones; whether the situations in which a constructive trust arises are those, and only those, where it genuinely should.

The possible bases for a constructive trusts are, however, sometimes all swept together in an assertion that such trusts arise where good conscience so requires.[18] A formula of this kind, providing no information as to when good conscience does so require, does not effectively identify a common factor by reference to which the law imposes constructive trusts. But unlike the theses discussed hitherto, it should not be read as attempting to do so. Instead, it stands for the proposition that a constructive trust will be found where the individual court, in its discretion, thinks fit. (The discretion need not be limitless, of course.) The view that constructive trusts

---

[16] Liberal property theory, via its predicates proprietary inertia and *nemo dat quod non habet*; a concern to counteract the 'principal–agent problem' besetting agency, trusts, and similar otherwise useful devices, and an analogous problem arising between a vendor and a purchaser especially of land; a concern to protect someone who will otherwise have been irretrievably prejudiced by relying on another's word; and the implications of family relationships. Beyond these, there is the goal of vindicating expectations associated with some uses of proprietary estoppel, identified in section 18.4; but, as noted there, it is hard to regard that goal as proper.

[17] See eg D Waters et al *Waters' Law of Trusts in Canada* 3rd edn (2005) 455.

[18] eg *Hussey v Palmer* [1972] 1 WLR 1286, 1289–90, Lord Denning MR: 'it is a trust imposed by law whenever justice and good conscience require it. It is a liberal process, founded upon large principles of equity, to be applied in cases where the defendant cannot conscientiously keep the property for himself alone, but ought to allow another to have the property or a share in it.'

can arise via the explicit exercise of judicial discretion in this way refers to such trusts as 'remedial constructive trusts', to which we now turn.

15.3 REMEDIAL CONSTRUCTIVE TRUSTS: WHAT ARE THEY?

Discussion of 'remedial constructive trusts' is hampered by a lack of agreement as to what the term means. Three principal different meanings can be identified, which will be explored below, though further variants may be discoverable and are certainly imaginable. 'Remedial' constructive trusts are contrasted with 'institutional' constructive trusts. The meaning of the latter term varies too, reflecting the particular contrast that is being made.

All the meanings of 'remedial constructive trusts' depict such things as trusts, in that they take a situation where a person holds some property and oblige him to treat it not as his own but as another's; and as constructive, in that they arise for some reason other than to vindicate a settlor's wish.

The first meaning[19] depicts them as arising automatically from the occurrence of certain significant facts—specifically, the fact that I, the present holder of some property, acquired it in such circumstances that the law sees me as thereby unjustly enriched at your expense—but as having no connection with the law of trusts beyond the proposition that I, therefore, hold the property for you. On this meaning, they differ from 'institutional' constructive trusts in that the key facts need not involve any prior relationship between us (but no more do some other constructive trusts, as Chapters 17 and 18 will show); and, more importantly, in that they oblige me only to transfer the property in question to you, rather than retaining it and behaving as a trustee so long as I do (but again, this is equally true of some other constructive trusts, as section 18.5 explains). This latter feature is said to make the remedial constructive trust a 'remedy', rather than a 'real trust'; so, saying that you have the benefit of this

---

[19] See eg American Law Institute *Restatement (First) of Restitution* (1937) §160 and Commentary, and *Restatement (Third) of Restitution and Unjust Enrichment Tentative Draft No 6* (2008) §55 and Commentary. The Restatements reflect the thinking of the scholar A W Scott. It is interesting, given the contrast drawn between remedial constructive trusts and 'real trusts', that Scott was a trusts specialist, as is the other doyen of the subject, the Canadian scholar D W M Waters. Despite this, however, it is hard to recognize the understanding of constructive trusts in English law essayed in their works, though perhaps it would have been easier at some point in the past.

'trust' is just another way of saying that you have a proprietary remedy. Regarded as a remedy, one might expect your 'trust' to operate only prospectively, ie from the time when the court grants it. Say that between the time of the key facts and the time when you succeed in your claim, I become insolvent: you should be unable to assert your claim to the property ahead of my general creditors. This view has, indeed, sometimes been taken.[20] But according to the dominant tradition, your 'trust' not only arises automatically from the occurrence of the key facts, but also—therefore—operates retrospectively, ie from the time of the key facts. So in the same example, you may indeed assert your claim to the property ahead of my ordinary creditors.[21] In this respect, then, your trust is just like a 'real trust', rather than a remedy, after all. This first meaning thus has an ambiguity embedded within its conceptual make-up, which has been a source of some awkwardness.[22]

The second meaning too sees the remedial constructive trust as a remedy rather than a 'real trust'. But it differs from the first meaning in seeing it as arising *not* automatically from the key facts—again, my ownership of some property when circumstances have occurred indicating that it should be yours, such as my acquisition of it via unjust enrichment at your expense[23]—but because a court decides, in its discretion, that the trust should arise.[24] This is the second meaning's headline characteristic. It may have emerged from a perception, or recollection, that your remedy could be personal rather than proprietary,[25] as much where the relevant property remains extant in my hands as (necessarily)

---

[20] Most famously, this was the conclusion reached, albeit via unsatisfactory reasoning, in *XL/Datacompp Inc v Wilson (In re Omegas Group Inc)* 16 F 3d 1443 (6th Cir 1994), United States. See further *Re Dow Corning Corp* 192 BR 428 (Bankr ED Mich 1996), United States.

[21] American Law Institute *Restatement (First) of Restitution* (1937) §160 and Commentary; *Restatement (Third) of Restitution and Unjust Enrichment Tentative Draft No 6* (2008) §55 and Commentary.

[22] See D Wright *The Remedial Constructive Trust* (1998) 267; C Rotherham *Proprietary Remedies in Context* (2002) 57–63; and further sources cited there.

[23] The decisions espousing the second meaning have focused principally on unjust enrichment, but not exclusively: see especially *Soulos v Korkontzilas* [1997] 2 SCR 217, Canada.

[24] For discussion, see *Re Esteem Settlement, Grupo Torras SA v Al Sabah* 2003 JLR 188, [136]–[151], Jersey.

[25] *Sorochan v Sorochan* [1986] 2 SCR 38, Canada; *Rawluk v Rawluk* [1990] 1 SCR 70, 103–8, Canada; *Peter v Beblow* [1993] 1 SCR 980, [24], [29], [34], Canada. A leading account of the first meaning contains a seed of the same idea, in asserting that, although the trust arises automatically from the key facts, a court should not enforce it if other (personal) remedies are adequate: American Law Institute *Restatement (First) of Restitution* (1937) §160, Comments *e–g*. This qualification to the first meaning is, however, played down in the more recent *Restatement (Third) of Restitution and Unjust Enrichment Tentative Draft No 6* (2008) §55 and Commentary.

where it does not.[26] But again, there is confusion about what ensues. According to one view, the court can decide whether or not to impose the trust (as opposed to granting a personal remedy), but, if it does, that trust necessarily operates—again, in this respect just like a 'real trust'—retrospectively, from the time of the key facts.[27] According to another view, however, the court should continue in its discretionary work, and finesse the trust's applicability.[28] In particular, the court may order that the trust should operate retrospectively, from the time of the key facts, but it may choose to have the trust operate only prospectively, from the moment of imposing it; or indeed, in some yet further manner, so as to affect some who previously gained a claim to the property, but not others.[29]

The third meaning adopts the second meaning's understanding that the 'trust' arises from the court's discretionary decision, rather than from the underlying key facts. It goes further, however, in rejecting the idea that there must be pre-defined key facts at all, whether in the way of unjust enrichment or anything else—though I must hold some property that ought to be yours, otherwise the response cannot take the form of a trust. Instead, it maintains that the court can impose the trust wherever it regards the facts before it as meriting this response. In other words, it treats not only the use of the 'trust' response, but also the identification of the cause of action itself, as a matter for the court's discretion. Perhaps the most famous identification of this meaning is to be found in the judgment of Lord Denning MR in *Hussey v Palmer*,[30] giving it the name 'new model' constructive trust.[31] There also exists a less transparent version

---

[26] Conversely, a trust can satisfactorily be imposed over property currently in the defendant's hands if this property can somehow be linked with the defendant's original enrichment by the claimant: *Peter v Beblow* [1993] 1 SCR 980, [25]–[41], Canada. But this same passage also shows how loose (and in the eye of the court, so discretionary) this linkage can be.

[27] *Rawluk v Rawluk* [1990] 1 SCR 70, 91–2, Canada.

[28] *Westdeutsche Landesbank Girozentrale v Islington LBC* [1996] AC 669, 716, Lord Browne-Wilkinson: 'The court by way of remedy might impose a constructive trust on a defendant who knowingly retains property of which the plaintiff has been unjustly deprived. Since the remedy can be tailored to the circumstances of the particular case, innocent third parties would not be prejudiced and restitutionary defences, such as change of position, are capable of being given effect.'

[29] See especially *Muschinski v Dodds* (1985) 160 CLR 583, 615, Australia, Deane J; D Waters in P Birks (ed) *The Frontiers of Liability, Volume 2* (1994) ch 13.

[30] [1972] 1 WLR 1286, 1289–90, quoted in n 18 above.

[31] See too *Gissing v Gissing* [1971] AC 886, 905, Lord Diplock: a constructive trust is created 'whenever the trustee has so conducted himself that it would be inequitable to allow him to deny to the cestui que trust a beneficial interest in the [property] acquired'; *Powell v Thompson* [1991] 1 NZLR 597, 615 (see too 605–6), New Zealand, Thomas J: 'in New Zealand the constructive trust has become a broad equitable remedy for reversing that which is inequitable

of this idea,[32] whereby a set of pre-defined key facts, such as an unjust enrichment, is required, but the requirement is constructed in such a way as to be only loosely constraining.[33]

Even those who are sympathetic to some notion of remedial constructive trusts generally regard the third meaning as a step too far in the direction of 'palm tree justice', ie towards dereliction of Rule of Law values.[34] On the other hand, the first meaning is fundamentally problematic: as we have seen, the vision of the constructive trust as a *remedy* is at odds with the dominant understanding of this meaning, whereby it arises automatically from, *and therefore from the time of,* the key facts. The most resilient vision of the remedial constructive trust, then, is that represented by the second meaning, and it is on this vision of the remedial constructive trust that the remainder of this section's discussion will therefore be focused. By this vision, to repeat, such a 'trust' is a proprietary remedy, responding

or unconscionable'; *Beatty v Guggenheim Exploration Co* 225 NY 380, 386 (1919), United States, Cardozo J: 'a constructive trust is the formula through which the conscience of equity finds expression.' But cf American Law Institute *Restatement (Third) of Restitution and Unjust Enrichment Tentative Draft No 6* (2008) §55, Comment *a*, reading Cardozo J's remark in a more 'prosaic' way, whereby the court is *not* required 'to determine *a priori* what equity and good conscience require in a particular case.'

[32] *Rawluk v Rawluk* [1990] 1 SCR 70, 102, Canada, McLachlin J: the remedial analysis of constructive trusts 'eliminates the need to find recognizable categories in which the constructive trust can be applied, relying instead on the more general concept of unjust enrichment arising from a contribution by one to property held in the name of the other to the detriment of the contributing party'. (And see too *Peter v Beblow* [1993] 1 SCR 980, [9], Canada.) Cf *Muschinski v Dodds* (1985) 160 CLR 583, 617, Australia, where Deane J rejects unjust enrichment as a basis for remedial constructive trusts, on the ground that (in that jurisdiction, at that time) 'unjust enrichment' was an insufficiently precise idea; only, however (620), to propose 'unconscionability' in its place, a suggestion taken up in *Baumgartner v Baumgartner* (1987) 164 CLR 137, 148, Australia. The apparent latitude of the latter concept may be deceptive, however; its meaning for the judgement is immediately explicated in a relatively precise way (149).

[33] Perhaps this is the home of D Wright *The Remedial Constructive Trust* (1998). Wright argues that a claimant's relief (whether in a form which others would describe as a 'remedial constructive trust' or otherwise) should be selected from a 'remedial smorgasbord', the selection being made by reference to an 'obligation continuum' and a 'remedy continuum'. The language suggests a relatively unconstrained approach to the identification of the facts that will elicit a particular remedy. It is clear, however, that Wright's aim is to promote not chaos in adjudication, but a more lucid, and therefore more stable, approach to it.

[34] See eg American Law Institute *Restatement (Third) of Restitution and Unjust Enrichment Tentative Draft No 6* (2008) §55 and Commentary; *Muschinski v Dodds* (1985) 160 CLR 583, 615–16, Australia; see too *Re Esteem Settlement, Grupo Torras SA v Al Sabah* 2003 JLR 188, [151](iv), Jersey. As a matter of principle, however, it is not obvious why one should simultaneously espouse highly discretionary relief (which *Muschinski v Dodds* does, though the American *Restatement* does not), while eschewing discretion as to the cause of action.

to pre-defined key facts—an established cause of action—but imposed by the court if, and (in the fullest version of it) to the extent that, the court in its discretion so decides. On this account, the contrasting 'institutional' constructive trust is likewise a response to pre-defined key facts, but it arises automatically from them, and from the time of them, with no discretionary judicial mediation.

Of course, this account overstates the contrast between remedial and institutional constructive trusts, mainly as a result of portraying the latter in an unrealistic way. It may well be less than certain whether the required key facts are present, either because the evidence is unclear or because discovering these 'facts' requires the application of an evaluative concept, such as 'in good faith'. Then, the court will in effect have a discretion whether to find even an institutional constructive trust. But there do remain differences between this and a remedial constructive trust. A court dealing with a remedial constructive trust will have a discretion even where the facts are clear. Even when the facts are unclear, the discretion in an institutional constructive trust case does not involve the overt consideration of the right outcome that is essential to the deployment of a remedial constructive trust. And even where the recognition of an institutional constructive trust involves a discretion in this way, the court's choices will be only to find the trust to have arisen from the time of the facts, with all that that will entail, or to find it not to have arisen at all: whereas, as we have seen, on the fullest understanding of this vision, a court wielding a remedial constructive trust has discretion to finesse every detail of its applicability. Say I own our family home in circumstances such that you deserve a share in it,[35] but before you claim, I mortgage the house to a bank. An institutional constructive trust arising on these facts would give you an interest pre-dating, and thus commonly unaffected by, the bank's;[36] the mortgage takes effect only against the remainder of the property, which will be unwelcome news to the bank. A court deploying a remedial constructive trust would, however, have a discretion whether to award you your share free of the bank's interest, or subject to it, or even perhaps in some manner between these two extremes.

So much for the possible visions of remedial constructive trusts; now to their place in the extant law.

---

[35] See section 18.3.
[36] This is in fact the law: *Williams & Glyn's Bank Ltd v Boland* [1981] AC 487.

15.4 REMEDIAL CONSTRUCTIVE TRUSTS: THEIR PLACE IN THE LAW

Remedial constructive trusts of some description are undoubtedly recognized and operated in many, if not all, common law countries. In particular, take the traditional version of the first meaning, whereby a remedial constructive trust arises automatically from pre-defined key facts, and operates simply to oblige the trustee to transfer the property in question to the beneficiary. This describes, or comes close to describing,[37] a number of the kinds of constructive trust recognized by English law, though they are not usually referred to as 'remedial'.

It is fair to say, however, that the vision of remedial constructive trusts on which we are mainly focusing, that involving a discretion as to the imposition of the trust, is more narrowly accepted. It is found most definitely in the United States and Canada, but even there, the exact vision of such trusts under discussion, involving a discretion to finesse every detail of the trust's applicability, is to be found more in speculative than in authoritative discourse.[38] Does it, or might it in future, also form part of English law?

There certainly exists material supportive of the possibility. A notable judicial statement[39] in this vein expressed concern that, on established understandings, constructive trusts automatically affect third parties, as explained in section 15.3; and commended the way that a discretion to finesse the trust's applicability allows third parties to be protected, without forsaking a proprietary response altogether.[40] Not long afterwards,

---

[37] In some of English law's constructive trusts, the obligation may be to transfer the property to the original or a replacement trustee, rather than to the beneficiary; but this does not seem crucially different. Likewise, in contrast to the traditional understanding of this type of remedial constructive trust, most of English law's constructive trusts respond to something other than unjust enrichment (though cf *Chase Manhattan Bank NA v Israel-British Bank (London) Ltd* [1981] Ch 105; see section 17.1); but again, this does not seem crucial.

[38] The closest rule to it being that recognized in *Rawluk v Rawluk* [1990] 1 SCR 70, 91–2, Canada, described at n 32 above.

[39] *Westdeutsche Landesbank Girozentrale v Islington LBC* [1996] AC 669, 716. For earlier support, see *Metall und Rohstoff AG v Donaldson Lufkin & Jenrette Inc* [1990] 1 QB 391, 478–9.

[40] See too *Lord Napier and Ettrick v Hunter* [1993] AC 713 and *Ocular Sciences Ltd v Aspect Vision Care Ltd* [1997] RPC 289, 414–16. In both, the court seemed to think that it could impose a trust on the defendant, but opted for a different remedy instead, on the basis that a trust would have an inappropriate impact. Although the reasoning is not put

however, remedial constructive trusts were judicially disparaged,[41] in terms that some perceived (with satisfaction) as fatal to their future prospects.[42] But, although that is sometimes taken to be the current position,[43] they appear in fact to have survived. Recently, they have been depicted judicially as not merely an attractive possibility for the future, but an already established feature of English law.[44,45]

Since remedial constructive trusts are presumably not vampires, the reason for their refusal to die in English law seems likely to be that they do, in fact, possess merit. Section 15.5 explores that question. It is important, too, to appreciate that the leading judicial rejection of them—in *Re Polly Peck International plc (in administration) (No 2)*[46]—was not elicited by the vision of remedial constructive trusts currently under discussion. Instead, it was aimed against an argument that the court should impose such a trust ad hoc, rather than in response to pre-defined key facts—that is, should adopt the third vision described above, ie the 'new model' constructive trust; while at the same time not hesitating to impose the trust retrospectively, ie make it effective even against third parties whose rights pre-dated the order. The argument was audacious, and its rejection quite unsurprising—but not, therefore, necessarily to be read

in terms of 'remedial constructive trusts', it uses the same essential idea of a discretion as to response.

[41] *Re Polly Peck International plc (in administration) (No 2)* [1998] 3 All ER 812.

[42] See especially P Birks (1998) 12 TLI 202. See too P Birks in P Birks (ed) *The Frontiers of Liability, Volume 2* (1994) ch 16.

[43] See eg *Sinclair Investments (UK) Ltd v Versailles Trade Finance Ltd (in administrative receivership)* [2010] EWHC 1614 (Ch), [23], [60].

[44] *Thorner v Major* [2009] 1 WLR 776, [20], Lord Scott. It is not completely clear how his Lordship sees such trusts, but probably as allowing a discretionary response to the facts which generate liability in proprietary estoppel (see section 18.4)—against the background that, unlike most judges, he does not view relief in proprietary estoppel as discretionary in its own right (*ibid*, and *Cobbe v Yeoman's Row Management Ltd* [2008] 1 WLR 1752, [14], [16]). If so, he is thinking in terms of what we are referring to as the second vision of remedial constructive trusts. See too T Etherton [2008] CLJ 265 and [2009] Conv 104, arguing that the remedial constructive trust was introduced into English law—without the term being used—by *Stack v Dowden* [2007] 2 AC 432 (see section 18.3), in order to allow discretionary relief in cases of unjust enrichment. This is a possible reading of at least one aspect of that decision, though note that the discretion seems to extend only to the quantum of the remedy, not to the timing of its applicability. It most certainly operates from the time of the key facts: *Williams & Glyn's Bank Ltd v Boland* [1981] AC 487.

[45] See too *Henry v Henry* [2010] 1 All ER 988, [47], [56], contemplating that a claim in proprietary estoppel (see section 18.4), in principle capable of binding a transferee of the property to which it relates, may yield a different remedy against the transferee than it would have yielded against the transferor—a phenomenon not there referred to as a 'remedial constructive trust', but (at least if involving an outcome identifiable as a trust at all) surely exactly that.

[46] [1998] 3 All ER 812.

as requiring so negative a reaction to our preferred, second, vision of remedial constructive trusts.[47]

15.5 REMEDIAL CONSTRUCTIVE TRUSTS: THEIR DESIRABILITY

The principal stated objection to the remedial constructive trust—even to our favoured vision of it—is that, with its element of discretion, it operates to produce departures from established property rights, on the say-so of judges rather than of Parliament.[48] Take the example above, regarding our family home. If the law were to operate by remedial constructive trust, and the court accepted your claim to a share in the family home but decided not to make it effective against the bank, then you might see your right to your share as to that extent confiscated. Equally, if the court did decide to make your right effective against the bank, the bank might see the court as having confiscated its rights under the mortgage.

But the remedial constructive trust is to be seen as producing departures from established property rights in this way only so long as one regards the property rights in question as established before admitting the remedial constructive trust to the story.[49] If the remedial constructive trust—or more especially, what it stands for, above all the possibility of priority between rights being finessed on the say-so of judges—is seen as an original feature of the law, our understanding of property rights changes: we see them as necessarily relative in this way. Then, it is impossible to say that you suffer judicial 'confiscation', with that word's connotation of something improper, if your claim to a share in the family home is not made effective against the bank: the only right you ever had is one that allows for the possibility of this happening. Likewise the bank and its mortgage rights.

---

[47] Cf *Re Goldcorp Exchange Ltd (in receivership)* [1995] 1 AC 74, 99, 104. The same argument was made as in *Re Polly Peck International plc (in administration) (No 2)* [1998] 3 All ER 812, and likewise rejected. But the court was careful to focus its rejection on the precise argument, rather than on the whole idea of remedial constructive trusts.

[48] See eg *Re Polly Peck International plc (in administration) (No 2)* [1998] 3 All ER 812, 830–1.

[49] This is the view of property rights taken by Lord Hope in *Fisher v Brooker* [2009] 1 WLR 1764, [8]: 'There is no concept in our law that is more absolute than a right of property. Where it exists, it is for the owner to exercise it as he pleases. He does not need the permission of the court, nor is it subject to the exercise of the court's discretion.' The word 'property' can certainly be taken as emblematic of this position, but, as the text explains, it does not follow that the law does or should adopt the latter.

So the fundamental idea involved is an intelligible one. The question really is whether it is substantively attractive or indeed acceptable. That is, whether we should approve or otherwise of the idea that the profiling of rights—the settling of their ambit, and their precedence amongst themselves—should lie in the discretion of (necessarily) judges, rather than being fixed by rules, and adjusted, if at all, by the legislature.[50]

The first point to note is that the distinction between rules and discretions is relative: propositions expressed as rules often, indeed normally or even inevitably, have latitude within them; while avowed discretions are normally operated according to discernible (though not necessarily desirable) patterns. Nevertheless, there remains a spectrum about the extent to which the law preordains its reaction to particular facts, and the terms 'rules' and 'discretions' can intelligibly be used to denote its two halves.

Rules, then, cater better than discretions to 'Rule of Law' values, notably the value that like cases should be treated alike (and unlike cases differently) and the value that those subject to the law should be able to know its impact on them so as to be able to conduct their affairs accordingly. Rules are also likely to be the product of more extended and circumspect reflection than discretionary determinations, and may make for more efficient disposal of disputes than discretionary techniques (though if the rules are complex and parties can appeal against alleged misapplications of them, the opposite may be true). If adjustments are to be made to the existing rules, leaving this to the legislature has most of these same benefits.

The game is not all one way, however. Discretions allow greater scope for the parties to a dispute to be involved in the process of its judicial resolution (though rules may make it easier for them to negotiate out of court); in contexts where the appropriate position for the law depends on

---

[50] On a general level, see R Dworkin *Taking Rights Seriously* (1977); D Galligan *Discretionary Powers* (1986); K Hawkins (ed) *The Uses of Discretion* (1992). As regards remedial constructive trusts in particular, see S Gardner in P Birks (ed) *The Frontiers of Liability, Volume 2* (1994) ch 14; and, outstandingly, C Rotherham *Proprietary Remedies in Context* (2002) chs 1–3. Rotherham depicts the idea of 'established property rights' as a symbol, standing for the idea that judges should have nothing to do with matters of property distribution, which according to this idea lie in the distinct domain of politics; argues that judges use the rhetoric of the institutional constructive trust as a way of fictionally protecting this symbol while they in reality subvert it, routinely addressing such matters; and sees the remedial constructive trust as a more truthful expression of the reality. But there remains the question whether *there is indeed value* (if not necessarily all-conquering value) in the idea that judges should eschew matters of property distribution; the text below suggests so, alluding to Rule of Law and other considerations. Rotherham may pay insufficient attention to this question. He does (ch 4), however, consider the rather different question of the principles by which a judicial distributive discretion might proceed—though without, perhaps, reaching a wholly secure conclusion.

weighing the significance of a number of disparate factors, discretions better allow for the achievement of that position in individual cases; and discretions allow the law to feel its way towards the development of a rule when the right shape for that rule is not at first apparent.

It follows that neither position is preferable to the other across the board; one can be more attractive than the other according to the degree of resonance that the considerations just outlined have in the particular context in question.[51] For example, if the factors influencing one's view of the appropriate legal response are few and easily weighed, and an adverse legal outcome is especially damaging, the value that like cases should be treated alike may be overwhelmingly important. If the parties to a particular kind of dispute are typically adept at negotiating their own settlements, as for example shipping companies are, it will be most helpful for the law to give a clear, easily discoverable statement of the starting point for those negotiations (and to ensure that any change in that statement operates only for the future and is given full publicity). If the parties typically need their negotiations to be moderated and if necessary shaped by an outsider such as a judge, however, that outsider needs to be given the authority to do this shaping. This may be characteristic of family breakdowns.

A particular consideration arises in the cases where English law currently deploys constructive trusts, as described in the Chapters 17 and 18. The facts generating such trusts are in many cases unlikely to be visible to those with whom the trustee continues to deal. When the existence of the trust eventually comes to light, therefore, it will confound the assumptions on which they conducted those dealings. For example, if our family home is in my sole name and I mortgage it, the bank will assume that the house's whole value is at my disposal as security for its loan, and will decide how much to lend me accordingly. If it emerges that you had a share in the house all along, under a constructive trust,[52] that share's immunity to the bank's rights may mean that the value of the loan is greater than that of the security. Or if a company raises even unsecured loans to develop a site that is its only asset, its creditors will be dismayed to find that it holds that asset on constructive trust for another company for which it was a fiduciary.[53]

---

[51] Such a contextual way of thinking about the matter is adopted in *Re Esteem Settlement, Grupo Torras SA v Al Sabah* 2003 JLR 188, [148], Jersey, referring to the 'great store' that 'the customary law of Jersey, with its influence from the civil law, has always placed . . . on matters of title and proprietary rights'.　　　[52] See section 18.3.

[53] See sections 17.3–17.4.

It is surely desirable to avoid such states of affairs. Proceeding remedially, in order to be able to declare that any such trust shall not affect a third party, is an obvious means of doing so. But it is a rather crude means, for it operates via a kind of judgement of Solomon between the third party and the claimant himself. As we have already noted, it is true that, conceptually, there is no reason why property rights must be absolute; that is, why as between you and the third party, there must be one winner, who takes all. But substantively, your claims may both be such that we should like you each to do so. Even at its best, the remedial constructive trust rarely does better than divide the available spoils between you both, thereby doing full justice to neither.

So it is worth exploring whether other, more round-about, strategies for balancing or reconciling the competing interests are possible. In some contexts it may make sense to accord the beneficiary of a constructive trust a firm proprietary interest, but require him to register it against the trustee's name or title to the property in question, so that others dealing with the trustee can know of it. In other contexts, eg that of family property, a rule requiring registration would be inept (as largely unknown or meaningless to those at whom it is directed), so a different approach is called for. This might, for instance, involve incentivizing banks to ensure that possible constructive trust claimants are alerted to and involved in any mortgage dealings, and leaving them to bear the risk (as the party best placed to spread the loss) of any cases that slip through the net. This is, in fact, largely the effect of the present law.[54]

---

[54] Land Registration Act 2002 Sch 3 para 2; *Williams & Glyn's Bank Ltd v Boland* [1981] AC 487; *Bristol and West Building Society v Henning* [1985] 1 WLR 778; *Barclays Bank plc v O'Brien* [1994] 1 AC 180.

16

Resulting Trusts

In this chapter, we move on to the other category of non-express trust, namely resulting trusts.

16.1 THE NATURE OF RESULTING TRUSTS

Semantically, a 'resulting' trust is a trust whose beneficiary is also the person from whom the trustee acquired the trust property: a beneficial interest 'results', ie jumps back, to him.[1] Conventionally, however, the term 'resulting trust' is not used to describe every trust of this pattern. Normal usage of the term excludes the case where the trust arises because of this person's own stipulation that it should, ie is an express trust to this effect, he being its settlor.[2]

As we noted in section 15.1, the Law of Property Act 1925 s 53(2) exempts constructive trusts from the formality requirements imposed by s 53(1): and is right to do so because constructive trusts can arise, by definition, in circumstances such that no one may realize the fact, and so be in a position to comply with a formality requirement. Section 53(2) also exempts resulting trusts. It is right to do so only because resulting trusts are like constructive trusts in this respect. And they are like constructive trusts in this respect only because of the usage just referred to, confining the term 'resulting trust' to trusts of the required pattern but arising for reasons other than a settlor's own stipulation. If the term extended to trusts arising from a settlor's own stipulation, it would include cases where s 53(1) could perfectly well be complied with.

---

[1] In *Re Printers and Transferrers Amalgamated Trades Protection Society* [1899] Ch 184 a trust in favour of persons other than the provider of the trust property was described as a 'resulting trust', but this usage is incorrect.

[2] Such as arises in the context of a pension fund trust, or of the arrangement under which the lender of money has the borrower hold it on trust for him, with a right or duty to expend it in a particular way (*Barclay's Bank Ltd v Quistclose Investments Ltd* [1970] AC 567). *Smith v Cooke* [1891] AC 297, 299, however, supports the inclusion of such trusts.

It is tempting to conclude that a resulting trust is therefore any trust whose beneficiary is also the person from whom the trustee acquired the trust property, and that arises 'because some other legally significant circumstances are present', as our 'definition' has it. That is, that a resulting trust is any constructive trust whose beneficiary happens also to be the source of the trust property. More would remain to be said about why we should want to distinguish these particular constructive trusts from others—what is special about them. That theme will be pursued in section 16.4. First, however, we must acknowledge that this vision is at variance with the current law, as established by the House of Lords, particularly by Lord Browne-Wilkinson, in *Westdeutsche Landesbank Girozentrale v Islington LBC*.[3]

16.2 WESTDEUTSCHE: TYPES OF RESULTING TRUST

According to Lord Browne-Wilkinson, a resulting trust can arise in two, but only two, classes of case.[4]

The first is where I transfer property to you on an express trust, but my stipulations do not determine what is to happen in at least some eventualities. I become the beneficiary to the extent of that omission: this is the resulting trust. Say I transfer property to you, making clear that you are to be its trustee, but continuing, 'I'll tell you later what to do with it': you hold it on trust for me.[5] Or say I transfer property to you on trust for Adam for his life, with no stipulation as to what should happen after his death: you hold it for Adam for life, and for me thereafter. Or say I transfer property to you on trust for my descendants, and the trust is to some extent invalid for perpetuity:[6] you hold for my descendants so far as that is permitted, and otherwise for me. Cases of this kind can be referred to as 'incomplete express trust' cases.

The other class of case is where I transfer property to you gratuitously[7] rather than by way of sale or loan, and you cannot establish that

---

[3] [1996] AC 669, 708. The rule there stated was however subsequently ignored in *Air Jamaica Ltd v Charlton* [1999] 1 WLR 1399, 1412 and *Twinsectra Ltd v Yardley* [1999] Lloyd's Rep Bank 438, 457: see n 47 below.

[4] The two classes were formerly labelled 'automatic' and 'presumed' respectively: *Re Vandervell's Trusts (No 2)* [1974] Ch 269, 289, Megarry J. The term 'automatic' is inconsistent with Lord Browne-Wilkinson's view, discussed in section 16.3, that all resulting trusts are based on intention.   [5] *Re Boyes* (1884) 26 Ch D 531; *Vandervell v IRC* [1967] 2 AC 291.

[6] See section 2.5.

[7] Or 'voluntarily'—you, the gratuitous transferee, being a 'volunteer'.

my transfer was a gift: you hold it on (resulting) trust for me.[8] A variant on this is the case where I pay a third party to transfer property to you, again gratuitously so far as you are concerned, ie for no consideration on your part: again, if you cannot establish that I procured the transfer as a gift to you, you hold the property on (resulting) trust for me.[9] The common factor is that I am the provider of the property. These cases may be called 'gratuitous transfer' cases. You can establish that my transfer was a gift, so as to displace the resulting trust, either by evidence that this was my intention, or by invoking the 'presumption of advancement',[10] by which a gratuitous transfer that you cannot otherwise prove to have been a gift is nonetheless taken as one if I am your husband,[11] or your father,[12] or I stand *in loco parentis* to you.[13] But both the rule whereby a gratuitous transfer otherwise generates a resulting trust, and the presumption of advancement, reflect a set of bygone practices and concerns.[14] Their practical significance has accordingly diminished to almost nil,[15] and their very place in the law has been queried or indeed denied.[16]

Give or take such doubts about the place of the gratuitous transfer class in today's law, these two classes of case have always been regarded as the

---

[8] *Dyer v Dyer* (1788) 2 Cox Eq 92; *The Venture* [1908] P 218.

[9] If you and I each pay part of the price, the presumption is that you hold on trust for both of us, in proportion to our shares in the price.

[10] See further J Glister in C Mitchell (ed) *Constructive and Resulting Trusts* (2010) ch 10. The Equality Act 2010 s 199 provides for the abolition of this presumption (though cf J Glister (2010) 73 MLR 807), but has not yet been brought into effect.

[11] *Kingdon v Bridges* (1688) 2 Vern 67.

[12] *Grey v Grey* (1677) 2 Sw 594. According to a number of Commonwealth cases also if I am your mother (eg *Nelson v Nelson* (1995) 184 CLR 538, Australia); but according to English law not in this case (*Bennet v Bennet* (1879) 10 Ch D 474), though the relationship will count as strong evidence in favour of a gift.

[13] *Powys v Mansfield* (1835) 3 Myl & Cr 359.   [14] See further section 3.7.

[15] *Fowkes v Pascoe* (1875) LR 10 Ch App 343; *Bennet v Bennet* (1879) 10 Ch D 474; *Standing v Bowring* (1885) 31 Ch D 282. '*Almost* nil', however, because they still dictate outcomes when the evidence to rebut them cannot be adduced because it involves an illegality: *Tinsley v Milligan* [1994] 1 AC 340; *Tribe v Tribe* [1996] Ch 107. Cf Law Commission *The Illegality Defence* (Law Com No 320, 2010) Part 2.

[16] See *Tinsley v Milligan* [1994] 1 AC 340, 371 and *Lohia v Lohia* [2001] EWCA Civ 1691, [21]–[26], pointing to the Law of Property Act 1925 s 60(3) (also *Fowkes v Pascoe* (1875) LR 10 Ch App 343, 348), regarding the presumption applicable to a gratuitous transfer of land; *Pettitt v Pettitt* [1970] AC 777, 793, 811, 824, regarding the presumption of advancement between husband and wife; and *Stack v Dowden* [2007] 2 AC 432, [31], [59]–[60], regarding both presumptions in the context of family homes (though note that this implicitly denies the relevance of s 60(3)). Cf however *Antoni v Antoni* [2007] UKPC 10, asserting the continued vitality of the presumption of advancement between father and child. For an argument that the presumption of advancement is contrary to the European Convention on Human Rights, see G Andrews [2007] Conv 340. See further R Chambers in C Mitchell (ed) *Constructive and Resulting Trusts* (2010) ch 9, 268–76.

salient instances of resulting trusts. But Lord Browne-Wilkinson's ruling affirmatively excludes trusts arising in situations of other kinds, which previous authority had treated as resulting trusts too. In these latter situations, the very transfer of the property is unsatisfactory in some way, such that, although it has technically taken place—ie the transferee has indeed become the owner of the property—we, and the law, prefer to say that it has not, by reckoning that the transferee holds the property on trust for the transferor.[17] Such a situation may occur where the transferor does not intend to transfer the property at all, as where his land is, by some process of which he is unaware, re-registered in the transferee's name; where he does intend to transfer the property, but the transfer is impermissible; and to some extent also where he does intend to transfer the property, but there is something wrong with that intention, as where he acts under duress, or is mistaken as to some crucial circumstance.[18] Let us call these 'unsatisfactory transfer' cases. One might think, and the earlier decisions say, that the trusts arising in them are resulting trusts, as the transferee holds the property on trust for the person from whom he acquires it, for reasons other than the latter's own stipulation to this effect. But according to Lord Browne-Wilkinson's account—limiting 'resulting trusts' to the two categories discussed above—they cannot be resulting trusts. He does not, however, aver that they do not arise at all. Apparently, they continue to do so, but as constructive trusts instead.[19]

16.3 *WESTDEUTSCHE*: THE RATIONALE OF RESULTING TRUSTS

As well as this statement of when resulting trusts can arise, Lord Browne-Wilkinson also makes a more abstract comment on the point: namely, that they arise in effectuation of the common intention of the transferor and

---

[17] The trust is recognized, and labelled 'resulting', in *Ryall v Ryall* (1739) 1 Atk 59; *Lane v Dighton* (1762) Amb 409; *Agip (Africa) Ltd v Jackson* [1990] Ch 265, 290; *El Ajou v Dollar Land Holdings plc* [1993] 3 All ER 717, 734; perhaps *Hodgson v Marks* [1971] Ch 892, 933.

[18] See further section 17.1.

[19] See *Westdeutsche Landesbank Girozentrale v Islington LBC* [1996] AC 669, 715–16, holding that a constructive trust arises in my favour when I transfer money to you by mistake (as in *Chase Manhattan Bank NA v Israel-British Bank (London) Ltd* [1981] Ch 105, at any rate so long as you know of my mistake), and when you acquire my coins by stealing them and mixing them with your own; see further section 17.1. See too, more recently, *Collings v Lee* [2001] 2 All ER 332, where a re-registration of land, obtained by fraud, was reversed by the imposition of a trust in favour of the previous owner; the judgment asserts, at 336, 'whether the trust should be characterised as implied, resulting or constructive is a matter of no importance'.

transferee.[20] He does not quite say so directly, but we may assume that he regards this comment as also indicating *why* such trusts arise. It differentiates resulting trusts radically from constructive trusts, which, as explained in section 15.1, certainly do not arise so as to effectuate intentions,[21] and in particular accounts for his refusal to accept as resulting trusts the trusts that arise in 'unsatisfactory transfer' cases. In the latter, we know that the transferor does not intend the transferee to hold the property in question on trust for him, as he either intends the transfer to be absolute, or does not intend it to occur at all.[22] Unfortunately, his Lordship's position also has difficulty in satisfactorily capturing and explaining even the 'gratuitous transfer' and 'incomplete express trust' cases, which he must believe instantiate it.

The intention that his Lordship demands is evidently a presumed rather than an actual one. The transferors in the 'incomplete express trust' and 'gratuitous transfer' cases do not actually intend to establish trusts, and neither do their transferees. Indeed, if they did, it would be hard to point to the differentiation which normal usage, and s 53 of the Law of Property Act 1925, assume to exist between resulting trusts and express trusts. But even reference to a *presumed* intention puts pressure on that differentiation. As we saw in Chapter 3, the settlor's intention is found on the basis of a presumption, rather than naturalistically, in a number of express trust cases. Indeed, remember the reasons for requiring formality, explored in section 5.1: above all the promotion of certainty in respect of the transaction's occurrence and its content. In respect of these reasons, trusts based on a presumed intention—or an implied one—are actually more problematic than those based on a properly articulated intention. If it is right to demand formality in respect of the latter, then, it is certainly wrong to exempt the former.

---

[20] *Westdeutsche Landesbank Girozentrale v Islington LBC* [1996] AC 669, 708. His Lordship refers with approval to W Swadling (1996) 16 LS 133. In that article, however, Swadling contends only that, as a matter of history/authority, the presumption in a gratuitous transfer case is of an intention that the transferee should hold the property on trust for the transferor. He does not suggest, as Lord Browne-Wilkinson does, that such an intention is required for all resulting trusts. See further now W Swadling (2008) 124 LQR 72.

[21] One type of constructive trust (that regarding a family home) may effectuate the common intention of the beneficiary and trustee. To the extent that this is true, however, it is unsupportable. See section 18.3.

[22] This was the *ratio* of the decision in *Westdeutsche Landesbank Girozentrale v Islington LBC* [1996] AC 669. The claimant bank transferred money to the defendant local authority in circumstances such that it was *ultra vires* for the latter to accept it. Arguably, then, the bank's intention to do this was 'unsatisfactory'. Nonetheless, it *was* the bank's intention; the bank certainly had no intention to establish a trust. So it could not substantiate its contention that the local authority held the money on resulting trust.

Lord Browne-Wilkinson does not explain the basis for presuming the necessary common intention. The answer is perhaps that this intention is the one the transferor and transferee would have held in the relevant circumstances, if they had thought about the matter. It follows that if we can say the transferor and/or transferee would *not* have intended a trust for the transferor to arise, there will be no room for a presumed intention to the contrary, and so, on this reckoning, there cannot be a resulting trust. So if the courts have in fact found resulting trusts where the transferor and/or transferee would not have wanted them, the basis for these trusts cannot lie in a presumed common intention. And this appears to be the case.

Take first the assertion that a resulting trust arises only if the *transferee* of the property would have intended it to. It is hard to see why he should so intend. Indeed, since in the absence of a resulting trust he would retain the property for himself, there is every reason why he should not. But in no other case does a trust arise from the intentions of its trustee,[23] and Lord Browne-Wilkinson gives no explanation for taking the contrary view here. Perhaps the demand is less for intention (implying concurrence) than for knowledge (with no such implication) on the trustee's part, for Lord Browne-Wilkinson, in the same decision,[24] asserted the latter to be essential to all trusts. In section 1.13, however, we doubted the latter view too.

So let us leave his Lordship's reference to the intention of the *transferee* aside, as probably no more than a slip. It is at first sight more plausible that the *transferor* would want a resulting trust where he makes a gratuitous transfer that is not proved to be a gift, or an incomplete express trust. But it is not always so.

Vandervell v IRC[25] involved an incomplete express trust. The claim that a resulting trust arose was made by the revenue authorities, seeking to recover the tax that the transferor/settlor owed if this claim was right; the settlor, seeking to escape paying the tax, argued *against* a resulting trust. The House of Lords held that a resulting trust arose. This decision is authority, therefore, that a resulting trust can arise even where the transferor would not have intended it to. As a decision of the House of Lords, Lord Browne-Wilkinson would surely have had to make an explicit statement if he meant to depart from it. No such statement is to be found,

---

[23] A person can opt out of being a trustee, as explained in section 11.1, but only by divesting himself of the trust property, so that the trust is not defeated thereby. Further, as noted in n 21 above, although constructive trusts of family property are said to depend partly on the intentions of their trustee, this is doubtful.

[24] *Westdeutsche Landesbank Girozentrale v Islington LBC* [1996] AC 669, 705–6, 715.

[25] [1967] 2 AC 291. See too *Re Gillingham Bus Disaster Fund* [1958] Ch 300, 310.

however. Even in the absence of such authority, indeed, the law would have to have *some* rule aimed at a situation of this kind; and if this cannot involve a resulting trust, for want of the intention that Lord Browne-Wilkinson claims to be requisite, it is a mystery what form it could take.

So far as gratuitous transfers are concerned, everything depends upon what exactly is presumed. Three principal views have been advanced about this, and each can point to some degree of support in the cases. Say I make a gratuitous transfer to you.[26] On the first view, I am presumed to intend you to hold the property on trust for me, and the trust arises in effectuation of that intention.[27] This view is aligned with Lord Browne-Wilkinson's understanding that a resulting trust reflects an intention on the part of the transferor (and also transferee, but we are overlooking that). On the second view, however, the presumption is that I did not intend you to take the property for your own benefit, and the trust arises out of this want of intention.[28] On the third view, meanwhile, the trust again arises out of a want of intention on my part that you should have the property for your own benefit, but there is no presumption of such a want of intention: the 'presumption' is of the trust itself, the word denoting simply the law's imposition of it.[29] If either of these latter two views is accepted, it cannot be said that a resulting trust 'effectuates an intention' on the part of the transferor.

The first of these views is thus compatible with an understanding that a resulting trust arises so as to reflect an intention on the part of the transferor that it should do so, while the second and third views are not. But even if we adopt that first view (we shall consider the merits of the three views in section 16.5), it is clear that, taking everything together, Lord Browne-Wilkinson's analysis of resulting trusts cannot be accepted. His reference to the transferee is simply unsupportable. His reference to the transferor might in theory have mapped onto the 'incomplete express trust' and

---

[26] According to J Penner in C Mitchell (ed) *Constructive and Resulting Trusts* (2010) ch 8, 238–41, a trust is presumed to arise even where the transfer is not gratuitous, but occurs by way of a sale or loan—though the presumption will routinely rebutted in such cases, so as to be de facto confined to the gratuitous case. This is problematic, however: there seems no reason whatsoever why a trust should be presumed in such cases, indeed every reason why it should not.   [27] See W Swadling (2008) 124 LQR 72.

[28] See R Chambers *Resulting Trusts* (1997) ch 1; J Penner in C Mitchell (ed) *Constructive and Resulting Trusts* (2010) ch 8, 241–57. To make sense, this view must be adjusted so that I have no intention that you should take the property either for your own benefit *or in any other behalf:* see section 16.6 below. But this adjustment does not affect the point being made here, that a trust arising on this basis is not one (presumed to be) intended by the transferor.

[29] See R Chambers in C Mitchell (ed) *Constructive and Resulting Trusts* (2010) ch 9, 276–85.

'gratuitous transfer' cases, while excluding the 'unsatisfactory transfer' case, which his Lordship himself regards as outside the category. But on examination of the materials, while his reference to the transferor may (on the first view) be tenable in the 'gratuitous transfer' case, it is untenable in the 'incomplete express trust' case. Moreover, if his Lordship were right, we should find it hard to differentiate resulting trusts from express trusts, in the way that we must differentiate them if we are to make sense of the two categories' differing treatment in point of, for example, formalities (section 5.5) and duties (section 18.5).

So, despite its authoritative status, Lord Browne-Wilkinson's account of resulting trusts is indefensible. If we therefore reject it, however, what account should we give instead?[30]

16.4 PROPRIETARY INERTIA

As we have just seen, it is impossible to explain all, or perhaps any, resulting trusts by ascribing them to the transferor's intentions (let alone the transferee's too). The obvious, indeed logically the only possible, alternative is the second basis for trusts identified in our initial 'definition', namely the effect of 'other legally significant circumstances'. The implication is that resulting trusts are a species of constructive trust after all. One might say, simply, that they are those constructive trusts where the trustee holds property for the person from whom he acquired it, but that does not take us far enough. Other species of constructive trust, such as those to be discussed in Chapters 17 and 18, are separated from one another at least partly by reference to the distinctive 'legally significant circumstances' that give rise to them. So with the species known as resulting trusts too, we must go on to say what are the 'legally significant circumstances' that generate them, and why these circumstances should do so.

---

[30] Lord Browne-Wilkinson's view that the trusts arising in 'incomplete express trust' and 'gratuitous transfer' cases are resulting, while those arising in 'unsatisfactory transfer' cases are constructive, could be captured in another way: by saying that resulting trusts arise where I intend to transfer the property in question to you, while constructive trusts arise where I do not so intend, though a transfer does in fact occur. (This leaves out of account the case where I intend to transfer the property to you, but my intention is vitiated. As we shall see in section 17.1, however, a trust probably does not arise in this case at all, so this creates no difficulty.) This suggestion connects with his Lordship's assertion that resulting trusts, unlike constructive trusts, reflect an intention on my (and your) part to establish a trust: it is only where I intend the transfer in the first place that I have a space in which so to shape its terms. In the vacuum left by the discrediting of that assertion, we might be tempted to fall back on it. While avoiding the problems that the text identifies with that assertion, however, this suggestion takes us nowhere. For in itself, it offers no reason—or, since it involves separating the two categories, reasons—why the trusts in question should arise at all.

It is suggested that the best answer runs as follows. The transferee of some property should hold it on trust for the transferor, aside from the case where the transferor so stipulates, whenever the transferor has not demonstrably chosen to give his property away and succeeded in doing so. This idea is in turn justified by the insight that whenever someone has not demonstrably chosen to give his property away and succeeded in doing so, he should remain its owner. Call the latter insight 'proprietary inertia'.

Proprietary inertia is rooted in a liberal vision of the institution of property. To give an owner maximal freedom in the disposition of his assets, it is necessary maximally to treat them as for him alone to dispose of.[31] Proprietary inertia operates in its simplest form where the owner in no sense loses his title: if you steal my pen, say, it merely remains mine.[32] But the insight operates also in the more complex case, generated by the possibilities of the trust device, where the legal title has effectively been transferred; but its previous owner has neither (intentionally and successfully) conferred beneficial ownership on the transferee nor (likewise) alienated it in some other direction.[33] The logic of the insight is that in such a situation the previous owner should be treated as himself retaining beneficial ownership. This desideratum is achieved in the face of the effective transfer, by ruling that the transferee of the legal title holds it on trust for the previous owner.[34]

16.5 PROPRIETARY INERTIA AND THE CASES OF RESULTING TRUSTS

The resulting trust that arises in the case of an incomplete express trust is readily explained in terms of proprietary inertia. If I transfer property

---

[31] If there were no rivals to this liberal theory, we would not accept the possibility of property being lost to its previous owner in any other way. But in the real world considerations ascribable to other theories call for this and are accepted. For example, we have to pay taxes even if we do not wish to, in causes broadly perceivable as utilitarian or communitarian. Statements of the proprietary inertia insight should be read as aimed only at the sphere governed by liberal theory.

[32] For this as the central case of proprietary inertia, the resulting trust being an extension from it, see *Re Vandervell's Trusts (No 2)* [1974] Ch 269, 290, Megarry J: 'Whether a legal estate, an equitable interest or anything else, what a man fails to dispose of remains his... [I]f the owner of a legal estate or interest... fails to dispose of anything at all, no question of any resulting trust can arise.'

[33] The text says 'alienated it in some other direction', rather than simply 'conferred it on someone else', to allow for the possibility of a purpose trust, charitable or otherwise.

[34] J Penner in C Mitchell (ed) *Constructive and Resulting Trusts* (2010) ch 8, 257–66 adopts what appears to be a substantially similar vision, while developing and describing it in rather different terms. Cf J Mee *ibid* ch 7; see n 45 below.

to you on an incomplete express trust, there exists, to the extent of the incompleteness, a situation of my not intentionally and successfully having given my property away. The insight's corollary, that I should to that extent remain the owner, is achieved by the imposition of a resulting trust.[35]

The resulting trust arising in the case of a gratuitous transfer is more problematic. Remember the three views of it set out in section 16.3. On the second and third views, we again encounter proprietary inertia. On the second, although I (the transferor) have transferred the property to you (the transferee), it is presumed that I do not intend you to have it for your own benefit (or for anyone else's). Other than to the extent of transferring the legal title, therefore, I have not chosen to give my property away and succeeded in doing so, and the ensuing trust for me can be explained as responding to that. On the third view, I transfer the property to you with, having no discoverable successful intentions on the subject, no reason for doing so. When it is said that I have 'no reason' for making the transfer, the message is not that we know it to be a gift, though nobody can understand why I should have made it. The stipulation that I have 'no discoverable successful intentions' for my transfer means rather that we have no warrant for treating it as a gift or any other form of beneficial transfer. Once again, then, except to the extent of transferring the legal title to you, I have not chosen to give my property away and succeeded in doing so; producing a situation of proprietary inertia, to which the resulting trust is the response. By contrast, however, in the first view regarding 'gratuitous transfer' trusts, the basis of the trust is my presumed intention that you should hold the property on trust for me. In this vision, my actions are fully accounted for, leaving no space within which to say I have not chosen to give my property away and succeeded in doing so. The trust is not, therefore, the product of proprietary inertia.

To assess the match between 'gratuitous transfer' resulting trusts and proprietary inertia, we thus need to take a position between these three views. Each has a degree of support in the case law.[36] Rather than trying

---

[35] Except where the express trust is charitable, when (unless the failure was initial and there was no general charitable intent) the property is instead applied cy près, ie to an analogous charitable purpose: see sections 6.1, 10.6. This departure from the liberally based proprietary inertia thesis can be explained on the utilitarian and/or communitarian grounds to which charitable trusts especially appeal: see section 6.2.

[36] See in particular W Swadling (2008) 124 LQR 72; R Chambers *Resulting Trusts* (1997) ch 1; J Penner in C Mitchell (ed) *Constructive and Resulting Trusts* (2010) ch 8, 241–57; R Chambers *Ibid* ch 9, 276–85. There is of course variability in the extent to which these reflect *Westdeutsche Landesbank Girozentrale v Islington LBC* [1996] AC 669 itself.

to adjudicate between them on that score, then, we should consider their sustainability in principle. Unfortunately, they all present difficulties.

The first view certainly appears historically authentic, reflecting the commonest intention actually held by those making gratuitous transfers, generally of land, in the late Middle Ages and for a time afterwards.[37] This view is otherwise beset with difficulties, however. The intention it presumes no longer rings true; to us, a gratuitous transfer is overwhelmingly likely to be meant as a gift. Further,[38] on this view, we must presume not only the intention described, but also the expression of that intention alongside the transfer: an unexpressed intention cannot generate a trust. Yet it will always be possible to prove that there was no such expression, for if it were otherwise, we should not be thinking in terms of a resulting trust in the first place. If we do succeed in surmounting this problem, moreover, a trust arising in this way is (as noted in section 16.3) more 'express' than 'resulting', and so does not merit the special formalities treatment accorded to resulting trusts, introduced by the Statute of Frauds 1677 and re-enacted in s 53(2) of the Law of Property Act 1925. We should feel justified in rejecting this view, therefore.

The second view escapes the latter objections, but proposes an even less plausible presumption as to a gratuitous transferor's intentions. It is certainly possible that someone should gratuitously transfer property to another with no successful intentions at all as to its beneficial destination; indeed, incomplete express trusts involve just such a state of affairs. It does, however, seem extraordinary to *presume* this characterization of gratuitous transfers, both because, once again, they are in fact generally gifts, and because the state of mind proposed is so nihilistic.[39] It too seems unacceptable, therefore.

The difficulty with the third view is substantial, but quite different. This view escapes all the objections discussed so far, but only because it envisages *no presumption at all* as to the transferor's intentions. In contrast to the second view, it makes no claim that, in making a gratuitous transfer, I probably had no intentions as to the transfer's purport. It merely states

[37] See A Simpson *A History of the Land Law* 2nd edn (1986) 77–9.

[38] See J Penner in C Mitchell (ed) *Constructive and Resulting Trusts* (2010) ch 8, 249–56; R Chambers *ibid* ch 9, 279–80.

[39] There is, however, a way in which one or other of the first two views might be supported, despite their practical implausibility. As explained in section 3.7, the presumption may reflect, not a likely real intention, but some non-facilitative predilection, such as paternalism, or dynasticism. (If the presumption is viewed in this way, too, the ensuing trust is arguably not express, removing the worry about its relationship with the formality rules.) Unfortunately, however, on this view of the presumption, there is once again scant modern reason to accept it at all, in either the first or the second form.

the obvious: that, in the event that no successful intentions can be found on my part concerning the purport of my transfer (whether it should benefit you, or someone else, or me, or no one), I must be taken to have made the transfer without any purport. But whilst the third view is thus saved from the embarrassments besetting the other two views, the rule it describes is simultaneously left in search of a reason to be called a 'presumption' at all. The proposed reconciliation is that the 'presumption' is not of an intention on the part of the transferor at all, as the first and second views take it, but of the trust that arises in the event of a purport-less gratuitous transfer itself.[40] In other words, when we say that the trust is 'presumed', we mean simply that, in the relevant circumstances, it is imposed, by the law. This is not a very satisfactory usage of the word 'presumed', but neither is it impossible, and it does correspond to the way that the judges themselves sometimes use it.[41]

The third view thus appears to emerge as the best of an unhappy lot. As already noted, this view clearly allows the trusts it describes to be seen as the product of proprietary inertia: if I gratuitously transfer property to you without known purport, I have, obviously, not demonstrably chosen to give my property away and succeeded in doing so. So both the two most familiar types of resulting trusts—those arising in the case of an incomplete express trust, and of a gratuitous transfer that cannot be shown to have any other purport—can be understood in terms of the proprietary inertia analysis.

That analysis also, however, accounts for, and so suggests that we regard as resulting trusts too, the trusts arising in 'unsatisfactory transfer' cases—which, as we saw in section 16.2, Lord Browne-Wilkinson declines, contrary to earlier authority, to accept as resulting trusts, though he does accept them as constructive trusts. Remember that such trusts arise where the law treats me as having transferred property to you despite my having no intention to do so, as where my land is, without my knowledge, re-registered in your name; where I do intend to transfer the property, but the transfer is impermissible; and to some extent also where I intentionally transfer property to you, but my intention is impaired by mistake, duress, misrepresentation or the like. It seems clear that the basis on which such trusts arise is that I did not intentionally and successfully confer the benefit of the property on you, or in any other quarter—that

---

[40] See R Chambers in C Mitchell (ed) *Constructive and Resulting Trusts* (2010) ch 9, 278–9, 280–5.

[41] See eg *Sayre v Hughes* (1868) LR 5 Eq 376, 380; *Re Vandervell's Trusts (No 2)* [1974] Ch 269, 294.

is, once again, proprietary inertia—meaning that they are properly to be seen as resulting trusts. But given Lord Browne-Wilkinson's characterization of them as constructive, further discussion of them is postponed to section 17.1, where we begin to look at the different kinds of constructive trust. Although thus inelegant from a viewpoint internal to the category of resulting trusts, his Lordship's position poses no fundamental problem for the present analysis, which regards resulting trusts as a species of constructive trusts anyway.

16.6 PROPRIETARY INERTIA: FURTHER EXPLANATION

The proprietary inertia analysis proposed here was developed from two other suggestions as to the basis for resulting trusts. These other suggestions, however, have certain problems, which the proprietary inertia insight is designed to avoid.

The first of these other suggestions is the 'proprietary arithmetic' thesis, developed by Hackney.[42] According to it, a resulting trust arises because a transferor of property necessarily (as a matter of 'arithmetic') retains so much of the beneficial entitlement to it as he has not given away (by giving it absolutely to the transferee, or by establishing a complete express trust of it). Operating at the level of legal doctrine, this formulation is problematic in the way it presents a beneficial interest as existing in the settlor's hands even before the transfer, ie at the time when he was absolute legal owner. The contrary view, that beneficial interests exist as the correlatives of trustees' duties[43] and so cannot exist before the transfer to the resulting trustee, is more generally favoured.[44] The proprietary inertia insight avoids this difficulty. Operating at the level of political theory, this insight merely observes that I should not be taken to have conferred benefits in other quarters except by voluntary disposition, and to the extent that I am not so taken, I should be treated as remaining owner myself. It is indifferent whether the legal modalities aimed at achieving this conceive me as remaining beneficial owner throughout,

---

[42] J Hackney *Understanding Equity and Trusts* (1987) 153–4. [43] See section 12.2.
[44] See eg *Commissioner of Stamp Duties (Queensland) v Livingston* [1965] AC 694, 712; *Westdeutsche Landesbank Girozentrale v Islington LBC* [1996] AC 669, 706. So in *DKLR Holding Co (No 2) Pty Ltd v Commissioner of Stamp Duties* (1982) 40 ALR 1, Australia, where, unusually, it made a practical difference (for tax reasons) whether the resulting trust interest remained in the transferor throughout or arose by detraction from the transferee, the court held the latter.

or, in accordance with the prevailing view, as newly becoming beneficial owner when the occasion arises.[45]

The second of the suggestions from which the proprietary inertia analysis derives is principally the work of Chambers.[46] It portrays resulting trusts as generated by a lack of intention on the part of a transferor that the transferee should have the benefit of the property transferred.[47] Thus, one who transfers property to a trustee on an incomplete express trust does not intend the trustee to have the undisposed-of benefit; and one who makes a gratuitous transfer is either to be presumed not to intend the recipient to enjoy the property beneficially (the second view regarding the 'gratuitous transfer' case, explained in sections 16.3 and 16.5),[48] or, making no such presumption but if in fact we simply have no information as to his intentions, by definition does not intend the recipient to enjoy the property beneficially (the third, and on the whole preferable, view).[49]

The similarity between Chambers's account and the proprietary inertia thesis is clear: the former talks of the owner 'not intending the transferee to have the benefit' of the property, while the latter talks of the owner of property 'not voluntarily conferring the benefit' of it in another quarter. The proprietary inertia thesis is, however, preferable for two reasons. First, because it is more explicit about *why* this situation should generate a resulting trust (because to the extent that the owner has not conferred the benefit of the property elsewhere, it should remain his), and about the basis upon which we should agree that in turn to be the case (the

---

[45] J Mee in C Mitchell (ed) *Constructive and Resulting Trusts* (2010) ch 7, 214–21 objects to the proprietary arithmetic thesis in a subtler way. While sensitively noting that the transferor has traditionally been portrayed as 'retaining' his pre-transfer interest, as proposed by the proprietary arithmetic thesis, he points out that this interest *differs* in certain details from his interest as beneficiary of a resulting trust, on account of how trusts operate. (This observation resonates with eg *Nelson v Greening & Sykes (Builders) Ltd* [2007] EWCA 1358, [49]–[58], see section 5.7; and especially the minority position in *Baker v Archer-Shee* [1927] AC 844, see section 12.3.) For the reason given in the text, however, the proprietary inertia analysis is undisturbed by this objection too. If I do not intentionally and successfully give away my property, it ought to remain mine. If the law nonetheless passes it to you, a resulting trust arises so as bring about—strictly, to come *as close as the trust device allows* to bringing about—that it does so.

[46] R Chambers *Resulting Trusts* (1997) (see further R Chambers in A Burrows and A Rodger (eds) *Mapping the Law—Essays in Memory of Peter Birks* (2006) ch 13). Chambers's analysis owes much in turn to P Birks in S Goldstein (ed) *Equity and Contemporary Legal Developments* (1992) 335.

[47] This view was adopted by the Privy Council in *Air Jamaica Ltd v Charlton* [1999] 1 WLR 1399, 1412, and by the Court of Appeal in *Twinsectra Ltd v Yardley* [1999] Lloyd's Rep Bank 438, 457, and might therefore be considered to represent the current law. But those decisions made no reference to the position taken by the House of Lords in *Westdeutsche Landesbank Girozentrale v Islington LBC* [1996] AC 669, described in sections 16.2–16.3, so cannot be regarded as authoritative.   [48] R Chambers *Resulting Trusts* (1997) ch 1.

[49] R Chambers in C Mitchell (ed) *Constructive and Resulting Trusts* (2010) ch 9, 276–85.

liberal vision of property). Secondly, because of its statement that, when I transfer to you, a resulting trust is negatived by my intention to confer the benefit not only on you but also in any other quarter. It is this feature of the thesis that precludes a resulting trust where I transfer property to you as trustee of a complete express trust for some other person(s) or purpose(s). At face value, Chambers's account seems to demand a resulting trust even in the latter situation, for there too I transfer to you, not intending you to take beneficially. That conclusion is unthinkable, of course; the account cannot but be amended accordingly.[50] Unfortunately following the literal terms of the account, however, the Privy Council has asserted that there is a resulting trust for me wherever I transfer property to you and do not intend you to have it, even despite an intention on my part to abandon my interest, ie to relinquish it as *bona vacantia* to the Crown.[51] Assuming that I am legally able to abandon my interest,[52] the proprietary inertia analysis produces the opposite conclusion: since I intended to confer the benefit in some other quarter,[53] there is no resulting trust.

---

[50] Perhaps we should say that if I transfer property to you to hold on trust for some other person(s) or purpose(s), the beneficial entitlement is not part of that which I transfer to you, so it cannot result to me. But this approach seems to assume that the beneficial entitlement was separate from the legal title in my hands; a conception not generally favoured: see n 44 above.

[51] *Air Jamaica Ltd v Charlton* [1999] 1 WLR 1399, 1412. To justify its finding that the transferor had an interest under a resulting trust *at the date of the claim*, moreover, the Privy Council must further have assumed that such an interest cannot be given away after it has arisen. That assumption is contradicted by *Re Vandervell's Trusts (No 2)* [1974] Ch 269, where (though there was a difficulty about formality: see section 5.7) there was a successful disposition of an existing resulting trust interest.

[52] Authority (*Re West Sussex Constabulary's Widows, Children and Benevolent (1930) Fund Trusts* [1971] Ch 1) holds that I am, but R Chambers *Resulting Trusts* (1997) 58–66 contends that I am not. The Privy Council did not rely on the latter argument, however.

[53] Note that saying 'I intentionally and successfully confer the benefit in some other quarter; specifically, I abandon it' is not the same as saying 'I would not have wanted a resulting trust if I had thought about it'. The former precludes a resulting trust; the latter does not, either in law (*Re Gillingham Bus Disaster Fund* [1958] Ch 300; *Vandervell v IRC* [1967] 2 AC 291: see text at n 25 above) or in the terms of the proprietary inertia thesis. An inferred case of the former may however sometimes more truthfully consist in the latter: the intention to render the property ownerless in *Re West Sussex Constabulary's Widows, Children and Benevolent (1930) Fund Trusts* [1971] Ch 1 might be seen in this way.

17

Constructive Trusts 2

We turn finally to consider a number of the situations in which a constructive trust occurs in English law, and the grounds on which it does so. On account of its volume, this topic is divided between two chapters, this and Chapter 18. As will be seen, the constructive trusts considered in the present chapter arise on one of two bases (liberal property theory, via its predicates proprietary inertia and *nemo dat quod non habet*; and a concern to counteract the 'principal–agent problem' besetting agency, trusts, and similar otherwise useful devices, and an analogous problem arising between a vendor and a purchaser especially of land); while those considered in Chapter 18 arise principally on one of two other bases (a concern to protect someone who will otherwise have been irretrievably prejudiced by relying on another's word; and the implications of family relationships).[1] The division is, however, one of convenience only. Chapter 18 also contains a section (section 18.5) considering the duties that apply to trustees of constructive, and also resulting, trusts.

17.1 UNSATISFACTORY TRANSFERS

Sections 16.4–16.6 developed the idea of 'proprietary inertia', whereby if I own some property, and do not demonstrably choose to give it away and succeed in doing so, I should remain its owner.[2] Usually, there is no more to be said. If you snatch my book, for example, it simply remains mine. Sometimes, though, the law rules that you do become owner of the property, but gives expression to proprietary inertia instead by going on to say that you hold the property on trust for me.

---

[1] Beyond these, there is the goal of vindicating expectations associated with some uses of proprietary estoppel, identified in section 18.4; but, as noted there, it is hard to regard that goal as proper.

[2] There are of course legitimate qualifications to this position, where the law is justified in passing my property to another when I do not so intend: eg if my property has to be taken to pay my debts, or by way of taxation.

We should expect the law to treat all trusts ascribable to proprietary inertia alike. In fact, as section 16.2 explained, the governing authority— *Westdeutsche Landesbank Girozentrale v Islington LBC*[3]—divides them into two classes. It gives the label 'resulting trusts' to those arising in the 'incomplete express trust' and 'gratuitous transfer' scenarios, ie those arising where I make you trustee of the property, but without effectively stipulating for whom or for what; and where I transfer the property to you by way of neither sale nor loan, and you cannot prove it to be a gift. In these scenarios, I have definitely transferred the title to the property, but in the one way or the other I have not demonstrably chosen to give it away beneficially, so ought to remain its owner to that extent. On the other hand, where proprietary inertia requires a trust in any other case, that trust is labelled a 'constructive trust'. This chapter being about constructive trusts, we shall avoid further allusion to the former class, but shall explore the latter.

In section 16.2 we referred to this residual context as the 'unsatisfactory transfer' case. Its characteristic is that (to quote section 16.2) 'the very transfer of the property is unsatisfactory in some way, such that, although it has technically taken place—ie the transferee has indeed become the owner of the property—we, and the law, prefer to say that it has not, by reckoning that the transferee holds the property on trust for the transferor.[4] Such a situation may occur where the transferor does not intend to transfer the property at all...; where he does intend to transfer the property, but the transfer is impermissible; and to some extent also where he does intend to transfer the property, but there is something wrong with that intention...' This description now requires elaboration.

Let us begin with the instance where the transferor does not intend to transfer the property at all, yet the law treats him as having done so, while nonetheless acknowledging the unsatisfactoriness of this by saying that the transferee holds on trust for him. Say you steal my coins. Normally, you will not become their owner at all—that is, proprietary inertia operates in its simplest manner. But if you go on to mix the coins with your own, ownership does pass from me to you. As it is impossible to say which of the coins came from me, the law holds that I can no longer claim to be their owner; so you are.[5] The result is thus a technical but unintended

---

[3] [1996] AC 669, 708, 716.

[4] *Ryall v Ryall* (1739) 1 Atk 59; *Lane v Dighton* (1762) Amb 409; *Agip (Africa) Ltd v Jackson* [1990] Ch 265, 290; *El Ajou v Dollar Land Holdings plc* [1993] 3 All ER 717, 734; perhaps *Hodgson v Marks* [1971] Ch 892, 933.

[5] Though L Smith *The Law of Tracing* (1997) 162–71 argues that this reading of the key decision (*Taylor v Plumer* (1815) 3 M & S 562) is wrong, and that I can in fact assert ownership of a proportionate part of the mixture.

transfer. The law imposes a constructive trust, to the effect that you hold
the mixture on trust for yourself and me in proportion to the value of our
contributions to the mixture.[6] Or say you procure, without my knowledge,
that my land is re-registered in your name. The register is conclusive as to
ownership, so again there is a technical but unintended transfer. You hold
the land on constructive trust for me.[7]

Now consider the two instances where I transfer property to you intentionally. In the instance where my intention is vitiated, ie flawed—say
because I acted mistakenly, or under duress or undue influence or in certain other similar circumstances[8]—the flawed quality of my intention is
recognized by a rule allowing me to rescind the transfer, ie reverse its
effects. If I do so, proprietary inertia logic becomes applicable, since the
foundation for your acquisition of the property—my intention—has now
been removed. So although you for the moment still hold the legal title
to the transferred property, you hold it on constructive trust for me. And
that trust appears to operate retrospectively, so that you are treated as having held the property on trust for me from the outset.[9] By the same token,
if I transfer property to you intentionally but the law treats the transfer,
though nominally effective, as impermissible to the extent that it should
never have occurred,[10] it seems logical that you should hold the property

---

[6] *Westdeutsche Landesbank Girozentrale v Islington LBC* [1996] AC 669, 716. There, however, the trust is analysed in terms not of proprietary inertia, but of your fraud. This analysis
is doubtful. It would leave the case as one of the type discussed below, where I do intend to
pass the property but my intention is flawed. This does not accurately capture what happens
in the theft scenario, and also, in imposing a constructive trust immediately, would contravene
the rule regarding the 'flawed intention' case stated at n 8 below. See *Shalson v Russo* [2005]
Ch 281, [109]–[117].

[7] *Collings v Lee* [2001] 2 All ER 332. (At 336 it is said, 'whether the trust should be characterised as implied, resulting or constructive is a matter of no importance'; but we are treating
it as constructive for the reasons given in section 16.2.) The previous owner was in fact duped
into transferring the land into the transferee's name. The court treated this as showing that
the previous owner lacked any intention to transfer to the transferee, and that is how the case is
treated in the text. But it would also have been possible to say that the transfer to the transferee
was intended, but that that intention was flawed, making the case of the type discussed below.
Consider also *Lawrence v Metropolitan Police Commissioner* [1972] AC 626; *DPP v Gomez*
[1993] AC 442; *R v Hinks* [2001] 2 AC 241, where theft was committed when the thief dishonestly induced the victim to transfer the property. The victim certainly had an intention to
transfer; it is unclear whether this intention was legally regarded as vitiated; but the fact that
theft was committed may suggest that a constructive trust should have arisen anyway.

[8] See further C Rotherham *Proprietary Remedies in Context* (2002) ch 6.

[9] So, for example, I collect any profits you have meanwhile made from it (section 17.4),
and can trace through any mixture you may have made with it (section 17.5): *El Ajou v Dollar
Land Holdings plc* [1993] 3 All ER 717, 734 (the trust being there referred to as resulting, but
we are treating it as constructive for the reasons given in section 16.2); *Shalson v Russo* [2005]
Ch 281, [121]–[127].

[10] Such a transfer is sometimes described as 'void', but 'void' more normally denotes the
situation where the purported transfer is wholly ineffective. As indicated in the text, we are

on constructive trust for me.[11] This too is the result of proprietary inertia. Remember the statement of proprietary inertia offered in section 16.4: 'The transferee of some property should hold it on trust for the transferor, aside from the case where the transferor so stipulates, whenever the transferor has not demonstrably chosen to give his property away and succeeded in doing so.' If my transfer to you, while intended and nominally effective, is impermissible to this extent, I have not 'succeeded' in giving my property away.

There is, however, controversy over the position, in the instance where I have a vitiated intention, during the period *before* (or indeed, unless) I rescind. The prevailing judicial view is that you do not yet hold the transferred property on trust for me.[12] But an argument has been made to the contrary: that even without rescission, a flawed intention should be regarded as no intention, producing a straightforwardly unintended transfer and so, for reasons of proprietary inertia, a constructive trust.[13] The issue at stake here is this. If—contrary to the authorities—such a trust were to arise whenever I have a flawed intention, regardless of rescission, it would essentially arise in most of the core cases in which you owe me a restitutionary liability: those where I transfer property to you in circumstances such that you are unjustly enriched thereby. The result would

---

concerned rather with the situation where the transfer is *nominally* effective, ie the transferee becomes the legal owner of the property in question, but a constructive trust arises so as to reverse this.

[11] This was the position in *Westdeutsche Landesbank Girozentrale v Islington LBC* [1996] AC 669 itself. The transfer was intended and nominally effective, but was *ultra vires* the transferor, a local authority. The transferor sought to reclaim the property in question on the basis that it was therefore held by the transferee on resulting trust, but failed: as explained in section 16.2, 'resulting trusts' were treated as arising only in 'incomplete express trust' and 'gratuitous transfer' cases, and the present facts represented neither of these. No claim was made on the basis of a constructive trust (*ibid* 703), so the decision does not stand against the position taken in the text.

[12] *Guinness plc v Saunders* [1990] 2 AC 663, 698; *Lonrho plc v Fayed (No 2)* [1992] 1 WLR 1, 11–12; *Collings v Lee* [2001] 2 All ER 332, 337; *Twinsectra Ltd v Yardley* [2002] 2 AC 164, [91]; *Shalson v Russo* [2005] Ch 281, [106]–[119]; P Millett (1998) 114 LQR 399, 402, 413. *Westdeutsche Landesbank Girozentrale v Islington LBC* [1996] AC 669, 689–90, 709, 718, 720, 738 appears to like effect. To the contrary effect, however, is *Chase Manhattan Bank NA v Israel-British Bank (London) Ltd* [1981] Ch 105, approved by Lord Browne-Wilkinson in *Westdeutsche Landesbank Girozentrale v Islington LBC ibid* 715–16, so long as the transferee does or should know of the vitiating circumstance (this being, in his Lordship's view, a precondition for any trust to arise: see section 1.13); but cf *Shalson v Russo* [2005] Ch 281, [118].

[13] P Birks in S Goldstein (ed) *Equity and Contemporary Legal Developments* (1992) 335; R Chambers *Resulting Trusts* (1997) chs 5 and 6 come to this conclusion, via an analysis similar, though not identical, to proprietary inertia, and referring to the trust in question as resulting rather than constructive, a point explored below. See further C Webb in C Mitchell (ed) *Constructive and Resulting Trusts* (2010) ch 11.

be to establish a proprietary obligation as the standard response to unjust enrichment;[14] which would be surprising. Other things being equal, if you receive property from me in the kind of circumstances under discussion, you certainly have to repay me its value.[15] But this obligation is a merely personal one, not carrying the advantages for me (such as priority in your insolvency) of the proprietary obligations associated with trusts.[16] These advantages hold dangers for other parties, especially your other creditors; saying that you hold the transferred asset on constructive trust withdraws it from the pool of your property available for distribution among the latter. Indeed, apparently reflecting such considerations, the law imposes certain limitations on my right to rescind.[17] If any transfer made on the basis of a flawed intention gave rise to a constructive trust, these limitations would be undermined. So it is intuitively understandable, if perhaps not yet fully explained as a matter of principle,[18] that the trust response should be less extensively available, as the authorities insist is the case.

It makes a difference to our thinking about this point, however, that Lord Browne-Wilkinson in *Westdeutsche Landesbank Girozentrale v Islington LBC*[19] insists on treating 'unsatisfactory transfer' trusts as constructive rather than resulting. As we saw in section 16.5, such trusts share the same basis—proprietary inertia—as the trusts that arise in 'incomplete express trust' and 'gratuitous transfer' cases, and so could well have been grouped together with these, as resulting trusts. Lord Browne-Wilkinson's position seems to have been influenced by the thought that, as constructive trusts, they might be *remedial* constructive trusts,[20] ie applicable by the courts discretionarily—there being no tradition of discretion in resulting trusts. In particular, this would allow their impact on third parties, such

---

[14] See P Birks *Unjust Enrichment* 2nd edn (2005) ch 8.

[15] On mistaken payments, for example, see *Morgan v Ashcroft* [1938] 1 KB 49; *Barclays Bank Ltd v W J Simms (Southern) Ltd* [1980] QB 677; *Kleinwort Benson Ltd v Lincoln City Council* [1999] 2 AC 349.   [16] See sections 1.9, 12.1.

[17] For example, an unexercised right to rescind will lapse if the transferor, knowing of the flaw, concedes the transaction's effectiveness, or delays unacceptably ('is guilty of laches') in rescinding it. In some circumstances, the right will not be exercisable if a court regards monetary redress to the transferor as adequate remedy (Misrepresentation Act 1967 s 2(2)). And it will be ineffective not only (like a constructive trust) against a bona fide purchaser for value of a legal interest in the property transferred, but (except if the property is registered land: Land Registration Act 2002 s 116) also against such a purchaser of an equitable right in the property: *Phillips v Phillips* (1861) 4 De GF & J 208; *Latec Investments Ltd v Hotel Terrigal Pty Ltd* (1965) 113 CLR 265, Australia (cf D O'Sullivan (2002) 118 LQR 296).

[18] Compare C Rotherham *Proprietary Remedies in Context* (2002) 149–52; B Häcker [2009] CLJ 324; C Webb in C Mitchell (ed) *Constructive and Resulting Trusts* (2010) ch 11, 328–32.

[19] [1996] AC 669, 708, 716.

[20] [1996] AC 669, 716. For remedial constructive trusts, see sections 15.3–15.5.

as creditors, to be mediated as might seem appropriate in the individual case. This, in turn, would facilitate their extension into the mainstream restitutionary area just discussed. By contrast, the argument that trusts arise in all 'unsatisfactory transfer' cases—including those comprising the mainstream restitutionary area—is made especially by commentators who simultaneously insist that such trusts should be seen as resulting.[21] In coupling these two positions, these commentators may seek to ensure that the law of restitution is conducted on a non-discretionary basis. They may favour this on account of political predilections, of the kinds identified in section 15.5, against remedial constructive trusts in general.[22] The holding of such predilections is understandable, but it needs to be recognized that, as Lord Browne-Wilkinson saw, they make it the more difficult to accept proprietary relief for unjust enrichment at all.

17.2 RECEIPT OF ILLICITLY TRANSFERRED TRUST PROPERTY

Say I, a trustee for Adam, acting outside my authority,[23] transfer the trust's assets to you. Unless you are a bona fide purchaser of them for value and without notice of their provenance, you in turn will hold them on constructive trust for Adam.[24]

As we saw in section 12.1, all trusts have some proprietary obligations, which affect persons who take the property to which those obligations relate in the way that you do here. These proprietary obligations include the duty to respect the fact that the property is not beneficially your own. To say that you take the property on a constructive trust is simply another way of expressing this.

---

[21] See especially P Birks in S Goldstein (ed) *Equity and Contemporary Legal Developments* (1992) 335; R Chambers *Resulting Trusts* (1997) chs 5 and 6.

[22] See especially P Birks in P Birks (ed) *The Frontiers of Liability Volume 2* (1994) ch 16, and (1998) 12 TLI 202.

[23] That is (see section 12.1), I transfer the assets to you neither as a proper recipient of the property in question (notably, a beneficiary), nor in circumstances that overreach the trust, ie fall within my authority to treat the assets as investments, selling them and buying others in their place (see section 7.4).

[24] According to Lord Browne-Wilkinson in *Westdeutsche Landesbank Girozentrale v Islington LBC* [1996] AC 669, 707, this situation is only to be termed a 'trust' if you are aware that I held the property on trust, but that view is doubtful: see section 1.13. His Lordship accepts that a recipient lacking such awareness does not simply become absolute owner; in his view, in this (innominate) situation the recipient may not treat the property as his own, ie must give it up if called upon to do so.

The basis of this constructive trust is the reflection that I cannot give you more than I have myself, often put in the Latin form, '*nemo dat quod non habet*'. If in my hands the assets have a set of obligations attached to them, which is what it means to say that those obligations are proprietary,[25] I cannot give the assets to you shorn of those obligations, because in that form the assets are not mine to give.[26] The reflection is rooted in liberal property theory, to which we have already made reference.[27] The obligations attached to the assets reflect other interests existing in them.[28] Letting me deal with the assets only to the extent that they are mine respects the monopoly over the disposal of those interests that the liberal vision of property accords *their* owner(s).

But note that you will not be bound, ie a constructive trust will not arise in this way, if you are a bona fide purchaser of the property in question, for value, and without notice of its being trust property transferred without authority.[29] Then, you cannot be affected by trust obligations relating to the property. Left vulnerable to the constructive trust are those who buy with notice of their purchase's provenance; and those who take the property as a gift ('volunteers'), whether they have notice or not. But those who buy trust property innocently are protected. This rule is of course logically incompatible with the proposition that I cannot give you more than I have myself. The fact that the transferee is a bona fide purchaser does not alter the transferring trustees' inability to transfer the property shorn of its proprietary obligations. It is explicable on the ground that the liberal vision underlying the usual rule can be overridden where more powerful considerations so require: and here a more powerful consideration, namely a desire to facilitate trade (by removing traps from the path of the bona fide purchaser), does so require.

If the original trust was an express trust, is the trust under discussion really a constructive trust, as asserted here; or are you, the recipient, simply bound by the original express trust? Certainly, the reason you are a trustee is that, when you acquired the property, you incurred the obligation to hold it on trust, which obligation sprang—in this case—from the original settlor's intention. So to that extent, the trust against you can sensibly be

---

[25] See sections 1.9, 12.1.   [26] *Re Nisbet and Potts' Contract* [1906] 1 Ch 386.

[27] See sections 2.2, 16.4.

[28] In section 12.1 we struggled to see why trust obligations should be proprietary; before, in section 12.3, speculating that it might be because such obligations traditionally reflected (equitable) ownership on the part of the beneficiaries: the beneficiaries' ownership necessarily connoting that the assets are not the trustees' to give away.

[29] For 'notice', see *Sinclair Investments (UK) Ltd v Versailles Trade Finance Ltd (in administrative receivership)* [2010] EWHC 1614 (Ch), [82]–[98].

regarded as express.[30] On the other hand, you do not simply substitute for me as trustee of the express trust. A legitimately substituted trustee of the original express trust would take over all the obligations that I previously had. That is, if (as is normal) I had an obligation to manage and invest the trust property, and if (as is very common) I had an obligation to exercise discretions,[31] a substituted trustee would take over those obligations, as well as the basic obligation to treat the property not as his own but as the trust's. In the context we are discussing, however, that would be an inappropriate outturn, as you were not selected to undertake the trusteeship by reference to your suitability to carry out those obligations, as an express trustee, whether original or substitute, would be.[32] And indeed, it is thought that such obligations are personal, so that the (proprietary) obligations by which you are affected are only those of respecting the fact that the property is not beneficially your own and of keeping it safe pending the transfer, either to the beneficiaries or to freshly appointed trustees, that you may be called upon to make.[33] Regarding the trust against you as constructive reflects this discontinuity with the original express trust.[34]

17.3 PERMITTED ACQUISITIONS BY FIDUCIARIES

A fiduciary who is authorized to receive property on his principal's behalf, and who does so, will hold it on constructive trust for the principal.

The idea of a fiduciary was introduced in section 1.10. Remember that a fiduciary is someone—such as a solicitor, stockbroker, employee, agent, company director, business partner, or (at any rate express) trustee—whose role is to serve the interests of another. A person who finds himself in the role of fiduciary incurs duties designed to put detail into the idea of 'serve the interests of another'.[35] One of these duties dictates that where

---

[30] Sometimes, however, the original trust will be constructive. Then, there will be no reason to doubt that the trust against you is also constructive.

[31] See Chs 7 and 9 respectively.   [32] Cf section 11.8.   [33] See section 12.1.

[34] Cf L Smith in P Birks and A Pretto (eds) *Breach of Trust* (2002) ch 5.

[35] According to J Edelman (2010) 126 LQR 302 this is an incorrect way of putting the matter. Rather, he regards a fiduciary's duties—such as that described in the text, and also in section 17.4—as arising where they are voluntarily undertaken by someone (whether expressly or impliedly), who in consequence becomes 'a fiduciary'. This view may be questioned, however. First, because it seems at least artificial to regard some who are known to be fiduciaries as voluntarily undertaking that position: see eg *English v Dedham Vale Properties Ltd* [1978] 1 WLR 93, where one who purported to act on behalf of another, without in fact being appointed by the latter to do so, was held a fiduciary; *M(K) v M(H)* [1992] 3 SCR 6, Canada, where a parent was treated as a fiduciary for his child. Secondly, because it is fanciful to see even those who

the fiduciary acquires property on behalf of his principal, he will hold it on trust for the latter.

There are two situations in which a fiduciary might, with authorization, acquire property on his principal's behalf. One is where he already holds property on trust for the principal (which many, though not all, fiduciaries do: trustees themselves, for example), and then that property yields some proceeds ('fruits'), which too come into his hands. He will hold those proceeds likewise on trust. Say the assets of a trust, held by the trustee, comprise some company shares. If a dividend is paid on those shares, it will come to the trustee as the holder of the shares; and he will hold it on trust in the same way. Or say the trustee sells the shares, something that trustees are normally authorized to do. The money he receives (and anything in which he reinvests it, such as new shares) will likewise be held on trust. The original trust may have been express or constructive (a secret trust, for example), but the trust of the proceeds will be constructive. The trust arises not, like an express trust, because the person transferring the property to the trustee so intends (this may or may not be the case), but because of the fiduciary's obligation to receive the property for his principal.

The other situation of this kind is where the fiduciary is authorized to receive, on his principal's behalf, property which the principal would otherwise have had to receive directly. An agent arranging the sale of his principal's goods will commonly be authorized also to receive the buyer's payment for them, for example. In some cases, the fiduciary's terms of engagement leave him to treat the incoming property as his own, and thus to mix it with his own property, eg by running a single bank account, with liability only to reimburse the principal its value. Because in this instance the fiduciary has no duties regarding the use of the particular property received on the principal's behalf, there is no trust of it.[36] In other cases, however, the fiduciary will be required to treat the property as the principal's, and so, in particular, not to mix it with his own. Here he will have duties regarding the particular property, and a trust does

---

enter voluntarily into fiduciary roles as always—necessarily, on Edelman's view—voluntarily undertaking the duties in question, especially the controversially onerous anti-distraction duties (see section 11.10) and obligation to account (sections 13.3–13.8). It is easier to see these duties as imposed by the law for policy reasons: in particular, as explained below and in those other sections, so as to facilitate the use of agents, trusts, etc, by countering the principal–agent problem that could otherwise arise. Hence the position taken in the text.

[36] This will usually be the sensible construction where incoming payments are expected to fund continued trading by the agent; saying that he holds them on trust would destroy the necessary liquidity: *King v Hutton* [1899] 2 QB 555, [1900] 2 QB 504.

arise. For example, say I sell my house. The purchase money normally comes not directly to me, but to my solicitor. The solicitor is expected not merely to reimburse me, but to treat the money in question as mine. So he will, after making certain deductions,[37] hold it on constructive trust for me.[38]

This constructive trust reflects the fiduciary's duty: he is obliged to hold the incoming property for his principal, and the trust means that he does so. The trust can also be understood by reference to the fiduciary's duty to account. As explained in section 13.8, if a fiduciary takes for himself property that he ought to take for his principal, the latter can choose to ignore the breach and assert that the fiduciary holds the property for him after all. So here, if the fiduciary receiving property on his principal's account were to try to take it for himself, the principal could—and doubtless would—claim it after all: so reproducing the rule under discussion. To point this out is hardly to explain the rule, however; merely to notice (with relief) its convergence with another rule covering the same ground. The explanation, of both rules therefore, is that they form part of the law's response to the 'principal–agent problem' that besets the (otherwise advantageous) use of a fiduciary, as explained in section 1.10. When an agency arrangement or trust leaves a fiduciary to receive property that should in principle be the principal's, the principal is exposed to the risk of potential difficulties in recovering it from the fiduciary, starting with the fact that the principal may not even know of the property's existence or arrival. Unless corrected, this consideration would reduce the attractiveness of using agents and trusts. One way in which the law supplies correction is by ruling that, unless it is arranged otherwise, a payment reaching the fiduciary is immediately held by him on constructive trust for the principal (alias, can be claimed as held on such a trust if the fiduciary tries to have it otherwise).

17.4 WRONGFUL ACQUISITIONS BY FIDUCIARIES

If a fiduciary holds property for his principal (as a trustee does, for his beneficiaries), but wrongfully takes that property for himself, a constructive trust will arise so that he holds it for his principal after all. Say I am your trustee, and hold shares in that capacity. If I wrongfully procure a transfer

---

[37] The sums needed to repay my outstanding mortgage, to meet his own and the estate agent's costs, and to pay for any house I am buying.   [38] *Brown v IRC* [1965] AC 244.

of the shares into my personal name, so that they apparently become mine absolutely, a constructive trust will arise whereby I hold them on trust for you after all.[39]

In this case, the fiduciary wrongfully—that is, in breach of his duty to his principal—acquires property *that he previously held for his principal*. But sometimes, he may wrongfully acquire property *from elsewhere*. Say again that I am trustee for you, but this time that I take a bribe calculated to influence my choice of investments for the trust assets. In doing so, I breach my duty, discussed in section 11.10, not to allow myself to enter into situations where I might be distracted from serving your best interests. Likewise if you are a property developer, and you employ me to seek out suitable sites for you, and in the course of my work I find a site that you might like; the same duty requires me not to buy it for myself without first asking your permission.[40] Or if I am your solicitor and, approaching on your behalf a company in which you are invested, I learn something that suggests that a further investment in the company will be profitable to you; I must not make such an investment with my own money, without first asking your permission.[41] In a case of this kind, I certainly cannot keep any gain I make from my wrongful act. There is no doubt that I must account to you for it, and so pay over to you the amount by which I would otherwise do so. It is controversial, however, whether a constructive trust also arises, whereby I hold the very property in question (the bribe, the development site, the investment) on trust for you. The difference becomes visible if, for example, I go bankrupt, or use the property in question to make further profits. Only if I hold the property on a constructive trust will you take it as such, rather than having to claim alongside my other creditors, or be entitled to those further profits.

The controversy lies in the fact that the authorities point both ways. The net effect of the English decisions—the most prominent being *Lister & Co v Stubbs*[42]—is that in this type of case (that where a fiduciary wrongfully acquires property that he did not previously hold for his principal), there is no constructive trust, only a personal liability to pay over the amount of the gain. On the other hand, the relatively recent decision of the Privy Council in *A-G for Hong Kong v Reid*,[43] applying what the

---

[39] *Ibid.*

[40] *Industrial Development Consultants Ltd v Cooley* [1972] 1 WLR 443 is similar.

[41] *Boardman v Phipps* [1967] 2 AC 46 is similar.

[42] (1890) 45 Ch D 1. Others are reviewed in *Sinclair Investments (UK) Ltd v Versailles Trade Finance Ltd (in administrative receivership)* [2010] EWHC 1614 (Ch), [23]–[80], before it is concluded that, as a matter of precedent, this view represents current English law.

[43] [1994] 1 AC 324.

court considered to be English law, concluded that a constructive trust does indeed arise.

If the English decisions are correct, then, a constructive trust arises where I wrongfully acquire property which I previously held for you, but not where I wrongfully acquire property from elsewhere. It takes little imagination to see this distinction as a likely cause of difficulty, for the crucial question of whether I previously held the property for you does not always yield a clean answer. How, for example, should we see the case where I previously hold property for you, but wrongfully appropriate the fruits of that property to myself? Again, in a decision where a solicitor, approaching on his client's behalf a company in which the latter was invested, acquired information on the basis of which he then made a profitable investment for himself, some of the judges treated the information as itself property which the solicitor held for his client.[44] If this perception is correct, it takes matters across the line between the two kinds of case, so as to entitle the client to a constructive trust when he would otherwise be restricted to a personal remedy. Others of the judges in the decision in fact denied the perception.[45] But the dissension illustrates the potential difficulty of making the point crucial.

In fact, as a matter of conventional doctrinal principle, the two kinds of case should be treated alike, a constructive trust arising in both. In the first kind of case, where the fiduciary's wrong is to take to himself property that he previously held for his principal, the trust arises because, as explained in section 13.8, the principal can treat the fiduciary's otherwise wrongful act as rightful, so turning any acquisition resulting from that act into one made by the fiduciary on the principal's behalf—this result being achieved by the subjection of the acquisition to a constructive trust, in the same manner as was described in section 17.3. In the second kind of case, where the fiduciary's wrong is to allow himself to enter into a situation where he might be distracted from serving his principal's best interests, the same analysis applies, again subjecting any resultant acquisition to a constructive trust.[46] In these terms, then, the view taken by the Privy

---

[44] *Boardman v Phipps* [1967] 2 AC 46, 106–11 (Lord Hodson), and perhaps 102–3 (Lord Cohen). *Quaere* whether an *opportunity* could likewise be viewed as property, so as to say that I benefit from the use of previously held trust property where, in the course of seeking development sites for you, I seize the chance to acquire one for myself.

[45] *Boardman v Phipps* [1967] 2 AC 46, 89–91 (Lord Dilhorne), 127–9 (Lord Upjohn).

[46] See *A-G for Hong Kong v Reid* [1994] 1 AC 324, 337 (though cf at 331 for other, unsatisfactory, reasoning: see S Gardner [1995] CLJ 60); P Millett in S Degeling and J Edelman (eds) *Equity in Commercial Law* (2005) ch 12, 324. For further reflections, see C Rotherham *Proprietary Remedies in Context* (2002) ch 9.

Council in *A-G for Hong Kong v Reid*[47] should therefore be preferred to that representing current English law.

However, this feature of the duty to account itself requires justification. As also explained in section 13.8, it should be seen as a response to the principal–agent problem, aiming to redress the inherent weakness of the position which the principal otherwise occupies *vis-à-vis* the fiduciary, in that the latter has control over the former's property and affairs. The rule generating a constructive trust over any acquisition made under these circumstances, in either kind of case, provides the strongest possible way of doing so, for the effect is that, from the outset, the acquisition belongs not to the fiduciary but to the principal. But whilst thus understandable, the rule may be objectionable from other viewpoints.[48] In particular, as we saw in section 11.10, the duty that the fiduciary breaches in the second kind of case—the duty against distraction—may itself be too hard on fiduciaries,[49] and may even do a disservice to principals, in preventing a useful alignment between principal's interest and the fiduciary's self-interest.[50] If this is the case, enforcing the duty by means of a constructive trust makes matters worse. No such squeamishness seems called for when the acquisition in question is a bribe, however.

17.5 UNAUTHORIZED EXCHANGES AND MIXTURES

Say a trustee holds property on trust[51] for certain objects. Without authorization to do so, he exchanges that property for other assets ('exchange products'), for example by using trust money to buy a car for himself. Or else he mixes it with other property—his own, perhaps, or that of another trust of which he is trustee—in such a way as to make it indistinguishable, for example by paying trust money into a bank account already containing funds of his own.[52] In acting in such ways without authorization, the

---

[47] [1994] 1 AC 324.

[48] See further R Goode (1987) 103 LQR 433, 441–6; P Watts (1994) 110 LQR 178.

[49] Cf *Boardman v Phipps* [1967] 2 AC 46, 124, where Lord Upjohn dissented from a decision that a solicitor had broken his duty to avoid distraction by his own interests, wishing to limit the duty to cases of a 'real sensible possibility of conflict' between the fiduciary's interests and his principal's.   [50] W Bishop and D Prentice (1983) 46 MLR 289.

[51] The trust can be express, resulting, or constructive. So the rules considered in this section can be applied, for example, where a fiduciary exchanges or mixes property that he holds on constructive trust for his principal (see sections 17.3–17.4).

[52] Technically, this involves not only a mixture but also an exchange: the money is paid to the bank, in return for a credit in the trustee's name. Nothing in the present discussion turns on the point.

trustee breaks his duty to safeguard the trust property,[53] and will of course
have to make good any resulting loss, or hand over any profit. However, the
law also rules that he holds the car, or an appropriate part of the mixture,
on constructive trust for the objects of the trust from which the original
property came.[54] (Of course, the objects will want to point to this constructive trust only if the exchange product, or the appropriate part of
the mixture, is worth more than the property used to acquire it, or if the
trustee has become insolvent.[55] Otherwise, they will do better to require
the trustee to make good the loss he has occasioned.)

The objects' ability to claim trust rights over exchange products and
mixtures in this way is known as 'tracing':[56] the objects can 'trace' the
original property into the car, or the appropriate part of the mixture.

It is sometimes asserted that tracing is a matter of finding the asset, if
any, in which the value involved in the original asset is currently located;
the legal treatment of that asset remaining a distinct question, to be
addressed as a separate exercise, labelled 'claiming'.[57] On this view, therefore, this section is wrong to depict tracing as *giving rise to* a (constructive)
trust. The assertion is incoherent, however. To speak of the 'location' of
the 'value' in question makes it sound as though the issue is one of physical topography; but this cannot be other than a metaphor. In truth, the
issue is a normative one: 'value' can be seen as 'located' in a particular
asset—that is, the asset can be made the subject of tracing—whenever this
should be the case. To know whether it should be the case, we must first
establish the reason why we want to know. And that reason is this: we are
considering using some rule to determine the asset's treatment, and need
to say whether the asset is one to which the rule deserves to apply. The
allegedly separate idea of 'claiming' thus contains information crucial to
the determination of the 'location' of the 'value'. In the present context,
we propose to treat the asset as trust property, with all that that entails;[58]

---

[53] See section 7.2. The trustee may be a constructive trustee; the duty to keep the property
safe applies equally to such a person: section 18.5.

[54] Arguably this occurs also when the trustee buys the car on credit, then uses trust money
to repay the debt ('backwards tracing'): L Smith [1995] CLJ 290; cf C Rotherham *Proprietary
Remedies in Context* (2002) 122–5. English law has not unequivocally accepted this argument: *Bishopsgate Investment Management Ltd v Homan* [1995] Ch 211, 217, 221–2; *Foskett v
McKeown* [1998] Ch 265, 283–4, 289, 296.   [55] See sections 1.9, 12.1.

[56] See further L Smith *The Law of Tracing* (1997); C Rotherham *Proprietary Remedies in
Context* (2002) ch 5.

[57] *Boscawen v Bajwa* [1996] 1 WLR 328, 334; *Foskett v McKeown* [2001] 1 AC 102, 128–9;
L Smith *The Law of Tracing* (1997) 10–14.

[58] It might entail any assertion to which it is necessary that the asset be trust property: not
only the standard trust claims, but for example the application of the Theft Act 1968 s 5(2),
determining what counts as a 'theft' of trust property.

so we need to decide whether the asset deserves to be regarded as trust property.[59] The answer is not inevitable. We, and the law, could regard the exchanged or mixed property as simply lost (as we certainly do when the trustee exchanges trust property for something ephemeral, such as a holiday), leaving the objects no alternative but to claim compensation for that loss. To say that, on the contrary, it is possible to trace into the exchange product or the appropriate part of the mixture—ie to say that a constructive trust arises over the latter—we must be able to justify why this should be the case.

The juridically authentic explanation of this constructive trust derives it from the objects' right to an account from the trustee who lost (exchanged or mixed) the original trust property.[60] As explained in section 13.8, this right entitles the objects to adopt the transaction in question as one made by the trustee on their behalf, allowing them to claim the benefit of it by saying that the trustee holds the resultant assets on trust for them. But this understanding takes us no further forward, as then we need to justify why the right to an account should operate in this way. As also explained in section 13.8, the justification seems to be, once again, to counteract the principal–agent problem. The fact that a trustee has legal title to, and usually custody of, the trust assets, but no personal stake in their proper treatment, is a source of vulnerability for the objects. An aspect of that vulnerability is the practical possibility it generates of the trustee improperly exchanging or mixing the trust assets. The strength of the trust device is enhanced if the degree of the vulnerability can be lessened. Rules allowing a trust to be asserted over unauthorized exchange products, or the appropriate part of an unauthorized mixture, have that effect. They bolster the duty to keep the trust property intact in the same way as the rule explained in section 17.4, generating a constructive trust where a fiduciary diverts to himself property that he holds for his principal (and also, correctly speaking, where he wrongfully acquires property from elsewhere). That is, they seek as far as possible to prevent the trustee from gaining from a breach.[61]

---

[59] So if the question of tracing arises in other contexts, the rules might deserve to be the same as those developed here, but that cannot be pre-supposed. Certainly, there is a tradition of tracing by somewhat different rules in certain common law contexts (see L Smith *The Law of Tracing* (1997) 162–74); whether rightly or wrongly, is a matter not relevant to the present discussion.

[60] See *Foskett v McKeown* [2001] 1 AC 102, 130–1; also P Millett in S Degeling and J Edelman (eds) *Equity in Commercial Law* (2005) ch 12, 315. Notice that the argument is incompatible with the view that 'claiming' is separate from 'tracing': it allows the objects to trace precisely by treating them as able to claim the exchange product or mixture.

[61] For a rival explanation, in terms of the trustee's being unjustly enriched at the objects' expense, see A Burrows (2001) 117 LQR 412; P Birks *Unjust Enrichment* 2nd edn (2005)

In principle, then, the traceable property—the exchange product, and the 'appropriate part' of the mixture—comprises (only) that property that would otherwise represent an illicit gain to the trustee.

So far as exchange products are concerned, this idea is simple enough to apply. Say I, who am trustee for you, improperly spend £500 of trust assets on a painting. The trust assets' exchange product is the painting, so I now hold the painting on constructive trust for you.[62] Likewise, if I go on to resell the painting for £5,000, the £5,000 is the exchange product of the painting, so I now hold it on constructive trust for you. In either scenario, you could of course require me to make good the £500 that I took from the trust. But if that were your only recourse against me, leaving me to keep the profit, I would have an incentive to misuse trust property. Treating the painting as trust property bolsters my duty not to do so, and so strengthens the duty's correction of your vulnerability, by removing that incentive in the most thorough possible manner. If however I can resell the painting only for £5, I certainly hold that £5 on trust for you, but as to the remaining £495 that I improperly spent, there is no alternative but to require me to make good the loss: there is no corresponding asset in my hands that can be the subject of a constructive trust.

Rather more needs to be said about the position regarding mixtures.

If the mixture is made up entirely of property drawn from the trustee's trusts, this will of course mean that the whole of it is caught by the constructive trust, and the only question will be how to divide it between the contributing trusts. But if some of the mixture derives from the trustee's own property, the question will be how much of it would otherwise be the trustee's illicit gain. The law in fact normally answers these two questions in the same, quite unsurprising, way, namely: the mixture is treated as belonging to its contributors in proportion to the values of their respective contributions, ie 'pro rata', or '*pari passu*'.[63] Say I mix £500 that I hold on trust for you, with £1,000 of my own money. I will therefore hold the resultant £1,500 on constructive trust, our respective beneficial entitlements reflecting the ratio of our inputs to the mixture. So I am entitled to two thirds, you to one third. Or say I mix £500 that I hold on trust for you, with £1,000 that I hold on trust for Adam. I will hold the resultant £1,500 on constructive trust for you and Adam in the ratio 1:2.

34–7. This explanation might be understood either as replacing that in terms of the objects' right to an account, or as providing another reason why that right should have the shape it does.

[62] *Foskett v McKeown* [2001] 1 AC 102, 130.   [63] *Ibid* 109–10, 130–2.

So long as the value of the mixture is simply the sum of the inputs to it, this rule gives each contributor an entitlement worth the same as his contribution (thus, you get back your £500). But if the mixture rises or falls in value, the rule means that the contributors proportionately share the profits or losses too. The mixture itself could change in value in this way, but more often the question arises as a result of expenditure from the mixture—remember, exchange products belong to the person whose assets were used to acquire them. Say, then, that I take the mixture of £1,500 that I hold in the proportions 1:2 for you and myself, or for you and for Adam, and spend £600 of it on a painting. I will now hold both the £900 remaining in the mixture, and the painting, one third for you, two thirds for myself or Adam. So if the painting turns out to be worth £6,000, you are now entitled to £2,300 (£2,000 being your third of the painting, £300 your third of the remaining £900); and Adam or I to £4,600 (£4,000 in respect of the painting, £600 out of the £900). Whereas if the painting turns out to be worthless, you are entitled only to £300 (from the remaining £900), Adam or I to £600 (likewise).[64]

Two qualifications are however required to this essentially simple picture of the law regarding mixtures.

First, a different rule may apply if the mixture is made by way of sequential payments into an ordinary current bank account, though only in the case where it is a mixture of the assets of two (or more) innocent parties: as where I take £500 that I hold on trust for you, and £1,000 that I hold on trust for Adam, and pay these sums in that order into such an account.[65] If I then make withdrawals from the account, they may

---

[64] In principle, the shares ought to be recalculated every time a new addition to the mixture changes the proportions: a technique known as 'rolling *pari passu*'. Say I mix £500 of your money and £1,000 of my own; then use £600 to buy a painting, leaving £900; then add £1,500 belonging to Adam; then use the entire £2,400 to buy another painting. By rolling *pari passu*, I hold the first painting for you and myself (alone) in the proportions 1:2; the second painting for you, myself, and Adam in the proportions 1:2:5. This approach is approved in *Shalson v Russo* [2005] Ch 281, [149]–[150]. But in *Barlow Clowes International Ltd v Vaughan* [1992] 4 All ER 22, the court regarded it as too complicated, and proceeded as though all the contributions to the mixture were simultaneous (see too, though there is no discussion, *Commerzbank AG v IMB Morgan Plc* [2004] EWHC 2771 (Ch)). This would mean you, me, and Adam sharing both paintings in the proportions 1:2:3.

[65] An equivalent situation (see *Sinclair v Brougham* [1914] AC 398, 443, 445–6, 448; *Re Diplock's Estate* [1948] Ch 465, 523–6, 531–2, 539, 554) is that where I take £500 that I hold on trust for you, and pay it into my own bank account, which already holds £1,000 of my own money, *when I do not know, and have no reason to know, that I hold the £500 on trust for you* (as especially where the original trustee transfers trust property to me as a gift). Since my innocence means that I do not breach my duty to safeguard your trust property (section 14.3), the mixture is again of the assets of two innocent parties. Because I was nonetheless trustee of

be reckoned as taking the funds from the account in the order in which I paid them into it: 'first in, first out'. So, for example, if I withdraw £600, leaving £900 behind, these sums are no longer seen as belonging to you and Adam in the ratio 1:2; rather, the £600 is seen as containing your entire £500 plus £100 of Adam's, the remaining £900 as wholly Adam's. Say I then spend the £600 on a painting: I hold this on trust for you and Adam in proportions reflecting your shares in the £600: ie 5:1 in your favour. So if the painting turns out to be worth £6,000, you are entitled to £5,000 of this, Adam to the other £1,000; whereas if it turns out to be worthless, you both get nothing. Either way, the £900 left in the account remains Adam's. This pattern of outcomes can only be described as arbitrary.

This 'first in, first out' rule was originally developed in a different context.[66] At one time, it was applied also in the case where a trustee wrongfully uses sequential payments into a bank account to mix trust money with his own,[67] but later it was disavowed there.[68] Although the authorities say that it still applies where the contributors to the mixture are all innocent,[69] it has been disparaged here too by both commentators[70] and judges:[71] understandably, in view of the arbitrary results it can produce, as we have just seen. Even in this context, moreover, its application has been narrowed. It has been said to apply only where proportionate reckoning is technically difficult;[72] where the contributors, alerted to the issue, would

the £500 for you, however, I still hold the mixture on constructive trust. (Cf the view of Lord Browne-Wilkinson in *Westdeutsche Landesbank Girozentrale v Islington LBC* [1996] AC 669, 705–6, 715, that a trust cannot arise at all unless and until the trustee knows the facts giving rise to it. As explained in section 1.13, this is probably aimed at producing the same result, that a person *cannot be liable for breach of trust* without such knowledge. But it would mean that I hold neither the £500 nor the mixture on trust at all before attaining such knowledge, making it difficult to say that one to whom I transfer it during that time shall himself take it on trust, in the manner explained in section 17.2.)

[66] See *Clayton's case* (1817) 1 Mer 572; explained, L Smith *The Law of Tracing* (1997) 185–9.   [67] *Pennell v Deffell* (1853) 4 De GM & G 372.

[68] *Re Hallett's Estate* (1879) 13 Ch D 696.

[69] *Re Stenning* [1895] 2 Ch 433; *Re Diplock's Estate* [1948] Ch 465, 554.

[70] See eg L Smith *The Law of Tracing* (1997) 189–94.

[71] See especially *Barlow Clowes International Ltd v Vaughan* [1992] 4 All ER 22, 43–6.

[72] *Re Diplock's Estate* [1948] Ch 465, 554. However, *pari passu* tracing is likely to be technically difficult only in its rolling form (see n 64); and the alternative resort in that case is to treat all the contributions as simultaneous (*ibid*). Conversely, moreover, *Barlow Clowes International Ltd v Vaughan* [1992] 4 All ER 22, 39 and *Commerzbank AG v IMB Morgan Plc* [2004] EWHC 2771 (Ch), [49]–[50] suggest that the tables are turned—*pari passu* tracing is used in preference to 'first in, first out'—if the *latter* is 'inconvenient'. The impression given by all this, that the rules alter to suit the judges' convenience, is unnerving.

not have intended otherwise;[73] and where it would not produce injustice.[74] This may well, of course, be never.

The second qualification to the usual *pari passu* rule is this. Where a trustee mixes trust property with his own, in breach of his duty to safe-guard the trust property,[75] the trust objects have an additional option. Instead of claiming a proportionate share of the mixture or its proceeds, they can choose to claim a 'charge' over the mixture or its proceeds, for the amount that their trust contributed to the mixture.[76] Say I mix £500 that I knowingly hold on trust for you, with £1,000 of my own money. As already explained, I will hold the resultant £1,500 on constructive trust for you and myself in the ratio 1:2. But you can also claim a charge over the £1,500 for your contribution of £500. So long as the value of the mixture remains £1,500, it will make no difference which approach you choose to take. The difference emerges if there is a rise in the value of the mixture and its proceeds, in which case you will do better to claim your due pro-portion; or a fall, when you will do better to claim your charge. Say I use the £1,500 to buy a picture. If it turns out to be worth £3,000, claiming your due proportion of this—one third—will bring you £1,000, whereas asserting your charge over it will entitle you to only £500. But if the pic-ture turns out to be worth only £900, claiming your due proportion will bring you only £300, whilst asserting your charge will entitle you to your original £500.[77] Likewise if I simply fritter away £600 from the mixture, leaving £900 in it.

A charge is not the same kind of right as that enjoyed by the object of a trust in that capacity, ie a beneficial interest. If I owe you a certain sum of money, you have a charge if your right to recover that sum is secured on some asset belonging to me. This situation differs from a trust in that, to the extent that it is not required to pay off what I owe you, the asset in question remains my own—whereas if I held it on trust for you, I could

---

[73] *Barlow Clowes International Ltd v Vaughan* [1992] 4 All ER 22; *Russell-Cooke Trust Co v Prentis* [2003] 2 All ER 479, [55]–[58].

[74] *Barlow Clowes International Ltd v Vaughan* [1992] 4 All ER 22, 39; *Commerzbank AG v IMB Morgan Plc* [2004] EWHC 2771 (Ch), [50]. Note the curious assumption that a rule can be disapplied if it gives an unfortunate result.

[75] That is, this rule does not apply where the contributors to the mixture are all innocent (ie are all trusts, or are one or more trusts plus an innocent trustee): *Foskett v McKeown* [2001] 1 AC 102, 132.

[76] *Re Oatway* [1903] 2 Ch 356; *Foskett v McKeown* [2001] 1 AC 102, 130–2.

[77] If the value falls below the trust's contribution—as where the picture turns out to be worth only £300—you will have a charge for £500 over the £300. In practical terms, obviously, this will yield you only £300. But it is still better than claiming your due proportion, which is worth only £100.

have no personal interest in it.[78] So if the right under discussion in the previous paragraph really is a charge, it strictly does not belong in this chapter, which is about constructive trusts, though it is convenient to discuss it here, so as to complete the treatment of tracing. There is, however, some doubt whether it is really is a charge.

Certainly, the right is normally referred to as a charge,[79] and it is possible to go some way towards explaining it as such. Where I mix £500 that I knowingly hold on trust for you with money of my own, I breach my duty to keep your money safe, and become liable to restore £500 to your trust. Instead of requiring me to do so, we have already seen that you are entitled (so as most thoroughly to attack the principal–agent problem) to treat the transaction in question as one made on your behalf, and so adopt its consequences for yourself.[80] So, instead of requiring me to repay the £500 to your trust, you can choose to claim your due proportion of the mixture containing the £500, or its proceeds…or else to say that I took the £500 as a loan to myself, at interest, and secured for maximum safety: this being your charge for £500.[81] But this reasoning does not justify the entire rule as it stands. If it were correct, the charge should attach to *any* asset I hold, in that you could have insisted that my loan be secured in that way. This view was indeed taken in one decision,[82] but it came as a surprise, and was subsequently doubted.[83] The more conventional view is that the charge attaches only to the mixture and its proceeds, not to other assets that I independently own; not even to assets that I may subsequently add to the mixture, this detail being known as the 'lowest intermediate balance rule'.[84]

---

[78] Section 1.10. If I hold only a portion of the asset for you, the rest for myself (as with the constructive trust yielded by the *pari passu* approach to tracing), I likewise hold that portion entirely for you. I do not hold the asset as my own, subject only to your right to resort to it in order to produce the particular sum I owe you.

[79] Or 'lien', which has a similar meaning.   [80] See section 13.8.

[81] *Foskett v McKeown* [2001] 1 AC 102, 130–1; J Penner *The Law of Trusts* 7th edn (2010) 363–4. For less focused judicial explanations, see *Sinclair v Brougham* [1914] AC 398, 422; *Re Diplock's Estate* [1948] Ch 465, 526.

[82] *Space Investments Ltd v Canadian Imperial Bank of Commerce Trust Co (Bahamas) Ltd* [1986] 1 WLR 1072, 1074. The view may be understood also on a 'swollen assets' basis, whereby you can claim a right in my property if the latter has been swelled by the absorption of your property, this being an alternative way of explaining tracing generally: see C Rotherham *Proprietary Remedies in Context* (2002) 108–14.

[83] *Re Goldcorp Exchange Ltd (in receivership)* [1995] 1 AC 74, 108–10; *Director of the Serious Fraud Office v Lexi Holdings Plc (in administration)* [2009] QB 376, [48]–[51].

[84] *James Roscoe (Bolton) Ltd v Winder* [1915] 1 Ch 62; *Bishopsgate Investment Management Ltd v Homan* [1995] Ch 211, 220.

This difficulty suggests that the 'charge' needs to be understood in a different way. And this may be possible, by saying that where I have split the mixture into parts (say by spending some of it and saving the rest; or by spending all of it, but on different purchases), you do not have to be satisfied with your proportionate share of the extant assets: instead, you can 'cherry-pick'. That is, you can point to your contribution as being the money used to generate any of the parts, and then claim the part(s) in question as yours. On this view, then, your right is not a charge after all. It is once more a beneficial interest under a constructive trust—one whose size is determined, however, not by proportionate reckoning, but in the manner just described.

So say again that I mix £1,000 of my own money with £500 that I knowingly hold on trust for you, then fritter away £600 of the resultant £1,500, leaving £900. Rather than accepting that I hold the £900 on trust for you and myself in proportion to our contributions, ie 1:2, you can point to your £500 in that £900, meaning that I hold the £900 for you and myself in the ratio 5:4. In this example, the outcome is the same whether we think in terms of 'cherry-picking' or of a charge, and of course this overlap is necessary, as 'cherry-picking' has to explain the effect that is otherwise referred to as a 'charge'.[85] But on different facts, the two analyses diverge. 'Cherry-picking' does, while a charge does not, allow you also to take the benefit of any increase in the assets' value. Say I spend the remaining £900 in the above example on a painting, which turns out to be worth £9,000. Your charge over the painting would be only for £500. Your *pari passu* proportion of it is one third, giving you £3,000. But if you can 'cherry-pick', you can say that, of the £900 used to buy the painting, £500 was yours, meaning I now hold the painting for you and me in the ratio 5:4, giving you £5,000.

The 'cherry-picking' analysis may sometimes be detectable in the wording of the relevant judgments,[86] and it can certainly be justified in

---

[85] But compare the case where I spend the £1,500 on a painting, which turns out to be worth only £900. The idea that 'you can point to your £500' in that £900 seems less plausible here: the £1,500 must have comprised the entirety of our respective contributions, so your share of the painting can only be one third, ie £300. On these facts, then, the only way to show that you have a right worth £500 may be via the idea of a charge.

[86] Passages in *Re Oatway* [1903] 2 Ch 356, 360, and in *Foskett v McKeown* [2001] 1 AC 102, 132 can be read thus. It may not be supportable to do so, however, for the surrounding text in both cases uses the word 'charge'. For an earlier experiment in the same direction, see *Re Hallett's Estate* (1879) 13 Ch D 696, 727, holding that withdrawals from the mixture are ascribed first to the trustee, up to the value of his contribution, and only then to the trust objects. On the facts of that case, where part of the mixture was withdrawn and the withdrawals were squandered, this reasoning meant that the surviving value was reserved for the

principle. If those wronged by a breach of trust are entitled (so as most thoroughly to attack the principal–agent problem) to treat the transaction in question as one made on their behalf, and so take its consequences for themselves, they should be able to say that such-and-such an asset remaining in, or acquired from, the mixture represents the current location of their contribution.[87] Moreover, if we see the right in question in this way, rather than as a charge, we solve our problem with the rule, noted above, that your right is restricted to the mixture and its proceeds, not to other assets I may independently own or indeed may subsequently add to the mixture (the 'lowest intermediate balance rule'). You obviously cannot point to a particular £500 remaining in or spent from the mixture as yours, if the value of the mixture had previously fallen below £500. But we encounter difficulty in another direction. Where the extant assets are worth the same as or more than the value of the inputs to the mixture, 'cherry-picking' should, as we have seen, sometimes be more beneficial to the trust objects not only than a charge, but also than a proportionate reckoning.[88] If 'cherry-picking' is the law, therefore, we would expect it (unless the relevant facts have never occurred, which seems unlikely) to show up in decisions accordingly. But there appear to be no such decisions in English law.[89] The position regarding this aspect of tracing remains ultimately mysterious, therefore.

---

objects; *and if all the value had survived, but later withdrawals had gained in value, it would have given that gain to the objects, after the manner of 'cherry-picking'*. In a case where the only surviving value was concentrated in the early withdrawals or their proceeds, however, the reasoning would have benefited the trustee at the expense of the objects. When such facts later arose, in *Re Oatway* [1903] 2 Ch 356, the reasoning was (therefore) abandoned in favour of the charge/'cherry-picking' analysis described in the text.

[87]   L Smith *The Law of Tracing* (1997) 77–80, 199–203, essays a different justification: a rule of evidence whereby, if someone wrongfully creates an evidential difficulty (as by mixing assets that he holds on trust), that difficulty can be resolved by taking any reasonable inferences against him (as, where he himself contributed part of the mixture, by allowing 'cherry-picking' against him). See too *Sinclair Investments (UK) Ltd v Versailles Trade Finance Ltd (in administrative receivership)* [2010] EWHC 1614 (Ch), [146]–[157]. But this rule, or at any rate its role in the present context, appears to be rejected in *Director of the Serious Fraud Office v Lexi Holdings Plc (in administration)* [2009] QB 376, [52]–[55]. In any event, the rule must itself be founded on normative considerations, so pointing to it offers no advantage.

[88]   This is not the case, however, where there is a single extant asset: eg where the entire mixture is used to buy a single painting. This was the situation in *Foskett v McKeown* [2001] 1 AC 102 itself.

[89]   'Cherry-picking' was essentially approved, but not in the end applied, in *Shalson v Russo* [2005] Ch 281, [143]–[146]. But it appears inconsistent with the way that the relevant right is analysed in *Director of the Serious Fraud Office v Lexi Holdings Plc (in administration)* [2009] QB 376, [36]–[40], namely as a charge in the strict sense.

17.6 ANTICIPATED TRANSFERS

When the owner of certain kinds of property, especially land, contracts to sell that property to a buyer, and the buyer has paid the money for it[90] but the title has not yet been formally transferred to him, the seller holds it on constructive trust for the buyer.[91] Similarly where the seller does not have the property at the time of the contract, ie contracts to transfer 'after-acquired' property: when he acquires it, he immediately holds it on constructive trust for the buyer.[92]

This means, for example, that if a seller of land goes bankrupt before the formal transfer takes place, the land is not seized as part of his assets to pay his debts. Or if the seller gives the land to someone else, the buyer's entitlement goes with it and can be enforced against the new owner. Likewise if a seller of after-acquired property goes bankrupt after acquiring the property, or transfers it to a third party.

This constructive trust springs from the doctrine 'equity looks upon that as done which ought to be done'.[93] The seller ought, under the circumstances, to transfer the land to the buyer. We know this because a court would order specific performance of the contract to transfer,[94] ie would force the seller actually to transfer the land in question to the buyer. But for the moment the transferor is still in fact the owner of it. The legal device for treating the land as transferred to the buyer at the same time as it is still owned by the seller is to say that the seller holds it on trust for the buyer. To the extent provided by the trust, the contract is thus made to perform itself.

To point to the doctrine just mentioned does not provide a satisfying account of the reason for such trusts, however. We are left wanting to

---

[90] Some of the effects of a trust arise earlier in the transaction than this, but the further back one goes the more qualified the purchaser's interest becomes (*Lysaght v Edwards* (1876) 2 Ch D 499), and hesitation arises over calling the vendor's obligations exactly a 'constructive *trust*': A Oakley *Constructive Trusts* 3rd edn (1997) ch 6.

[91] See generally *Englewood Properties Ltd v Patel* [2005] 1 WLR 1961, [40]–[58]. Where the contract is for the grant of a proprietary interest less than ownership (eg a lease), the law again anticipates the formal grant of the interest (regarding the prospective lessee as already having a lease): *Walsh v Lonsdale* (1881) 21 Ch D 9. But since in such cases the grantor is to retain an interest in the land or other asset in question (eg as landlord), the upshot is not a *trust* for the grantee.

[92] *Holroyd v Marshall* (1860) 10 HLC 191; *Tailby v Official Receiver* (1888) 13 App Cas 523; *Pullan v Koe* [1913] 1 Ch 9; *Re Lind* [1915] 2 Ch 345.

[93] Also known as 'conversion', though that term has other meanings too.

[94] Implying that if for any reason the court would or could not order specific performance, the trust will not arise. The role of this factor is however variable and controversial: S Gardner (1987) 7 OJLS 60.

know *why* equity should 'look upon as done that which ought to be done'. Instead of making the contract perform itself, why does it not leave the seller as absolute owner until he makes the actual transfer to the buyer, simply allowing the buyer to sue him if he fails to do so? The constructive trust is more advantageous to a buyer than a mere right to enforce the contract (which would not give the buyer priority in the seller's bankruptcy, or allow him to retrieve the property from a third party): but why should the law extend such advantages?

The historically correct explanation seems to be as follows. At the time when the constructive trust rule was invented, the remedies for breach of contract remained under-developed. A buyer of property other than land, to whom the property had not yet been delivered, was able to claim it because he was nonetheless regarded as its owner: the law treated the contract itself as effecting the transfer. The law could not however treat the contract itself as effecting the transfer of land, for land could be transferred only by a physical act, known as 'livery of seisin', such as the handing over of a clod of earth. This left a buyer of land, let down by the seller, without a remedy. One was however developed. Something like a transfer without livery of seisin could be brought about, and was, by ruling that the seller held the land on constructive trust[95] for the buyer. The disappointed buyer could then sue his seller on this constructive trust.[96]

This class of constructive trust cannot be justified on this basis today, however, for in the meantime the law's remedies for breach of contract have been more fully developed, and the constructive trust is no longer needed so as to give the buyer any claim at all. We are seeking a justification for the trust's effect of giving the buyer rights superior to those that he would enjoy if confined to his ordinary contractual claim.[97]

There may be such a justification. It would be similar to that encountered in sections 17.3–17.5. There, we saw how the law uses constructive trusts to counter the principal–agent problem—the problem that arises when a principal uses a fiduciary, so that he cannot closely control, and has reason to be concerned about, the fiduciary's activities on his behalf. A not dissimilar sort of problem arises in the present context. In some kinds of transactions, especially those involving land, progress towards formal

---

[95] At the time in question, the term was 'use'.

[96] S Gardner (1987) 7 OJLS 60, 74–81. Thus 'specific performance' of a sale of land was not an order to a seller to perform his contract, so much as an order to a trustee to transfer the trust's subject matter to the beneficiary. The largely automatic availability of the latter kind of order explains why specific performance is nowadays routinely available to enforce a contract to buy land, when it is only exceptionally available to enforce other kinds of contract.

[97] See further C Rotherham *Proprietary Remedies in Context* (2002) ch 8.

transfer is typically slow and to some extent outside the parties' control.[98] The buyer remains more vulnerable than his counterpart in the case of a simple sale because he cannot take the purchased property immediately, or even quickly, in hand: he is forced to rely on the seller's behaving properly towards him for the typically quite lengthy period until he can. A buyer of after-acquired property is similarly vulnerable as having to rely on the seller for a potentially substantial time before he can take the property: until the property is ultimately transferred (and even when the seller does acquire the property, the buyer will not necessarily know of this so as to move to claim it), the seller may encounter temptations to repent of his contract with the buyer, or otherwise, most obviously through insolvency, become a less reliable trading partner than the buyer had reason to think him when the contract was made. The constructive trust rule can be justified as being an effort on the law's part to reduce the buyer's vulnerability in such cases, and so to render such transactions more commercially attractive.[99]

---

[98] The completion of a land sale, for example, will wait on steps to be taken by the parties' lawyers and perhaps financiers and by the state land registry.

[99] Note that the parties can agree to exclude the trust or certain of its implications. In particular, the trust shifts the risk (eg of the bought house being burned down) from seller to buyer. This effect is not nowadays practically favoured (Law Commission *Transfer of Land: Risk of Damage after Contract for Sale* (Law Com No 191, 1990)), and is normally excluded by the terms of the contract.

18

Constructive Trusts 3

This chapter covers the remaining types of constructive trust considered in this book, and finishes with a section (section 18.5) considering the duties that apply to trustees of constructive, and also resulting, trusts.

18.1 TRANSFERS SUBJECT TO AN UNDERTAKING

Where you transfer property to me on the faith of an undertaking I give you to hold it on a certain trust, a constructive trust arises against me in the shape of that trust, thus holding me to my undertaking. Of course, it is usually unnecessary to point to this constructive trust; your act of transferring the property to me on the basis that I will hold it on the trust in question will normally generate an effective *express* trust, regardless of whether I so undertake. But sometimes, to create an effective express trust, you need to comply with formality requirements. As was noted in Chapter 5, this is the case where the transfer is *inter vivos* but is of land, when the trust needs to be expressed in signed writing;[1] or where the transfer is to take effect on your death, when the trust needs to be expressed in a valid will.[2] If you fail to comply with these requirements, your trust will not be effective as an express trust. But if you transfer the property to me on the faith of my undertaking to hold it on the trust, I will be bound by a constructive trust to the same effect, as explained in section 5.6. Where the transfer occurs on your death, this constructive trust is known as a 'secret trust'. Where the transfer is *inter vivos* but

---

[1] Law of Property Act 1925 s 53(1)(b).
[2] Wills Act 1837 s 9, as amended by Administration of Justice Act 1982 s 17, requiring writing, signed and witnessed.

the property in question is land, we refer to the relevant leading cases, perhaps *Rochefoucauld v Boustead*[3] and certainly *Bannister v Bannister*.[4]

In section 5.6, we reviewed certain other explanations that have been essayed for secret trusts and their *inter vivos* counterparts, but rejected these, accepting only that now under consideration. Traditionally, the latter has been expressed along the lines that these trusts arise in order to prevent 'fraud'. But this account of it does not suffice. It leaves us wondering exactly what features in the facts represent the 'fraud', and why a constructive trust is the appropriate response to those features. Or more directly—omitting what is ultimately an unnecessary reference to 'fraud'—what features in the facts elicit the constructive trust, and why.

The best answer runs as follows.[5] The law is concerned to prevent the transferor being prejudiced, ie made worse off than he was initially, by believing in and acting upon the transferee's promise. In the abstract, the law's response is not to hold the transferee to his promise without demur (the normal bases for doing that being by definition absent), but to hold him to it to the extent that that is necessary if the transferor is not to be worse off, when it is not fulfilled, by having relied on it.[6] In the area under discussion, if the undertaking does not take effect, the transferor will be prejudiced by relying on the transferee's undertaking if he has meanwhile lost his opportunity to make his intended disposition by way of an effective express trust. The transferee should therefore be allowed to go back on his undertaking to the extent that it is possible to recreate that opportunity. To the extent that it is not, the law should hold the transferee to his undertaking.[7]

It is important to be precise about what 'that opportunity' means. First, it means the opportunity to establish the trust with effect from the date on which it was originally intended to arise. Secondly, it does not mean

---

[3] [1897] 1 Ch 196. 'Perhaps', because this decision may have taken a different approach, noted and criticized in section 5.6. See further W Swadling in C Mitchell (ed) *Constructive and Resulting Trusts* (2010) ch 3.

[4] [1948] 2 All ER 133. *Hodgson v Marks* [1971] Ch 892 is similar; and see too *De Bruyne v De Bruyne* [2010] EWCA Civ 519, [35]–[54].

[5] For further examination, see S Gardner in C Mitchell (ed) *Constructive and Resulting Trusts* (2010) ch 2. A different account is given by B McFarlane (2004) 120 LQR 667.

[6] *Tool Metal Manufacturing Co Ltd v Tungsten Electric Co Ltd* [1955] 1 WLR 766.

[7] In *De Bruyne v De Bruyne* [2010] EWCA Civ 519, [51], it is said that this kind of constructive trust does not depend on reliance on the part of the beneficiary. That is obviously correct; the required reliance is that of the transferor. (Sometimes, of course, the transferor and the beneficiary are the same person, as in *Bannister v Bannister* [1948] 2 All ER 133.)

the opportunity for the transferor to change his mind and instead make no trust or a different one. He has lost this opportunity equally if the transferee honours his undertaking, and in fact lost it by trying to make the disposition at all. It seems in fact not to be possible to recreate the opportunity, so defined. In particular, it cannot be recreated by literally revesting the property in the transferor and leaving him now to subject it to an effective express trust in accordance with his intentions. That response would meet neither of the above points, and moreover it would be futile in the situation, as in all testamentary cases and some *inter vivos* ones, where the transferor has died in the meantime. As it is thus not possible to restore to the transferor the opportunity effectively to make his trust that he had before he relied on the transferee's undertaking, he will have been prejudiced, if the undertaking is not fulfilled, by his reliance upon it. To negate that prejudice, the law must enforce the undertaking, ie must regard the transferee as holding the property on a (constructive) trust in the terms that he agreed with the transferor.

The rule under discussion also operates outside the sphere of trusts. If I undertake that I will accept some property from you on certain terms *that do not themselves amount to my holding it on trust*, and you transfer the property to me on the faith of that undertaking, an obligation once again arises against me, requiring me to keep to the agreed terms. Say you own a large estate, and allow an old lady to live in one of its cottages for the rest of her life. You sell the estate to me. The lady's right to stay in the cottage does not in itself bind me, because it is merely a contract between her and you, which the doctrine of privity of contract prevents from affecting others. In my dealings with you, however, I undertake to honour the old lady's position. I am obliged to do so.[8] By transferring the estate to me in reliance on my promise to honour the old lady's position, you have lost the opportunity to protect her in some other way, so you will be injured unless my promise is enforced.

In this case, my promise was not to hold the property on trust for the old lady; rather, it was to allow her to live in the cottage. But the authorities[9]

---

[8] *Binions v Evans* [1972] Ch 359, 368–9; *Swiss Bank Corporation v Lloyds Bank Ltd* [1979] Ch 548, 571; *Lyus v Prowsa Developments Ltd* [1982] 1 WLR 1044; *Ashburn Anstalt v Arnold* [1989] Ch 1, 22–6. The example given involves a contract between the transferor and the person who benefits from the transferee's obligation (the old lady), and that feature is to be found in these cases. But it seems unnecessary. Say you sell the estate to me after taking a promise from me that I will allow my elderly mother to move into and remain in the cottage. There is no contract between her and you, but your reliance on my promise nonetheless loses you the opportunity to provide for her otherwise, so I should be bound in the same way.

[9] *Binions v Evans* [1972] Ch 359, 368–9; *Swiss Bank Corporation v Lloyds Bank Ltd* [1979] Ch 548, 571; *Lyus v Prowsa Developments Ltd* [1982] 1 WLR 1044; *Ashburn Anstalt v Arnold* [1989] Ch 1, 22–6.

refer to my obligation in this case as a 'constructive trust' in just the same way as we find where the promise was to hold on trust. This must be incorrect, however. In the latter situation, my obligation—tracking my promise—should indeed be a trust. But in the former, my obligation—again tracking my promise—should *not* be a trust. Referring to it as a trust is inaccurate in two respects. First, we saw in section 1.10 that it is part of the nature of trusts that the trustee, whilst holding the legal title to the trust property, is subject to duties that leave no room for a personal interest. But in the doctrine under discussion, my obligation is simply to use the property in the specified way: to allow the old lady to remain in the cottage, for example. In all other respects, I owe no duties as to my use of the property, and so can enjoy it as my own. In particular, if I were to sell the property, the proceeds would be mine. So I evidently have a personal interest in the trust property. Secondly, as we saw in section 1.9, trust obligations are proprietary, ie are attached to the property and so affect it in the hands of a recipient from the original trustee. If a trust arises in the situation under discussion, therefore, the duty owed to the beneficiary (in the example, the duty to allow the old lady to stay in the cottage) should be proprietary. Yet while you were her landlord, her rights were merely personal ones against you. It is odd that a person's rights should change their quality in this way, by virtue of a transaction, the transfer of the property to the purchaser upon the faith of his promise, to which that person is not even a party.[10] In fact, it seems more likely that no such change occurs: that the obligation generated by a transferee's undertaking is proprietary where the right which he undertakes to honour is a proprietary one (such as a trust), but personal where that right is itself personal.[11]

So although it is right that an obligation should arise on the basis under discussion against someone who acquires property having undertaken to use it in a certain way, that obligation should only be a 'trust' if the undertaking was to hold on trust.

---

[10] At one time, this oddity in fact led the courts to decide that someone in the position of the old lady (a contractual licensee) must have had proprietary, rather than personal (merely contractual), rights all along, even in her original relationship with me. See *DHN Food Distributors Ltd v Tower Hamlets LBC* [1976] 1 WLR 852; *Re Sharpe (a bankrupt)* [1980] 1 WLR 219. This view was disapproved, albeit without advertence to the difficulty that had caused it, in *Ashburn Anstalt v Arnold* [1989] Ch 1.

[11] The authorities do not explicitly state this position, but (aside from those referred to in n 10) are consistent with it. See *Lyus v Prowsa Developments Ltd* [1982] 1 WLR 1044; *Chattey v Farndale Holdings Inc* (1996) 75 P & CR 298.

18.2 FURTHER RELIANCE-BASED RULES

Some further rules operate in essentially the same way, generating a constructive trust where I undertake to hold some property on trust for you or some other person, and, in reliance on my undertaking, you forego your opportunity to bring about this result in some more secure manner.[12] These further rules are those associated with the decisions in *Neale v Willis*[13] and *Pallant v Morgan*,[14] and with mutual wills.

In *Neale v Willis*,[15] a woman lent some money to her son-in-law to help him buy a house, on the understanding that he would have the house put not simply into his own name, but into the joint names of himself and his wife, the woman's daughter. When he in fact had the house put into his own name alone, a constructive trust arose, under which he was obliged to hold it in accordance with his undertaking, for himself and his wife equally. Relying on his informal undertaking, his mother-in-law forewent the opportunity that her initial bargaining-power (he sought a loan, remember) gave her more effectively to secure an interest for her daughter. When he went back on his undertaking, she therefore suffered a loss for which he was responsible. To rectify this, he was required to honour his undertaking: that is, a constructive trust was imposed on the lines of the arrangement he had agreed to set up.

Notice that in *Neale v Willis*,[16] the son-in-law acquired the house not from his mother-in-law, in the manner found in section 18.1, but from an outside source. In terms of the explanation offered here, this difference is unimportant. Whether the mother-in-law helped the son-in-law acquire the property from outside, or transferred it to him herself, she relied on his undertaking to share it with her daughter, and so forewent the opportunity she previously had to achieve this more securely. Acquisition from an outside source is also to be found in the doctrine in *Pallant v Morgan*.[17] The latter deals with the case where you and I are interested in purchasing the same property, and agree that, instead of competing for it (which would only drive the price up), I alone will bid for it, but shall, assuming I succeed in acquiring it, share it in some way with you. If I do acquire the property but then renege on our agreement and seek to deny you your share, a constructive trust arises whereby I am held to my agreement after

---

[12] Again, see S Gardner in C Mitchell (ed) *Constructive and Resulting Trusts* (2010) ch 2.
[13] (1968) 19 P & CR 836.   [14] [1953] Ch 43.   [15] (1968) 19 P & CR 836.
[16] *Ibid.*
[17] [1953] Ch 43. There are other decisions to the same effect, most notably *Chattock v Muller* (1878) LR 8 Ch D 177; *Banner Homes Group Plc v Luff Developments Ltd* [2000] Ch 372.

all. Your initial ability to bid against me meant that you could damage me, in particular by making me pay a higher price for the property; you therefore had a bargaining chip, on the basis of which you could have struck a firmer deal with me for a share in the property. You gave up that bargaining chip when, on the strength of our agreement, you failed to bid without insisting on such a firmer deal. If I can now dishonour that agreement, I have caused you a loss.[18] To prevent that, I must be held to our agreement after all; that is, I must hold the property in question on a constructive trust for myself and you on the lines of our agreement.

Finally, mutual wills.[19] Say you and I agree to make wills aimed at ultimately leaving some property to Adam, and agree also not to resile from that plan (as the revocability of wills, before death, would otherwise permit us to). Say then that you die before me, having complied with this agreement. The upshot is that any property of mine to which our agreement applies is held by me, from the moment of your death, on constructive trust for Adam. Usually, the agreement is that you will leave some property to me, and that I in turn will leave it to Adam. But this feature is not necessary, and the arrangement may simply be that we shall each leave property to Adam.[20]

The latter variant shows that, in contrast to all the contexts discussed thus far, mutual wills need involve no transfer of property at all. Once again, this difference is unimportant. The key point is that, relying on my undertaking to leave certain property—whether received from you or from someone else, or mine all along—to Adam, you forego the opportunity you previously had to provide as you wished for Adam. If I now resile from the agreement, you will be worse off than if we had never made it. In order to prevent that, the law holds me to the agreement. And since the agreement obliges me to make Adam the owner of property in my hands, this means my holding the property on (constructive) trust for Adam.[21]

---

[18] Chadwick LJ in *Banner Homes Group Plc v Luff Developments Ltd* [2000] Ch 372, 388, 398–9, 401 asserts that loss is not always present in a case of this type, and that loss cannot therefore be part of the reason for the imposition of a constructive trust. He was, however, thinking only of the loss of the opportunity *to secure the property in question outright*, which was certainly absent from some of the cases. He appears to overlook the different kind of loss—the loss of the opportunity *to secure a firm joint arrangement*—on which the text focuses.

[19] The common basis of mutual wills and secret trusts is noted in *Re Cleaver (deceased)* [1981] 1 WLR 939.   [20] *Re Dale (deceased)* [1994] Ch 31.

[21] Sometimes, because this is the nature of the agreement, I will hold the property on trust for myself and Adam; and sometimes again the size of the two shares will be for me to decide (with limits or otherwise). The latter arrangement seems to involve a power of appointment in my own favour, though other, more problematic, concepts are sometimes invoked. See *Birmingham v Renfrew* (1937) 57 CLR 666, Australia; *Re Cleaver (deceased)* [1981] 1 WLR

Between them, the doctrines discussed in this and section 18.1 thus cover a range of situations in which, in reliance on my undertaking to deal with some property in a particular way, you forego your opportunity to oblige me more securely to do so, and so suffer loss if I resile. The law corrects that loss by requiring me to honour my undertaking after all. If my undertaking is to allow you or someone else a beneficial right in the property, the result will be that I hold the property in question on constructive trust to that effect. It is odd, and unsatisfactory, that the various doctrines remain fragmented, dealing each with a particular context, rather than being drawn together into a single understanding.

18.3 FAMILY HOMES

Say you and I have a family relationship (whether married or unmarried, same sex or otherwise, as sexual partners or otherwise). If our house is in my name alone, with no express trust giving you an interest in it,[22] prima facie it belongs entirely to me: ie I do not hold it on trust at all. But if we have a 'common intention' that you should have some interest in it while I have the remainder, a constructive trust arises, under which I instead hold it on trust for the two of us in accordance with that intention.[23] Similarly, if the house is in our joint names, but again with no express trust indicating what our shares in it shall be,[24] prima facie it belongs to us in equal proportions: ie we hold it on trust for ourselves in equal proportions.[25] But once more, if we have a 'common intention' to share it in some other proportions, such as 67:33, a constructive trust arises under which we instead hold it on trust for ourselves in those other proportions. These propositions were established by the House of Lords in *Stack v Dowden*,[26] building upon, though in some respects changing direction from, certain

---

939; *Re Goodchild (deceased)* [1996] 1 WLR 694; also *Ottaway v Norman* [1972] Ch 698, a secret trust case on similar lines.

[22] As the trust's subject matter would be land (the house), such a trust would of course have to be in writing: Law of Property Act 1925 s 53(1)(b). See section 5.4.

[23] Your interest could even be 100 per cent, leaving nothing for me, in which case I would hold it on trust for you alone. More usually, however, we would both have shares; often, though not always, equal ones.

[24] Such a situation should be unusual. If a house is transferred to two (or more) people, the paperwork (satisfying the writing requirement) will normally make clear what are their interests in it: most straightforwardly, that they hold it on trust for themselves in equal proportions.

[25] *Stack v Dowden* [2007] 2 AC 432, [54]–[58].   [26] [2007] 2 AC 432.

earlier authority.[27] (Before *Stack v Dowden*,[28] there used also to be a requirement for you to act in reliance upon the common intention.[29] This requirement was however omitted from the doctrine's restatement in that decision.)

At first sight, the propositions seem straightforward enough, ruling simply that a constructive trust will arise where, and to the extent that, we so agree. There is, however, a complication. To be sure, the crucial 'common intention' may take the form of a genuine agreement between us— whether express, ie made in explicit discussion between us, or implied in the way we have conducted ourselves. But in the view of some, it may alternatively be invented by the court. *Stack v Dowden*,[30] while ultimately ambiguous on the point (everything depending on the precise sense in which the judges there used the word 'imputed'), certainly contains passages supportive of this view. Subsequent judicial treatments have vacillated over the matter. The authoritative position at the time of writing[31] requires a genuine 'common intention', not accepting its invention. The matter is due to go to the Supreme Court in spring 2011. Even if held to represent the authentic law, however, a requirement of a genuine common intention will be hard to sustain in practice. This was certainly the experience before *Stack v Dowden*,[32] when a genuine common intention was in theory required;[33] in practice, the courts used to find such intentions on weak,[34] or indeed incredible,[35] grounds,[36] and as regards the quantification of any interest had ceased even to pretend to do so.[37]

And rightly so. It is of course generally appropriate, on libertarian grounds, to allow people to arrange their own affairs (as via a genuine common intention) rather than having an arrangement imposed upon them (as via an invented one). But the context under discussion, that of family homes, is one in which people will not normally devise their own arrangements; and, crucially, the very reason for this—the parties'

---

[27] Principally *Gissing v Gissing* [1971] AC 886; *Lloyds Bank plc v Rosset* [1991] 1 AC 107 (an earlier decision, *Pettitt v Pettitt* [1970] AC 777, sheds little light). See on these S Gardner (1993) 109 LQR 263; J Mee *The Property Rights of Cohabitees* (1999); C Rotherham *Proprietary Remedies in Context* (2002) ch 10.

[28] [2007] 2 AC 432.   [29] *Lloyds Bank Plc v Rosset* [1991] 1 AC 107, 132.

[30] [2007] 2 AC 432; see especially [17]–[22], [60]–[61].

[31] *Jones v Kernott* [2010] 1 WLR 2401. The text reflects the position of the majority in the Court of Appeal; but a dissenting judgment, and the judgment in the High Court took the opposite view, ie permitted invention.   [32] [2007] 2 AC 432.

[33] *Gissing v Gissing* [1971] AC 886, 904.

[34] *Hammond v Mitchell* [1991] 1 WLR 1127; *Stokes v Anderson* [1991] 1 FLR 391.

[35] *Eves v Eves* [1975] 1 WLR 1338; *Grant v Edwards* [1986] Ch 638.

[36] See further S Gardner (1993) 109 LQR 263.

[37] *Midland Bank Plc v Cooke* [1995] 4 All ER 562; *Oxley v Hiscock* [2005] Fam 211.

familial trust in one another—also warrants the law's intervention none-theless. Unless the law reacts to such trust as much as to genuine common intention, those who put their faith in the former rather than the latter will lose out. The law would thus discourage their choice (or, one might more sensitively say, their assumptions about family life), and so commit itself to a vision of human existence at odds with that which, in the fam-ily context, we surely recognize and approve. The (official or unofficial) invention of 'common intention' is the vehicle by which the law has hith-erto reacted to familial trust. The adoption of this vehicle makes sense, of course, only because the area's rhetoric has traditionally been dominated by the libertarian value of genuine common intention. Especially as the whole point is that that value should *not* dominate, it would be preferable in principle no longer to invent 'common intentions', but to acknowledge that an outcome is simply being imposed.

To return, however, to the juridical position. Under *Stack v Dowden*,[38] a judge considering the discovery of an implied common intention should attend to the parties' 'whole course of conduct in relation to [the property]'.[39] This rule is unproblematic; one would hardly expect any other position.[40] If the common intention can be invented, the judge must once again look to the parties' 'whole course of conduct'. In this context, however, the rule is deeply problematic. For the judge may attend assidu-ously to the parties' 'whole course of conduct', but still have no means of knowing what intention to invent, because the proposition says noth-ing about the normative significance of the conduct in question. Say, for example, that we are a couple; you go out to work while I keep house for us; your earnings meet the mortgage repayments on our house and all our other bills. What intention is to be invented on account of this? That because it is your earnings that have paid for the house, it should be yours

[38] [2007] 2 AC 432.

[39] *Abbott v Abbott* [2007] UKPC 53, [5], [6]. This means more or less everything: *Stack v Dowden* [2007] 2 AC 432, [69]–[70].

[40] Though the rule was in fact previously otherwise. Under *Lloyds Bank plc v Rosset* [1991] 1 AC 107, 133, the only permitted evidence of an implied common intention was 'direct contri-butions to the purchase price [of the house in question] . . . , whether initially or by payment of mortgage instalments'. The artificiality and strictness of this rule made it unpopular, so it was sometimes ignored (as in *Le Foe v Le Foe* [2001] FLR 970), or else by-passed by the fictitious discovery of an *express* common intention, to which no such rule applied (as in *Eves v Eves* [1975] 1 WLR 1338; *Grant v Edwards* [1986] Ch 638). Nevertheless, the rule may possibly still apply to the sole question whether, in a case where the house is in my name alone (*not* in the case where it is in both our names), you should have an interest in it (*not* to the further question of the size of that interest): *Stack v Dowden* [2007] 2 AC 432, [63]. But there is no reason why there should be a different rule (let alone such an unfortunate one) for this one aspect of the matter, so the possibility is best discounted.

alone? Or that because we worked as a team, each making out own contribution to the success of our family, it should belong to us in equal proportions? Or indeed something else again? The answer is that the judge should invent whatever intention gives effect to the law's aim in this area. That, however, takes us no further forward, as it begs the question, 'What is the law's aim?' This question could be answered in a variety of ways, but the cases—assuming they truly involve invented common intentions at all, though this does seem to be the case—seem to disclose a pattern.[41]

This pattern distinguishes between two kinds of relationship: those that may be labelled 'materially communal', and others. A materially communal relationship is one in which the parties pool their resources, such as where one of them goes out to work and meets the bills, while the other runs the home and looks after the children; or where each goes out to work and they share the bills and the other necessary tasks, but it does not matter to them who contributes what. Marriage and civil partnership virtually of necessity represent materially communal relationships, but an unmarried family relationship, of any description (ie whether between sexual or platonic partners, siblings, parent and child, whatever), could do so too. A joint bank account is a good, though probably not an infallible, indicator of such a relationship. A non-materially communal relationship, by contrast, is one in which the parties do attach importance to who contributes what.

The suggestion is that in the case of a non-materially communal relationship, the law will award the parties such shares in the home (announce that the nominal owner(s) hold it on constructive trust for the parties in such proportions) as reflect their respective contributions to its acquisition.[42] In the case of a materially communal relationship, however, the parties' shares are determined not by their contributions, but by the implications of their relationship.[43] Generally, these implications have required the house to be shared equally.[44] In one case, however, a different

---

[41] S Gardner (2008) 124 LQR 422; see also *An Introduction to Land Law* 2nd edn (2009) 132–44.

[42] Thus *Stack v Dowden* [2007] 2 AC 432 itself, where the claimant contributed 65 per cent of the cost of acquiring the family home, and emerged with a 65 per cent share in it.

[43] It is principally because this area of it thus accesses the implications of the parties' relationship that the doctrine applies specifically to family homes, rather than more generally. Other kinds of constructive trust arise from the implications of other kinds of relationship, however: notably, the relationship between a fiduciary and his principal. Cf sections 17.3–17.4.

[44] Thus *Abbott v Abbott* [2008] 1 FLR 1451. Likewise *Fowler v Barron* [2008] 2 FCR 1. There, the house was in the parties' joint names, giving them prima facie equal shares in it. Despite their unequal contributions to its acquisition, these shares were left undisturbed.

outcome was reached.[45] Although here too the parties shared the house equally during the currency of the relationship, the issue before the court was as to their interests 15 years after the relationship had broken down and the defendant had moved out and bought another house of his own. The court held that the former family home now belonged 90 per cent to the claimant, 10 per cent to the defendant. This outcome had nothing to do with the parties' contributions to the acquisition of the house, which were approximately equal. Rather, it meant that the combined net value of the two houses was divided more or less equally between the parties, just as would almost certainly have been the outcome if they had been married, and the court had applied the ancillary relief jurisdiction that operates after a divorce.[46]

The scheme just described is intelligible, but it has difficulties of principle. In particular, in requiring a judge to say whether any given relationship is materially communal or not, it demands a simple appreciation of something that is often a most complex and elusive phenomenon, and quite possibly one that is the subject of disagreement or justifiable dissatisfaction among those party to it.[47] And in the form where it de facto applies the matrimonial ancillary relief jurisdiction to unmarried relationships, it does something at which legislators have hitherto baulked, for fear of the implications for 'the sanctity of marriage'.[48]

To recap, however: a constructive trust will arise under *Stack v Dowden*[49] from the parties' common intention, genuine or perhaps (but hopefully) invented; and, if permissible at all, the invention exercise may be conducted according to the scheme just described, for all the latter's

---

[45] *Jones v Kernott* [2010] 1 WLR 2401. As explained in n 31, however, the majority in the Court of Appeal in this case declined to invent a common intention at all, and found no genuine one, so maintained the 50:50 shares deducible from the fact that the house had been acquired in the parties' joint names. The text describes the position taken by the dissenting judge in the Court of Appeal and the two judges below.

[46] Matrimonial Causes Act 1973 s 24. See S Gardner and K Davidson (2011) 127 LQR 13.

[47] A Bottomley in S Bright and J Dewar (eds) *Land Law—Themes and Perspectives* (1998) ch 8; cf M Harding [2009] Conv 309.

[48] The Law Commission has proposed a new statutory scheme for unmarried relationships: *Cohabitation: The Financial Consequences of Relationship Breakdown* (Law Com No 307, 2007). The scheme is markedly less holistic than the ancillary relief jurisdiction that operates at the end of a marriage or civil partnership, and, as explained in the text, presently too at the end of a materially communal unmarried relationship. Thus, it would merely recoup a party for losses suffered, or advantages conferred on the other party, as a result of the former's contribution to the relationship. In 2008, the Government indicated that it would not seek to legislate on the basis of this proposal until it had discovered and considered the impact of the somewhat analogous Family Law (Scotland) Act 2006. For this, see F Wasoff et al *Legal practitioners' perspectives on the cohabitation provisions of the Family Law (Scotland) Act 2006* (2010), <http://www.crfr.ac.uk/researchprojects/rp_cohabitation.html>.   [49] [2007] 2 AC 432.

difficulties. We must now consider the question whether it is supportable for, specifically, *constructive trusts* to arise in this way.[50] As we shall see, the answer may be yes, but it is far from straightforward to show this.

Where the house is solely in my name, my evincing a *genuine* intention to give you an interest in it will in principle produce that result, as a declaration of an express trust. But to be effective, my declaration needs to be put in writing, because of the rule requiring express trusts of land to be made in this way;[51] and the type of case with which we are concerned is, by definition, that where this requirement is not met. Likewise, where the house is in our joint names, my genuine common intention to enlarge your interest in it, if expressed, will also in principle have that effect, but again, the relevant rule requires writing.[52] It is true that the doctrine under discussion requires a *common* intention, ie that you share my intention: but that makes no difference, either to the effectiveness of my intention in principle, or to its ineffectiveness for want of writing. There is no basis in authority (other than the material being considered) for suggesting that your sharing my intention should achieve, via a constructive trust, what my unwritten unilateral intention failed to; and there seems to be no reason of principle why it should. The position might well be different, of course, if you act to your detriment in reasonable reliance on my offer. Then, I should be responsible for your loss, and you should have a right against me calculated to correct that loss. Under appropriate circumstances—those needed to invoke *Bannister v Bannister*[53]—this right should and does take the form of a constructive trust reflecting the common intention. As noted above, the doctrine under discussion used to have a requirement of action in reliance,[54] and so could be explained in that way. This requirement was however omitted from the doctrine's restatement in *Stack v Dowden*.[55] Its omission makes sense if this restatement also introduced the possibility of the common intention being invented; for one cannot rely on an intention that does not really exist. But it should have been retained for the case where the common intention is genuine, as offering a basis for the constructive trust that we find.

---

[50] See further S Gardner (2008) 124 LQR 422, 434–44; C Rotherham *Proprietary Remedies in Context* (2002) 230–44.   [51] Law of Property Act 1925 s 53(1)(b): see section 5.4.

[52] Law of Property Act 1925 s 53(1)(c): see section 5.7.

[53] [1948] 2 All ER 133. See sections 5.6, 18.1. On the account given there, a constructive trust reflecting the common intention should arise only if, by way of reliance, you forego another opportunity to secure the intended interest (or perhaps an interest of equivalent value in some other property). This will sometimes, but not always, be the case.

[54] *Lloyds Bank Plc v Rosset* [1991] 1 AC 107, 132.   [55] [2007] 2 AC 432.

Turning to the case where resort is had—if this is permissible—to an *invented* common intention, it is necessary to distinguish between the different ways in which the courts have interpreted that idea, as outlined above. Where, our relationship not being materially communal, they impose a constructive trust reflecting our respective contributions to the cost of acquiring the house, the basis for that constructive trust may be the correction of unjust enrichment. Say the house is solely in my name, but I pay only 60 per cent of its cost, while you contribute the remainder. Unless the position is corrected, I am clearly enriched at your expense to the extent of your contribution. Assuming however that you do not contribute by way of a gift or loan to me on the one hand, and that I do not force or trick you into contributing on the other, it is less clear whether that enrichment is unjust.[56] It is certainly unjust if you contribute under the impression that you already have, or are going to get, an (enlarged) interest in the house, and that impression turns out to be false: but such cases will probably involve a genuine common intention, and be dealt with via that. In the case where common intention is to be imputed, you are likely to have contributed with no particular thoughts at all. It is contentious whether an enrichment gained under such circumstances counts as unjust. The answer depends on whether 'absence of basis' renders an enrichment unjust in English law, which is controversial—though the material under discussion may be among the evidence suggesting that it does. Even if the enrichment counts as unjust, moreover, it is contentious whether the redress for this should take the form of a constructive trust, ie proprietary as opposed to personal restitution (an order that I give you the value of my enrichment). The pattern of availability of proprietary restitution is an area of perhaps even greater controversy.[57]

Remember, however, that where our relationship is (or was) materially communal, an invented common intention seems instead to be used—and so a constructive trust will arise—to reflect the imperatives of that relationship. An obligation can certainly be erected on such a basis: it is, after all, the basis also of the matrimonial ancillary relief jurisdiction, which one version of our doctrine mimics. And if that obligation involves saying that (some of) my property ought to be yours, it appropriately takes the form of a constructive trust.

Although thus (just about) doctrinally explicable, however, the constructive trusts found in these family property cases—whether on the basis of a genuine or an invented common intention—are problematic in

---

[56] On whether an enrichment counts as 'unjust', see further P Birks *Unjust Enrichment* 2nd edn (2005) ch 6.   [57] See further P Birks *Unjust Enrichment* 2nd edn (2005) ch 8.

another way. They come into effect on the basis of what are often quite nebulous events, notably the formation of a genuine common intention or the formation or breakdown of a materially communal relationship. As was explained in section 15.3, the ordinary type of constructive trust, ie an 'institutional' constructive trust, takes effect from the time of the facts that give rise to it. It can thus bind third parties who acquire interests in the property in question after that time.[58] If those facts are nebulous, it is hard to pin this time down, or indeed to say whether a trust has arisen at all. The results are that third parties are at risk from obligations they will have difficulty in spotting, and that the market suffers from the caution that they have to show so as to avoid that risk. As further explained in section 15.3, a solution is to use a remedial constructive trust instead. A remedial constructive trust can be made to take effect only from the date of the court order imposing it, and/or selectively among those who might be affected. The cases thus far, however, have assumed that the constructive trust in operation here is an institutional one.[59]

Such a remedial constructive trust must be distinguished from another idea, which is different but sometimes given the same name.[60] This is the idea that an obligation should arise not on a pre-ordained basis (even if contested, or focusing on nebulous facts), but on the basis of whatever attracts the individual judge on the day. Such an approach is of course contrary to the Rule of Law. It may however be discernible as regards the invention of common intentions (if this is permissible at all) in the area under discussion. Although the discussion above presents a reasonably defined scheme (involving different kinds of relationships), this scheme is largely constructed from what the courts have done, rather than what they have said in their judgments. It is possible, therefore, that the courts themselves do not recognize it or indeed any rival to it as representing the law, but regard it as open to the individual judge, operating via the invention of a common intention, to take any approach he finds appealing. If anything, by referring us only to the implications of the parties' 'whole

---

[58] Section 12.1.

[59] See especially *Williams & Glyn's Bank Ltd v Boland* [1981] AC 487. Cf T Etherton [2008] CLJ 265 and [2009] Conv 104, who sees the constructive trust as remedial, though *quaere* how he circumnavigates the latter decision. (His writing suggests that he also sees this constructive trust as always based on unjust enrichment, whereas the text argues that this is the case only in non-materially communal cases; but perhaps he is focusing only on *Stack v Dowden* [2007] 2 AC 432 itself, this being such a case, if it involves an invented common intention at all.)

[60] This is the 'third meaning' of remedial constructive trust discussed in section 15.3, advanced in *Hussey v Palmer* [1972] 1 WLR 1286, 1289–90.

course of conduct' and leaving these in the eye of the beholder, *Stack v Dowden*[61] itself regrettably supports this understanding.

18.4 PROPRIETARY ESTOPPEL

Constructive trusts can arise also through the doctrine of proprietary estoppel.

This doctrine is not well defined, and indeed the courts have tended positively to eschew precise statements of it.[62] But in broad terms, it gives you a claim if, with my encouragement or acquiescence, you reasonably believe that you have or are going to get a right affecting my property, and act in detrimental reliance on this belief, so that it would be unconscionable to leave matters as they stand. Say I am elderly and becoming infirm. You (perhaps you are a relative, or a neighbour, or my lodger) start to look after me. Out of gratitude, I promise to leave you my house in my will, and you continue looking after me. But then I fail to keep my promise: that is, I die without bequeathing my house to you. Assuming I am thought to have behaved unconscionably in this, you will have a claim against me (or rather, since by this point I am no longer alive, against my estate).[63]

It is hard to say what relief your claim will yield; the relevant decisions do not tell a straightforward story about the principle(s) involved;[64] some suggestions will be advanced below. In some cases it has meant the enforcement of my promise—in this example, ordering me (or my estate) to transfer the property in question to you;[65] in others, an order that I (or my estate) should allow you some other right in or over the property in question;[66] in others again, an order that I (or my estate) should pay you a

---

[61] [2007] 2 AC 432.

[62] See *Taylors Fashions Ltd v Liverpool Victoria Trustees Co Ltd* [1982] QB 133n, 151–2; *Gillett v Holt* [2001] Ch 210, 225. A crisper approach may have been taken (along somewhat unexpected lines, indeed) in *Cobbe v Yeoman's Row Management Ltd* [2008] 1 WLR 1752, but *Thorner v Major* [2009] 1 WLR 776 seems to represent a reversion to the previous position.

[63] Facts of this kind are to be found in a number of estoppel decisions, including *Re Basham* [1986] 1 WLR 1498; *Campbell v Griffin* [2001] EWCA Civ 990; *Jennings v Rice* [2002] EWCA Civ 159; *Ottey v Grundy* [2003] EWCA Civ 1176. Not far away are *Greasley v Cooke* [1980] 1 WLR 1306; *Gillett v Holt* [2001] Ch 210; *Thorner v Major* [2009] 1 WLR 776.

[64] The principal authority is *Jennings v Rice* [2002] EWCA Civ 159, but it neither offers an easily-assimilated statement, nor has been universally adopted. For exploration, see S Gardner (1999) 115 LQR 438 and (2006) 122 LQR 492.

[65] As in *Dillwyn v Llewelyn* (1862) 4 De GF & J 517; *Pascoe v Turner* [1979] 1 WLR 431; *Re Basham* [1986] 1 WLR 1498; *Thorner v Major* [2009] 1 WLR 776.

[66] As in *Inwards v Baker* [1965] 2 QB 29; *Sledmore v Dalby* (1996) 72 P & CR 196.

sum of money.[67] Your entitlement to your order, however, is back-dated to the time of the underlying facts.[68] So if the order confers on you a right in the nature of a beneficial interest—that is, either the entire ownership of the property in question,[69] or some fraction of (for example, a half share in) that ownership—this back-dating means that I hold the property to that extent on (constructive) trust for you, from that time. On the other hand, if the order turns out not to give you a beneficial interest (for example, where it requires me to pay you a sum of money), your interim right against me cannot be described as a trust, and so falls outside the scope of this book.[70] The estoppel doctrine itself operates in the same manner either way, however, and we shall continue to discuss it as a whole.

Given its demand that you reasonably believe in a right over my property, with my encouragement or acquiescence, and rely on that belief to your detriment, proprietary estoppel might seem an instance of the familiar project of redressing loss suffered in reasonable reliance on another's undertaking.[71] The usual means of relieving a reliance loss is, of course, monetary compensation. As we saw in sections 18.1–18.2, however, the loss in question may sometimes be the foregoing of the opportunity to bring about the subject of the undertaking in a more secure way. Then, 'redressing your reliance loss' involves enforcing my undertaking; and where the undertaking is to allow a beneficial entitlement, this will mean generating a constructive trust, in the manner described there. Proprietary estoppel claims do indeed sometimes result in relief along these lines,[72] and indeed

---

[67] As in *Campbell v Griffin* [2001] EWCA Civ 990; *Jennings v Rice* [2002] EWCA Civ 159; *Ottey v Grundy* [2003] EWCA Civ 1176.

[68] Where the claim relates to a right over land of registered title, this is made clear by the Land Registration Act 2002 s 116(a). Although the case law is a little disorderly, however, it is probably also true more generally.

[69] As in eg *Dillwyn v Llewelyn* (1862) 4 De GF & J 517; *Pascoe v Turner* [1979] 1 WLR 431.

[70] But cf *Yaxley v Gotts* [2000] Ch 162; *Kinane v Mackie-Conteh* [2005] EWCA Civ 45. Here, where proprietary estoppel yielded a non-beneficial interest (respectively, a lease and a charge), a 'constructive trust' was nonetheless said to arise. But the constructive trust was invoked not for its own sake, but as a device aimed at escaping a formality requirement under the Law of Property (Miscellaneous Provisions) Act 1989 s 2. (As well as conceptually inaccurate, the device was in fact unnecessary: see M Dixon [2005] Conv 247; B McFarlane [2005] Conv 501. The very possibility of escaping s 2 via proprietary estoppel was later denied by Lord Scott in *Cobbe v Yeoman's Row Management Ltd* [2008] 1 WLR 1752, [29], but without reference to the decisions just mentioned, these being followed in preference to Lord Scott's view in *Brightlingsea Haven Ltd v Morris* [2008] EWHC 1928 (QB), [40]–[55].)

[71] On reflection, however, the demand that your belief be in *a right over my property* does not mesh with this account. Your loss merits redress just as much if incurred in reasonable reliance on my promise of any other kind of advantage.

[72] Monetary compensation for reliance loss was given in *Dodsworth v Dodsworth* (1973) 228 EG 1115; *Burrows and Burrows v Sharp* (1989) 23 HLR 82; *Baker v Baker* [1993] 2 FLR 247. Representations were enforced, in a manner ascribable to the 'loss of opportunity'

in this guise, proprietary estoppel may be seen as the generalized doctrine to that effect, appealed for at the end of section 18.2. Decisions to this effect are sporadic, however: other awards, even if involving monetary compensation or the enforcement of the defendant's undertaking, cannot be seen as redressing the claimant's reliance loss.[73] These indicate the application of the doctrine to some other end or ends.

In fact, two other ends are discernible.[74] One is the enforcement of the defendant's undertaking, not simply where this equates to the claimant's reliance loss but for its own sake.[75] The other is the enforcement of the implications, in the prevailing circumstances, of the parties' personal relationship[76]—as, for example, where an elderly couple promised to bequeath their house to their lodger in return for the care he took of them, but failed to do so: the lodger was awarded, not the house itself, but such a sum of money as would enable him to rehouse himself at the sort of level he enjoyed before the couple's deaths.[77] Of these two projects, the latter is in principle unproblematic, involving essentially the same sort of thinking (the vision of the parties' relationship as itself creating obligations between them) as we saw, in connection with the use of invented 'common intentions' regarding family homes, in section 18.3. The former, however, is not obviously proper. For an undertaking to be legally enforceable, it must normally be embedded in a contract and supported by consideration: requirements that an estoppel claim may well not meet. Further, a contract to give an interest in land, which is the subject matter of most

---

phenomenon, in *Crabb v Arun DC* [1976] Ch 179 and perhaps also (though it may be a strained reading) *Re Basham* [1986] 1 WLR 1498; *Wayling v Jones* (1995) 69 P & CR 170; *Thorner v Major* [2009] 1 WLR 776.

[73] For monetary awards not aimed at reliance loss, see for example *Campbell v Griffin* [2001] EWCA Civ 990; *Jennings v Rice* [2002] EWCA Civ 159; *Ottey v Grundy* [2003] EWCA Civ 1176. For enforcement of the representation where the claimant had not discernibly suffered a loss of opportunity, see for example *Dillwyn v Llewelyn* (1862) 4 De GF & J 517; *Pascoe v Turner* [1979] 1 WLR 431.

[74] See further S Gardner *An Introduction to Land Law* 2nd edn (2009) 112–20.

[75] As in *Dillwyn v Llewelyn* (1862) 4 De GF & J 517.

[76] As in *Pascoe v Turner* [1979] 1 WLR 431; *Sledmore v Dalby* (1996) 72 P & CR 196; *Campbell v Griffin* [2001] EWCA Civ 990; *Jennings v Rice* [2002] EWCA Civ 159; *Ottey v Grundy* [2003] EWCA Civ 1176. There exists further evidence of this project, in the form of decisions taking estoppel's official requirements less than seriously—the point being that these requirements (an undertaking, detrimental reliance, etc) are irrelevant to a project of enforcing the implications of the parties' relationship. Such decisions include especially *Greasley v Cooke* [1980] 1 WLR 1306; *Re Basham* [1986] 1 WLR 1498; *Wayling v Jones* (1995) 69 P & CR 170; *Gillett v Holt* [2001] Ch 210: in all of which the parties had a relationship which itself held implications for the situation that had arisen.

[77] *Campbell v Griffin* [2001] EWCA Civ 990.

estoppel claims, must normally be put in writing:[78] a requirement that, again, an estoppel claim may well not meet. It seems unsupportable that an undertaking lacking these requirements should be enforceable nonetheless, via estoppel.[79]

18.5 DUTIES IN CONSTRUCTIVE AND RESULTING TRUSTS

Having thus taken stock of resulting (in Chapter 16) and constructive trusts, and in particular of some the main kinds of the latter, we can finally turn to the duties that bear upon the trustees of such trusts.

Section 7.1 discussed trustees' duties generally. It was explained that in all trusts, by their very nature, the trustee is under a basic duty to respect the fact that the property is not beneficially his own—which may mean only that he must transfer it, if asked to do so, to the beneficiaries if they have immediate rights to it, or to fresh trustees. The discussion went on to review the more extensive duties that characterize most express trusts, for there would generally be no point in establishing a trust requiring the trustee simply to hand the assets over again: above all, then, duties regarding the distribution of the assets in some more complex manner, and their safeguarding and management (investment, etc) pending such distribution.

It is sometimes said that resulting and constructive trusts are quite different:[80] that they involve only the basic duty to transfer the trust property to the object(s). This notion assumes that such trusts are not about the retention and complex distribution of their assets. One can certainly see the thought behind this assumption. Take for example the situation where I hold property on express trust for certain objects and, without authority to do so, transfer it to you (and you are not a bona fide purchaser for value without notice of its provenance). You hold the property on constructive trust for the objects, as explained in section 17.2. In concrete terms, however, this means that you are obliged to return it to me (or, perhaps more likely given my unsatisfactory performance, to someone

---

[78] Law of Property (Miscellaneous Provisions) Act 1989 s 2.

[79] For discussion of these issues around the case of *Crabb v Arun DC* [1976] Ch 179, see P Atiyah (1976) 92 LQR 174; P Millett (1976) 92 LQR 342.

[80] *Lord Napier and Ettrick v Hunter* [1993] AC 713, 738, 744, 752, however, appears to assume the opposite: that the duties in such trusts are identical with those found in express trusts. This really is implausible, for the reasons given in the text. For a more cautious assumption see *Westdeutsche Landesbank Girozentrale v Islington LBC* [1996] AC 669, 703.

appointed trustee in my place), or else to the objects themselves, if they are immediately entitled. There is no expectation that you should manage it into the future, and undertake its distribution.

But as we shall see, this is not—indeed, cannot be—the whole picture. Unfortunately, however, the area is relatively unexplored, whether by judges or by commentators. Some of what follows is therefore suggested from first principles rather than derived from authority.

In the first place, even in the case of a constructive trust such as that just mentioned, the trustee will in practice often not hand over the relevant assets immediately, sometimes for good reason. There is therefore a space in which issues of safeguarding could arise. It seems plausible in principle that the trustee even in such a rudimentary kind of trust is required to take reasonable care of the trust assets, once he knows or should know the facts generating the trust. And this appears to be the law. As we saw in section 14.3, he is under these circumstances liable (in 'knowing receipt') to make good the loss if, failing to take care of the assets, he loses them.[81] And if he exchanges the assets, or mixes them indistinguishably with other property that he holds, the resultant gain to himself counts as having occurred through a breach of trust, yielding a further constructive trust enabling the objects to trace into the exchange-product or mixture (or, in appropriate cases, to assert a charge over it), in the manner described in section 17.5.[82]

It would be surprising, however, if the trustee of such a constructive trust incurred further duties, requiring him to manage the assets in question more actively—in particular, to invest them—or to promote the

---

[81] C Mitchell and S Watterson in C Mitchell (ed) *Constructive and Resulting Trusts* (2010) ch 4, 138–9 prefer to speak in terms of the trustee having to account for the trust property and not being relieved. This vision is criticized in section 13.4.

[82] See *A-G for Hong Kong v Reid* [1994] 1 AC 324, where a fiduciary took bribes; held them (as it was decided: section 17.4) on constructive trust; and therefore, it was assumed, likewise held on constructive trust some houses acquired either solely or partly using them. Similarly *Re Diplock's Estate* [1948] Ch 465, where unauthorized payments were made from a testator's estate (analogous to a trust) to bodies which, therefore (section 17.2), held them on constructive trust; and so, when they exchanged these payments for or mixed them with other assets, held the exchange products and mixtures on constructive trust too. However, there is a problem with this decision. The argument in the text observes that tracing depends on a constructive trust arising from a breach of the trustee's duty to safeguard the trust assets (*Foskett v McKeown* [2001] 1 AC 102, 130–1; see section 17.5), and, by noticing instances of tracing against those who were only constructive trustees in the first place, concludes that such trustees too incur this duty. But surely they *breach* it only if they know, or should know, that they hold the assets on trust at all? (See section 14.3.) Which the recipient bodies in *Re Diplock's Estate* did not. Perhaps the case was wrongly decided to this extent.

objects' interests, avoiding any distractions.[83] But a number of types of constructive trust are aimed not at the simple transfer of the assets in this way, but at their retention and deployment by the trustee over an extended period, exactly after the manner of an express trust; and here we should expect more extensive duties. Take especially those constructive trusts that replace an express trust in the manner explained in sections 18.1–18.2. The most famous of them, a 'secret trust',[84] arises where you die, leaving property to me after securing my promise to hold it on what would, were it not for your non-compliance with the relevant formality rules, be a straightforward express trust. Although the trust is a constructive one, I am bound under it to adhere to those terms—that is, I am in effect bound to operate the failed express trust. It seems never to have been suggested that my duties differ from those that I should have incurred if I had literally come under the express trust. Certainly, it is hard to imagine that there is no duty of safe-keeping, and it is easy to believe that there should be more active duties of management and even investment too; and, there seems no real reason not to add, duties of loyalty and anti-distraction duties as well.[85]

We can think about resulting trusts in a similar way.[86] Say I transfer property to you on an express trust 'for Adam', but there is no such person as Adam. You will hold the property on resulting trust for me. This resulting trust allows me to require you to transfer the property back to me without further ado. Following what was said above, therefore, we should expect you to have a duty to safeguard the property pending this

---

[83] See eg L Smith in P Birks (ed) *Privacy and Loyalty* (1997) ch 9, 262-7; though such duties were assumed to arise in *Ultraframe (UK) Ltd v Fielding* [2005] EWHC 1638 (Ch), [1577]–[1588]. Of course, such duties of selfless service and avoidance of distraction may arise for their own sake, rather than as a product of the presence of a trust. Say I am your solicitor. If I receive property in that capacity, I hold it on constructive trust for you: see sections 17.3–17.4. But I owe you such duties in any case, as a consequence of our very relationship, whether or not such a constructive trust would itself so entail (or indeed, arises at all)—in fact, it is these duties that generate the constructive trust in the first place. For a solicitor's fiduciary duties, see especially *Boardman v Phipps* [1967] 2 AC 46.   [84] See section 5.6.

[85] J Edelman (2010) 126 LQR 302, relying on a substantial number of judicial statements to like effect, argues that these duties are incurred only by someone who—expressly or impliedly—voluntarily undertakes them. On this view (which is not beyond challenge, however), they should arise only in those constructive trusts whose formula involves an undertaking by the trustee. These include the constructive trusts singled out in the text, though not for the reason identified there; but also, presumably, the more short-term constructive trusts arising against fiduciaries (see sections 17.3–17.4), whom Edelman sees as earning that title precisely because they voluntarily incur such duties.

[86] See generally R Chambers *Resulting Trusts* (1997) chs 8, 9. Chambers's treatment is, however, coloured by his overall thesis that resulting trusts are a general means of effecting restitution.

transfer back, but nothing more. But say instead that I transfer property to you on trust 'for Adam for his life, thereafter to Briony for her life, thereafter to Caitlin', but there is no such person as Caitlin. Here, a resulting trust arises whereby I am the ultimate beneficiary in Caitlin's place, but the express trust's provisions in favour of Adam and Briony remain good. So you incur all the duties associated with the latter—duties not only to safeguard the property, but also to manage and invest it, deploy it as instructed in favour of the beneficiaries in turn, promote the objects' interests selflessly and avoid distraction; and it is hard to think that your duties towards me, taking Caitlin's place, can be any different.

One type of long-haul constructive trust requires separate thought, however. This is the constructive trust that arises over a family home, as described in section 18.3. Say our family home is in my name alone, but a constructive trust arises whereby I hold it for myself and you. The trust cannot require me to straightway transfer your share to you, ie sell the house and give you your due portion of the proceeds: this would contradict the very point that the house is our family home.[87] Although the question will never arise in practice, it seems plausible in principle that I should incur a duty to safeguard it—but presumably not a duty to manage the property more actively, in particular to treat it as an investment. It seems far-fetched too to think of me as coming under duties to serve the objects selflessly and avoid distractions, though once again the matter will rarely be put to the practical test.[88]

---

[87] Of course, sale and division of proceeds will commonly be what is needed when such cases come to court, for this occurs usually in the context of our separation. The presence of my own share, however, means you cannot simply demand such relief even under these circumstances: if I oppose it, the court will have to decide between us, under the Trusts of Land and Appointment of Trustees Act 1996 s 14.

[88] It would do so if, say, I bought the next-door house too, without obtaining your agreement. This might be a move not open to an express trustee of our house, as involving a conflict between his personal interest and his duty selflessly to promote the interests of the trust objects, as the combined value of the two plots might be greater than the sum of their individual values, making the acquisition a potentially attractive one for the trust itself.

Index